ESSAYS ON CONTRACT

ESSAYS ON CONTRACT

P. S. ATIYAH

CLARENDON PRESS · OXFORD

Oxford University Press, Walton Street, Oxford OX2 6DP
Oxford New York Toronto
Delhi Bombay Calcutta Madras Karachi
Kuala Lumpur Singapore Hong Kong Tokyo
Nairobi Dar es Salaam Cape Town
Melbourne Auckland Madrid
and associated companies in
Berlin Ibadan

Oxford is a trade mark of Oxford University Press

First issued as a paperback (with corrections), 1988
Reprinted (with a new chapter), 1990 (twice), 1994

Published in the United States
by Oxford University Press Inc., New York

British Library Cataloguing in Publication Data
Atiyah, P. S. (Patrick Selim),
Essays on contract.
1. England. Contracts. Law
I. Title
ISBN 0-19-825444-X

Library of Congress Cataloging in Publication Data
Atiyah, P. S.
Essays on contract / P. S. Atiyah.
'Reprinted with a new chapter'—T.p. verso.
Includes bibliographical references.
1. Contracts—Great Britain.   I. Title.
KD1554.A973   1990   346.41'02—dc20   [344.1062]   90-30541
ISBN 0-19-825444-X

Printed and bound in Great Britain by
Biddles Ltd, Guildford and King's Lynn

Preface

This collection of essays brings together most of my writings on contract law and theory which have been published in academic journals over a period of almost twenty years. Putting these pieces together has enabled me to see many relationships which had formerly escaped me, and even if today I am less confident of some of the answers than I used to be, I am (I believe) more sure of the nature of some of the major questions. All the essays have been brought up to date and revised, some substantially so, and there are several completely new sections. In particular, I have taken the opportunity to comment on some of the criticisms of the original essays, and I have explored more thoroughly than before the grounds for, and the desirability of, awards of expectation damages in actions based on promises (Essay 7) and on misrepresentations (Essay 10).

Essay 1 is based on some remarks originally made, first at a Workshop at the Institute of Advanced Legal Studies in London in 1982, and again, in a slightly different form, at a Workshop at the University of Toronto in the same year, and later published in the *Canadian Journal of Business Law*. Essay 2 is a slightly revised reprint of an article originally published in the *Law Quarterly Review* for 1978, with a substantial postscript in which I attempt to answer some of my critics. Essay 3 is an extract, suitably edited, from my Oliver Wendell Holmes lecture, delivered at the Harvard Law School in 1981 and originally published in the *Boston University Law Review* for 1983. Essay 4 comes from a review essay originally published in the *Duke Law Journal* for 1983. Essay 5 is an expanded version of the Eighth Annual Viscount Bennett Lecture delivered at the University of New Brunswick in 1984, and originally published in *The Legal Mind: Essays for Tony Honoré*, ed. Neil MacCormick and Peter Birks. Essay 6 is a rewritten version of my review article of Charles Fried's *Contract as Promise: A Theory of Contractual Obligation*, first published in the *Harvard Law Review* for 1981. Essay 7 is a much expanded and rewritten version of my review article of Kronman and Posner, *The Economics of Contract Law*, first published in the *International Review of Law and Economics* for 1981. Essay 8 is a revised version of the inaugural lecture I gave at the Australian National University, Canberra, in 1971, and originally published by the Australian National University Press; it includes some comments by way of reply to Professor Treitel's critique of the original version. Essay 9 is a revised version of an article originally published in the *Ottowa Law Review* for 1968. Essay 10 is a substantially revised version of an article first published in the *Alberta Law Review* for 1971, and Essay 11 is a version of the Fifteenth Cecil Wright Memorial Lecture given at the University of Toronto in 1983 and later published in the *University of Toronto Law Journal* for 1985.

I am grateful for permission to reproduce these works to Stevens and Co., Ltd., publishers of the *Law Quarterly Review*, the *Boston University Law Review*, the *Duke Law Journal*, the Harvard Law Review Association, Butterworth and Co., Ltd., publishers of the *International Review of Law and Economics*, the *Ottowa Law Review*, the *Alberta Law Review* and the University of Toronto Press.

The opportunity has been taken in this reprint to correct a few misprints and minor errors. The book by myself and R. S. Summers, *Form and Substance in Anglo-American Law*, referred to in the following pages as 'forthcoming' has now been published by the Clarendon Press, Oxford.

In this reprint the opportunity has been taken to add, as a new Essay 12, a version of my Cassel lecture on 'Freedom of Contract and the New Right', which was given at the University of Stockholm in May 1988.

St John's College, Oxford.   P.S.A.
                                                               October 1988

Contents

I

The Modern Role of Contract Law

Definitions of legal concepts are today somewhat unfashionable, so neither lawyers nor legal theorists are likely to spend much time worrying over the correct definition of the concept of 'contract'. But there are in fact some very important issues latent in our conception of contract, and lawyers have a strong tendency to assume there is one paradigm of contract, the rules of which are therefore assumed to be generally applicable to all cases which fall within the scope of contract law. I shall have more to say in Essay 2 about this traditional paradigm, but I propose in this essay to adopt a somewhat different tack, and instead of attempting to construct a paradigm of contract, to make some more general remarks about the 'role' of modern contract law. What, then, to put the question bluntly, is contract law all about? The traditional answer, of course, is that contract law is 'about' contracts, in the same way (for example) that railway law is 'about' railways, or shipping law is 'about' ships. But this presupposes that a 'contract', like a railway or a ship, is itself something which exists outside the law, and that it can be recognized and defined, at least in general terms, without the use of the law itself. This 'Lockean' Natural Law idea, though it has sometimes been endorsed in modern times (for example, by Lon Fuller[1]), is surely untenable. While 'exchange'—simultaneous exchange—may exist in a pre-legal or non-legal world, contract is crucially different from mere exchange. Contract involves futurity and the concept of obligation; and although one can discuss non-legal obligations in a general sort of way and posit their existence as moral or social phenomena, it is not easy today to disentangle the extent of the interaction between legal and moral ideas about contract. It thus seems impossible to assume that the concept of contract itself today can be said to exist outside the arena of law, and that the law merely regulates this pre-existing phenomenon. Only with the aid of the law itself can we know what contract law is about, and what a contract is.

It might be more plausible to suggest that at least contract law is 'about' such extra-legal phenomena as promises and agreements, be-

[1] See L. Fuller, *Principles of Social Order*, ed. Kenneth I. Winston (Duke University Press, NC, 1981), at p. 174, and Essay 4 below, p. 76.

cause it may seem that these at least can be recognized to exist outside
the law. Surely, it may be urged, we can all recognize an agreement or
a promise without the aid of the law; and then, it may be thought, we
can conclude that contract law is 'about' promises and agreements. But
it turns out on further examination that even these concepts have a
substantial infusion of law already in them. Take first the concept of a
promise, surely the easier of the two. Nearly all theorists and philosophers who have written about 'the practice of promising' take it
pretty much for granted that promising is a social or non-legal institution or practice, and that it is therefore possible to analyse the
constituent elements of a promise by careful study of the use of language, and of social custom.[1]

But even these writers acknowledge that there are many difficult
problems at the borderline of the concept of promising. For example,
it is unclear whether a promise is 'really' a promise if it is not communicated to anyone. If someone writes down a promise and sticks the
document in a drawer without showing it to anyone, is that a promise?
Or again, even if a promise is communicated, suppose it is not accepted
by the person to whom it is addressed, does it then no longer 'count' as
a promise? Or was it never even a promise before acceptance? Again, it
is unclear if a promise can relate to a matter of fact, rather than to
some future action to be performed by the promisor. So also, it may
be uncertain if a 'promise' to do something which is, or turns out to
be, impossible, is 'really' a promise at all. All these problems—and
many more could be put—may seem to be mere quibbles; they may
seem to be merely marginal points about fringe cases. Surely, it may be
insisted, the paradigm of a promise is clear enough in its essentials.

While it must be acknowledged that this is indeed a very widely held
view, it seems to me that there is a more fundamental problem about
identifying the non-legal phenomenon of promise, which does seem to
go to the very roots of the concept, and not merely to be a quibble about
the marginal elements. This problem concerns the question whether a
putative promise 'really' is, or 'counts as' a promise, when there seems
no good reason *other than the bare promise itself*, for recognizing that
the promise creates an obligation. Generally speaking, this problem
has not been recognized as a serious difficulty by theorists (if indeed it

---

[1] See, for a general discussion of the philosophical problems concerning promising,
P. S. Atiyah, *Promises, Morals and Law* (Oxford, 1981) and the literature referred to
there. For a particularly thorough attempt to analyse the non-legal elements of a promise,
see J. R. Searle, 'What is a Speech Act?', in *The Philosophy of Language*, ed. J. R. Searle
(Oxford, 1971).

is recognized at all), perhaps for the simple reason that it is rare to find promises being made where there is no good reason for recognizing the existence of an obligation, apart altogether from the fact that a promise has been made. Many promises, for example, are made in order to obtain something of value from the person addressed, the promisee. And once that thing has been obtained, it seems clearly right that there should be some sort of obligation upon the promisor, which is partly at least due to the very fact that he has received what he wanted. So also, other promises are made which, even if they are not designed to produce some benefit for the promisor, are intended to, or calculated to, induce the promisee to act on the promise in some way or another. And if a person does act in reliance on another in a way which the other ought to anticipate, that also seems a good reason for the creation or recognition of an obligation, quite apart from the express promise which led to the act of reliance.

Most theorists and lawyers would say that these problems do not concern the existence of a promise as a non-legal phenomenon, but at most affect its legal enforceability. The crucial issue then may turn upon whether a bare promise can or should create a (non-legal) obligation even where the promise is made without any good reason whatever, and even though no actions in reliance have been induced by the promise. If such a bare promise is thought to create a non-legal obligation even in these extreme circumstances, then a promise ought to be capable of recognition and identification without recourse to the law itself. It seems clear to me, however, that this view cannot be sustained, whether we are searching for a descriptive or a normative theory of the concept of promising. From a descriptive perspective, my view is that the great storehouse of legal decisions concerning con-tractual obligations (using this term in a broad sense for the present) illustrates that at no time in our legal history has a bare promise been regarded, without more, as sufficient to create a legal obligation; and furthermore, this limitation on legal effectiveness is itself largely based on moral considerations. That is to say, the circumstances in which the law denies that a putative promise creates a legal obligation are usually (though certainly not always) circumstances in which ordinary persons would often themselves feel extremely dubious, to put it at the lowest, as to whether there exists a moral or social obligation; and if that is the case, then it seems to me no great step to suggest that in many such circumstances, we would often be doubtful of the propriety of referring to the putative promise as a 'real' promise at all.

Normatively speaking, it seems to me equally clear that it is quite impossible to affirm that all promises *ought* to create moral or social obligations, without any regard to the reasons for the making of the promise, or the consequences which have ensued from its being made. No doubt a strong general principle to this effect can be justified from a normative viewpoint, and in Essay 5 I try to explain the great advantages which ensue from treating bare promises as binding legal obligations, without looking behind them (to see why they were made) or after them (to see whether they have been relied upon). But there must always remain some circumstances in which we do need to ask why a promise was made, or what has been done in consequence of its having been made, before we can sensibly say that it creates an obligation. In these circumstances, much weight is going to be placed on these other considerations, and the promise itself may then turn out not to be capable of generating an obligation of its own force.

The upshot of all this is that I am extremely dubious about the possibility of understanding contract law in terms of a set of rules 'about' promises; in my view, the law of contract is a set of rules (and other normative principles) concerning the creation of obligations, in which the law itself has refined and made use of the concept of a promise. Today, it is no doubt very difficult to disentangle the legal and moral elements in our everyday usage of the concept of promising, but it seems to me utterly wrong to try to draw a sharp line between them, as though the law itself is not, and ought not to be, based on moral ideals.

Much the same conclusion must follow if we try to analyse the concept of agreement, and suggest (as most definitions of contract used by English lawyers would suggest) that a contract is definable in terms of legally enforceable agreements. Here again, the moment we try to analyse the concept of an agreement, difficulties will be seen to ensue. What kinds of agreement are in question? Clearly not all agreements can form the basis of a contract, for instance, where one person (say a judge) agrees with the views of another (another judge). So a contract must be about certain kinds of agreements. Then again, there must be questions about how a putative agreement is to be made, before it is to 'count' as a 'real' agreement, and so on. In particular, there is often great difficulty over the concept of an 'implied agreement'. Some people see 'implied agreements' everywhere. The social contractarians, for instance, saw the very existence of the State as being the result of an 'implied agreement', and Blackstone saw the obligation to obey the law generally as being the result of an 'implied agreement'. But others may insist that these are not 'true' agreements, but artificial constructs. Ultimately, the same conclusion must emerge as if we try to explain contract law in terms of promises. In particular, we must face the question whether a putative agreement is a 'real' agreement if (for instance) there seems no good reason for the agreement to have been made at all—at least by one party—if (for instance) it is a very unfair, or one-sided, or even irrational agreement for one of the parties to have made. Here too, most theorists and lawyers would prefer to keep these two issues separate. The first question, they would urge, is whether there is, simply *is*, an agreement, as a pure matter of fact; the second question is whether that agreement ought to be legally recognized as creating an obligation, or perhaps ought even to be recognized as creating a moral obligation. Again, this view seems to me to be wrong, both descriptively and normatively. I do not believe we can identify such a thing as an 'agreement' as a pure matter of fact: an agreement is a social or moral or legal construct, and is therefore necessarily already imbued with our social or moral or legal ideals. Nor do I think it desirable that we should try to create an ethical or legal world in which the recognition of an agreement becomes a pure matter of fact, even though I acknowledge that there are very strong grounds—as in the case of promises—for going a long way down this road.

Returning, then, to the problem of trying to identify what the role of contract law is in modern societies, it seems to me that we are reduced to thinking of contract law as 'about' fairly broad areas of human interaction such as 'co-operative activity'. In dealing with co-operative activity we find a number of core elements, arrayed in different patterns, with greater emphasis sometimes on this element and sometimes on another. In particular, we find the three elements of consent, reciprocity of benefit, and reliance as key elements in much co-operative activity. All this means, I suggest, that we should not think of contract law as 'about' *one* central paradigmatic type of conduct, but about clusters of typical *situations*. So we are looking for situations rather than simple transactions. There are *families* of situations, related to each other, much as there are 'family' resemblances among games, in Wittgenstein's famous example. It is incorrect today to think of contract law as having one central core with clusters of differences around the edges. If we take as our starting-point the classical model of contract (which is discussed further in Essay 2), we can focus on five characteristics (there may be others). Thus we have the (1) discrete, (2) two-party, (3) commercial, (4) executory, (5) exchange.

Moving away from the first characteristic, we encounter a cluster of family situations which concern continuous relationships or continuing series of exchanges rather than discrete events (of course, the line between a discrete event and a continuing relationship is itself a blurred line). Some continuing relationships depart only marginally from the classical model, for example output and requirement contracts. Some are more different, for example landlord-tenant relationships, franchise dealerships, employment contracts. These are still clearly recognizable contracts in modern law, though the landlord-tenant relationship has (at least in England) precious few of the features of freedom of contract which we associate with classical law. Other continuing relations, again, go beyond the traditional frontiers of contract law, for example husband and wife relationships, or cohabitation relationships without marriage. Here we reach the frontiers of traditional contract law, though paradoxically modern courts have occasionally been able to step in here. And in matrimonial cases contract law may step in when the marriage breaks down. Here, as in cohabitation cases, recognizable contract norms are used by the courts even where contract law itself is not thought applicable, for example ideas of agreement, exchanges of benefit, detrimental reliance, and so on, are all present and useful in some of these situations. Another type of continuing relationship, the employer-trade union relationship is, in the United States and Canada, on the fringes of contract law, and contract norms are often imported into the relationship. But in England, as is well known, *the law* and especially the law of contract, tends to be excluded altogether from this relationship. It operates, or at least has until very recently operated, in 'a state of nature', with results we are all familiar with.

We can move away from the classical model of contract in another direction, and look at multiparty relationships. These subdivide into other clusters of family situations. For instance one can have a discrete multiparty transaction, though these are not common. More typically we find multiparty relationships which have some institutional form, for example the partnership, the company, the social club. Here the relationships between the members are again on the frontiers of contract law as now perceived. The multiparty nature of these relations creates important differences from the classical model, for example it creates a need for institutional (that is, in effect, constitutional) arrangements, which in turn creates a need for the quasi-legislative possibility of having legal duties modified without the consent of one of the parties. Contract law has had a lot of trouble with these cases for fairly obvious reasons. As one looks at well-defined bodies with clearly set out institutional arrangements, divisions of power, and so on, one sees dimly in the background the next stage, or set of relationships, which of course is that of the State itself. Here we move into the realm of political theory with its 'social contract' traditions. This may seem completely divorced from 'legal' contractual ideas, but that would perhaps be too narrow a view. Assuming that contractual norms are what link together the various clusters of family situations in modern law, it would not be difficult to find in constitutional law and political conventions a good deal of support for, and much use of, many of these same norms.

Consent of the governed is said to be the basis of the democratic state as of contractual relations. Reliance ideas underlie many well accepted political conventions (for example against retrospective legislation) and the notion of a fair exchange of benefits constantly comes up in political debate no less than in the law. Many of the problems of modern politics can be seen in semi-contractual terms. A major and topical question of this type concerns the question whether it would be wrong to abolish the indexation of civil servants' pensions—do they have a sort of contractual right to this? Furthermore, one of the major problems of modern contract law is the extent to which redistributive ideas (derived from the political stage) have a valid role to play in the market. It is the basic assumption that they do not which underlies much of the modern law-and-economics literature in the United States.

Another family relationship, or cluster of relationships, is the discrete non-commercial situation. Here we have simple cases such as private sales of second-hand cars and house-purchase transactions where both parties are non-commercial parties. It is, of course, a question whether one should treat the commercial–consumer transaction as a separate one from the commercial–commercial deal, or the consumer–consumer transaction. The Unfair Contract Terms Act 1977 does, for various purposes, recognize three different categories corresponding roughly to these three classes. From these cases one can slide readily into the non-discrete relationship between a commercial party and a non-commercial party as in the consumer credit transaction, or the ordinary contract of employment.

Another cluster of situations is found when we move away from the paradigm of the executory transaction and recognize that the law is often called upon to deal with events that have happened, after they have happened, and it uses contractual ideas and norms to sort out a mess (a quasi-accident situation) or to decide how to distribute a windfall (a restitution situation in some cases, but not necessarily—for example where a matrimonial home has increased in value, and the parties split up). Here again contract norms, such as reliance and exchange of benefit ideas have often been used, and are relevant to the ultimate disposal of these problems. An offshoot of the benefit side is the involuntary exchange, of which there are a great many examples in modern times, though not yet recognized or treated as part of 'the law of contract' in most instances.

Finally, if we take exchange as one of the central elements of the classical model of contract, one can see how another cluster of situations concerns less exchange-orientated situations, for example charitable donations, unbargained-for reliance cases, and so on. Perhaps testation, with its close association with (non-exchange) contracts fits in here also. The lesson of all this, it seems to me, is that we must try to extricate ourselves from the tendency to see contract as a monolithic phenomenon. Although there are inter-relationships between many clusters of situations with which contract law deals, it does not follow that all these clusters have close family resemblances to all the others. Cluster A may be related to B which is related to C and so on, but there may be little relationship between cluster A and cluster D. This is, I think, why it is possible, on the one hand, to continue to believe that one important cluster of situations (the typical commercial exchange contract) retains and will always retain certain distinctive features associated traditionally with 'contract law', and at the same time to recognize that contract law as a whole—that is, many other clusters of situations—is increasingly merging with tort law into a general law of obligations.

Although this idea of the merger of contract and tort has become pretty trite in recent years and is, indeed, increasingly evident in the case law of modern times, many lawyers and theorists intuitively feel hostile to it because they continue to insist that contract law is 'based' on agreements or voluntarily incurred obligations, while tort law is 'based' on legally imposed obligations. It should by now be apparent that this hostility is misconceived. Parts of contract law—the law regulating standard commercial transactions—for instance, will always be remote from parts of tort law—for instance, the law relating to assaults. But it is of course equally true that parts of tort law like assault are today remote from other parts, like liability for defamation or liability for economic loss in negligence. It is equally true that even in dealing with standard commercial transactions the law will use, and has probably always used, collective ideas of justice and fairness to fill in many of the gaps in the relationship between the parties, to interpret the express contractual terms they have used, and to fashion the appropriate remedies when there is a breach.

There seem to be two reasons why today it is evident that contract and tort are merging. First, because the use of collective values to impose solutions on the parties in cases of contract has become less illegitimate than it used to seem under the influence of classical contract theory; and secondly, at a more technical and doctrinal level, because modern judges are happier with the fluidity of tort techniques than they are with the perceived rigidities and inadequacies of contract law.[1] Hence tort law is increasingly used to resolve problems which could equally be resolved by contract law if the judges were more willing than they seem to be to adapt contract law to modern ideas and values. This is, perhaps, itself an indication of the need to break away from the idea of the one central paradigm of contract law, because it may well be this which inhibits the judges from developing contract law as freely as they are willing to develop tort law.

[1] This question of technique is discussed further in Essay 9.

Contracts, Promises, and the Law of Obligations

For at least a hundred years—and in many respects for more like twice that time—common lawyers have operated within a particular conceptual framework governing the law of obligations. Within this framework, the fundamental distinction has been that between obligations which are voluntarily assumed, and obligations which are imposed by law. The former constitute the law of contract, the latter fall within the purview of the law of tort. There is, in addition, that somewhat anomalous body of law which came to be known as the law of quasi-contract or, in more modern times, as the law of restitution. This body of law was accommodated within the new conceptual framework by the academic lawyers and jurists from the 1860s onwards, and, after a considerable time-lag, their ideas came to be part of the accepted orthodoxies. The law of quasi-contract, it came to be said, was part of the law of obligations which did not arise from voluntary acts of the will, but from positive rules of law. Quasi-contract thus took its place alongside tort law on one side of the great divide. Contract alone remained on the other side. Nobody ever paid much attention to the place of the law of trusts in this scheme of things. Equity, after all, was a peculiarly English invention and theorizing about the law of obligations was very much a Roman and subsequently a Continental fashion. It is true that much time and trouble was devoted to the problem of fitting equitable obligations into another typically Roman distinction, namely that dividing a *jus in rem* from a *jus in personam*. But nobody seems to have troubled over-much about the place of equitable obligations in the great divide between voluntarily assumed and legally imposed obligations.

These broad distinctions reflected a set of values and ways of thought which also exercised a most profound influence on the conceptual pattern which was imposed on contract law itself. Contractual obligations came to be treated as being almost exclusively about promises, agreements, intentions, acts of will. The function of the law came to be seen as that of merely giving effect to the private autonomy of contracting parties to make their own legal arrangements. It is, of course, well known, indeed, has become part of the modern orthodoxy, that the private autonomy, this extreme freedom of contract, came to be abused by parties with greater bargaining power, and has been curtailed in a variety of ways, both by legislative activity and by the judges themselves. That is a familiar story and I do not wish to pursue it here. What I do wish to discuss is the conceptual framework of contract and its place in the law of obligations as a whole. I want to suggest that, despite the increasing attacks upon freedom of contract, and the great divide between contract and tort, the conceptual apparatus which still dominates legal thinking on these issues is the apparatus of the nineteenth century. It goes, indeed, far beyond the law itself. Our very processes of thought, our language in political, moral, or philosophical debate, is still dominated by this nineteenth-century heritage to an extent which, I venture to suggest, is rarely appreciated. I want to suggest, further, that this conceptual apparatus is not based on any objective truths, it does not derive from any eternal verities. It is the result, quite specifically, of a nineteenth-century heritage, an amalgam of classical economics, of Benthamite radicalism, of liberal political ideals, and of the law itself, created and moulded in the shadow of these movements. The result, I will argue, is that our basic conceptual apparatus, the fundamental characterizations and divisions which we impose on the phenomena with which we deal, reflect not the values of our own times, but those of the last century. It is true that they reflect much that many will still think most admirable about the nineteenth century, the liberal tradition, the belief in the value and rights of the individual, adherence to an economic and social system which had the confidence to reward enterprise, initiative, and success. But to recognize that many of the values of our society today are opposed to much that was admirable in the last century is not to denigrate our predecessors. And to argue the case for revising our concepts so that they conform more closely to the values of today involves no judgment that those values are better than the values of yesterday. Indeed, the revision may prove useful to those who think otherwise, for it will bring into greater relief precisely what is involved in today's values.

It is time to turn away from these generalities, and I propose to begin by spending a few moments on the paradigm of modern contract theory. If we were asked today to indulge in the fashionable exercise of constructing a model of a typical contract, I suspect most common lawyers would come up with something like this. A typical contract is,

Essay 2

first, a bilateral executory agreement. It consists of an exchange of promises; the exchange is deliberately carried through, by the process of offer and acceptance, with the intention of creating a binding deal. When the offer is accepted, the agreement is consummated, and a contract comes into existence before anything is actually done by the parties. No performance is required, no benefit has to be rendered, no act of detrimental reliance is needed, to create the obligation. The contract is binding because the parties intend to be bound; it is their will, or intention, which creates the liability. It is true that the law has this technical requirement known as the doctrine of consideration, but, except in rare and special cases, mutual promises are consideration for each other, and therefore the model, by definition, complies with the requirement of consideration. When the contract is made, it binds each party to performance, or, in default, to a liability to pay damages in lieu. Prima facie these damages will represent the value of the innocent party's disappointed expectations. The plaintiff may, therefore, bring suit on a wholly executory contract, for example, because the defendant has attempted to cancel his offer or acceptance, or to withdraw from the contract, and may recover damages for his disappointed expectations even though he has not relied upon the contract in any way, and even though the defendant has received no benefit under it. The whole model is suffused with the idea that the fundamental purpose of contract law is to give effect—within limits of course—to the intentions of the parties. It is their decision, and their free choice, which makes the contract binding, and determines its interpretation, and its result in the event of breach. It is, of course, a commonplace today that all legal obligations are, in the last resort, obligations created or at least recognized by the law, but the classical model of contract is easily enough adjusted to take account of this truism. The law of contract, it is said, consists of power-conferring rules. The law provides facilities for private parties to make use of if they so wish. Those who wish to create legal obligations have only to comply with a simple set of rules and the result will be recognized by the law. The function of the law itself in all this is largely neutral in a moral and a distributive sense.

There is no doubt that this model has been of astonishing power. For a hundred years it has had no serious rival. Today many lawyers would probably want to qualify it, or modify it in a variety of respects. Many would admit, perhaps insist, that the model is primarily useful in connection with the business transaction, and that it does not fit the consumer transaction, or the family arrangement, or other agreements which cannot be characterized as business deals. Even in transactions among businessmen, many lawyers will want to qualify this model. At the least many will recognize that the role of free choice on the part of contracting parties has declined, and that courts may, in the interests of justice as they perceive it, sometimes impose solutions in the teeth of contracting parties' intent. But making all allowances for the necessary qualifications, I do not think it would be seriously disputed that this is the paradigm model of contract which we have inherited from nineteenth-century lawyers. Indeed, a glance at the contract textbooks will confirm that the model is still alive and well.

The pervasiveness of this model is attested by the closely parallel set of ideas and values which underlie social and philosophical ideas about promises. The binding force of promises, the nature of promissory liability, the role of implication, the idea of a background set of conventions and practices enabling promises to be made, all these and many other topics have been the subject of much debate and discussion among moralists and philosophers. Perhaps it is not surprising that the model of promissory theory most widely adhered to among philosophers appears to correspond very closely to the model of contractual liability sketched above.

Before proceeding further to examine the reality of this model of contract, it is worth pausing to consider some of its underlying presuppositions which are rarely made explicit. The first of these is that the classical model assumes that contract law is fundamentally about what parties *intend*, and not about what they do. Here again, of course, qualifications, and important qualifications, have to be made. It is the manifestation of intention and not actual intention that matters most; and what the parties do is obviously crucial in measuring the extent to which performance falls short of promise. Nevertheless, classical contract theory assumes that contractual obligations are created by the intention of the parties and not by their actions. The classical model is thus concerned with executory arrangements, with forward-looking planning. Contracts have a chronology, a time sequence, as can be seen by looking at the Table of Contents of any contract textbook published in the last hundred years. They are created first, and performed (or not performed) thereafter. In this respect, of course, contractual obligations necessarily differ from those on the other side of the great divide. The law of torts and the law of quasi-contract are concerned with what parties do. It is human action, or inaction, which leads to liability in tort or in restitution. Among other results, this means that contract lawyers focus on a different time sequence. In tort, or in restitutionary claims, it is the causing of damage or injury on the one hand, or the rendering of benefits on the other, which is the immediate object of interest. In contract, likewise, damage or injury may be caused, or benefits rendered, but it is not these consequences or the actions giving rise to them which are the focus of attention of the classical model. It is the intention of the parties which (it is assumed) must necessarily precede the causing of the damage or the rendering of the benefits, and which is therefore the source of the obligation. I will suggest later that this difference in the time which is the focus of attention has led, not merely to an exaggeration of the role of intentional conduct in the creation of contractual obligations, but also to a minimization of the role of intentional conduct in the creation of other forms of obligation.

The second presupposition of the classical model of contract is that a contract is a *thing*, which has some kind of objective existence prior to any performance or any act of the parties.[1] Of all the examples of legal reification, none is surely more powerful than this. A contract is a thing which is 'made', is 'broken', is 'discharged'. So powerful is this reification that most lawyers see nothing odd about the notion of anticipatory repudiation, that is, about the idea that a promise can be treated as broken even before its performance is due. The tendency to reify legal concepts is, in the case of contract, given powerful impetus by the fact that so many contractual arrangements are in written form. Even today, lawyers constantly use the words 'the contract' to signify both the legal relations created by the law, and the piece of paper in which those relations (or some of them) are expressed. Here again, there is a profound difference in the lawyer's way of looking at legal obligations on the other side of the great divide. A contract may be a 'thing' but nobody would conceptualize a quasi-contract or a tort as a thing. One reason why the tendency to reify the concept of contract has had important results is that it has reinforced the respect for the private autonomy of the contractual relationship. If a contract is a thing created by the contracting parties, it is easier to see it as a relationship within defined and limited parameters. Within these parameters, concepts such as fairness, justice, reasonableness seem to have less room to operate than they do with diffuse concepts like tort or quasi-contract.

The third presupposition of the classical model of contract concerns the function of the court in the enforcement of contracts. I take it as

[1] See Arthur Leff, 'Contract as Thing', 19 *Am. U. Law Rev.* 131 (1970).

axiomatic that, in principle, the judicial process is designed to serve either or both of two important social ends. The first is, by the threat of penalties or the promise of rewards, to encourage the citizenry to comply with socially desired standards of behaviour. And the second is to provide machinery for the settlement of disputes by peaceful and fair means. Now the classical model of contract, with its emphasis on intentional conduct and future planning, presupposes that the first of these two goals is the primary function of the courts in dealing with contractual litigation. The purpose of contract law is to encourage people to pay their debts, keep their promises, and generally be truthful in their dealings with each other. The enforcement of contracts, like the protection of property and the punishment of crime, is thus perceived as important primarily for its deterrent or hortatory purpose. It is no coincidence that these were historically linked together as the essential functions of the state even by Adam Smith and the classical economists. By contrast, other parts of the law of obligations are more likely to be dominated by the dispute-settlement functions of the courts, rather than by their deterrent or hortatory functions. In the law of quasi-contract, in particular, the court is almost invariably called upon to deal with a problem by resolving a conflict of equities. Some misfire has occurred, some untoward and unplanned benefit has been rendered. Is it right that the beneficiary should pay for it, or are there grounds on which it is more just that he should be permitted to retain an unpaid-for benefit? It is not generally regarded as an important function of the court to discourage (for example) people from paying debts twice over, or rendering benefits to another without ensuring that there has been an agreement to pay for them.

Similarly with the modern law of torts, the importance of the deterrent function of the law has declined at the expense of the dispute-settlement function. Increasingly, the emphasis is on the function of the court in dealing with what are essentially perceived as accidents. The court must patch up a dispute, pick up the pieces after an accident, resolve a difficult conflict of equities, but the court is primarily concerned with *these* parties in this particular situation, and not with threatening sanctions or offering rewards to future parties. Although some lawyers would still be prepared to defend the idea that the law of negligence has a value in discouraging negligent conduct, there can be no denying the decline in the relative importance of this aspect of the law. In the ordinary running-down action, in particular, it has for some years been a commonplace that the presence of third-party insurance on the one hand, and of criminal sanctions on the other, have tended to make the law of torts almost exclusively concerned with compensating the plaintiff rather than deterring future defendants. The fact that so much modern scholarship in the law-and-economics area has attempted to rehabilitate the centrality of the deterrent function of tort law goes some way to confirming this point, because this new scholarship is closely related to the revival of ideological support for *laissez-faire* economics and the classical model of contract.

The fourth presupposition of the classical model of contract is that there is indeed one model, that it is possible and useful to think still in terms of general principles of contract. The continued vitality of our textbooks and of our university law courses on contract attest to the faith which lawyers still have in the generalizing effect of the concept of contract. We know, of course, that most contracts fall into particular categories which have their own rules and qualifications derogating from the general law. There are, for example, special rules applicable to contracts of employment, consumer credit contracts, consumer sales, leases, mortgages, insurance contracts, house purchase, matrimonial agreements, and many others. Indeed, there are few contracts today which are not governed by specific rules which in some measure derogate from the general law. But none of this has shaken the power of the classical model of contract. This model is, without doubt, based on an economic model, that of the free market. Historically there is every reason to believe that the classical model grew up under the influence of the classical economists and of the philosophical radicals. There is no need to subscribe to the crude and exaggerated myth that these nineteenth-century thinkers wanted to reduce all relationships to economic terms, or to encourage a purely materialist approach to all human motivation. But it is true that many of them saw much in the classical contract model which they felt was both admirable and applicable far beyond the commercial sphere. They thought it desirable that men should learn to order their lives according to some definite plan, that they should be encouraged to aim for particular goals, that they should co-operate with others in attempting to seek those goals, that those who let down their fellows should be made to pay the cost of doing so; they thought it desirable that men should be free to develop their skills and ambitions, and they accepted the natural corollary that some would rise and some would sink. It was partly for these reasons (though there were certainly others too) that the classical model of contract was so unified and, no doubt, it was partly its unity which gave it so much power.

In the law itself, it was the nineteenth century which very largely saw the supersession of the importance of special kinds of contract by the general principles of contract. It was, of course, an Age of Principles— principles of morality, principles of political economy, principles of justice, and principles of law. When Addison published his *Treatise on Contracts* in 1847 he insisted that contract law was not a mere collection of positive rules but was founded 'upon the broad and general principles of universal law'. Indeed, he went further: 'The law of contracts', he wrote in his Preface, 'may justly indeed be said to be a universal law adapted to all times and races, and all places and circumstances, being founded upon those great and fundamental principles of right and wrong deduced from natural reason which are immutable and eternal.' Naturally, a concept of contract which could dismiss all differences of time and place, of circumstances and people, had no need for trivial distinctions between sale and hire-purchase, mortgages and leases, commercial and consumer contracts. Nor was there at this time the smallest hint that perhaps (as argued in Essay 1) the law of contract was used for a variety of disparate types of situations with only a series of family resemblances to connect them.

It is necessary now to cast a somewhat more critical eye at this conceptual structure. How far does it stand up to more detailed examination? Is it reconcilable with the value systems of the modern world and, in particular, of modern England? Is it even reconcilable with the developments in positive law which have taken place within this conceptual framework? Is it true that contractual obligatations normally arise from agreements or exchanges of promises? How far is it true to suggest that contracts are intentionally made with a view to future performance? To what extent is it correct to regard contractual liability as depending on voluntary assumed obligations? To what extent is it possible to adhere to the very concept of a single basic model of contract?

Let me begin with this last question. If we look at the law as it is stated in the books and the case-law we shall see that the concept of contract is applied in a very wide range of situations and to a very large variety of relationships. In Essay 1 I argued that these different types of relationships could not sensibly be treated as simple variations of a single paradigm. Before it is possible to construct a model even of a typical or paradigm case of contract it is necessary to have some idea of what it is that we are trying to achieve. Typical of what? Paradigm of what? Quite apart from the circular nature of the definitional problem, it is hard to understand how one is to measure the typicality of a particular relationship. If we are concerned with the most *numerous* types of transaction then presumably the typical contract would be the bus ride, the train journey, or the supermarket purchase. But even this is somewhat speculative and only empirical research could actually tell us what are the most commonly made transactions. Alternatively, we may be concerned with the value of the transactions we are examining. Commercial transactions are doubtless typically of greater individual value than consumer transactions; but it is not at all clear whether they are of greater aggregate value, nor is it clear how one could measure these relative values, or why the answer should matter. And anyhow commercial transactions are so far removed from the ordinary experience of most persons that it is hard to believe a contractual model based on the commercial transaction would today have a wide and pervasive application outside the particular sphere of business. It is, surely, an everyday observation that (for instance) one cannot apply the law of the market-place to matrimonial or parental relationships— hence abolition of actions for breach of promise, and the proposal of the Warnock Committee to ban surrogate parent contracts. But, as noted in Essay 1, this is also true of a wide variety of other kinds of relationships, some of which may have more of a commercial flavour than family cases. A third possible criterion for identifying the typical contract (which may have had more weight than perhaps it should) is the practical experience of lawyers. Doubtless city solicitors and barristers in London have more to do with commercial contracts than any other types of transactions or relationships dealt with by contract law; but if we looked at the totality of legal experience, it would surely emerge that the ordinary house-purchase-mortgage transaction was the one dealt with in greatest numbers by the legal profession. But even if we could succeed in identifying the largest class of contracts dealt with by lawyers, why should this be entitled to tell us what is the typical contract, on the basis of which we should construct our legal paradigms?

The truth is, I would suggest, that there is no such thing as a typical contract at all. Moreover, modern society has plainly rejected the values of the market outside the relatively narrow area in which the market is permitted to operate. The classical model of contract thus continues to exist though with much less content or application than would justify treating the model as the paradigm even of voluntarily incurred obligations. The principles of contract law sometimes govern new or marginal or residuary situations, but it is hard to see in what sense they can continue to be called *general* principles. They remain general only by default, only because they are being superseded by detailed *ad hoc* rules lacking any principle, or by new principles of narrow scope and application.

Let me turn now to a more challenging question. To what extent is it true to say that contractual liabilities arise from agreement or promises or depend on the voluntary assumption of obligation? I want to begin by suggesting that the power of the classical model here derives largely from its stress on the executory contract. If two parties do exchange promises to carry out some performance at a future date, and if, immediately on the exchange of promises, a binding legal obligation comes at once into existence, then it seems inexorably to follow that the obligation is created by the agreement, by the intention of the parties. If they have done nothing to implement the agreement, if no actions have followed the exchange of promises, then manifestly the legal obligation cannot arise from anything except the exchange of promises. Thus far the classical model appears to be impregnable. But closer examination suggests that the area of impregnability is really rather small.

The first point to note is that wholly executory contracts are rarer, more ephemeral in practice, and somewhat less binding than the classical model of contract would suggest. In the classical model, as I have suggested, the executory transaction lies at the very heart of contract. It is precisely because the classical model largely defines contract in terms of executory transactions that it necessarily locates the source of contractual liability in what the parties intend rather than in what they do. But large numbers of contracts are regularly made in which the making and the performance, or at least part performance, are simultaneous or practically simultaneous events. Consider such simple transactions as the boarding of a bus, or a purchase of goods in a supermarket, or a loan of money. Is it really sensible to characterize these transactions as agreements or exchanges of promises? Is it meaningful or useful to claim that a person who boards a bus is promising to pay his fare? If so, would it not be just as meaningful to say that when he descends from the bus and crosses the road he promises to cross with all due care for the safety of other road users? I do not, of course, deny that all these transactions involve some element of voluntary conduct. People do not generally board buses, buy goods in a supermarket, or borrow money in their sleep. But they involve much else besides voluntary conduct. They usually involve the rendering of some benefit, or actions of detrimental reliance, or both. A person who is carried by a bus from point A to point B after voluntarily boarding the bus can normally be presumed to have derived some benefit from the arrangements. Does his liability to pay his fare have nothing to do with this element of benefit? A person who borrows money and actually receives the loan is, according to the classical model of contract, liable to repay the money merely because he promised to repay it. The fact that he received the money appears to be largely irrelevant. It is not, indeed, wholly irrelevant in law, because of the doctrine of consideration, but in the classical model it is the intention or agreement or promise which is the source of the liability and not the consideration. The consideration is either a historical anachronism, a meaningless technicality, or, if it has any rational function at all today, it is merely to provide evidence of the seriousness of a promise. Thus a person who borrows £100 is liable to repay it because he has promised; the actual receipt of the money is merely evidence of the seriousness of the promise.

If we look at a normative system not encumbered by the doctrine of consideration—say the moral basis of promissory liability—the position is even more starkly clear. An obligation to perform a promise to pay £100 is generally considered to be precisely the same whether the promise is to make a gift or to repay a loan. Since the basis of the obligation lies in the promise in both cases it makes not a particle of difference that in the former case the promisor receives nothing for his money, while in the latter case he has already received full value. Is it not evident that there is some grotesque distortion here? Consider next the possibility of detrimental reliance by the promisee. Is it not manifest that a person who has actually worsened his position by reliance on a promise has a more powerful case for redress than one who has not acted in reliance on the promise at all? A person who has not relied on a promise (nor paid for it) may suffer a disappointment of his expectations, but he does not actually suffer a pecuniary loss. The disappointment of an expectation may of course be treated as a species of loss by definition, as indeed, the law generally does treat it, if the expectation derives from contract. But no definitional jugglery can actually equate the position of the party who suffers a diminution of his assets in reliance on a promise, and a person who suffers no such diminution.

But this is not all, for both in morality and in law the rendering of benefits and actions of detrimental reliance can give rise to obligations even where there was no promise at all. The law of restitution is almost entirely concerned with situations in which one party is entitled to recompense for a benefit received by another from him, or at his expense, even though the latter made no promise to pay for it. The receipt of a benefit is thus in some cases a sufficient ground for liability even without an agreement or promise to repay. Of course, the law of restitution has 'nothing at all' to do with the law of contract, as classical contract theory (at least in its maturest form) tells us. But that is itself, as I shall suggest later, an idea which is quite unacceptable, both historically and analytically. And if the law of restitution concerns liability for the restitution of uncovenanted benefits, the law of torts and the law of trusts frequently provide redress for acts of reliance performed in the absence of an express promise. Moreover, the law of contract itself, together with associated parts of the law sometimes characterized as distinct sets of rules, provides many examples of provisions plainly designed for the protection of acts of reasonable reliance, rather than for the imposition of promissory liability. The law of misrepresentation, of warranty, of estoppel and promissory estoppel, no matter how they are conceptualized, provide many illustrations of what can only be rationally regarded as reliance-based liability.

And so far I have said nothing about one of the most obvious bodies of legal doctrine which is not easy to reconcile with the theory that contractual and promissory obligations rest on voluntary obligation. I refer, of course, to the so-called 'objective-test' theory of contractual liability. Every law student is taught from his earliest days that contractual intent is not really what it seems; actual subjective intent is normally irrelevant. It is the appearance, the manifestation of intent that matters. Whenever a person is held bound by a promise or a contract contrary to his actual intent or understanding, it is plain that the liability is based not on some notion of a voluntary assumption of obligation, but on something else. And most frequently it will be found that that something else is the element of reasonable reliance.[1] One party relies on a reasonable construction of an offer, or he accepts an offer, reasonably thinking it is still open when the offeror has revoked

---

[1] For a discussion of the *Centrovincial* case which is hostile to my thesis, see Essay 7, p. 173.

it but failed to communicate his revocation. All this is standard stuff but I suggest that cases of this type have for too long been regarded as of marginal importance only, as not affecting the fundamental basis and theory of liability. In a simple world of simple promises and contracts this might have been an acceptable perspective. But the arrival of written contracts, and above all the standard printed form, has surely rendered this approach much less defensible. A party who signs an elaborate printed document is almost invariably held bound by it not because of anything he intended; he is bound in the teeth of his intention and understandings except in some very exceptional cases of fraud or the like. The truth is he is bound not so much because of what he intends but because of what he does. Like the man who is bound to pay his fare because he boards a bus, the man who signs a written contract is liable because of what he does rather than what he intends. And he is liable because of what he does for the good reason that other parties are likely to rely upon what he does in ways which are reasonable and even necessary by the standards of our society.

What I suggest, then, is that wherever benefits are obtained, wherever acts of reasonable reliance take place, obligations may arise, both morally and in law. These obligations are by no means confined to cases where explicit promises are given, for they may arise in cases where we would imply a promise, but they also arise in many cases where any attempt to imply a promise would be nothing but a bare fiction. The man who boards a bus without any intention of paying for his fare is bound to pay it though it is difficult to see what reality there can be in claiming that he impliedly promises to pay. The man who signs a document without reading it does not make an implied any more than an express promise in any genuine sense. Now I want next to suggest that these cases of benefits received or of action in reliance, are more common than is suggested by our conventional image of the legal world. In conventional contract theory, the paradigm of contract is the executory arrangement. Executory contract theory has totally subsumed liabilities and obligations which arise from the receipt of benefits or from acts of reasonable reliance. But in practice, the wholly executory transaction is nothing like such a paradigm as it appears in the books. I have already said something of the difficulties involved in the very concept of a paradigm in this context, but the most cursory look at the world and at the law will reveal that many types of transactions do not fit the model of the wholly executory arrangement at all. Vast numbers of transactions are not in any real sense binding prior to something being done by one or both of the parties. This may partly reflect the fact that lawyers have traditionally implied promises very easily from transactions, and that in consequence today there are many situations in which the lawyer would assert that an executory arrangement involves implied mutual promises while the parties themselves might very well deny that they had promised anything at all. The language of consumer transactions, in particular, is not couched in terms of promises. People 'book' holidays, or air reservations, they 'order' goods, they 'accept' estimates, and so on. Even in business circles this sort of terminology is more common than the express language of promises and undertakings. Whether language of this kind is treated as creating an obligation is traditionally thought of as depending upon whether the language is tantamount to being promissory. But it is at least arguable that in many cases of this nature the reality is otherwise. Frequently, both in law and in moral discourse we appear to determine whether there should be an obligation first, and then decide how the language should be construed afterwards. And it follows that the existence or non-existence of the obligation is then being decided independently of the existence of any promise.

Much the same occurs where conduct rather than language is in question. Consider a recent example of the creation of what is, in essence, a new species of liability. The courts have recently decided that a local authority which is guilty of negligence in supervising the construction of a house in accordance with the Building Regulations may be liable to an ultimate purchaser of the house.[1] The liability is, of course, a liability in tort. Now that the liability is established as a matter of law, it would not seem unreasonable or odd to say that a local authority impliedly undertakes or promises to exercise due care in supervising the construction of houses. But it would have been difficult to argue for the existence of such an implied undertaking or promise prior to the establishment of legal liability. Here it is clear that the liability is first created on independent grounds, and the implication of a promise can then be read into the conduct which leads to the liability.

It is not always appreciated, I suspect, how easy it is to interpret transactions or arrangements as binding or not binding in their inception, according to the predilections of the interpreter. Consider a simple case like *Queen* v. *Demers*[2] which came before the Privy Council in

---

[1] *Dutton* v. *Bognor Regis UC* [1972] 1 QB 373; *Anns* v. *Merton London B.C.* [1978] AC 728.

[2] [1900] AC 103.

1900. Here was an arrangement between a colonial government and a printer for printing government publications for eight years. Disputes led to the cancellation of the arrangement by the government whereupon protracted litigation took place in the colonial courts. In the Privy Council the whole case was disposed of in a judgment consisting of one paragraph by the 'discovery' that the transaction involved no promise on the part of the government. The only obligation on the government's part was to pay for the work actually done in accordance with the contract. In other words the transaction was viewed not as a binding executory arrangement but as an agreement on the terms which would govern any work actually carried out. The estate agency cases in this century, though they gave rise to more difficulty, involved, in effect, the same considerations. It came ultimately to be held that to appoint a person as an estate agent to sell a property did not create a binding future obligation.[1] The obligation was only to pay for services rendered after they had been rendered. These interpretations were neither necessary nor inevitable. Indeed, in one case they overturned the views of the lower courts and in the other case, the House of Lords departed from a long line of decisions dating back to the mid-nineteenth century.[2] The differing decisions represent, I suspect, a difference in the values attached to the concept of binding executory arrangements on the one hand, and the freedom to change one's mind on the other.

It is also worth reflecting on how, once again, the question whether a person has made a promise may depend upon whether he is under an obligation rather than vice versa. Consider the variety of circumstances in which the modern consumer is accorded the right to withdraw from wholly executory arrangements. These rights are sometimes accorded by statute, but more often by social and commercial custom. Whether a consumer is 'bound' by revocable arrangements of this kind depends thus on the law or on such custom; whether he has made a promise, whether his language or conduct can sensibly be interpreted as promissory can only be decided after it has been settled whether he is liable or bound. Even the use of plainly promissory language does not necessarily settle the issue. For, if rights of withdrawal do exist, then a promise can easily be construed as being subject to such rights. There is nothing

---

[1] *Luxor Ltd.* v. *Cooper* [1941] AC 108. See Essay 8 for an extended discussion of this case.

[2] The view that an estate agency contract is bilateral, restricting the client from changing his mind, is also followed by some American states, see e.g. *Marchiondo* v. *Scheck* 432 P. 2d 405 (1967) but compare *Hutchinson* v. *Dobson-Bainbridge Realty Co.* 217 SW 2d 6 (1946).

very odd about such a possibility which closely resembles the common case where a contract provides for unilateral variation of some of its provisions, and any promises must be read subject to such variations.

Now I must repeat that I am not arguing that consent, promise, intention, voluntary conduct, are irrelevant to the creation of obligations even where an element of reciprocal benefit is present, or some act of reasonable reliance has taken place. In the first place, where liability arises out of conduct rather than from the voluntary assumption of an obligation, the conduct itself is usually of a voluntary character. Even if liability on a part-executed arrangement can properly be said to be benefit-based rather than promise-based, a man is normally entitled to choose what benefits he will accept—normally, though by no means invariably. Similarly, with reliance-based liability; it is normally open to a person to warn others that they are not to rely upon him, but must trust to their own judgment. Obviously this raises difficulty where a person wants to have his cake and eat it, where he wants to influence others to behave in a certain manner but wants also to disclaim responsibility for their doing so. There is little doubt that in such circumstances the trend is towards insisting on the imposition of responsibility. The striking down of exemption clauses and disclaimers of liability are evidence of the unacceptability of these attempts to have things both ways. This trend may reflect the increased emphasis on reliance and the declining stress on free choice.

But secondly, and much more important, I would argue that even where obligations can be said to be primarily benefit-based or reliance-based, explicit promises may have a valuable role to play. I referred earlier to the conventional wisdom of English common lawyers which some decades ago suggested that the only rational function of the doctrine of consideration was to serve as evidence of the seriousness of a promise. I now want to suggest that the truth lies more closely in the precise converse of this assertion. Where obligations arise out of the rendering of benefits or from acts of reasonable reliance, the presence of an explicit promise may, I suggest, serve valuable evidentiary purposes. Consider the simple example of a loan of money which I referred to earlier as an illustration of a liability which could not, without distortion, be viewed as purely promissory. The presence of an explicit promise may nevertheless serve valuable evidentiary purposes. First, it helps to avoid doubt about the nature of the transaction. The possibility of a gift is ruled out by the express promise to repay. Then it helps clarify who the parties to the transaction may be, for the handing of money by A to B may create a loan from X to Y where A and B are acting as agents or in a transaction of any complexity. An explicit promise may resolve any ambiguities about such matters. Then again an explicit promise may help settle many minor or ancillary terms, and it is worth reflecting on how and why this is the case. Suppose, for example, that the borrower promises to repay the loan with interest at a specified rate. In the sort of society we live in, it can be taken for granted that a loan should normally carry some rate of interest, and in the absence of an agreed rate, the fixing of the rate would fall to the court in the last resort. What would the court do? The court would, of course, endeavour to fix on a just or reasonable rate of interest having regard to all the circumstances. Here again, therefore, the explicit promise to pay a specified rate does not seem to create the obligation, which would exist anyhow, but to give it precision. And the reason why it gives it precision is, surely, that it functions very like a conclusive admission. If the court is to search for a fair and reasonable rate of interest, the rate which the borrower has agreed to pay is good evidence that that is in fact the fair and reasonable rate. Good evidence, but not, at least not always, conclusive evidence. For if the agreed rate of interest is extortionate, or if it has been obtained by fraud or misrepresentation the promise to pay will not bind.

There are, indeed, some cases in which the evidentiary value of promises has already been distinctly recognized by the courts. Naturally enough, given the classical model of contract, these cases concern situations in which an independent legal obligation already exists. For example, where a person promises to pay for valuable services previously rendered to him—the so-called past consideration cases—the promise may be treated as evidence of the value of those services.[1] And again, where services are rendered in pursuance of a contract which turns out to be invalid for some technical reason, the value of the services may nevertheless be recovered and the contract can be treated as evidence of that value.[2]

It may, of course, be said that these cases are no illustration of the general nature of contractual liability, but on the contrary serve to illustrate the difference between contractual and other forms of liability. For (it may be urged) the whole point of contractual liability is to permit parties to determine conclusively their own obligations. The promise creates the liability, and does not merely evidence it. In non-

[1] *Stewart* v. *Casey* [1892] 1 Ch 104.
[2] *Way* v. *Latilla* [1937] 3 All ER 759.

contractual cases, *per contra*, the duty is in the first instance created by the law; and the promise cannot be treated as creating the obligation. But I suggest that this analysis is the result of treating the executory contract as the paradigm of contract, the heritage of the classical law which I have already criticized. In the part-executed transaction, as I have argued, it is in fact frequently the case that there would be a liability even apart from any express or implied promise. Promises are not a necessary condition of the existence of a liability or the creation of an obligation. The performance by one party of acts which are beneficial to the other, the rendering of services to another, for instance, would normally be thought of as creating some sort of obligation even in the absence of a promise. Similarly, acts of reasonable reliance would often create liability in tort, or by way of trust, or other equitable obligation, even where there is no express or implied promise. Indeed, did not the whole law of trusts arise because property was entrusted to other hands, usually no doubt because of some understanding that the trustee would behave in a certain fashion? In circumstances of this kind, therefore, where obligations would normally be thought of as arising from what has been done, rather than from what has been said, there seems to me no difficulty in regarding promises as having primarily an evidentiary role.

Treating explicit promises as prima-facie evidence, and as strong prima-facie evidence of the fairness of a transaction, of the appropriate price to be paid for goods and services, is an indispensable tool of efficient administration in a free market society. For any other rule would leave it open to a dissatisfied party to any and every transaction to appeal to a judge to upset an agreed price and fix a new one. But, it may be urged, the law does not treat promises as only prima-facie evidence of the fairness of a transaction, or of the terms which should bind the parties; in most circumstances, a promise is treated as conclusive of these matters. If I am right in thinking that the role of the promise is thus limited it is incumbent on me to explain why promises are normally treated as conclusive of most of these questions, and this task I attempt in Essay 5. Here I will content myself with pointing out that promises are never treated as wholly conclusive in law. All promises and contracts are defeasible in *some* circumstances. A promise or agreement extorted by violence is no evidence of the fairness of a transaction, and is therefore naturally set aside by the courts. Promises given as a result of certain types of mistake may likewise be set aside. Alternatively, the courts may uphold the validity of the exchange but adjust the obligations of the parties (for example by implying appropriate terms) so as to ensure, so far as possible, that the exchange is a fair or reasonable one, despite the disparity between the literal obligations assumed by the parties.[1] But the *extent* of the indefeasibility of a promise, the *extent* to which it is to be treated as a conclusive admission of the fairness and reasonableness of the terms of an exchange, is a much less simple proposition. The extent to which the courts and the law are prepared to go in treating promises as defeasible, or merely as prima-facie rather than conclusive evidence of the fairness of in exchange, is obviously something determined by the degree of paternalism which commends itself to the society and the judiciary in question. A society which believes in allowing the skilful and knowledgeable to reap the rewards of their skill and knowledge is likely to have a higher regard for the sanctity of promises than a society which wishes to protect the weak and foolish from the skilful and knowledgeable. As we shall see, this point is a good deal more important in the case of executory transactions.

So far I have been trying to place the part-executed and the wholly-executed transaction more firmly back into the central role of contract, and to suggest that the classical model, based on will theory and the executory transaction, does not fit a large part of law and life. But in the case of wholly executory arrangements, it may seem that things are different. If a person is liable, morally or legally, on a wholly executory arrangement, if he is liable on a promise prior to the receipt of any benefit, and prior to any act of reliance by the promisee, then it would seem that the liability must be promise-based and nothing else. Morally, few would doubt that, prima facie at least, a promise is *per se* binding; and lawyers, while insisting on the requirement of consideration, would largely agree with the moralists. Now the requirement of consideration or, at least, the satisfaction of that requirement, in the case of the wholly executory contract, is one of the puzzles of the common law. A, let us say, orders goods from B, to be specially made to his requirements. The next day, A discovers he can buy what he wants ready-made elsewhere and cancels the order. B, let it be supposed, has so far done nothing whatever under the contract. There is no doubt in law that B can hold A liable and sue him for damages without having to lift a finger to perform his part of the contract. A receives no benefit, B suffers no detriment, no reliance, and yet he is entitled to damages. How can this be so, and how is it that common lawyers have continued

[1] See Essay 11.

to define the doctrine of consideration in terms of benefit and detriment when this definition does not fit the paradigm case of classical contract theory?

The answer to this conundrum, which led to a vast quantity of ponderous legal literature, particularly in America, early in this century, lies, I suggest, deep in our legal history. The story is long and complex and I have no space here to explore it fully. But in essence I believe it is correct to say that, until the end of the eighteenth and beginning of the nineteenth century, the recognition and enforcement of executory contracts was a very different thing from what it is today. In modern law, the plaintiff who sues on a wholly executory transaction obtains damages for his lost expectations, the difference, roughly speaking, between the value to him of the defendant's performance, and the cost to him of his own performance. He makes, in effect, his profit on the transaction without actually having to go through with the transaction. This was not generally the law until very late in the eighteenth century, and it only reached its full development in the nineteenth century. In earlier times the plaintiff who sued on an executory transaction generally remained bound to perform himself, or to pay damages for his own non-performance in the future. The enforcement of an executory contract thus still envisaged an exchange being carried through, benefit for benefit. The defendant might have to pay damages for his non-performance now, but he paid the full value of his performance in the expectation that he would in due course receive the plaintiff's performance. Thus consideration in the form of benefit would always actually pass. If it had not passed before the plaintiff sued, it would still be due afterwards.[1] There was, except in some special and rare instances, no possibility of a plaintiff obtaining damages without any performance himself, without any actual benefit or detriment.[2]

Now as we know, in modern law, all this is different. A plaintiff is unquestionably entitled to expectation damages for breach of an executory contract, without any actual consideration passing. There is no need to show any actual benefit, any detrimental reliance. The

---

[1] These rules were entangled with the independent covenant rules which also remained in the law till late in the eighteenth century. It was because the plaintiff remained liable on his own promise that non-performance by him did not generally prevent him suing the defendant; see generally, my *The Rise and Fall of Freedom of Contract*, (Oxford, 1979, hereafter cited as *Freedom of Contract*), pp. 208–12, 424–5.

[2] Cases of breach of promise of marriage and also wagers were not uncommon exceptions, but these shared the peculiarity that they could not be part executed contracts. Moreover, the independent covenant rules could not have applied to them for obvious reasons.

modern law is squared with the doctrine of consideration by saying that the mere promises constitute consideration for each other. That indeed was what judges had been saying since the time of Elizabeth I, but it has not generally been perceived what an enormous difference has come over the practical import of this formula. For in the reign of Elizabeth I, a promise was good consideration for a promise precisely because both promises had to be performed. In our modern law, a plaintiff's promise is good consideration for the defendant's promise even though the plaintiff is discharged from performing his promise by the defendant's breach. It is only since these rules grew up, therefore, that liability on the wholly executory contract has truly become promise-based, rather than benefit or reliance-based.

But although this form of liability must be treated as promise-based, we are entitled to ask how extensive it is in relation to the rest of the law, and whether it deserves to occupy the central role in contract and even in promissory theory that it occupies today. It is, I think, worth observing that wholly executory contracts are generally nothing like as binding in practice as legal theory might suggest. Consumers and even businessmen often expect to be able to cancel executory agreements with the minimum of penalty, paying perhaps only for actual expenses laid out in reliance on the promise. And such reliance expenditures would, by definition, not exist if the arrangements were still wholly executory. And even in strict law, it must be stressed that the expectations protected by executory contracts are limited. They are not generally expectations of performance but expectations of profit. Where there is no difference in the market price of the goods or services which are the subject of the contract, and the market price of comparable goods or services, the contract may in law be broken with impunity. In practice this must comprise a high proportion of cases in which executory arrangements are broken. Then again, the binding force of wholly executory contracts is normally of an ephemeral nature. Executory contracts do not normally remain executory for very long. Even if made well before the time for performance, the whole purpose of making them is frequently to enable the parties to make preliminary arrangements in confident reliance on reciprocal performance. Thus action in reliance is likely to follow hard on the heels of the making of most executory contracts, and it is only in the rare cases where cancellation is sought very soon after making the contract, or where, despite the lapse of some longer period of time, no action in reliance has been commenced, that the source of the obligation has to be rested in the promise alone. Whatever the paradigm of actual contract may be, there can be no doubt that the paradigm of a *breach of contract* is not the breach of a wholly executory contract. And this surely reflects the intentions of most parties who enter into executory contracts. The primary purpose of making such a contract is usually to agree upon the terms which are to regulate a contemplated exchange, when and if it is carried through; it is surely—at least in most instances—a subordinate and less obvious purpose that the contract binds both parties to see that the exchange is indeed carried through.

If this is correct, it is not difficult to see how, even in the case of wholly executory arrangements, the principal functions of the promise are evidentiary, as they are in the case of the executed or part-executed arrangement. For when the parties begin to carry through the exchange which they have contracted about, obligations would anyhow arise even in the absence of the contract. The transaction would then become part executed and, as before, there is no reason why obligations should not then arise even in the absence of promises. It is, therefore, only in relation to the bare, unperformed, unpaid-for, and unrelied-upon promise, or contract, that the evidentiary theory of promissory or contractual liability cannot be supported. Upon what, then, does liability rest in such circumstances? Wherein is the source of the obligation?

To stress the limited nature of the issue I must again draw attention to the fact that promises, especially when given as part of some mutual arrangement, do not usually remain unrelied upon for very long. And there are, of course, obvious and complex issues involved in defining what is meant by action in reliance for these purposes. Does it include inaction? Does it include opportunity cost, that is the loss or cost incurred by the promisee through failure to search for and make alternative arrangements which he might have made if this particular contract had not been made? Does a sort of generalized action in reliance serve as sufficient to take the case out of the category of the wholly executory arrangement? These are important and difficult questions but I want to put them aside here and face squarely up to the case where there is no reliance of any kind at all; and equally as I have said, where there has been no payment, no benefit rendered or received.

Perhaps an illustration is in order. Let me take an example discussed by Sir James Fitzjames Stephen in the first number of the *Law Quarterly Review* in 1885:[1]

A wanted to take a furnished house, expecting to have to pass the summer in

[1] 1 *Law Q. Rev.* 1, (1885).

London. He made a verbal agreement to take the house of B, a friend and a man in his own position in life, who was going out of town. The day after the agreement was made, A was ordered to return to his appointment in India instantly. A, being thus prevented from occupying the house, asked B to release him from his agreement, which I think most men in B's position would have done, as nothing had been done under it, and B had been put to no expense or inconvenience. B, however, refused. A reminded B of the Statute of Frauds, but added, that having given his word, he would if required, fulfil his agreement, whatever he might think of B's conduct. In this case I think A did his duty as a man of honour.

To a lawyer, this case is clear. A contract was made, and if it was not for the Statute of Frauds, the contract would be binding. Moreover, the modern lawyer is likely to share the moral perspective of Stephen himself. A contract is morally binding as well as legally binding, even though it is purely executory and nothing has been paid, nothing been done under the arrangement.[1] These conclusions do not appear to me to be as self-evident as they have seemed to most Englishmen at least since the days of the seventeenth century Natural Lawyers. But it is anyhow worth observing that the most celebrated of the modern Natural Lawyers offered some argument in support of their views about the inherently binding nature of promises and executory contracts. To Grotius,[2] the right to bind oneself by promise or contract necessarily followed from the power to dispose of property. For to bind oneself by a promise was to dispose of a right, to give the promisee here and now a right over the promisor's liberty or future assets. To him, this appeared a less significant form of disposition and therefore necessarily included in the power of presently disposing of property. Today, this argument simply looks fallacious. No doubt the power to bind oneself as to a future disposition of property is similar to the power to bind oneself by a present disposition; but the two things are not the same, and there is no logical ground for supposing that one must follow from the other.

Samuel Pufendorf, second only to Grotius himself as the founder of seventeenth-century Natural Law, devoted a good deal more attention to the binding nature of bare promises or executory contracts.[3] Like many a modern philosopher, he argued that the tendency of promises to be relied upon, of men to place their faith in promises, was the

[1] An earlier generation of lawyers may not have agreed with this. Cf Bayley J. in *Ridout* v. *Bristow* (1830) 1 Cr. and J. 231, 235: 'It is just that a promise to pay that which I am under no legal or moral obligation to pay should be considered as nudum pactum.'

[2] *De Jure Belli ac Pacis*, Book II, ch. XI.

[3] *De Jure Naturae et Gentium*, Book III, ch. V, §11.

principal justification for treating them as binding. But he added that it would be dangerous to argue that a promise was not binding unless and until it was in fact relied upon. Although in such a case the promisee is no worse off than he would have been if no promise had ever been made, men's duties are not confined to refraining from causing actual harm, actual loss to their fellow-men. Men are, in addition, bound to strive always to further the interests of their fellows, and therefore even a bare unrelied-upon promise is naturally binding. It must be said that this looks somewhat thin and unconvincing today. It is hard to relate these generalized duties to one's fellow-men with the particular obligation deriving from a promise. If there is any substance to the argument, it may be thought to support the evidentiary nature of promises. For the argument, is in effect, that the promise gives precision, clarity and individualized shape to the pre-existing general obligation, owed to the world at large.

If we put aside these historical texts and seek more satisfying arguments for the binding nature of bare promises and contracts, we will, I think, be surprised to discover how little attention has been devoted to them by the common lawyers. Apart from the celebrated article by Fuller and Perdue in the *Yale Law Journal* now fifty years old,[1] little of value has been written on the question. The modern, and perhaps even, by now, the traditional legal view would probably be that promises and executory contracts give rise to reasonable expectations and that it is the function of the law to protect reasonable expectations. But this is itself a somewhat circular justification. We all have a large number of expectations, many of which are perfectly reasonable, but only a few of them are protected by the law. Besides, the reasonableness of an expectation is itself something which turns largely upon whether it is in fact protected. If the law did not protect expectations arising from a wholly executory arrangement, then it would be less reasonable to entertain such expectations, or at any rate to entertain them as entitlements. Wherever the law does give a person the right to change his mind and withdraw from some executory arrangement, any expectations which the other party had ought to be discounted to reflect the right of withdrawal; and if the promisee omitted to discount them, his expectations would hardly be said to be 'reasonable', at least in the sense of deserving protection.[2]

Then again, the explanation appears to prove too much. For reason-

---

[1] 'The Reliance Interest in Contract Damages', 46 *Yale L J* 52 and 373 (1936).
[2] See Essay 7.

able expectations may arise from assertions or representations of fact as much as from promises. Yet the law seldom or never protects such expectations unless and until they have been acted upon. If we can, as I think we should, conceptually equate the idea of action in reliance on representations with the notion of detrimental reliance as a consideration in the case of promises, then we must recognize that representations can only give rise to a contractual-type obligation in the case of a part-executed transaction. And this remains true even in the extreme case of fraud. No matter what expectations are thereby generated, a person who tells a downright and deliberate falsehood is not subject to legal obligations unless and until someone suffers loss through acting upon it. Indeed, even when it is acted upon, it is widely thought that the measure of any consequent liability is fixed by the extent of the reliance losses and not by the expectations generated. This, at least, is said to be the measure of damages in tort for fraud, although it is certainly not the measure in cases classified as warranty or estoppel. It is, perhaps, possible that the explanation for this otherwise puzzling distinction between the law's treatment of promises and assertions lies in the too ready acceptance of the idea that words or conduct are in practice easily classifiable as the one or the other. Perhaps the reality is that in more cases than lawyers are willing to admit, words or conduct are classified as promises or assertions precisely because in the particular circumstances the expectations aroused are, or are not, felt worthy of protection.[1] But if this is the case, then it is clear that we cannot defend the protection of bare expectations by pointing to the fact that they derived from a promise.

Another puzzling feature of the law's willingness to protect bare expectations is that a disappointed expectation is a psychological rather than a pecuniary injury, and the law is generally sparing in its willingness to award compensation for injuries or losses which are neither physical nor pecuniary. And if it should be urged that, at least in the commercial sphere, expectation damages are more widely justifiable, a problem might then arise about the extent to which companies and other commercial bodies can be said to suffer from a disappointment of their expectations. If disappointment is a psychological phenomenon can a company suffer disappointment? Now I would not suggest that the disappointment of reasonable expectations is no ground at all for holding contracts or promises to be binding. To raise an expectation

---

[1] See also Essay 10 where I discuss the use of 'implied promises' as a way of imposing liability for misrepresentation in certain situations.

and then to decline to fulfil it is in some measure to worsen the position of the promisee, certainly an individual promisee. Prima facie this is something that should be avoided, other things being equal. But I am bound to say that it does appear to me to be a very weak ground for the enforcement of executory contracts, and one that could very easily be counter-balanced by proof that other things are not equal. In the example discussed by Stephen, it might well be thought by most people that the inconvenience to the promisor of being held to his contract would be enough to outweigh the prima facie desirability of not disappointing the promisee.

The second possible argument for upholding executory contracts is the argument from principle. Executory contracts are made so that the parties can rely upon each other and take the necessary preliminary steps to performance. The whole point of such contracts is that they invite reliance. Therefore, it may be urged, even if there *has in fact been no reliance yet*, it is desirable that the principle of upholding the sanctity of contracts should be maintained. Supporters of this argument, however, must explain why a shift in the onus of proof would not meet the case. Certainly, it may be justifiable to throw upon the promisor the burden of showing that the promisee has not yet acted upon the promise; but if in fact he can show this, or if it is conceded, can the argument on principle be maintained? What principle is it that requires contracts to be held binding because they may be relied upon where in fact it is conclusively demonstrated that the particular contract has not been relied upon? Here again, I do not think the argument is as weak as it may look. Contracting parties will not always know whether the other party has relied upon the contract, and it may be undesirable to encourage the promisor to take the chance that the promisee has not yet acted in reliance. And even if, to take the strongest case, as in Stephen's example, the promisor knows that the promisee has not yet acted upon the contract, the argument on principle is not necessarily to be discounted. There is a case for saying that the sanctity of a general principle is likely to be better maintained if people are generally persuaded to observe it as a matter of principle, without pausing to examine, in every case, whether the reasons justifying the principle cover the case in hand. Further, there is the court to consider as well as the promisee. The court, when called upon to enforce a contract, may err if it permits the promisor to escape liability because it thinks the promisee has not relied upon the promise; and we may believe that such reliance is so probable, and sometimes so difficult of proof, that it is better not to open the question for factual examination in every case with the resulting cost and possibility of error which this would entail.

Then again, for reasons I elaborate in Essay 5, it is sometimes better to insist on the application of a rule even where the reasons for the rule do not operate in the circumstances of the particular case. But a heavy onus rests on those who assert that this is indeed the case because it involves an argument which is not congenial to our times, and smacks of fetishism, or formalism. Nor is it an argument which seems to carry much weight with the public or our legislators in modern times. Given the temper of the times there may well be difficulty in maintaining the line between holding a promise to be binding because it may be relied upon and holding it binding because it has been relied upon.

The third possible argument in support of the executory contract concerns the case where the contract is a deliberate exercise in risk allocation. Where the primary purpose of a contract is to shift a risk of some future possibility from one party to another, and where, in particular, the risk is thereby shifted to a party who in a commercial sense is better able to take the risk, or to take avoiding action against the risk eventuating, there appears to be a strong economic case for the executory contract. I believe that this argument lies at the heart of the historical development of the binding executory contract in English law, but it is imperative to note the limits upon its application. It is very far from being true that all contracts, even all executory contracts, are exercises in risk allocation. Frequently, it is the interpretation of the law which converts a simple postponed exchange into a risk-allocation exercise, rather than any deliberate intent of the parties. In the example given by Stephen, which was discussed above, it seems clear that the risk of being recalled to India was simply not present to the mind of the promisor, or presumably the promisee either. In such circumstances, therefore, the transaction is not (or not necessarily) *designed* to allocate the relevant risk. It is the law which interprets the transaction as having allocated those risks. It is also far from being always the case that the purpose of an executory contract is to shift a risk to a party whose business it is to handle such risks and who can, therefore, be assumed to be generally more efficient at handling them. Indeed, the clearest and most widespread example of a contract of a risk-allocation character is the simple bet, which involves no such economically efficient transfer of risk. Even business contracts frequently partake of the nature of a bet in so far as they allocate future risks, though in these cases there is a greater likelihood of some economic or social purpose being served inasmuch as the risk is likely to be shifted to a party better able to handle it.

I suggested earlier that the extent to which promises are treated as conclusive evidence of the fairness of transactions must reflect the degree of paternalism in any society. I must now observe that if the primary justification for the enforcement of executory contracts is that they are risk-allocation devices, then it follows that the enforcement of such contracts raises profoundly value-laden questions. The justification for the executory contract becomes, in effect, an economic justification, an argument for greater economic efficiency. The purpose of enforcing such contracts is that of facilitating the use of greater skill, intelligence, foresight, knowledge, and perhaps even resources by those who possess these advantages. To the extent that the law refuses to recognize the binding force of executory transactions in order to protect the weak, the foolish, the improvident or those who lack bargaining power, it must necessarily weaken the incentives and indeed the power of those not suffering these disadvantages. I must not be thought to be arguing for or against developments of this nature in the law. There has been during recent decades no shortage of arguments in favour of a greater willingness to protect contracting parties from their own follies and weaknesses. But more recently still there are signs that lawyers and even the public at large may be coming to appreciate the inevitable costs associated with such protection.

Let me illustrate the point by referring to the simple case, which from time to time receives extensive discussion in the media, of the house-purchase transaction. As everyone knows, the almost invariable practice in England is for such transactions to be entered into, in the first instance, 'subject to contract', which means that the initial agreement lacks binding legal force. Of course, as a matter of legal doctrine, this is explained by reference to the intention of the parties, but I have little doubt that the great majority of buyers and sellers regard the result as prescribed by the law and not as subject to their own intentions at all. The substance of the matter is that the legal profession has devised a procedure which prevents parties from binding themselves to an executory arrangement in most instances until they have had ample opportunity to consult their solicitors and make any necessary financial arrangements. The result naturally protects those who are less able and skilful at managing their affairs from making a commitment which turns out to be disadvantageous. But it inevitably does so by depriving those who are perfectly capable of managing their affairs, of the opportunity of using their skills. The dilemma seems to be inescapable. The economic arguments for the binding executory contract, like those in favour of the institution of property itself, involve a tendency to a perpetuation of existing inequalities. To strike down, or limit the binding force of executory contracts in order to protect some people from their own folly or ignorance is, by contrast, a redistributive device, and like all such devices must impose costs as well as benefits.

The fourth argument, which I have left to the last, for the binding executory contract is the moral argument. It is simple and appealing to argue that promises are morally obligatory, and that this remains the case whether they have been paid for, or relied upon, or not. But as the case for the morally binding nature of promises is examined more closely, it bears a curious resemblance to the case for the binding nature of legal contracts rather than offering an independent reason in support of the law. One of the most commonly adduced reasons for arguing that promises are morally binding is that they have a tendency to be relied upon. We then find it being argued that, if that is the only justification, it is a somewhat circular one. For if promises were not binding, they might not be relied upon.[1] And again, it is argued that if the tendency to rely on promises is the source of their binding character, what of the case where reliance is distinctly disproved? The argument on principle, too, has generated a debate among philosophers which closely parallels the legal and social issues hinted at previously. Principles may be useful as rules of thumb but if it is shown that, in some particular case, adherence to the principle produces worse results than non-adherence, is it not merely rule-worship to insist on maintaining the sanctity of the principle?[2]

Then, too, there is the legal argument that a promise to do something which the promisor is already bound to do cannot (anyhow in some circumstances) constitute a valid consideration for a contract. A close parallel to this is to be found in the writings of some philosophers who argue, like J. R. Searle, that a promise to do something which the promisor was going to do anyhow is not really a promise at all.[3] And finally, the argument that executory contracts may be risk-allocation devices has its parallel in the writings of philosophers like John Rawls

---

[1] See e.g. Warnock, *The Object of Morality* (London, 1971), pp. 99–100.

[2] See e.g. J. J. C. Smart, 'Extreme and Restricted Utilitarianism', 6 *Phil Q*. 344, 348–9 (1956).

[3] See 'What is a Speech Act?' in The Philosophy of Language ed. J. R. Searle (Oxford, 1971), pp. 49–50; J. Rawls, 'Two Concepts of Rules', 64 *Phil. Rev.* 1 (1955).

and H. L. A. Hart who argue that to promise is to deliberately take part in a social practice, accepting the benefits of that practice and therefore necessarily subordinating oneself to its burdens.[1]

But when all is said, I do not find the moral contribution to the problem to be a very satisfying one. For moralists and philosophers, like the lawyers themselves, have not generally perceived the need to separate off the wholly executory arrangement for independent justification. Virtually all discussion of the source of contractual and promissory obligation, in law and in morality, has failed to draw the all important distinction between promises and contracts which rest purely in intention, and promises and contracts which depend partly on action. Surely, nobody can doubt that morally speaking promises are more strongly binding where payment has already been received, or where there is a clear and significant act in reliance which would worsen the position of the promisee if the promise were not performed. And just as I have suggested that, in the law of part-executed contracts, explicit promises may play a useful evidentiary role, so it may be suggested that promises themselves are frequently of an evidentiary character. The purpose of a promise, far from being, as is so often assumed, to create some wholly independent source of an obligation, is frequently to bolster up an already existing duty. Promises help to clarify, to quantify, to give precision to moral obligations, many of which already exist or would arise anyhow from the performance of acts which are contemplated or invited by the promise. The promise which is given without any independent reason for it is a peculiarity, just as the wholly executory contract is a legal peculiarity. Is it pure coincidence that the phrase, a 'gratuitous promise', means both a promise without payment and a promise without reason? Could it then be that the refusal of English law to recognize the binding force of executory gratuitous promises is not the peculiarity, the idiosyncrasy it has so long been thought to be? Might it not be that the real oddity lies in the belief that a bare promise creates a moral obligation and should create a legal obligation, without any inquiry into the reason for which the promise was given, or the effect that the promise has had?

These arguments, of course, require much greater development than they can be given here; but enough has been said to show that, if they stand up to further examination, they should suffice to dethrone the

---

[1] H. L. A. Hart, 'Legal and Moral Obligation,' in Essays in Moral Philosophy, ed. Melden (Seattle and London, 1958); 'Are there any Natural Rights?' 64 *Phil. Rev.* 175 (1955).

executory contract from the central place which it occupies in contract theory. The consequences of this would be to require some drastic redrawing of the lines of the conceptual structure of contractual and promissory obligation. In the first place, the distinction between contract and restitution would surely come crashing to the ground. This distinction was not anyhow indigenous to English law. It is well known that, until the middle of the nineteenth century at least, the common lawyers distinguished between express and implied contracts, not between contracts and quasi-contracts. To the early common lawyers, the important point in common between express and implied contracts was that both usually involved a claim for payment or reimbursement for a benefit which had been conferred by the plaintiff on the defendant. Whether the defendant had promised to pay for that benefit was a secondary question. In the nineteenth century, when the executory contract became the pivotal key to the law of obligations, when will theory flourished, and when, we may add, renewed study of the classics reminded common lawyers of the Roman law distinctions and terminology, the old common law distinction fell into disrepute. The process began with academics and writers like John Austin, Henry Maine and Martin Leake. Will theory, which emphasized the importance of free choice and the voluntary creation of obligations, was plainly inconsistent with the indigenous common law. The newer ideas got into the books and—after the lapse of a couple of generations— into the Law Reports. They passed into orthodoxy. Everybody (myself included) began to say that quasi-contracts had nothing to do with contracts. The contract textbooks expelled the subject. Universities have begun to run separate courses on the Law of Restitution. Plainly, if the part-executed contract is to replace the executory contract as the centre piece of contract theory, we shall have to turn our back on these exciting new ideas. We may then discover that, far from being new, they derive from the intellectual climate of the early nineteenth century. Free choice in all things, rational planning, calculated risk assessment, and the severest limitation of the active role of state and judge, these are the themes which underlie the distinction between contract and restitution. It is scarcely necessary to add that they are the themes of the last century, although it is also necessary to add that there have been some signs of resurgence in belief in the ideology of freedom of contract in the past decade or so.

A similar fate may well await the distinction between contract and tort when once the executory contract is removed from the central place in the law of obligations. I have already suggested that our nineteenth-century heritage has led us to place undue emphasis on the extent to which contractual obligations depend upon intentions and the voluntary assumption of liability. But is it not equally true that, perhaps by way of reaction, tort theory has swung too far in the opposite direction? In their reaction away from contract, lawyers and judges have tended to stress the positive nature of tortious liability. Tort duties are imposed by law, not assumed by the parties. They are the reflection of society's standards of fairness and reasonableness and not the result of deliberate submission to a mutual binding arrangement, and so on. I want to suggest that all this has tended to draw far too sharp a line between contract and tort. It is not true that consent, intention, voluntary conduct are irrelevant to tort liabilities. The modern law of negligence is, in many respects, an offshoot of nineteenth-century contract law. Historically, the tort of negligence which dominates modern tort law grew almost entirely out of contractual-type arrangements. Personal injury actions brought against occupiers of premises, against employers, against railway companies were the forerunners of the modern running-down case. The road accident between strangers was not the typical tort action of the last century. And even today it remains true that nearly all tort liabilities arise in the course of the performance of voluntary actions. A person who negligently injures another while driving his car is voluntarily on the road, voluntarily driving his car, and may be said to submit himself to the requirements of the law with as much or as little truth as the seller of goods. The liability of the bus company to pedestrians or other road users does not, in this perspective, differ significantly from its liability to passengers inside the bus. In both cases, I suggest, liability arises primarily from what is voluntarily done, from the element of reciprocal benefit and from the fact of reliance.

It is, of course, true that the sharp distinctions drawn by the law between tortious and contractual liability have, over the years, led to various accretions of positive law. In particular, contractual liability is often stricter than tortious liability. The seller of defective goods is liable even without proof of negligence for any injury caused by the goods to someone who can claim that he has contracted to buy them. But this distinction is, in a way, an illustration of the theme I am attempting to develop. For here too, lawyers and reformers are rejecting the traditional approach. Most lawyers would today prefer to decide what the obligations of a vendor of goods should be, and would then construe his behaviour to support those obligations. Thus if it is thought, as it widely is, that a vendor of defective goods should be strictly liable to anyone who uses the goods and not only to those who buy the goods, the vendor can be said to give an implied warranty that his goods will be safe. But this implied warranty does not necessarily mean that the vendor is thought to voluntarily accept that liability; he voluntarily sells the goods, and the liability is imposed upon him. If we ask, further, why the obligations should be imposed, we will find, in most cases, that the twin elements of benefit and detriment underlie the judgment. In this particular case, for instance, it would be widely agreed that the vendor gets the benefit of the sale, that the purchaser or user relies upon him to distribute goods which are not dangerous, and that these two factors, together with the fact that the sale is a voluntary transaction, suffice to justify the obligation.

It is worth considering another example, where tort law is concerned primarily with the waiver or reduction of legal obligations, rather than its creation. The liability of a car driver to a passenger has, both in this country, and still more overseas, given rise to many shifts and devices for restricting the application of the normal rules of negligence. Whether this has been done by the former legislative exemption from carrying insurance to cover liability to passengers, or by invocation of the maxim *volenti non fit injuria,* or by denial of a duty of care, or by restricting liability to cases of gross negligence, it is surely not far-fetched to see the benefit to the passenger as the heart of the problem. The passenger who is a mere guest (as opposed to the fare-paying passenger) is deriving a gratuitous benefit from being carried in the vehicle. Is it right that he should be permitted to look this gift-horse in the mouth and sue the driver in the event of injury in an accident? The fact that an emphatic affirmative answer has, at least in this country, now been given to this question, does not, I think, detract from the value of this illustration.

I do not, of course, want to suggest that the whole law of obligations can be rewritten in terms of a few simple principles drawn from the notions of benefit and reliance. Society and social and economic relationships are too complex in the modern industrial world for over-simplifications of this nature. But what I do want to suggest is that the great divide between duties which are voluntarily assumed and duties which are imposed by law is itself one of these over-simplifications. A more adequate and more unifying conceptual structure for the law of obligations can be built around the interrelationship between the concepts of reciprocal benefits, acts of reasonable reliance, and voluntary human conduct.

POSTSCRIPT: A REPLY TO MY CRITICS

Since this essay was first written in 1977, many of the questions I discussed there have been the subject of extensive debate and controversy. My own views, first on the historical origins of these matters were set forth at some length in my *The Rise and Fall of Freedom of Contract* (1979), and secondly on the philosophical foundations of promissory liability (on the assumption that contract law is indeed about the enforcement of promises) in *Promises, Morals and Law* (1981). But this essay still encapsulates my ideas in a sufficiently succinct form that I have felt justified in reprinting it above, with only minor revisions. It is, however, appropriate that I should append to it some comments by way of reply to some of my leading critics. Amongst these must be numbered Professor Charles Fried, of the Harvard Law School, whose *Contract as Promise, A Theory of Contractual Obligation* (1981) was avowedly inspired in part by a desire to refute some of my views. I reviewed Professor Fried's book at some length in the *Harvard Law Review*, and that review has been substantially rewritten to appear as Essay 6 in the present collection. I shall not therefore say anything further about it here. I shall confine myself here to replying, necessarily briefly, to some of the criticisms of my views which have been published by Professor J. Raz,[1] Professor Peter Birks,[2] and Mr A. S. Burrows.[3]

Professor Raz has himself written extensively on the subject of promises, on practical reasoning, and on obligations, and has in the process developed a subtle theory of promising, as well as some extremely important ideas about (what I call in Essay 5) formal and substantive reasoning. On a great many issues, Professor Raz and I are very much in agreement. We agree in rejecting the notion that it is self-evident that a person is bound by his own voluntary undertakings, while being problematic how a person can be bound by any other kind of obligation. We agree in rejecting the notion that promises are binding, irrespective of their social context, as manifestations, in Professor Raz's words, 'of the sovereign will of a monadic individual'.

[1] In a review of my *Promises, Morals and Law*, in 95 *Harv. L. Rev.* 916 (1982).

[2] 'Restitution and the Freedom of Contract', [1983] *Current Legal Problems* 141.

[3] 'Contract, Tort and Restitution—A Satisfactory Division or Not', 99 *Law Q. Rev.* 216 (1983).

We agree that the purpose of contract law is not just to enforce promises; we agree that the legal protection of bare unrelied-on expectations is (at least) more difficult to justify, and that the expectation-damages measure is not obviously the appropriate remedy for a breach of contract, even if we differ in our reasons for this. He bases his view on Mill's harm principle, taking it to mean (as I understand him) that the disappointment of bare expectations is not such a harm as necessarily to call for the enforcement of the moral obligation to observe a promise, while I have chosen to argue that law and morality are much more closely linked in this regard, and that it is a mistake to believe that there is (or is often) a moral obligation (or a strong moral obligation) to observe a promise which has not been paid for or relied upon.

I need not pursue this difference between us at any length, because I believe that in the end very little divides us in this regard. I have always conceded that there is a 'positive morality' which holds that a promisor is prima facie under a moral obligation to keep his promise; and now that I have come to appreciate more clearly the great importance of (what I call in Essay 5) the nature of formal reasoning on issues like this, I would not dispute that normatively it is desirable that people at large should believe that promises ought to be kept. The purpose of my—possibly exaggerated—challenge to the very idea that a promise even creates a prima facie moral obligation, (especially in my *Promises, Morals and Law*) was to draw attention to a number of factors which experience of contract law led me to think were neglected by philosophical writngs about promises. In particular I wanted to draw attention to the facts that (1) many, if not most, promises are made as a way of obtaining something, and when that has been obtained, the case for enforcement, or obligatoriness, seems to me greatly enhanced; (2) that a promise invites reliance by virtue of some propositional content, and that once relied upon there is again a greatly enhanced case for treating the promise as binding; but that (3) an unpaid-for and unrelied-upon promise is an altogether different matter, and much less worthy of being treated as a source of moral or legal obligation.

When Professor Raz argues that an unpaid-for and unrelied-upon promise should not (or not necessarily) be legally binding because its breach may cause no 'harm' in the Millian sense, but that nevertheless such a promise is morally binding, he will probably find ready acceptance among many contemporary lawyers and philosophers. Yet if Mill's principle is itself in some sense a moral principle, then this argument concedes that there are moral grounds for not giving an unpaid-for and unrelied-upon promise that degree of bindingness which legal enforcement entails. It seems to me that we then end up with two kinds of obligations arising from promises, (1) those not worthy of legal enforcement, and (2) those which are. The moral (as well as the legal) force of the second kind surely must be greater than the moral force of the first, otherwise why should breach of the second carry this legal result while breach of the first does not? This seems to me so close to my own view that it is scarcely worthwhile to contest the remaining points of difference between us.

Professor Raz also argues that, despite the Millian principle, it is defensible (or may in some cases be defensible—I am not sure which view he takes) to enforce purely executory promises on the grounds (1) that this protects the practice of undertaking voluntary obligations, (2) that even the frustration of expectations may amount to a harm in the relevant sense, and (3) that leaving the court to search for reliance losses in every case may lead to expensive litigation and frequent judicial mistakes. All three of these arguments I have already made above, and were made in the original essay, though perhaps less clearly and strongly than they are now.

One other apparent difference of opinion between Professor Raz and myself concerns the distinction between contractual and tortious liability. In the original essay I argued (and this passage is unchanged above) that implied promises are very often invoked to justify the imposition of a liability which is not truly promissory. Thus I gave the example of the person who boards a bus, and suggested that if he is to be treated as having impliedly promised to pay his fare, then there is no reason why we should not regard him as impliedly promising to cross the road with due care when he alights from the bus. Professor Raz criticizes my position here, by insisting that there is a difference between these two sorts of obligation, which lies in the fact that the justificatory relevance of the knowledge of the person obliged differs in the two cases. In the case of the genuine promise, the promise (and the promisor's state of mind) are positive justifications for imposing liability; in the non-genuine case, the knowledge of the obligor that his conduct will involve him in obligations is not a positive justification for imposing the obligation upon him, but merely a negative justification for not allowing him to argue that it would be unjust to impose the obligation. The positive grounds for imposing the obligation lie elsewhere. Professor Raz adds to this his insistence that promising is only an extreme case of voluntary obligations, and he concludes by insisting that the function of contract law is not so much (or should not so much be) to enforce promises, as to protect the practice of voluntary undertakings and the individuals who give such undertakings.

Here again, it seems to me that little divides us in the end, despite Professor Raz's stress on the different nature of the justificatory relevance of the agent's knowledge in the two cases, a point on which I said nothing. I argued that stress on the voluntary nature of contractual liabilities had led lawyers and theorists to under-emphasize the importance of the voluntary elements in many other forms of liability as well. Professor Raz seems to agree with this, though he confines his remarks to the purposes of *contract* law, when it seems clear to me that the thrust of his argument relates to the whole law of obligations. If, as he asserts, promising is only a small sub-branch of voluntary undertaking, then the function of the law of obligations as a whole (or one such function anyhow) should be to protect such undertakings.

For my part, I am prepared to accept the point about justificatory relevance, though it seems to me clear that it can only be accepted via a theory (which Professor Raz has made elsewhere, and which I substantially adopt in Essay 5) about what I call formal reasons. But I doubt its practical importance, at any rate in this context. Even in many cases of quite genuine contractual obligations—say commercial contracts between businessmen—I think it will often be found that the language of express promising is avoided, but everyone proceeds in the knowledge that if they act in such-and-such a manner, legal obligations will be imposed upon them as a result.[1] And certainly, it seems to me clear that this will be the usual position in regard to all those parts of a legal relationship arising out of an express contract which do not themselves involve what Americans call the 'dickered terms'. Thus if Professor Raz wishes to treat these latter obligations as arising from voluntary undertakings, rather than promises, I would not disagree with him, though I would repeat that such voluntary conduct is also to be found in many situations leading to tortious liability (and restitutionary liability) and that the role of the voluntary nature of the conduct will vary according to the circumstances. Moreover, the two types of case will often (indeed, will typically) shade into each other so that any attempt to keep them separate in practice is likely to be impractical.[2]

I have two doubts about this result. The first is that I am less confident

[1] See the discussion in Essay 10, pp. 283–4 below.
[2] See below, pp. 282, 283–6.

of my ability to identify the elements of promissory liability outside the legal framework than Professor Raz or Professor Fried. So long as lawyers wish to treat contract law as more or less co-terminous with promising, it continues to be necessary to insist that promising does not have the essential voluntary characteristics which mark it off from other obligations that most lawyers seem to think. If lawyers could be educated to accept that a large part of the law of contract is not based on the idea of promise, then this would be less important. My second doubt goes in the other direction: if, as Professor Raz and I agree, there are circumstances in which formal reasoning (as I call it) justifies the imposition of obligations without penetration of the underlying reasons of substance, then this possibility, it is surely clear, must exist in some areas of voluntary obligation besides promising. If, when businessmen make contracts without using the language of express promises, but (for instance) sign conventional pieces of paper which are understood to be contractual, their liability is not to be regarded as promissory, it seems to be nevertheless clear that the same powerful reasons for refusing to reopen the transaction will exist as if they had used the express language of promising. It is doubtless partly for these reasons that lawyers have traditionally been so casual about penetrating the true nature of implied promises, and have been so free in treating obligations as contractual whether or not explicit promises can be found at their root. But if we are now to mark off promissory liability as something different from liability arising from non-promissory voluntary undertakings, then we will need to ask whether, and when, these latter obligations depend upon similar kinds of formal reasoning as promises themselves. I doubt whether Professor Raz would disagree with this in view of his own work on what I call formal reasons.

I turn now to make some comments on the powerful and elegant criticisms of my position made by Professor Birks. Professor Birks is concerned to defend the law of restitution against my attempts to deny it—as he thinks I do—independent status. He makes two major criticisms of my position. First, he rejects my view (expressed in *The Rise and Fall of Freedom of Contract* rather than in the above essay) that it is 'misconceived' to try to separate out the law of restitution from the law of contract. He suggests first that there is a logical distinction between restitutionary and contractual liability: restitution concerns the rules which require an unjustly enriched party to disgorge his enrichment. He must account for the amount by which he has been enriched, neither more nor less. This is not necessarily, or at all, the

same as the purpose of contract law which he takes to be the enforcement of compensation for breach. He concedes, however, that
though this may be a logically sound distinction it may possibly be so
inert as to be useless, though he then gives reasons for rejecting that
view also.

Professor Birks misunderstands my position when I say that the
attempt to separate out the law of restitution from the law of contract
is 'misconceived'. Unlike Professor Birks, I do not find the divisions
between the branches of the law to rest neatly upon fundamental theoretical or conceptual distinctions. The distinctions drawn between the
branches of the law seem to me to be drawn for purposes of pedagogy
and exposition, but precisely where the lines will be drawn often depends on historical accidents and traditions. I think it is 'misconceived'
to separate the law of restitution from the law of contract for two
reasons. First, because I believe that in the long run this will do damage
to the law of contract. If we try to put into the contractual 'basket'
only those parts of the law in which it is more or less plausible to
suggest that the results are in some sense determined by the parties'
mutual consent, then there are very real dangers that judges and other
lawyers will fail to appreciate that *all* the law of obligations is not based
on one set of values only—roughly those we associate with 'freedom of
contract'. That these dangers are real and not imaginary seems to me
to be demonstrated by the quite extraordinary freedom which the judges
allow themselves today in imposing liability in tort for negligence even
in contractual contexts, while denying themselves similar freedom in
cases where it is impossible to pray in aid tortious liability, even by
today's elastic standards.

It is for this reason that I made the point which Professor Birks
criticizes, that benefit-based liabilities appear to be surfacing in many
corners of the law, such as property law, family law, labour law, and
so on, and not merely in the law of restitution. In answer to this
Professor Birks makes a number of elegant and subtle points, to which
I must refer the reader, but (with respect) I do not think he does full
justice to the point I had in mind, though perhaps did not spell out
with sufficient explicitness. Take first the question of property law. I
had in mind two points: there are, it seems to me, a number of modern
cases in which obligations have been placed on the owners of property
simply because they are the owners of property—for instance, *Leakey*
v. *National Trust*,[1]—in a way which would not have been done in the

---

[1] [1980] QB 485.

last century. This sort of case seems to me to illustrate a moral idea, namely that property rights are a benefit which should carry corresponding obligations.

Then I had in mind a case like *Greenwood* v. *Bennett*[1] which seemed to me to illustrate a willingness to reduce, or cut down on, the property rights of an owner, in order to give effect to a moral ideal, that another party who had benefited an owner, even without his consent, should (in appropriate circumstances) be entitled to be paid for the value of that benefit. Again, it seems clear to me that this represents a change in value systems, as compared with the law of the last century. Property rights are less sacrosanct than they were: the rights of the property owner may have to give way to the conflicting rights of the benefit-conferer.

Similar decisions can be found in other branches of the law, as for instance, in family law cases where modern law would give a wife a share in the beneficial ownership of a family home because (for instance) she had benefited her husband—the legal owner—by work she had done, or contributions she had paid, towards the purchase of the house. Professor Birks attempts to deny the importance of such cases by arguing that they are equally relevant to the law of restitution and to other branches of the law. This fails to do justice to my point, which was that in these, and in many other cases, moral ideas have gained ground to the effect that those who confer benefits on others, *even without their consent or contract or agreement to pay* are often entitled to be recompensed. If contract lawyers do not study these cases, if they are never thought to be relevant in contract cases, if they are never cited as analogies in contract cases, then there is a serious danger that lawyers will continue to believe that modern contract law is based on one set of values to the exclusion of all others. Furthermore, as I try to demonstrate in detail in Essay 10, it seems to me that the law of misrepresentation, and especially the 'request' principle which is associated with it, is also closely related to certain 'benefit' ideas—that is, obligations are often imposed on one person to indemnify another where the former has requested the latter to do something for the benefit of the former. These liabilities are not restitutionary in Professor Birks's (or any) sense. Nor can they be assigned to any individual branch of the law. Yet (as I argue in Essay 10) it seems clear that the liabilities are substantially benefit-based.

Secondly, I think it misconceived to try to put aside restitutionary

[1] [1973] QB 195.

remedies when we study and teach contract law, for the obvious reason that the great majority of restitutionary claims arise out of failed or putative contracts. Professor Birks objects to my attempt to link (anyhow large parts of) contract and restitution under the generic rubric of 'benefit-based liability' because he suggests that this fails to distinguish between genuine resitutionary cases and cases where more or less than the value of the benefit will have to be paid, and this distinction can only be drawn in most cases according to whether the benefits have been conferred pursuant to a promise. But all this only goes to prove that all line drawing in the law involves an element of arbitrariness. Of course, if we incorporate the law of restitution within contract law we will have problems: there will be cases of restitution where there is no 'contractual element' at all, for instance conditional gifts—though that may only demonstrate that we need a wider conception of 'contract'. Equally, the appropriate remedy for what has happened will sometimes be fixed by looking to what the plaintiff has lost, whether by reliance or also in expectation, and sometimes by looking to what the defendant has gained; and lumping all these cases into one branch of the law may—though it need not—obscure these distinctions. But on the other hand, drawing a line between restitution and contract law also suffers from disadvantages: it fails to take account of the fragmentary nature of 'purely contractual' remedies for breach. One has only to consider what an enormous hole would exist in a student's grasp of contract law if he knew nothing about restitutionary remedies arising from breach or frustration or part performance.

But more fundamental than this is the difference between Professor Birks and myself on the question whether restitutionary remedies can appropriately be called 'contractual'. Again Professor Birks defends what must now be taken to be orthodoxy forcefully and skilfully. Contractual remedies, he insists, are remedies for breach, which involve compensating the injured party. Restitutionary remedies, though frequently overlapping with contractual ones in the context of contractual arrangements, do not depend upon breach, but on a different conceptual justification. I concede the power of this case, which is, of course, itself a part of the classical tradition (though modernized as to the role of restitution) to which I also conceded much power. But at the end of the day I remain unconvinced.

My continuing doubts stem from my inability to accept that most remedies for breach of contract are based on, or follow naturally or inexorably from, the making of the contract, or the intention of the parties. Undoubtedly this is sometimes the case, for instance, with an enforceable debt, or an enforceable liquidated damages clause. But in the great majority of cases, it seems to me clear that normal 'contractual' remedies are fashioned by the court. The rules as to when expectation damages are awardable, when reliance damages only can be obtained, rules as to remoteness, mitigation, and so on, rules as to whether the plaintiff can recover only for pecuniary loss, or can in addition recover for non-pecuniary items, or can recover exemplary damages, and a fortiori, of course, rules like those concerning penalties and equitable relief, just do not stem naturally from breach of contract. Consider, for instance, the simple problem raised by a sale of goods in which the buyer fails to pay the price. Can the seller sue for the price? As we all know, the answer is complex and subtle: sometimes such an action lies, and sometimes it does not. It is the law, the court, which decides whether to allow this remedy or not, and the reasons for the law have little to do with the intention of the parties. The intent of the parties is surely the same in all these cases. The buyer intends to pay the price if he gets the goods, but 'if he gets the goods' is a difficult concept which most buyers will not have stopped to analyse. That analysis is and must be provided by the court. But if this is the case with ordinary contractual remedies for breach, why cannot restitutionary remedies equally be treated as simply part of the total legal rules governing transactions or contracts which fail in some way or another? Sometimes restitutionary remedies are explicitly provided for ('the buyer is entitled to his money back without questions asked') just as contractual ones; sometimes, they are explicitly excluded just as other remedies are sometimes explicitly excluded; sometimes they are allowed by the law as more appropriate than reliance or expectation damages. Sometimes they are allowed as a possible alternative to exemplary damages. What is there in all this which requires us to treat restitutionary remedies in the contractual context as not being part of the law of contract, or (if that means something different) as not being 'contractual' in their nature?

As I have said, I do not deny that different lines can be drawn for purposes of study and exposition of the law. No doubt there is utility in studying a variety of restitutionary cases together: after all, the search for analogy in legal reasoning is always a search for unusual and different ways of classifying material and no one can doubt its utility. So I do not want to detract from the value of Professor Birks's (or anyone else's) 'high-powered postgraduate seminars' on the law of restitution. But I am concerned that these seminars should not be at the expense of a developed understanding of the law of contract.

Mr Burrows, in his article in the *Law Quarterly Review* for 1983, criticizes my views for reasons similar to those of Professor Birks, but in a more general fashion. The existing division of the law of obligations into three principal categories is, he argues, a satisfactory division because it separates at least most of the law based on the three most important principles of the law of obligations. These are, of course, (1) the fulfilment of expectations engendered by promises, (2) compensation for wrongful harm, and (3) the reversal of unjust enrichment. In addition, he criticizes me for suggesting that the protection of expectations is linked to the ideals of a *laissez-faire* society, for suggesting that the present law does not substantially reflect the distinction between expectation and reliance damages, and that promissory estoppel is a form of reliance-based liability.

A full refutation of these criticisms would require another full-length treatment, though I fear much of it would simply repeat things I have already said elsewhere. But as Mr Burrows's views probably represent a widely held orthodoxy, they deserve some response at this point.

I must start by stressing that the 'division' of the law into segments is an artificial exercise, and whether a particular division is satisfactory or not cannot really be answered until we know the purpose of the division. Obviously, as I have already suggested above, we can draw all sorts of different lines across the categories and cases of the law, depending on whether we wish to collect together all the material which has affinities for this purpose, or for that purpose. So, for example, someone who wishes to be a legal adviser to the personnel manager of a large organization will need to familiarize himself with *all* the law concerning the obligations of employers to their employees, and it will be of little concern to him (or his superiors) that some of these duties may be contractual and some tortious. Now it seems clear to me that the present 'division' of the law of obligations into the three familiar categories espoused by Mr Burrows is designed largely for purposes of exposition and pedagogy. It is useful to divide up a large and potentially unmanageable subject so that we can teach it and write books on it and examine on it. But the question then arises whether the material within each of these three categories has more in common than material which spills across the boundaries. It is this which I deny, and I remain entirely unpersuaded by Mr Burrows's attempt to defend the traditional divisions.

Take first the law of tort, and consider the extraordinarily heterogeneous collection of cases with which that law deals. It deals with bodily injury, with defamation, with deceit and misrepresentation, with malicious prosecution and wrongful imprisonment, with intimidation, and inducing breach of contract. To insist that all these areas of the law have in common the fact that they deal with 'compensation for wrongful harm' hardly explains why the law should lump them all into one category and treat them as one 'division' of the law. After all, there is a sense in which even breach of contract is designed to provide 'compensation for wrongful harm', and until we have defined our terms more carefully, we cannot use them to justify these divisions.

Next, consider how closely related many of the areas of tort law are to many areas of contract law, especially now that liability for economic loss, at least in certain circumstances, has become a recognized head of negligence liability. Deceit, misrepresentation, duress, inducing breach of contract, and negligence are all torts which may determine the obligations of contracting parties, or putative contracting parties. Nor do these torts only arise incidentally, as it were, in determining side isues in contractual relations. In one sense they are of absolutely fundamental importance: for instance, the torts of deceit and duress actually define the parameters of permissible conduct in the market-place, and the market is (as Mr Burrows rightly insists) still central to our law, and therefore to our legal theory. When we are told that a variation of a contract obtained by a threat to break that contract may be treated as invalid because it was obtained by duress or intimidation,[1] can it be seriously argued that the law of duress or intimidation is tort and concerned only with compensation for harms? Or again, consider how the expansion of modern tort law is beginning to impose duties on parties in a negotiating position who have not yet made a contract, as in *Esso* v. *Mardon*[2] and *Box* v. *Midland Bank*.[3] And what about a case like *Cornish* v. *Midland Bank*,[4] where the Court of Appeal suggested that a mere non-disclosure by one contracting party to another could be actionable in the tort of negligence, even where conventional contract doctrine has hesitated to impose a duty to disclose?[5] And to return for a moment to the law of restitution, is it not now becoming apparent

[1] See, for instance, *North Ocean Shipping Co. Ltd.* v. *Hyundai Construction Co. Ltd.*, (*The Atlantic Baron*) [1979] QB 705; *Pao On* v. *Lau Yiu* [1980] AC 614.

[2] [1976] QB 801.

[3] [1979] 2 Lloyd's Rep. 391.

[4] [1985] 3 All ER 513.

[5] See Chitty on *Contracts*, 25th edn., vol.ii, §4414.

that the principle of 'free acceptance' which is often used to fill in gaps in contract law is inadequate to do justice between the parties precisely because—following the traditional demarcation lines—the courts have been reluctant to impose duties on putative contracting parties?[1] In other words, it may be suggested that the traditional threefold classification breaks down in practice in handling the relationship of negotiating parties, precisely because the law has failed to grapple with the problems arising out of failed negotiations in a coherent and integrated manner.

Consider next how the combination of liability in negligence with liability for economic loss is leading to the further erosion of the privity of contract principle: is it really necessary today to do more than point to cases like *The Eurymedon*,[2] *Junior Books*,[3] *Lambert* v. *Lewis*,[4] *Ross* v. *Caunters*,[5] and *The Aliakmon*[6] to make the point that the existing division between contract and tort is—at least in these areas—quite artificial? More broadly, can one possibly understand the modern law of products liability or medical malpractice or other forms of professional liability without study of the rules of contract and tort in tandem?

The fundamental flaw in the traditional approach, as it is expounded by Mr Burrows (and in the liberal theory of contract which I discuss further in Essay 6), seems to me to be the view that contract law is largely about the enforcement of promises, and the protection of expectations engendered by promises. I cannot do more than repeat a point I have so frequently made elsewhere, that a very large part of modern contract law depends upon the creation of obligations which do not arise from promises, and upon the protection of reliance, rather than the protection of expectations. In connection with this last point I must add that Mr Burrows mistakes me in supposing that I believe the protection of expectations *per se* to be associated with the ideology of *laissez-faire*. Of course this is incorrect, and I have never said anything of the kind; the protection of expectations which are (for instance) denied by the terms of a contract (such as may be obtained under the

---

[1] See Ball, 'Work Carried out in Pursuance of Letters of Intent—Contract or Restitution?', 99 *Law Q. Rev.* 572 (1983).

[2] [1975] AC 154.

[3] [1982] AC 520.

[4] [1982] AC 225.

[5] [1980] Ch. 299.

[6] [1986] AC 785.

Unfair Contract Terms Act) is highly paternalistic. It is the protection of expectations deriving from promises which I regard as associated with a *laissez-faire* ideology, together with the related idea that a person who has *not* obtained a promise to protect himself cannot complain of the other party's behaviour. That is indeed a highly individualistic position, and is surely very closely linked with nineteenth century ideology. And that is why, as modern tort law imposes duties on parties who have made no promises, it is departing from the individualist, self-reliance stance, of traditional law.

I conclude with some comments about the extent to which existing law does (as Mr Burrows asserts) reflect the existing contract–tort distinction, at least in the realm of damages. Of course I concede that the general rule of contract law differs here from the general rule of tort law, and does indeed appear to be based on the notion that promises ought to be performed, and that therefore a promisee is entitled to have his expectations of performance protected. Nevertheless, it is unrealistic to assume that these 'general rules' reflect the reality of life, without more. As I have tried to point out elsewhere, consumers are very rarely held liable for expectation losses,[1] and there is plenty of evidence that, even in business transactions, commercial parties are often content with protection of their reliance losses in the event of breach.[2] One must beware of assuming that the 'general rules' of the law are actually translated into practice 'as a general rule'. I must also reiterate my view that the mitigation doctrine does in practice make an enormous dent in the theory that the promisee is entitled to full protection for his expectations. Mr Burrows tries to dispose of this point by further sub-categorization—the mitigation doctrine, he argues, adds a 'supplemental policy' to the protection of expectations. Perhaps so, but this policy runs counter to the policy of protecting contractual expectations, and pursuit of this second policy cannot but be at the expense of the first. And as to the doctrine of promissory estoppel, I cannot see how Mr Burrows can argue that this is designed to protect the expectations of the promisee when it seems to be pretty well established that the promisee will only be protected to the extent of his

---

[1] See my *Freedom of Contract*, pp. 754–759.

[2] See Macaulay,'Non-Contractual Relations in Business: A Preliminary Study', 28 *Am. Soc. Rev.* 55 (1963); Beale and Dugdale, 'Contracts Between Businessmen: Planning the Use of Contractual Remedies', 2 *Br. J. L. and Soc.* 45 (1975).

reliance, and not at all if his reliance is so trivial that it can be relatively easily undone.[1]

---

[1] See for instance, *The Post Chaser* [1982] 1 All ER 19. Of course it might be argued that this case did not turn upon a 'real' promise but upon conduct calculated to lead to reliance; but that is true of the great mass of promissory estoppel cases. A theory which separates out 'real' promises from objectively-defined promises would only account for a small part of the law of contract, the rest of which would then have to merge with tort.

3

Holmes and the Theory of Contract

1. Holmes's Theory of Legal Liability

In this essay I propose to examine Holmes's theory of contract, as revealed in *The Common Law* and elsewhere in his writings. At the heart of *The Common Law* is a theory of legal liability which Holmes expounded in Lecture II on the Criminal Law, Lectures III and IV on Torts, and Lectures VII, VIII, and IX on Contracts. Holmes must be one of the very few theorists of modern times who have argued for a general theory of legal liability embracing both the criminal and the civil law, and the contemporary English lawyer is certain to be deeply suspicious of his suggestion that 'the general principles of criminal and civil liability are the same.'[1] As this passage indicates, Holmes proffers his theory of liability as though he were engaged in a descriptive exercise, but in truth he does not distinguish between a descriptive and a normative theory. Here and there he admits that the precedents and authorities in support of his theory may be slender, but this does not shake his faith in his theory, which might therefore seem more normative in character. The theory is clearly perceived by Holmes as one that ought to, and does, underlie the law itself.

As is well known, Holmes's theory of liability rested on two interlocking principles. First, the primary purpose of the law is to 'induce external conformity to rule',[2] and second, personal moral blameworthiness is not generally an ingredient of liability.[3] I turn first to consider how Holmes applied these central principles to the case of contract. Naturally enough we find many of the same themes as in his theories of liability in the criminal law and in tort. There is, for a start, Holmes's hostility to the role of morals, expressed in extraordinarily vehement language in 'The Path of the Law'.[4] Morality helps put the cart before the horse and makes people think that it is morally wrong to break a contract, and that there is a duty to perform a contract. Not

---

[1] *The Common Law*, (M. DeW. Howe edn., 1963), p. 38.
[2] Ibid., p. 42.
[3] Ibid., pp. 42–3.
[4] Holmes complained that his own way of looking at the law of contracts 'stinks in the nostrils of those who think it advantageous to get as much ethics into the law as they can'. 10 *Harv. L. Rev.* 457, at p. 462 (1897).

so, says Holmes. The duty to perform a contract is imaginary, and
the right to the other party's performance is even more imaginary. A
contracting party has a choice—to perform or to pay damages for not
performing. To enter into a contract is not to assume any duty to
perform, and is thus analogous to committing a tort. Holmes thus
presents his marvellous apothegm: committing a contract is more or
less the same thing as committing a tort, except that in the former case
liability is conditional on non-performance.[1] A contract is, in effect, a
way of allocating a risk, the risk of non-performance or non-occurrence
of an event.[2] This, in Holmes's words, frees the subject from the 'super-
fluous theory that contract is a qualified subjection of one will to
another, a kind of limited slavery'.[3] Many of us today would share
Holmes's satisfaction at the dissolution of that quasi-metaphysical nonsense in his cynical acid. Holmes's theory of the nature of contractual
liability also leads to the conclusion that damages should be limited to
those that can reasonably be regarded as part of the risks assumed by
the defendant. So punitive damages can be ruled out, the contract-
breaker's motives become immaterial, and perhaps, more generally,
damages should be kept on the low side.

Lastly, Holmes's thoughts on contract focus on the external standards of liability and the unimportance of actual internal intention.
Mistake, fraud, and the like affect the validity of contract not by reason
of a deficiency in the will of the contracting parties, or a failure of
assent, but for other, more external reasons.[4] Holmes even made the
remarkable assertion that the 'true ground' of decision in the famous
case of *Raffles* v. *Wichelhaus*,[5] involving the steamship *Peerless*, was
'not that each party meant a different thing . . . but that each said a
different thing'.[6] As Grant Gilmore said, this was, 'even for Holmes an
extraordinary tour de force'.[7]

2. The Duty of Performance

Looking at all this, can an English common lawyer with the advantage

---

[1] See *Pollock–Holmes Letters* (ed. M. DeW. Howe, 1941, published in America under
the title, *Holmes–Pollock Letters*), vol. i, at p. 177, vol. ii, at pp. 199–200, 233.

[2] *The Common Law*, pp. 324–6.

[3] Ibid., p. 235.

[4] Ibid., pp. 245–6, 253. Such external reasons might include the fact that 'there is no
second party, or the two parties say different things, or essential terms seemingly consistent are really inconsistent as used'. Ibid., p. 246.

[5] (1864) 2 H. and C. 906.

[6] *The Common Law*, p. 242.

[7] *The Death of Contract* (1974), p. 41.

of a hundred years of hindsight endorse Mark DeWolfe Howe's verdict that '[t]he influence of the three lectures on contracts [in *The Common Law*] has been extraordinary and profound'?[1] I doubt it. English lawyers have never accepted Holmes's theory that there is no such thing as a duty to perform a contract, and this is not a matter of rejection *sub silentio*. Holmes's theory of contract is tolerably well known among contract scholars in England, and has been regarded by virtually all as a brilliant but wholly unsound paradox.[2]

Criticisms of the theory that there is no real duty to perform a contract have been offered on at least three planes. The first relies on actual English doctrine, the second is concerned with the reality of Holmes's theory as it relates to the functions of contract law, and the third takes a more jurisprudential form, and is thus often raised as part of a general critique of Holmes's whole position on the nature of legal rights. The chief difficulty with Holmes's theory according to the first criticism is simply its inconsistency with a large number of established rules of law. After all, was it not Holmes himself who once said that '[t]he first call of a theory of law is that it should fit the facts'?[3] For example, Equity sometimes decrees specific performance of contracts. Holmes's reaction to this is weak: he asserts that when he suggests that there is no duty to perform a contract, he is speaking only of the common law, and not of Equity, and, moreover, that even Equity never wholly[4] or literally[5] compels performance of a contract. Neither of these responses is satisfactory. A better answer might be to admit that where equitable intervention is a practical possibility, it makes sense to talk of a duty to perform a contract, but to observe that specific performance is a relatively rare remedy except in a limited class of contracts.

A whole collection of other contract rules, however, also presupposes the existence of a duty to perform. These include the tort of inducing a breach of contract, the doctrine of anticipatory breach, and the doctrine of frustration, all of which, at one time or another, Pollock called to

---

[1] *Justice Oliver Wendell Holmes: The Proving Years* (1963), p. 228.

[2] Pollock was the earliest and one of the most formidable critics of Holmes's analysis of contractual obligation. One of the entertaining features of the *Pollock–Holmes Letters* is the way in which the two old adversaries continually recurred to their positions on the theory. In all the long years of their correspondence, neither of them budged an inch.

[3] *The Common Law*, p. 167—suggesting therefore that Holmes saw the function of legal theory as primarily descriptive.

[4] *The Common Law*, pp. 235-6.

[5] Ibid.

Holmes's attention.[1] As far as I am aware, Holmes never attempted to explain how his theory could be reconciled with legal doctrines of this character. Moreover, other English lawyers have pointed out that Holmes's theory obscures an important distinction, namely the distinction between a promise which is clearly in the *alternative*, 'to do this *or* that', and a categorical promise where the alternative of damages is part of a remedial system and not part of the promise itself.[2]

Criticisms of the second kind often attack Holmes's theory for its unreality. Pollock, for instance, wrote: 'A man who bespeaks a coat of his tailor will scarcely be persuaded that he is only betting with the tailor that such a coat will not be made and delivered within a certain time. What he wants and means to have is the coat, not an insurance against not having a coat.'[3] Of a similar character are the criticisms of Henry Hart[4] and Lon Fuller[5] that Holmes's theory focuses too much on the judicial and remedial aspects of the law. Law exists in the outside world, not merely in the courts, and one of the functions of the law is to shape the moral consensus which actually controls men's conduct. So it is part of the duty of the judge who grants a remedy for breach of contract to encourage belief in the moral duty to perform a contract.

The third plane on which Holmes's theory has been criticized is a broad jurisprudential one. To anyone who has sympathies with the case for 'taking rights seriously', it is, of course, quite unacceptable to wash away rights and duties in cynical acid. There *is* an obligation to perform a contract, as there is an obligation to fulfil a promise. Even if it is not necessarily a moral obligation (because for instance, the law of contract may go beyond enforcing promises), the legal obligation is a real obligation, and it is *because* of this obligation that the law often provides a legal remedy to an aggrieved party.[6] Although English law has not, in recent years, shown much sign of being significantly influenced by such theories, even traditional English positivists like Professor H. L. A. Hart have subjected Holmes's theory of rights to much illuminating and critical analysis.[7]

It is not my purpose to re-examine Holmes's theory of contract in light of modern jurisprudential and philosophical thought; but it is at

---

[1] See also W. W. Buckland, *Some Reflections on Jurisprudence* (1945), pp. 97–8.
[2] Ibid.; see also J. Finnis, *Natural Law and Natural Rights*, (1980), p. 324.
[3] *Principles of Contract* (3rd edn., 1881), p. xix.
[4] 'Holmes' Positivism—An Addendum', 64 *Harv. L. Rev.* 929, at pp. 929–31 (1951).
[5] *The Law in Quest of Itself* (1940), pp. 135–8.
[6] John Finnis, op. cit., n. 2 above, p. 324.
[7] *The Concept of Law* (1961), pp. 38–41, 55–6, 132–7.

least appropriate to mention one criticism of Holmes's theory that also stems from some of the misgivings of modern jurists. Holmes's theory, like much of the realism for which he was responsible, requires that we simply ignore most of what judges actually write in their opinions. Now I am as willing as any realist to discount much of what is said in legal opinions on the ground that judges often intuitively feel their way to a conclusion, but are unable or unwilling to articulate very convincingly why they have reached a result. And I also entirely accept that the realist may see patterns in decisions that are not apparent if one only reads what judges say, and ignores what they do. But there are limits to this approach. If judges constantly describe the duty to perform a contract in moral terms and if they constantly devise rules which they justify by praying in aid the principle that a contract does impose a duty of performance, then the realist will not really understand how the law works if he ignores what the judges have to say. Even Holmes's own predictive theory of law would demand that we pay attention to judges' talk of the moral duty to perform a contract, if only to predict more successfully what judges will do in future cases at the margin. After all, one of the most powerful and valid lessons that the realists have taught us is the importance of studying what actually happens in court; Holmes's 'bad man' theory of law fails to take into account the simple fact that judges do not like bad men.[1] This in no way involves conceding victory to the theorist who sees the law in terms of morality; it only requires that we understand him better if we are to be true even to a predictive theory of law.

Thus far, I think these and similar criticisms of Holmes's theory of contract are justified. It seems to me, however, that there are nevertheless a number of insights in his theory that we should not overlook. First, the modern reformulation of contract theory, which owes so much to Lon Fuller's seminal article on the reliance interest,[2] takes as its starting-point the notions that the bindingness of a contract is a matter of degree and that it is impossible sensibly to discuss *how* binding a contract is until one knows what form of damages are likely to be awarded for its breach. Given Fuller's antipathy to Holmes's positivism, it may seem curious to cite Fuller's contract work in support of Holmes's view, but there is no escaping the fact that many of the most

---

[1] See Fuller, op. cit., p. 60, n. 5 above, at pp. 92–5; Henry Hart, op. cit., p. 60, n. 4 above, at pp. 932–3.

[2] 'The Reliance Interest in Contract Damages', 46 *Yale L.J.* 52, 373 (1936); see further, Essay 4 on Fuller's contract theory.

valuable developments in modern contract law and theory stem from this article by Fuller, which is itself built substantially on Holmesian foundations. Even though Fuller often reiterated that legal rights drew their inspiration from moral duties,[1] it was, curiously, he himself who first demonstrated the extent to which the rights of a contracting party are in practice *determined by* the differing kinds of damages that he may recover.

Much as the antipositivist may insist that the remedy of damages is a consequence of the right, the detailed and different forms that the remedy can take may tell us things about the right that we did not previously appreciate. For instance, the right to claim damages for expectation losses is less strongly protected than the right to claim damages for reliance losses; thus the duty to perform a contract— especially an executory contract—may not be as strong as we sometimes believe. Indeed, we are now more aware that in many cases, as for example, where there has been no change in the market, breach of an executory contract will not in practice give rise to any legal remedy at all.

Holmes in fact greatly understated one of the strongest arguments for his own theory when he said that '[t]he only universal consequence of a legally binding promise is, that the law makes the promisor pay damages if the promised event does not come to pass'.[2] This is, in truth, very far from being a universal consequence of a legally binding promise—the law only makes the promisor pay damages when the promisee has suffered what the law characterizes as a loss. The fact that lawyers and judges usually become involved in contract disputes only when some loss occurs seems to have obscured the reality that countless breaches of contract do not cause any recoverable loss at all. Let me cite just one modern English case that cannot but raise questions about the power and importance of the duty to perform an executory contract. In *Lazenby Garages* v. *Wright*[3] the defendant contracted with the plaintiff, a car dealer, to buy a second-hand car but, thinking better of it, refused to take delivery of the car. The dealer resold the car without dropping his price, but nevertheless sued for the loss of profit on the first sale. The court held that the dealer had suffered 'no loss', because a second-hand car was a unique object. The court refused to assume that the second buyer would have bought a different car if the

---

[1] See e.g. Fuller, *The Morality of Law* (1964), pp. 135-6.

[2] *The Common Law*, p. 236. Holmes may have intended this statement to be understood as limited to instances where loss in fact occurred. Since this qualification is so crucial, however, Holmes's point is greatly strengthened when full account is taken of it.

[3] [1976] 1 WLR 459.

first one had been delivered to the defendant. This reasoning is clearly open to challenge since it is unreal to regard the ordinary second-hand car, which commercially is almost a fungible, as a 'unique' object. But whether or not this case was 'rightly' decided, a decision of this character does seem to bear out some of Holmes's insights into contract theory. It reflects at least some doubt about the belief that there is always a moral duty to perform an executory contract. A realist can turn the tables on his Natural Law adversaries with decisions of this kind, for if the Natural Lawyer is entitled to infer the existence of a moral duty to perform from the fact that courts regularly penalise the failure to perform (not that many Natural Lawyers would make such an inference), then it is surely permissible to argue that decisions that refuse to penalize the failure to perform may predicate a belief that there is indeed no duty to perform.

Holmes's theory suggests a second insight. There are a number of transactions, which I suspect are far more common and important than most lawyers are apt to think, in which a contract may more readily be characterized as a joint act than as an agreement or an exchange of promises. One need only think of the ordinary supermarket cash purchase to appreciate how brainwashed we have become with regard to defining contracts in terms of agreements or promises. The man in the street would assume that when he buys something for cash in a supermarket, he is exchanging his money for the goods. Only the lawyer insists that this transaction is an exchange of promises, surely a grotesque example of the way in which we reinterpret facts to fit our concepts.

In cases of this kind, the transaction will for most practical purposes exhaust its legal significance once the exchange is completed, except in the rare case when the goods prove defective or dangerous. That potential liability seems more readily understood as a conditional liability arising from the sale, than as a breach of a promise. Indeed, very little difference exists between that sort of liability and the liability of the ordinary motorist for negligently injuring someone on the highway. The motorist chooses to drive knowing that by doing so, he will subject himself to certain legal responsibilities; the supermarket likewise chooses to sell its goods, knowing that by doing so, it also will become subject to certain legal responsibilities regarding the quality and fitness of the goods. Although these responsibilities may vary according to the circumstances of the sale, so may the duties of the motorist vary acccording to the circumstances of the road. I do not say that there are *no* differences between these types of legal liability, but only that the differences may be less important than the similarities. That, it seems to me, is one of the things Holmes was trying to say in his theory of contractual liability. This insight appears all the more valuable at a time when the conceptual separation of contract and tort seems to be disintegrating.[1]

The third insight that may be derived from Holmes's theory relates to his point about warranties and promises concerning events that are not within the control of the promisor, such as a promise that it shall rain tomorrow.[2] The starting-point for Holmes's theory seems to have been his criticism of the Indian Contract Act of 1872,[3] for overlooking the fact that not all promises relate to the future conduct of the promisor. The more complicated a contract, the less likely that its performance will lie entirely in the control of the promisor, and the less likely that it will consist entirely of promises as to future conduct. Most complex contracts involve warranties and undertakings as to the conduct of third parties. It may be too simplistic to assume that this disposes altogether of the possibility that the promisor has a moral duty to perform; but it is also too simplistic to think that the existence of such a moral duty itself disposes of the problems. For instance, it is not necessarily the intention of a warrantor to undertake to indemnify the promisee if the warranty is breached.[4] If that is not his intention, the nature of the 'duty' created by a warranty is mysterious indeed. The truth is that neither contract theory nor moral philosophy has yet given an adequate account of the source and nature of contractual duties in such cases.

Holmes's theory also suggests a fourth insight. Even if one main purpose of contract law is facultative, another important purpose of contract law is remedial, and it is not at all clear which is primary and which secondary.[5] The old dogma that courts do not make contracts for the parties is simply out of date. Courts often impose entire contracts on parties, and sometimes even declare non-parties to be subject to the burdens or entitled to the benefits of contracts made by others. Even

---

[1] For the views of Professor J. Raz on this question, and an attempted rebuttal of those views, see Essay 2, pp. 45–6, above.

[2] *The Common Law*, pp. 233–5.

[3] Holmes's interest in this Act presumably stemmed from the fact that it was drafted by Pollock, and was thought to be largely a codification of the English common law.

[4] This was, however, Corbin's theory about the nature of warranty: see Corbin on *Contracts*, vol.i, §14 (1963). See further on this, Essay 10.

[5] See further on this point, Essay 4, pp. 77–9 below.

more commonly, courts may impose their will upon parties by implying particular terms in contracts. I have elsewhere collected up a few of the better known of these instances in English law,[1] but the general picture is too well known to need repeating here. No doubt, arguments will continue indefinitely about the relative importance of the facultative and remedial functions; but one must at least admit that much of Holmes's theory about contract law makes reasonable sense with reference to the remedial role of the law. In these cases, parties have conducted themselves in such a way that the court imposes legal obligations on them that they never intended to assume, or thought they were assuming. Prior to the court's decision, their conduct simply could not have been determined to give rise to any particular legal duty. Although some primary duty may exist in these cases, this duty is more akin to the duty to provide redress for harms than that of an obligation to perform a contract.

Lastly, I wish to pose a question concerning the educational and persuasive function of the notion of a duty to perform a contract.[2] Holmes may have persuaded himself that there is no such thing as a duty to perform a contract, but merely a probability that a court will order damages to be paid for its breach. But he never seems to have asked himself whether it was desirable that everyone else should think the same way.[3] Even if the duty to perform a contract or to fulfil a promise turns out, on analysis, to be simply a mirage, is it best that everyone appreciates that truth? I will return to this question at the conclusion of this essay, and at this point will only say that I believe many English lawyers and judges would feel very uneasy about it. To some, no doubt, all demystification of the law is to be welcomed,[4] but to others, there remains a need for some mystique in the law, the power to persuade and cajole by emotive words rather than rational argument. Judges who habitually make reference to 'binding' contracts, or to moral duties and rights, may, although perhaps unconsciously, be making use of the emotive power of words to further a public policy. This policy, of course, rests upon the belief of judges that it is better that

[1] See my *Introduction to the Law of Contract* (3rd edn., 1981), pp. 58–61.

[2] I have previously raised this point elsewhere, see my *Freedom of Contract*, at pp. 357–8 and *Promises, Morals and Law*, pp. 84–5.

[3] For a possible hint that Holmes may not have thought this to be 'desirable', see M. Dew. Howe, op. cit., p. 59, n. 1 above, at p. 237 (citing Holmes's letter of 1919 to W. W. Cook).

[4] See e.g. H. L. A. Hart, 'Bentham and the Demystification of the Law,' 36 *Mod. L. Rev.* 2, at p. 2 (1973).

people comply with contracts than that they pay damages in lieu. I find it hard to believe that Holmes would have disagreed with this policy objective, and so therein perhaps lies the principal weakness of his theory of contract.

3. The Bargain Theory of Consideration and the External Standard of Liability

When we pass to consider Holmes's views on the doctrine of consideration and other central features of contractual liability, those areas in which he perhaps had the most profound influence on American law,[1] it seems difficult to avoid the conclusion that Holmes's theory was deeply embedded in inconsistency. What strikes one most forcibly at first reading of *The Common Law* is the emphasis Holmes gives to external standards of liability. Contract liability is not based on the subjection of one party to the other's will; it is a matter of risk allocation, with the risks allocated by the law, not by the promises.[2] Liability, as well as exemption from liability, depends on what a person says, and not on what he intends. Fraud, mistake, and other defences depend not on failures of will or defective assent, but on lack of the objective requirements of a contract. Even the distinction between contract and tort—so central to traditional nineteenth-century contract theorists—is not, says Holmes, 'found ready made'.[3] Yet, at the same time, there are many signs that Holmes could not wholly free himself of the basic contractual idea that liability ultimately turns on what the parties intend.

Consideration, of course, lies at the heart of this problem, and Holmes has been credited by several scholars with having invented the bargain theory of consideration.[4] Certainly, Holmes stated the theory forcefully and clearly: 'The root of the whole matter is the relation of reciprocal conventional inducement, each for the other, between consideration and promise.'[5] It is also clear that Holmes once again violated his own precepts by enunciating a theory that did not fit the

---

[1] This at least was Gilmore's view, see Grant Gilmore, *The Death of Contract* (1974), at pp. 14–15.

[2] *The Common Law*, at p. 302; *Pollock–Holmes Letters*, vol. i, at p. 177, vol. ii, at p. 233.

[3] *The Common Law*, p. 14.

[4] See Gilmore, op. cit., n. 1 above, pp. 19–21; cf. Dawson, *Gifts and Promises* (1980), p. 203.

[5] See *The Common Law*, p. 230.

facts—the authorities he cited in favour of his bargain theory were scanty in the extreme;[1] in fact, he conceded that there were many against him, but of the principle itself, he insisted, '[T]here can be little doubt'.[2]

In emphasizing the bargain nature of contractual exchange, and in formulating this theory of consideration, Holmes was surely marching in step with nineteenth century thought. The main characteristic of nineteenth century contractual theory was the treatment of the executory contract—the bargain for future performance—as paradigmatic.[3] The notion that contractual liability actually arose from what we call consideration, from either acts of detrimental reliance or the rendering of benefits, a notion that had been buried deep in the thinking of earlier generations[4], was seriously at odds with the idea that contracts could become binding by the mere will or intention of the parties. On these issues Holmes seems constantly to prevaricate between two inconsistent approaches. On the one hand, Holmes insisted that standards of liability are external, and that the intentions of the promisor count for naught; yet, on the other hand, he wanted to explain contracts exclusively in terms of the bargain, surely a highly subjective concept. The intention of the parties, for example, must determine whether an exchange is a bargain or merely (say) a pair of reciprocal gifts. Moreover, Holmes's theory of consideration determines whether consideration has been given by the way the parties have dealt with each other, and a modern lawyer would not hesitate to say that this depends on their intention. Holmes's biographer rejects the charge of inconsistency, claiming that it was not the actual intent of the parties that mattered here, or anywhere else, but their manifested intent.[5] I am sceptical about this, but in any event the fact remains that Holmes's whole approach downgraded the importance of consideration, and upgraded the importance of the promise. Consideration was, he repeatedly insisted, a mere form,[6] because anything which limited the creation of a liability as a result of the intent of the parties must be a

---

[1] Ibid., p. 231.

[2] Ibid., p. 293.

[3] See *Freedom of Contract*, pp. 419–48.

[4] See *Freedom of Contract*, pp. 1–7 and chapter 22; A. W. B. Simpson, *A History of the Common Law of Contract* (1975), pp. 454–8, 488.

[5] Howe, op. cit., p. 59, n. 1, at pp. 241–2.

[6] 'The Path of the Law' loc. cit., p. 57, n. 4 above, at p. 464 and Howe, op. cit., p. 59, n. 1, p. 233, quoting from a letter to Harriman in 1896. On this puzzling idea of contract as a mere form, see further Essay 4, p. 84, below, and more generally, Essay 5.

matter of form.[1] The promise, on the other hand, was the 'common element of all contracts'.[2]

There is no glimmer of recognition in Holmes's writings of the vital link that the doctrine of consideration, with its twin pillars of detrimental reliance and benefit, provided between contract and tort,[3] and between contract and restitution. On these issues, Holmes offered what became or what was then in process of becoming the new orthodoxy: reliance was not deserving of legal protection unless it was bargained for or paid for as part of a contract;[4] equally, Holmes adopted the new nineteenth-century orthodoxies on benefit,[5] quasi-contract, and restitution. The traditional category of quasi-contract, he insisted, included genuine implied-in-fact promises and also duties that were not contractual at all.[6] All this came straight from nineteenth-century theorists like Austin and Maine who were imbued with the notion that the fundamental dividing line in the law of obligations was that which separated consensual from non-consensual liabilities.[7] Had Holmes pursued his belief in external standards of liability as far as his biographer thinks he did, he might have perceived that the relationship between contract and other parts of the law of obligations could be found in the doctrine of consideration. In that event, Holmes would surely have been already preparing for the death of contract rather than, as Gilmore asserts, being primarily responsible for its birth.[8] The truth is that the novelty of Holmes's theory of contract has been greatly exaggerated. In most respects he takes his place with English writers and jurists of the last decade of the nineteenth century to whom contract was the key to the whole law of obligations.[9] Certainly, he placed more

---

[1] *The Common Law*, p. 215.   [2] Ibid., p. 227.

[3] Neither does Holmes recognize a link between the doctrine of consideration and other non-consensual liabilities, such as those which arise in the law of trusts, or through the application of doctrines like estoppel.

[4] See *Commonwealth* v. *Scituate Savings Bank* 137 Mass. 302 (1883).

[5] For example, Holmes accepted the late nineteenth-century view that past consideration was good (when so found) not because of the benefit received, but because of a pre-existing implied promise.

[6] See Holmes, 'Codes and the Arrangement of the Law', 5 *Am. L. Rev.* 1, p. 13 (1870), reprinted in 44 *Harv. L. Rev.*, 725, 736 (1931).

[7] See *Freedom of Contract*, at pp. 480-3.

[8] Since Gilmore's thesis was so exaggerated, it was presumably not intended to be taken too seriously. Even the suggestion that Holmes provided the first coherent statement of the classical common law of contract cannot seriously be sustained, see ibid, pp. 398-408.

[9] Thus Holmes's theory, despite his idiosyncratic rejection of the duty to perform, places him squarely in the classical tradition which saw contract entirely as the creation of the parties. Compare Essay 2.

emphasis on external manifestations of assent than many earlier writers had done, but in this respect also, he had largely been anticipated, as he had in tort law, by ruling English case law.[1]

Perhaps for this reason, Holmes's theory of contract had, I believe, much less influence in England than in America. The bargain theory of consideration, although almost adopted by Pollock,[2] and once approved in the House of Lords,[3] never took firm root in England. Although English theorists often flirted with it, the judges continued to protect unbargained-for reliance where it seemed just to do so even though theory might have suggested otherwise.[4] The objective approach to questions of assent was also increasingly adopted by English courts over the years,[5] but this was part of a general approach and probably owed nothing to Holmes.

4. Concluding Thoughts on *The Common Law*

So after this tour round Holmes's theory of liability, as set forth in *The Common Law* and other writings, what can be said in summary form, from the perspective of the English common lawyer? The answer, I fear, is that not much can be said that is likely to add to Holmes's reputation. On contract, Holmes is remembered for his brilliant but generally rejected paradox that there is no duty to perform a contract, and for his bargain theory of consideration, which has left little mark on English law. In this we may have been fortunate for the mark which the bargain theory left on America proved for some years, with the assistance of Williston, to be a troublesome stumbling-block to the adequate recognition of reliance interests. But the very fact that English lawyers have not yet reformulated their own contract theory to take account of the importance of reliance interests, may suggest that perhaps these developments in Anglo-American law were part of a broad

---

[1] See e.g. *Smith* v. *Hughes* (1871) LR 6 QB 597, 607; *Freeman* v. *Cooke* (1848) 2 Ex. 654, 662.

[2] In the third edition of his *Principles of Contract*, p. 179, Pollock defined consideration as 'the price for which the promise of the other is bought'. The essence of this definition was retained in all subsequent editions of the book. But it is unclear if this definition owed anything to Holmes. The definition first appeared in the third edition of Pollock's book; Pollock received his copy of *The Common Law* after his third edition was already in proof, and too late to add more than a few words in deference to Holmes in the Preface. See ibid., p. xi.

[3] See *Dunlop Pneumatic Tyre Co.* v. *Selfridge* [1915] AC 847, 855.

[4] *Freedom of Contract*, at pp. 460–4.

[5] For an extreme case of which Holmes might well have approved, see *Frederick E. Rose* v. *W. H. Pim & Co.* [1953] 2 QB 450. See also Essay 4, pp. 79–92.

tide of opinion, which owed little to any individual, however brilliant
or idiosyncratic.

Some forty and fifty years ago, the distinguished American scholars
Morris Cohen[1] and Lon Fuller[2] were already commenting that
Holmes's contribution to the actual developmnent of the common law
had been disappointing. From an English standpoint, this seems likely
to be the ultimate verdict of history as well. In fact, Holmes might very
well have acquiesced in this. As long ago as 1912, in referring to his
own book, Holmes wrote to Pollock saying, 'All books are dead in
twenty five years, but luckily the public does not always find it out.'[3]

5. Holmes the Judge through English Eyes

I return finally to the question I posed earlier, and it is a question which
needs to be pondered by anyone who feels an underlying sympathy
with Holmes's brand of extreme realism. If it is true that legal 'duties',
like the 'duty' to perform a contract, are just imaginary constructs,
artificial grammatical consequences from postulating what will happen
under certain contingencies—the 'apostasis of a prophecy' as Holmes
often called it—can we be indifferent to the possible spread of this
message? It is, I suspect, anxiety about this sort of question which
underlies the continued belief by many members of the English judiciary
that it is best if discussion of the creative powers of the judges is limited
to the *cognoscenti*. There is much evidence, for instance, that many
English judges believe that it would be desirable for the public to
continue to believe in the declaratory theory of law even though the
judges themselves have outgrown it.[4] The explanation for this may be
complex and speculative, but I believe that one underlying reason is
that English judges believe that it is necessary for the law to retain
some mystique, some mystery, and some permanence, if it is to hold its
persuasive power and emotive force over the public. Demystification
of the law is all very well, but the power of the law over the minds of
men will surely collapse if the process goes too far, and the public comes
to see law as a man-made instrument, lacking all moral authority,
good for this Parliament alone, and liable to be repealed by the next.

[1] 'Justice Holmes and the Nature of Law', 31 *Col. L. Rev.* 352 (1931).
[2] *The Law in Quest of Itself*, at pp. 62-3. However, in Essay 4 I suggest that Fuller
himself owed a lot to Holmes in respect of his own theory of contract, and that Fuller's
work indeed has been influential on the common law.
[3] *Pollock–Holmes Letters*, vol. i, p. 195.
[4] See Atiyah, 'Judges and Policy', 15 *Israel L. Rev.* 346 (1980); Alan Paterson, *The
Law Lords* (1982).

Moreover, *even if ,all this is true*, I believe many English judges would think it desirable that the public should not believe it. I have elsewhere criticized this Janus-like attitude,[1] though I understand and sympathize with the anxieties that lie behind it.

I ask myself: how would Holmes have responded to this sort of attitude? One feels sure that his fierce intellectual honesty would have led him to reject it without a moment's hesitation. If it is true that law has nothing behind it other than the 'can't helps' of the majority of 'the crowd', then Holmes would surely have emphatically protested at the idea that anyone should fool the crowd into thinking otherwise.[2] But that raises another question which I believe the English lawyer would want to pose: can constitutionalism and legality survive in a nation where everyone believes what Holmes believed, that there is no such thing as natural law, that moral ideas and rights are dissoluble in cynical acid, that law is the prophecy of court decisions proffered to the 'bad man', and that might is the nearest thing we have to right?[3] Holmes might have answered that question by suggesting that all would remain well if men were sufficiently rational to understand their own long term interests. He might have quoted his own words in his famous dissent in the case of *Abrams* v. *United States*:

[W]hen men have realized that time has upset many fighting faiths, they may come to believe even more than they believe the very foundations of their own conduct that the ultimate good desired is better reached by free trade in ideas— that the best test of truth is the power of the thought to get itself accepted in the competition of the market, and that truth is the only ground upon which their wishes can be safely carried out. That at any rate is the theory of our Constitution.[4]

Stirring words indeed, but surely wrong. The need for constitutional control of power arises because history suggests that it is very doubtful whether men *en masse* ever will come to realize these things. Surely *that* is the theory of the American constitution. That is why in a country

---

[1] Atiyah, 'Judges and Policy', see last note.

[2] Yet one anecdote has been told (for which no source is given) which suggests that, at least in his lighter moments, Holmes may not have been totally oblivious to the value of mystique. It is related that when Holmes first saw the huge Hopkinson portrait of him which today hangs in the Harvard Law School, he said, 'That isn't me, but it's a darn good thing for people to think it is'. See C. D. Bowen, *Yankee from Olympus* (1945), p. 408. I owe this reference to Jeffrey O'Connell.

[3] See Wyzanski, 'The Democracy of Justice Oliver Wendell Holmes', 7 *Vand. L. Rev.* 311, 319 (1954).

[4] 250 US 616, 630 (1919).

like Britain, which lacks constitutional restraints on majority power, the judges do not contemplate with equanimity the prospect of everyone coming to believe what Holmes believed. I trust that it is not *lèse majesté* to say that I cannot altogether blame them.

4

Fuller and the Theory of Contract

1. Contract as a Method of 'Social Ordering'

The late Lon Fuller was undoubtedly one of the most original, interesting, and profound legal thinkers of the present century. Generations of American contract students have been taught through his case-book, one of the finest examples of the art, and his famous article (co-authored with his student, William R. Perdue, Jr.) 'The Reliance Interest in Contract Damages',[1] has probably been the most influential single article in the entire history of modern contract scholarship, at any rate in the common law world.

Although he wrote widely on legal theory as well as on contract law, Fuller never expounded a systematic theory of contractual obligation. His two principal contributions to contract scholarship are the reliance article, and 'Consideration and Form', published in the *Columbia Law Review* in 1941.[2] In the third (1972) edition of his case-book, however, he included a section on 'The Role of Contract', which was later reprinted in the posthumous collection of essays, *The Principles of Social Order*, edited by Kenneth I. Winston.[3]

In this section Fuller discussed (as he had often done before) 'the principles of social ordering', and explained the relationship between one of these principles—contract—and the others. This discussion suggests that Fuller may well have regarded contract as the predominant principle, because it seems to be involved one way or another with all the others. His list of the principles of social ordering, as set out in this section of his case-book was, in his own words:

1. The co-ordination of expectations and actions that arise tacitly out of interaction, illustrated in 'customary law' and 'standard practice'.
2. Contract.
3. Property.
4. Officially declared law.
5. Adjudication.
6. Managerial direction.

[1] 46 *Yale LJ* 52, 373 (1936).
[2] 41 *Col. L. Rev.* 799 (1941).
[3] Duke University Press, Durham, NC, (1981).

7. Voting.
8. Mediation.
9. Deliberate resort to chance, 'tossing for it'.

Disclaiming any pretence at exhaustiveness, Fuller proceeds to show how the various principles may be interrelated and combined. He suggests that the principles fall into two broad categories, those which operate 'vertically'—for example legislation and managerial direction, and those which operate 'horizontally'—custom, contract, and so on. He then criticizes what he takes to be the modern tendency to see all social ordering as 'imposed from above', and proceeds to explain how contract relates to his other principles. His analysis leaves the reader in little doubt about Fuller's view of the relative importance of contract as a method of social ordering. Although he never specifically asserts that it is the 'most important', and indeed probably would have resisted the question as over-simplistic, absent clear criteria of importance, it certainly must rank among the more dominant.

Any doubts as to the primacy of contract are stilled by Fuller's repeated emphasis, in other contexts, on the essential purposiveness of all law. This point is clearly linked to his views on the value-laden nature of law, for purposiveness presupposes an idea or vision of what law *ought to be*. Throughout his writings Fuller reiterates the purposive nature of law, the rationality of the whole enterprise of law, and therefore, of all methods of ordering. Much of his writing on the 'inner morality of law', for instance, assumes that law is purposive. It is only this, he says, which justifies finding a 'tacit promise' by the legislator or government to judge the citizens' conduct in accordance with enacted law; otherwise he rightly finds no conceptual necessity to bind the legislator's or government's hands. A legislator whose purpose is to reduce his subjects to a state of neurotic despair could enact a law one day and order his citizens to be punished for complying with it the next; there is nothing contrary to logic in such an exercise in tyranny unless one first makes some basic assumptions about the purposes of legislation, and perhaps of law in general.[1]

When we come to Fuller's treatment of contract itself, it becomes perfectly clear that here too he sees contract as a principle of social ordering in the sense that it is a way of regulating *future* human interaction. There is no hint here of any possible secondary function, such as that of 'clearing up a mess', sorting out the results of accidental

---

[1] See *The Morality of Law*, revised edn., pp. 39-41 (1969).

and unintended interaction. Furthermore, it is an essential part of Fuller's conception of contract that it is an *autonomous* way of regulating future conduct. Parties regulate their own future conduct through contract; the regulation is not imposed on them. Fuller articulates this most clearly in 'Consideration and Form', in which he seeks to extricate the principle of private autonomy from some of the excesses of will theory. Thus he rejects the notion that private autonomy is somehow inconsistent with the objective interpretation of contracts,[1] although he does not fully develop this argument either here or elsewhere.

Fuller recognizes in the great reliance article that the measure of damages for breach of contract is not a purely logical corollary of the duty breached, and that expectation damages may be awarded partly as a 'prophylaxis' to deter contract breakers. This powerful and original insight seems somewhat at odds with his rejection of state aid to the enforcement of contracts, once voiced rather strongly in response to a suggestion of Llewellyn's.[2] Measuring damages by their deterrent effect demands that we recognize awards of expectation damages as policy decisions made by the courts as organs of the state. This may seem a matter of detail in Fuller's overall theory of contractual obligation. But in fact it reflects some deeper weaknesses and ambiguities, which are perhaps due in part to Fuller's failure ever to expound a systematic theory of contract. These difficulties with Fuller's theory can be classified into three groups.

2. Contract and Exchange.

When Fuller writes in general terms about the role of contract, and about the relationship of contract to other forms of social ordering, he is, I think, insufficiently clear about the distinction between contract and exchange; he also fails to disentangle adequately the separate elements in contract. Contract differs from mere exchange because it contains an element of futurity—what Ian Macneil calls 'presentiation'.[3] Contracts (or anyhow many contracts) *bind* people to future performances. Exchange can be a purely present transaction. The fact that contracts are often defined as consisting of an 'exchange of promises' must not obscure the fact that such an exchange necessarily looks

---

[1] 41 *Col. L. Rev.* at pp. 806-10.

[2] See *The Principles of Social Order*, p. 105.

[3] 'Restatement (Second) of Contracts and Presentiation', 60 *Va. L. Rev.* 589 (1974); 'The Many Futures of Contract', 47 *S. Cal. L. Rev.* 691 (1974).

to future performance, while many cash transactions involve nothing beyond a present simultaneous exchange—for example, a cash purchase in a supermarket. Of course, in modern law the extensive use of devices such as 'implied warranties' means that even a simultaneous exchange of goods for cash has an element of futurity in it; but this is not inherent in the exchange itself. Exchange without warranties is perfectly possible, and indeed such an exchange was regarded as the norm in early nineteenth-century law.

The difference between exchange and contract is quite an elementary distinction, but it is surprising how often it is overlooked. When Fuller rejects Bentham's insistence that contract derives its form and validity from society and law,[1] and asserts that the institution of contract 'functioned in some measure' before state laws 'existed or were even conceived of',[2] he seems to overlook this simple point. It is almost certain that exchange in some form antedates state and law, and it is true that vows and oaths were known in primitive societies. But almost all historians concede the emergence of executory contracts to be a relatively modern phenomenon.[3] Again, when Fuller argues that contract underpins nearly all the other methods of social ordering that he identifies,[4] he does not disentangle the various underlying bases of contractual obligation which he recognizes and discusses elsewhere, especially in 'Consideration and Form'.[5] Thus it is not always clear in *Principles of Social Order* whether he is discussing autonomy and consent, or expectations, or reliance, or unjust enrichment, or some unspecified mix of these factors when he finds contractual elements in various other forms of social ordering. For instance, the 'tacit promise' which he regards the legislator as making to his subjects may indeed be some kind of moral or political obligation, but calling it a promise does not adequately explain how it can be identified with express promises where the obligation has, at least traditionally, been seen as deriving from some element of autonomy or even from the will of the promisor.

---

[1] Bentham, *Works* (Bowring edn.) vol. i, 308-9, 333.

[2] *Principles of Social Order*, p. 174.

[3] See e.g. Maine, *Ancient Law* (1861); A.W.B. Simpson, *A History of the Common Law of Contract* (1975); J. H. Baker, 'Origins of the "Doctrine" of Consideration', in *On the Laws and Customs of England: Essays in Honour of Samuel E. Thorne* (1981), ed. M. S. Arnold, T. A. Green, and others; for anthropological evidence, see M. Gluckman, *The Ideas in Barotse Jurisprudence* (1965), p. 181 and *The Judicial Process Among the Barotse* (2nd edn., 1967), pp. 28, 30, 200, 440-2.

[4] *Principles of Social Order*, at pp. 175-80.

[5] 41 *Col. L. Rev.* at pp. 806-13.

3. The Facilitative and the Remedial Functions of Contract Law

Like many, indeed nearly all, liberal legal theorists, Fuller saw contract exclusively in terms of its facilitative function. He saw contract as an institution which enables people to plan their future relationships. Despite the importance Fuller attached to 'remedies' in the traditional narrow contractual sense, his writing demonstrates little recognition that contract might have a secondary or 'remedial' role to play in a broader and perhaps more significant sense of the concept of 'remedy'. In this broader sense, 'remedial' refers to the function a court exercises when it imposes on the parties a solution to a problem that goes beyond the natural or logical implications of the parties' own ordering. In the traditional and narrower sense, 'remedies' for breach of contract were thought to involve no interventionist action by the courts; a remedy by way of damages was merely the logical corollary of wrongful breach. In this broader sense of 'remedial', a court does not merely assist the parties to give effect to the inherent implications of their own arrangement when it provides a 'remedy'. It intervenes to deal with a situation in the nature of an accident, much in the way that tort law deals with accidents.

Although Fuller's own work on 'remedies' in the narrower sense demonstrates that damage awards depend on judicial policy choices rather than on the parties' own intentions, he never seems to have appreciated the full implications of this for the role of contract law more generally. Some modern scholars, by contrast, see one of the main functions of contract law as being to help to sort out the unintended and perhaps unforeseen results of past voluntary human interaction. Of course, what is 'foreseeable' and the specificity with which it is foreseen are matters of degree, and contracting parties can and often do try to take account of the unexpected and unintended in their private orderings.[1] But contracts simply do not contain provisions designed to deal with everything that occurs. In these circumstances, the private ordering would break down if it were not supplemented by the remedial role of the law in this broad sense: for example, where performance of a contract becomes impossible, where unforeseen difficulties arise, where fundamental changes occur in the background to some long-term contractual relationship, and so on. But it may also happen that the law can be used to sort out difficulties in a relationship never originally thought of as one of a legal-contractual character. Cohabitants who buy a house and then part, for instance, often leave the law with the

[1] *Principles of Social Order*, p. 181.

problem of deciding how the property is to be dealt with; other 'family arrangements' which the courts would never enforce while executory may simply cry out for some solution when property has been transferred without formal contractual arrangements and family disputes then occur.

These are just a few samples of the many cases that courts today decide under a variety of doctrinal headings—'implied contract', 'constructive trust', 'estoppel', and so on. Most of these cases can be dealt with as cases of contract if courts are sufficiently enterprising or counsel sufficiently ingenious in their pleadings; but they are plainly not examples of the sort of contracts that Fuller discusses in these essays as methods of social ordering. In these cases, the courts come in to clear up a mess after things have gone badly wrong in a relationship, not simply to enforce compliance with privately made arrangements.

No doubt what the courts do in these cases may help others to order their affairs better in the future, but it is typical of many of these cases— the cohabitant and many family cases, for example—that initially the parties have such trust in each other that they would never feel the need to spell out the legal implications of their relationships. Indeed, as Fuller recognized elsewhere,[1] to try to invoke formal contract in such cases often destroys the very trust on which the relationship is based.

Fuller does not seem to have been greatly interested in, if he recognized at all, this broader remedial role of contract law. He demonstrates basic hostility to an active judicial role when courts attempt 'to write contracts' as opposed to 'lay[ing] down rules about contracting.' Furthermore, his view of the proper limits of legislation tends to be of the traditionally narrow liberal variety: legislation should lay down a framework within which individuals can exercise their private autonomy.[2] All this seems to be extraordinarily narrow and restrictive. Why shouldn't the law provide assistance to parties to help them sort out their problems, especially when they have an ongoing relationship the continuance of which is important to the public? Many countries, for instance, provide labour mediators or arbitrators to help employers and unions resolve their differences when industrial disruption thre-

---

[1] Ibid., at p. 121.

[2] Ibid., at pp. 161-3. It is put even more strongly by Fuller's editor on p. 158: 'In Fuller's view, the only permissible form of legislation is the sort that lets individuals plan their own lives.' However, Professor Summers tells me that he has seen a letter in the Fuller archives in the Harvard Law School library, dated 10 May 1965, addressed to Professor Bedau of Tufts University, in which Fuller expressed support for legislation establishing public transportation systems.

atens. There are passages in 'The Forms and Limits of Adjudication'[1] from which it might be inferred that Fuller would not have been happy with even so modest an element of state initiative. It is even more necessary for the law to step in to help clear up a mess when normal relationships finally break down. Of course this is often done under a different legal heading—bankruptcy, for instance, or corporate liquidation. One can hardly suppose Fuller would have objected to state legal activity of this kind. Perhaps, therefore, Fuller would merely have found the use of the term 'contract' objectionable in this context.

It may appear ironic, in light of his emphasis on 'remedies' in the narrow sense in the reliance article, as well as in the opening chapter of his case-book, but it almost seems that Fuller would have preferred to define 'remedial contract law' as not part of the law of contract. Although this could be seen as a merely verbal issue, there are real dangers in imposing artificial definitional limits to a subject as important and central as contract law. I have suggested elsewhere[2] that this kind of definitional jugglery had serious consequences in the late nineteenth century, when judges persuaded themselves that 'pure' freedom of contract remained the fundamental ideal of the law by defining out of contract law any laws which interfered with freedom of contract. This led to an impoverished understanding of what was really happening to the law in the early part of this century, and, in some quarters, that danger still seems to be apparent.

4. The Relationship of Reliance to the Principle of Autonomy

One of the deepest and strangest ambivalences in Fuller's theory of contract arises from the relationship between reliance and the principle of autonomy. Fuller's great article on reliance was, of course, the starting-point for much modern reliance theory.[3] It opened up for discussion the whole relationship between the doctrine of consideration and the different types of damages awardable in contract. It was, I think, the first systematic demonstration of the relationship between promise, benefit, and detrimental reliance on the one side and expectation damages, restitution 'damages', and reliance damages on the other. But it also challenged the centuries-old orthodoxy which asserted

---

[1] *Principles of Social Order* at pp. 104-5.

[2] See my *Freedom of Contract*, at p. 405.

[3] It was preceded by some of Corbin's work, and especially article 90 of the (first) Restatement of Contracts, for which Corbin was largely responsible; but at that date reliance theory was almost exclusively directed to recognition of unbargained-for reliance as an alternative to consideration.

that contracts are enforced on the basis of principles of autonomy alone—or out of respect for the human will. For the first time since the seventeenth-century Natural Lawyers it was now seriously contended that contractual obligation could be seen as based primarily on actual or probable reliance by the promisee. What is so very curious is that Fuller never seems to have seen in his recognition of the importance of reliance any challenge to his respect for the priority of the principle of autonomy. In 'Consideration and Form' he actually refers to a number of cases in which 'a promisee has seriously, and according to ordinary standards of conduct, justifiably relied on a promise which the promisor expressly stipulated should impose no legal liability on him'.[1] In a footnote Fuller adds that in these cases 'the principle of reimbursing reliance is regarded as over-riding the principle of private autonomy'.[2] It is astonishing that Fuller should have left this point without further comment; the implications cry out for exploration. How can the reliance be *justifiable* when the 'promisor' disclaims responsibility for the consequences—unless, that is, one accepts that it is the court rather than the parties which has the responsibility for deciding when reliance is justifiable and, therefore, worthy of legal protection. Certainly, as Fuller does recognize, the result involves a reversal of the normal order of priority between reliance and autonomy as the controlling principle. But once this order is reversed in these cases we surely need a principle to tell us when and why it will be reversed in other cases. Indeed, perhaps we need a principle to explain why autonomy normally takes priority over reliance rather than the other way around.

Perhaps more fundamental still is the question whether reliance doctrine is tied to promissory obligation—rather than illustrating a much broader principle of social policy—in the way Fuller apparently assumed. Once again it is odd that Fuller never addressed this question, though he came tantalizingly close to it on several occasions. In the reliance article Fuller assumes almost throughout that the discussion concerns *promises*: the article chiefly addresses the question when and to what extent will promises be enforced because they have been or are likely to be relied on. It is true that he devotes a few pages[3] to liability for misrepresentation in order to demonstrate that here, too, a distinction can be drawn between the reliance interest and the expectation

---

[1] 41 *Col. L. Rev.* at p. 811.

[2] Ibid., at n. 16.

[3] 46 *Yale LJ* at pp. 406-10. For a recent case illustrating the way in which the difference between protecting expectation and reliance can arise in a misrepresentation case, see *Avon C.C.* v. *Howlett* [1983] 1 All ER 1073, discussed in Essay 10.

interest; and he also discusses other contractual problems from the same point of view, such as the effect of rejection of an offer.[1] But Fuller does not seem to appreciate the potential implications of the reliance idea in these extensions of promissory liability. Nowhere does he fully explore the question whether reliance on non-promissory language or conduct may not, of itself, be a ground for the imposition of liability, in which case the protection of reliance may be a principle of far wider importance than promise-based liability, or even contract itself.

This omission is all the more curious in light of Fuller's reference to the cases in which reliance has been allowed to override the autonomy principle, that is, where there is 'a promise which the promisor expressly stipulate[s] should impose no legal liability on him'.[2] But what kind of a promise is this? A strict positivist might insist that a person could morally bind himself by a non-legally binding promise; but it is an uphill task to argue that a person who disclaims all legal responsibility for reliance on his language is nevertheless making a morally binding commitment. And for Fuller, of all people, to say or imply that this could be the case is doubly puzzling. For Fuller would surely have said that a person who disclaims responsibility for reliance on his words quite clearly negatives the very moral responsibility which normally justifies the imposition of legal liability. Of course, so long as Fuller thought of reliance almost exclusively in conjunction with promises, it was more understandable that he continued to assume the primacy of the principle of private autonomy. A promise, after all, can be seen as, and indeed often is expressly couched in the form of, an *invitation to rely*. Hence the question whether the promisee was justified in relying as he did is often not even perceived—and does not seem to have been perceived by Fuller—as raising serious problems so long as reliance is tied to explicit promises. But even this oversight raises some fundamental questions. In particular, by permitting *unbargained-for reliance* to justify enforcement of a promise, the law necessarily embarks on a substantial redistributive exercise. The promisee is granted an entitlement to rely which he has not bought.

I will return to this point later.[3] Here I must pass to what is perhaps

---

[1] See Fuller and Eisenberg, *Basic Contract Law* (4th edn., 1981), p. 367. A recent English case is, so far as I am aware, the only illustration in the reports of the point here discussed by Fuller, viz., whether a rejection by an offeree terminates an offer when the rejection has not been acted upon, and is immediately retracted: *Marseille Fret SA* v. *D. Oltman Schiffarts* [1981] Com. LR 277 (held, yes it does).

[2] 41 *Col. L. Rev.*, p. 811, n. 16.   [3] See below, p. 89.

an even more serious implication of reliance theory once reliance becomes detached from promissory obligation. Once liability is imposed—for example, in tort, or via estoppel—for loss caused by justifiable reliance on language or conduct which cannot in any sense be regarded as promissory, the whole issue of justifiability of the reliance is opened up to a collective judgment. It cannot be asserted with even a modicum of plausibility that this kind of reliance—that is, reliance on non-promissory language or conduct—can be treated as giving rise to enforceable legal rights in some 'neutral' sort of way. There must be a community or court judgment not merely as to the 'reasonableness' of the reliance, as it is often put, but as to *the justifiability of the reliance so as to shift the risk of ill consequences away from the party relying.* Once reliance came to play the major role even in promissory cases which was ascribed to it by Fuller, it was almost inevitable that its role would expand into these areas of non-promissory language and conduct. Yet Fuller never seems to have shown awareness of what this might involve.

Fuller's failure to address the issues raised by reliance on non-promissory language or conduct is also surprising because he lays so much stress on tacit promises and on custom as a source of reciprocal expectations. Although it may remain possible to treat the protection of reliance on an express promise as a form of promissory liability, it becomes implausible if not impossible so to treat reliance on an implied or tacit promise. Of course we infer promises for a variety of different reasons, but Fuller never seems to have appreciated that one powerful motive that often impels the inference of a promise is simply the reliance of one party on the other. Rather than deciding that there has been justifiable reliance because of a tacit promise, we often infer a promise because we believe there has been justifiable reliance. Perhaps the reason why some of us may sympathize with Fuller's suggestion of an implicit promise by the legislator to judge citizens in accordance with his own laws is the fact that he has invited—indeed instructed—citizens to act in accordance with the laws. Having thus relied on the laws, having thus changed their position in many ways, it would be a monstrous injustice if the citizenry were then condemned for this very process. So the legislator may indeed be under the obligation which Fuller asserted, but it is not obvious that much is gained by classifying this as a promissory obligation. If it is promissory, then presumably (according to traditional views) it binds the legislator from the outset, but would it really be so iniquitous if the legislator were to enact a law, and then before it had come into force, or before anyone had relied upon it in any way, the law were repealed, and the contrary enacted?

In other words, we often imply the promise because we think there ought to be an obligation, not the other way round. Calling the obligation promissory then seems to legitimate the imposition of the obligation by invoking 'neutral' moral principles, but in reality 'we' feel —or most of us do—that there *should be* an obligation in this situation because of many of our basic presuppositions about liberalism, freedom, and the individual's role in society—presuppositions shared, of course, by Fuller. Recognizing openly why we want to impose such obligations is surely better than pretending that these are self-assumed obligations like those usually thought to arise from explicit promises. A similar analysis may be offered of the famous Wisconsin case, *Hoffman* v. *Red Owl Stores*,[1] in which the court imposed a reliance liability on the defendants for abruptly terminating negotiations with the plaintiff, during the course of which he had relied upon assurances given by the defendants that a deal would be forthcoming. As a result of these assurances the plaintiff had committed himself in various ways and suffered loss when no contract was ever concluded. Many commentators, following a Fullerian approach, assume that this case involved enforcement of some kind of an implied promise—to bargain in good faith, and indeed, rather more, since bad faith was explicitly negatived by the jury. Yet it is far from evident where this implied promise came from: the defendants could well have argued that they intended no such promise because the normal understanding of negotiating parties is that each acts at his own risk until a deal is concluded. It clearly follows from the court's decision that Red Owl owed a duty not to cause loss by failure to conclude the bargain, but it is hardly plausible to say that this duty arose from the defendants' intentions or from the parties' private ordering. It arose from the court's perception of the requirements of good faith, or the requirements of the normal bargaining process, even if this in turn was derived from normal understanding of commercial behaviour.

Fuller would, I think, have responded to this argument by saying that implied contracts or implied terms are based on normal understandings and that they are parasitic on normal transactions between people acting normally. Thus good faith in bargaining is the norm and the 'implication' of a duty to bargain in good faith is genuine.

Many lawyers would find this a defensible position, but there are

[1] 133 NW 2d 267 (1965). See also, p. 125, above.

serious difficulties in reconciling it with other facets of Fuller's theories. In particular, Fuller laid great stress on custom, practice, and reciprocal standards of behaviour as the substantive sources of obligation both in the case of enacted law and in the case of contract. Indeed, in dealing with enacted law he stresses the rationality and purposiveness of customary behaviour, and declares that 'we cannot understand "ordinary law"—that is, officially declared or enacted law—unless we first obtain an understanding of what is called customary law'.[1]

At this point there appears to be a close connection between Fuller's perception of law in general and his perception of contract—which, indeed, he often insisted was a sort of private law for the parties.[2] In both cases Fuller sees the informal normative rules of customary law or personal interactions as the primary source (in one sense) of the eventual obligations, perhaps as paradigmatic of public and private law respectively. In both cases the formal source, 'law' or 'contract', is then superimposed on the informal norms. Legislation thus becomes 'formal' law, a formal, official declaration of what is right; equally, contract itself then becomes a sort of 'form', a formal, authoritative determination of how the parties admit they ought to behave. In this connection it is important to note that Fuller's perception of customary law was far wider than, say, Llewellyn's perception of mercantile usage. Indeed, to Fuller, customary law seems to have been almost equivalent to what might be called social morality. Although Fuller never quite spells out this perception of the relation of express contract to implied contract or of the similarity between express contract and enacted or 'made' law, he gets within a whisker of doing so in 'Consideration and Form' when he discusses the role of moral obligation in the doctrine of consideration.[3] Far from being aberrant departures from principle, the cases upholding moral obligation as a consideration are, Fuller says, capable of rational defence:

When we say the defendant was morally obligated to do the thing promised, we in effect assert the existence of a substantive ground for enforcing the promise. In a broad sense, a similar line of reasoning justifies the special status accorded by law to contracts of exchange. Men *ought* to exchange goods and services; therefore when they enter contracts to that end, we enforce those contracts. . . . The court's conviction that the promisor ought to do the thing,

---

[1] *Principles of Social Order*, at p. 213.
[2] *Principles of Social Order*, p. 236.
[3] 41 *Col. L. Rev.*, at pp. 821-2.

plus the promisor's own admission of his obligation, may tilt the scales in favor of enforcement where neither standing alone would be sufficient.'[1]

This comes very close to saying that all contractual obligations are ultimately referable to prior substantive grounds of duty, and that the contract itself is merely a formal acknowledgment or admission of. that fact.[2] On this view, neither enacted law nor explicit contract is a paradigmatic source of law or legal obligation. They are only formal sources. The primary or substantive sources must be sought behind the formal sources. Of course, these substantive sources may lack qualities such as clarity and precision, which renders it inappropriate to give them legal validity without the addition of the subsequent formal process—in this case, express contract. But the whole thrust of Fuller's philosophy of law was to minimize the importance of the formal rules of legal validity; therefore, he probably would have played down the idea that the prior sources of obligation are in some sense less 'important' than the subsequent formal ones.

Fuller's discussion of the source of obligation for custom itself provides further confirmation of this. Why is customary law binding, whence the legitimacy of requiring parties to behave in accordance with custom? Fuller rejects the idea that this legitimacy can be based on a sense of obligation, or on a belief that the custom is binding—the *opinio necessitatis*. In clear cases, this is merely a tautology; where new customs are emerging, this doctrine gives no answer. Fuller turns for his solution to the promissory estoppel idea in article 90 of the first Restatement of Contracts:

As formulated to fit the problem at hand this principle would run along these (unfortunately somewhat complex) lines: Where by his actions toward B, A has (whatever his actual intentions may have been) given B reasonably to understand that he (A) will in the future in similar situations act in a similar manner, and B has, in some substantial way, prudently adjusted his affairs to the expectation that A will in the future act in accordance with this expectation then A is bound to follow the pattern set by his past actions toward B. This creates an obligation by A to B. If the pattern of interaction followed by A and B then spreads through the relevant community, a rule of general customary law will have been created. This rule will normally become part of a larger system, which will involve a complex network of reciprocal expectations. Absorption of the new rule into the larger system will, of course, be facilitated

[1] Ibid., p. 821.
[2] This theory is developed in my *Promises, Morals and Law* at chapters 5-7 (1981) and again, more directly pursuing this insight of Fuller's, in Essay 5.

by the fact that the interactions that gave rise to it took place within limits set
by that system and derived a part of their meaning for the parties from the
wider interactional context within which they occurred.[1]

At this point Fuller is in danger of being caught up in a vicious circle:
express contract, like 'made law', depends on, even arises out of, what
parties 'ought to be doing anyhow'; what they 'ought to be doing' is
complying with customary and traditional patterns of behaviour; these
are binding on them because they involve giving informal understandings of how they will behave and inducing others to rely 'prudently' on those understandings. But why do these 'informal
understandings' create obligations? To escape a *petitio principii* here
Fuller must surely go in one of two directions: he must choose between
the principle of private autonomy or a collective determination of what
is a 'prudent' or justifiable reliance on the language or behaviour of
another.

I cannot find in Fuller's work a clear indication of which road he
would ultimately have chosen. In many places he apparently views
collective judgments as to what is 'reasonable' or justifiable as parasitic
on normal, intentional behavior. For example, parties who mislead
others as to their intentions are thus held liable on an 'objective' interpretation of their behaviour, but this presupposes a world in which
people normally mean what they say.[2] On this view, one could argue
that 'implications' are parasitic on normal behaviour, normal intentions. But elsewhere in his writings Fuller seems to argue that normal
behaviour and normal intentions often fail to answer the questions
which face us in the law. For example, in the reliance article, Fuller
exposes the emptiness of the foreseeability rule in *Hadley* v. *Baxendale*:[3]

[I]t is clear that the test of foreseeability is less a definite test itself than a cover
for a developing set of tests. As in the case of all 'reasonable man' standards,
there is an element of circularity about the test of foreseeability. For what
items of damage should the court hold the defaulting promisor? Those which
he should as a reasonable man have foreseen. But what should he have foreseen
as a reasonable man? Those items of damage for which the court feels he ought
to pay.[4]

---

[1] *Principles of Social Order*, p. 227.
[2] A similar idea seems to underlie the argument offered by Professor J. Raz, 'Promises
in Morality and Law', 95 *Harv. L. Rev.* 916 (1982). See also Essay 7 (pp. 172–5, below)
as to the appropriate measure of damages in such cases.
[3] 9 Ex. 341 (1854).
[4] 46 *Yale LJ* at p. 85.

This element of circularity seems to me to extend to the whole relationship between explicit contract and imposed legal obligations. The meaning and nature of express promises take much of their substance from ideas of reasonableness, but ideas of reasonableness derive in part from normal patterns of purposive behaviour. There is, inevitably, action and reaction here: but which is paramount? Which is the paradigm and which is parasitic? The answer to this question will often not matter; however, it may matter when principles of autonomy and reasonable reliance conflict. It may also matter when the law draws on residuary principles or ideals for extensions and new developments.

It is comforting to rest on our familiar conceptions of freedom of contract to answer this question, but Fuller, again in the reliance article, shows how easy it is to reverse our notions of what is normal and what exceptional, just as it is to reverse our perception of what is paradigmatic and what parasitic. Thus in dealing with the distinction between busimess contracts, normally enforceable while still executory, and non-business contracts, which tend to be enforceable only after reliance, Fuller points out how easy it would be to 'base the whole law of contracts on a fundamental premise that only those promises which have been relied on will be enforced'.[1] All we need add is that 'the chief exception' to this principle will be the bilateral business agreement.

I have elsewhere developed the argument that the past century or thereabouts has seen a shift in the paradigm of contractual obligation.[2] In 'the age of freedom of contract'—wherever that is placed—the principle of private autonomy was supreme. 'Reasonableness' took its colour from that principle; therefore, 'objective' interpretations and 'justifiable' reliance were viewed as parasitic on the private autonomy principle. In particular, reliance was largely seen as justifiable if, and only if, it was based on a promise. Today, with the waning of the private autonomy principle, 'reasonableness' appears to be a more basic community judgment, drawing its sustenance less from private autonomy and more from collective moral ideas and even customary practices and redistributive ideologies. Private autonomy must now accommodate itself to reasonableness, rather than the other way round.

The result is that the notion of justifiable reliance may be gradually acquiring dominance over the private autonomy principle. Not all reliance on a promise is today seen as justifiable: for example, a promise by a consumer inserted in a contract in small print. Conversely, reliance

---

[1] Ibid., p. 70.
[2] *Freedom of Contract*, chapters 20-2.

on language and conduct is more often seen as justifiable even in the absence of a promise. Reliance has greatly developed as a source of liability in warranty law, in misrepresentation law, in products liability cases, in ordinary negligence actions, and of course in estoppel and promissory estoppel. Some of these forms of liability could be defended as liability on an 'implied promise', but many of them cannot be so explained without circularity or distortion. Many therefore illustrate the growing ascendancy of the reliance principle over the private autonomy principle. They also suggest that this ascendancy is deep-rooted, and is unlikely to be overturned by the apparent resurgence in the ideology of freedom of contract which has been observed in the Western world since the 1970s.

This process can be illustrated by looking to a recent decision, *Yianni* v. *Edwin Evans & Sons*.[1] The plaintiffs wanted to buy a house and applied for a loan to a building society. The building society, as customary, commissioned a valuation which was conducted by the defendant surveyors. The report being favourable, the building society lent the plaintiffs eighty per cent of the amount of the valuation. The plaintiffs did not see the defendants' valuation, which was shown only to the building society, but they paid the defendants' fee through the building society. The valuation turned out to be grossly excessive, the defendants having negligently failed to discover structural weaknesses in the house which had to be put right at a substantial cost. The plaintiffs recovered damages against the defendants for their negligence: the court held that the plaintiffs had reasonably and foreseeably relied on the valuation, even though they had not seen it, because they assumed that the house was worth at least the amount loaned to them.[2] There was, of course, no promise or warranty addressed by the defendants to the plaintiffs; indeed, the defendants clearly did not intend that their valuation should be made available to or be directly relied on by the plaintiffs, because they advised the plaintiffs to commission their own survey. Nor in all probability did the defendants charge a fee commensurate with the assumption of liability to the plaintiffs, because before this decision it had been widely assumed that surveyors were not liable in these circumstances, so it is fair to assume that they charged accordingly.

It seems clear enough that, if the principle of private autonomy was paramount, the defendants should not have been liable: they did not

[1] [1982] QB 438.
[2] See [1982] QB at 457.

intend to assume liability nor even to invite reliance by the plaintiffs. It is true, and was found as a fact, that the plaintiffs' reliance was in one sense foreseeable and reasonable because most buyers do not commission their own surveys but rely on the building society's willingness to lend as sufficient evidence of the value of the property. But although this reliance may thus be said to have been 'reasonable' it is hard to see how the plaintiffs could have been entitled to throw on the defendants the result of their reliance if traditional principles of contract had prevailed. Despite the argument of Professor Fried that there is no inconsistency between liberal insistence on the autonomy principle, and supplementing that principle with principles of tort (or restitution),[1] the inconsistency here seems plain for all to see. The plaintiffs had no 'right' or 'entitlement' to rely so as to hold the defendants liable for the consequences. They had not 'bought' such a right; although they had paid the defendants' fee, the fee clearly did not include any element of 'premium' to protect the plaintiffs against the risk which occurred. The decision in favour of the plaintiffs—and this is typical of many such cases today, both in England and America—stems from the shift from contractual and promissory doctrine to reliance or tort doctrine. Contract doctrine, at least when it was largely bargain-based, only protected paid-for reliance. The promisee had to buy the right to rely. Once the courts shift into reliance or tort doctrine, however, they in effect 'give' the right to rely to the plaintiff and are thus engaged in a redistributive exercise. Furthermore, they do so largely on the ground that the plaintiffs have relied in fact, and in a normal, customary—therefore foreseeable—manner. Factual, customary reliance becomes justifiable reliance and is thus converted into a legally protected reliance.

It is, of course, true that any decision awarding damages to an injured plaintiff in a tort case involves a distributive element; even the torts of battery or conversion of goods depend on recognition that the person injured had the 'entitlement' not to be injured by the battery or the conversion, and in that sense involve recognition that, as between the two parties, the entitlement is allocated to the victim. But in *Yianni*, and in any case in which the plaintiff is claiming reliance losses, there are two special features which make the distributive implications particularly striking. First, in the typical tort case the plaintiff has suffered a loss which is a social as well as a private cost, and traditionally tort law has been seen as having at least some concern for the avoidance or minimization of such social costs. But in the instant case, and in most

[1] See Essay 6.

typical reliance cases, the plaintiff has incurred a private cost which is not a social cost at all. The plaintiffs' loss in the instant case was offset, from the social viewpoint, by the corresponding gain to the seller of the property. Hence, the argument is purely about the allocation of the loss between the plaintiffs and the defendants, and the court could only shift the loss to the defendants by allocating to the plaintiffs a 'right to rely' to which they were not prima facie entitled.[1]

Of course, much the same may be said of plain theft where the gain to the thief counterbalances the loss to the owner, and the tort remedy can therefore only be granted by allocating the entitlement in question to the owner. However, in this situation, the allocation of the entitlement takes place in accordance with the pre-existing set of property laws, whereas in the case under discussion, the allocation of the right— at any rate on the first occasion such a decision is made[2] —involves a change from the pre-existing allocation of entitlements. Moreover, the change in allocation—the redistribution of rights—is particularly striking because it concerns an entitlement to a recognizable commodity which can be bought in the market, and could have been so bought by the present plaintiffs. They could have bought advice with 'a right to rely' on that advice, but they did not do so.

A second striking feature of decisions of this character is that the plaintiffs' loss or injury stems not only from the defendants' conduct or language, but more immediately from the plaintiffs' own free choice decision to act in reliance on that conduct. Because the defendants intended that the plaintiffs should not be entitled to shift the risk of such reliance to them and the plaintiffs likewise could not intelligibly have intended that their action in reliance should be at the defendants' risk, the allocation of the entitlement to rely to the plaintiffs clearly

---

[1] On the distinction between private and social cost in cases of this kind, see Bishop, 'Economic Loss in Tort', 2 *Ox. J. Leg. St.* 1 (1982); Rizzo, 'The Economic Loss Problem: A Comment on Bishop', ibid., at p. 197; Bishop, 'Economic Loss: A Reply to Professor Rizzo', ibid., at p. 207.

[2] Of course, once the decision is accepted and becomes known it can be assumed that surveyors will begin charging an appropriate premium for the extra risk they are forced to bear. Thus the long-term result of such decisions is not to make a free gift of the 'right to rely'; future buyers will have to pay for it, and thus in effect buy compulsory insurance against the risk involved. But there is much to be said in this sort of situation for compulsory insurance, and it could even be defended in terms of liberal or free market theory by pointing out how difficult it would be to obtain private insurance against such risks, in the absence of a legal duty of this kind.

violated the principle of private autonomy.[1] This result seems to me to illustrate very well the curious way in which the development of reliance doctrine—for which Fuller was substantially responsible—today clashes so violently with the principle of private autonomy which he so strongly favoured.

I would like to end by suggesting that there is a broad sense in which the protection of 'reasonable' reliance—perhaps even in the extended way illustrated above—ought not to cause serious anxiety to the modern liberal. F. A. Hayek has repeatedly warned us that non-contractual expectations (that is, in this context, non-bargained-for, or unpaid-for expectations) cannot be protected to the hilt without serious infringements of the rights of others.[2] My 'expectations' in my job, my income, the retention of the present value of my property, and so forth depend entirely on the assumption that other people will continue to behave in ways that I have no right to compel them to behave. The continuation of my job in a market society depends on a continuing demand for the services I can provide. If people's needs or tastes change, I may lose my job; my property may depreciate in value and so on. These results can only be avoided by freezing the existing economic arrangements in society in a way which would greatly benefit the haves at the expense of the have-nots. In any event, not all expectations can be fully protected because some people expect no relevant change, while others expect change beneficial to them.

On the other hand, it is surely one of the marks of a liberal society that revolutionary or even over-rapid change should be avoided where possible. Protecting reliance is, in a broad sense, a way of reconciling the need for change with the desire to avoid infliction of unnecessary suffering on those who lose by change. Protection of all non-contractual expectations (in the above sense) would be not only inconsistent with all change, it would be impossible for the reasons given above. But protection of at least some kinds of non-contractual reliance is not inconsistent with change. All it does is to cushion those liable to be most severely affected by the change. The radical or revolutionary may

---

[1] It must be admitted that these remarks may seem just as applicable to the case of fraud as they are to negligence. But a general allocation of an entitlement to rely on the *honesty* of those with whom we deal is one thing, and a general allocation of the right to rely on the *carefulness* of others is something else. Care has a market value, and usually has to be bought. But we do not usually allow people to trade in honesty.

[2] In particular, see his *Law, Legislation and Liberty*, vol. ii, *The Mirage of Social Justice* (1976), at pp. 114-25, 137-8, 140-1; see also T. Honoré, *Quest for Security: Employees, Tenants, Wives* (Hamlyn Lectures, 1982).

protest that this is merely a way of enabling 'the rich' to hang on to part of their wealth a little longer, but at the present day as much of the demand for this form of protection—job protection, income maintenance, and so on—comes from 'the poor' as from the rich. Perhaps Fuller, with his sympathy for Burkean gradualism, as well as his faith in the rationality and legitimacy of customary behaviour, would ultimately have come to see that his reliance principle could be justifiably extended to the non-promissory arena, and that once entrenched there it might often take priority even over the principle of private autonomy.

5

Form and Substance in Contract Law

1. Two Different Types of Legal Reasoning

Throughout the varied areas of law it is apparent that we encounter two different types of legal reasoning. There are, on the one hand, reasons of substance.[1] If we are, for instance, considering what rule should be formulated to govern a particular situation, we may weigh up a variety of arguments bearing on the desirability or the rightness of this rule, or that rule. If we are asking whether one person ought to pay damages to another we will weigh up a variety of considerations, some pointing in one direction and some in another, but these will mostly be reasons of substance bearing directly on the question. Did the defendant, for instance, commit a wrong against the plaintiff? Did his actions cause the plaintiff's injuries? And so on. Or again if we are trying to construct a procedure for the resolution of disputes, we can weigh up reasons for allowing the parties to adduce such and such evidence, or for allowing them to have such and such opportunities for appeal, reasons of substance bearing directly on the goals we are trying to achieve.

On the other hand, we often find ourselves giving effect to reasons of a different character, which I shall call formal reasons. In the paradigm case, a formal reason is a requirement for writing, or sealing, or perhaps for registration or attestation of some kind. When a document fails to comply with stipulated forms, the law may declare the document to be legally ineffective. A will, for instance, or a contract required to be in writing, may be declared void or unenforceable if the formalities are not observed. In such cases we do not stop as a rule (though there may be exceptions) to ask whether the failure to comply with the formal

---

[1] See R. S. Summers, 'Two Types of Substantive Reasons: The Core of a Theory of Common Law Justification', 63 *Cornell Law Rev.* 707 (1978). The distinctions I am drawing cut across those drawn by Professor Summers in this paper; however, elsewhere Professor Summers distinguishes between two working conceptions of the law as 'rules' and 'reason'. See, 'Working Conceptions of the Law', 1 *Law And Philosophy* 267 (1982). This distinction is closer to that which I draw in this paper. Since this paper was first written, Professor Summers and I have been engaged in a work (tentatively entitled *Form and Substance in Anglo-American Law*) which develops the present theme in several new dimensions.

requirements is outweighed by some other substantive reason in favour of giving legal force to the will or contract. Once the legal rule of ineffectiveness for lack of form is clearly established, the application of that rule shuts out from consideration the substantive arguments in favour of validity or enforcement. These formal reasons are typically thought of as associated with writing and written documents. But there are many other examples of similar kinds of reasons in the law even though we would not perhaps normally refer to them as formal reasons. For example, a judge who follows a binding precedent may do so without examining the substantive arguments in favour of the principle for which that precedent stands. If the precedent is truly binding on him, and if he loyally accepts the principle of *stare decisis*, he will not even pause to consider what substantive reasons may be given for an opposite decision. So far as he is concerned, the question cannot be properly considered at all. There is no question of weighing one set of factors against the other, no question of balancing the authority of precedent against the weight of the reasoning to be found in the particular precedent. The formal reason—that the precedent binds him—simply excludes from consideration any countervailing reason. Or again, take a case where a claim is defeated by the statute of limitations. Here also, if the statute is properly pleaded and is properly applicable, it shuts out of consideration all other factors. Prima facie at least, the court does not weigh up the strength of the plaintiff's case against the strength of the limitation plea. If the plea is good, all other argument is irrelevant.

The nature of reasons of this kind has been discussed and illuminated in an important series of works by Joseph Raz, but Professor Raz calls them 'second-order' reasons[1] or pre-emptive or protected reasons[2] rather than formal reasons as I intend to call them. Nothing of course turns on mere matters of terminology, but it is understandable why Professor Raz eschews the term I have chosen to use. Formal reasoning today has a bad name among lawyers; indeed, it is often treated as the same thing as formalistic reasoning as though these were both examples of bad reasoning ranging merely from the bad to the very bad. I do not deny that there are many examples, both in law and elsewhere, of formalistic reasoning which is indeed deplorable. But in my view we

[1] See Joseph Raz, *Practical Reason and Norms* (Hutchinson, London, 1975) especially at pp. 35-48 and 58-62; also, his *The Authority of Law* (Clarendon Press, Oxford, 1979), pp. 30-3.
[2] Raz, 'Authority and Justification' in 14 *Philosophy and Public Affairs* 3 (1985).

ought to distinguish between formal reasoning and formalistic reasoning. Formal reasoning is not *per se* unjustified or wrong, though formalistic reasoning is. Where reasons of substance ought to be considered by the decision-maker, and he refuses to consider them, any formal reasons he gives for his decision will be out of place and unjustifiable, and hence can fairly be called formalistic. A judge, for instance, who claims that he is bound to make a particular decision because of a prior precedent, even though the precedent is clearly distinguishable according to the accepted rules and practices governing these matters, is giving a formal reason which is not merely bad, but out of place. He is being formalistic. Similarly, a judge who woodenly applies a rule without even pausing to consider whether it is possible or justifiable for him to create an exception to the rule is reasoning in a formalistic manner. Nobody can deny that the law books are full of examples of formalistic reasoning of this kind. But the fact that formalistic reasons are always bad does not justify us in jumping to the conclusion that all formal reasoning is bad. Indeed, it is quite apparent that the law uses, and, I will argue, correctly uses, formal reasons in all sorts of situations.

Once we start looking at the law and legal reasoning in detail, we find a great many examples of formal reasons which cannot be condemned as bad or formalistic. Statutes, precedents, judgments, jury verdicts, and administrative decisions by statutory bodies all give rise to questions of this character; so too do marriage and contracts though in rather different ways. Although the case of contract is the one to which I mainly want to direct my attention, I shall try to set the issues in context by looking first at some of these other illustrations.

Let me take first some relatively simple examples about the sources of law. The simplest example of a formal reason for a decision is that it is required by a clear statutory provision. Where this is indeed the case, a judge who applies the statute has no cause to consider the substance or merits of the arguments. Within certain limits—and I shall come back to the question of limits in a moment—it is clear that the application of a simple statutory provision just excludes from consideration arguments which would be relevant in a purely common law inquiry, at least where no binding authority exists. It would be pointless to adduce arguments to suggest that the statute leads to unfair results, or odd results, or anomalous results. Again, within limits, it is pointless and impermissible to suggest that the application of the statute may not produce the result that the legislature intended. Still less is it permissible to argue that, whatever may have been the position when the statute was first passed, conditions have so changed, or even the composition of the legislature has so changed, that to give effect to the Act would be to decide contrary to present-day social or moral views, or contrary to the views of the majority in the present legislative assembly.[1] In all ordinary cases the statute is, and is intended to be, a formal source of law in the sense that it is intended to exclude from consideration countervailing arguments against the result which the statute dictates. The statute is not just one additional reason to be taken account of by the judge, which may tip the scales in one direction, or be overriden by contrary arguments. The statute shuts out contrary arguments.

Of course, as I have said, all this is only the case within certain limits. If a statute seems ambiguous, or unclear, or if it produces results which seem grossly anomalous or utterly absurd or perhaps even seriously unjust, then courts may avoid applying the statute. The limits within which judges do this vary from country to country, from time to time, and no doubt even from judge to judge. They have been much discussed by judges and writers. I do not propose to add to this discussion. For my purposes it is enough that there are some limits, and that everyone recognizes that there are such limits. If a statute could be disregarded by a judge whenever he felt that it led to a result which he would not have reached in the absence of the statute, then a statute would cease to be a formal source of law in the sense in which I am using the term. The reasons underlying the statute would simply be additional arguments to be considered along with all the other reasons of substance bearing on the case. But the fact that these reasons had been enshrined in a statute would not give them any primacy over other reasons.

Much the same is true of the system of precedent. According to the theory of the common law, some precedents are binding on some courts in the sense that the judges in the subsequent case are bound or obliged to follow the principle of the first case without examining the substantive arguments for and against the principle. Here, however, there tends to be rather more scepticism than there is with regard to statutes. As we all know, not everything that is said in a case is regarded as part of the *ratio decidendi* which is binding on subsequent judges; further, the subsequent court may be able to distinguish the earlier case; and in

---

[1] But see Calabresi, *A Common Law for the Age Of Statutes* (Harvard University Press, 1982).

any event, there are often rules and practices about the relative hierarchy of courts which entitle one court to declare precedents binding on another. Again, practice on these matters varies from country to country, time to time, and even judge to judge; and I would not underestimate the significance of these variations in practice. Moreover, I think it is probably true to say that, especially in well-tilled fields of law, a precedent is often treated as an additional reason for deciding in a certain way, rather than as a different kind of reason which shuts out of consideration all other reasons. But still, at the end of the day, wherever the common law operates, there must I think be some cases where a court feels obliged to follow a precedent of a higher court, solely and simply because that precedent is regarded as a formal source for decision, excluding from consideration all reasons of substance. Of course, if we turn away from the effect of precedents on lower courts, and consider their effect on other officials, or even on the citizens at large, it seems still more clear that precedents are habitually treated as formal sources of law binding on everyone, unless and until other courts pronounce on the issues. Once again, I do not forget the limits. Precedents are meant to be used intelligently. Counsel advising a client, even the ordinary citizen who reads a case—if that ever happens—may well say: 'Clearly this precedent is not going to be applied in this particular situation; the result is too absurd, and the judges never had that sort of case in mind.' But still, no matter within what limits the doctrine of precedent operates, it clearly amounts in some cases to a formal reason for subsequent decision making.

In the case of precedents, many lawyers have rebelled at the implications of the doctrine. Bentham, for instance, condemned the system of precedent as 'acting without reason, to the declared exclusion of reason and thereby in opposition to reason'.[1] And in more modern times, lawyers without number have protested—particularly perhaps in the United States—at the slavish following of precedents as an abdication of reason. In the case of statutes, the arguments tend to take a different form. Because the relationship between the legislature and the court is usually a constitutional datum or starting-point, there are few lawyers who protest at the abdication of reason required of a judge when he gives effect to a statute, at any rate, perhaps I should add, in England. But there are those, of course, who would press the argument that at least the application of a statute is designed to give effect to the

---

[1] See *Collected Works of Jeremy Bentham, Constitutional Code* (F. Rosen and J. H. Burns ed., 1983), vol. i, 434.

intentions of the legislature, and that therefore a statute should never be interpreted in a way which seems plainly contrary to what the legislature intended. Yet this certainly happens on occasion. Is this also to be condemned, as Bentham condemned the following of precedent, as 'acting . . . in opposition to reason'? At first sight it might indeed seem to deserve such condemnation. If a friend writes me a letter requesting me to do something for him, but, interpreting the letter in the manner of a Parke B., I do something quite different *even though my declared objective is to carry out his intention*, my action may seem indefensible, indeed incoherent. Yet surely this is not true of the action of a judge who sticks somewhat rigidly to the apparent meaning of a statute, even though he may think that the result is not what the legislature intended. Indeed a not unsophisticated defence of this approach was offered by Lord Simon of Glaisdale in the House of Lords in 1975 in the *Black-Clawson* case,[1] which concerned the interpretation of a statute giving effect to the report of a committee.

The true function of the court interpreting a statute, said Lord Simon, is not to ascertain what Parliament intended, but what is the meaning of the words used by Parliament. Conceding that this was not a self-evident juristic truth, Lord Simon nevertheless offered a spirited defence of this procedure. First, he insisted that if the courts were permitted to search for the intentions of Parliament outside the words of the statute itself, a great deal of time and cost would be wasted in the ransacking of additional material as to the intentions of Parliament. 'By concentrating on the meaning of what has been said, to the exclusion of what was meant to be said, the material for scrutiny is greatly reduced.'[2] Secondly, interpretation is concerned not merely with the intentions of the legislature but with the reasonable understandings and expectations of the citizen. Citizens, with or without their advisers, are entitled to look to an enactment as the source of the law, and to base their conduct on it, without having to concern themselves with questions about the intention of Parliament behind and beyond the words used. Thus the statute operates as a sort of barrier; it is the final expression of Parliament's intentions, and the reader and interpreter must confine himself in principle[3] to the words of the Act. Thirdly, Lord Simon went on to

---

[1] [1975] AC 591.

[2] Ibid. at p. 645.

[3] Of course exceptions are admitted. In the *Black-Clawson* case reference to the Report of a Committee was permitted though there was disagreement as to whether this was only permissible to identify the 'mischief' being aimed at, or also as a direct aid to the interpretation of the Act.

point out that, if the draftsman has done his job properly, the meaning of the words used should coincide with the intentions of the legislator. The last point is, of course, one of general application whenever the construction of a document is in issue. It is a reasonable starting-point—indeed, the only possible starting-point—that words mean what they mean, and that those who use words intend to convey what the words normally convey. In the great majority of cases this is almost certainly true; and we are likely to achieve more accurate results if we refuse to depart from this assumption, than if we open it to question in all cases. We may, of course, occasionally go wrong if we always insist that people mean what they say; but we are far more likely to go wrong if we always question whether they mean what they say. Indeed, it is arguable that we are more likely to go wrong even if we confine our-selves to the more moderate course of questioning whether they mean what they say only where there is some ground for thinking that perhaps they do not mean what they say.

Lord Simon's first two points are especially important to the very nature of formal reasons for decisions. The first is the question of cost. Even if we assume that there is such a thing as a parliamentary inten-tion, even leaving aside the theoretical and practical difficulties in know-ing what intentions to attribute to a legislative body of several hundred members, the fact is that it would take a great deal of valuable time to search for a true or real parliamentary intent, different from that ascertainable from the face of a statute. Suppose it is suggested, however, that this search need only take place where a statute is am-biguous or where the intent is not clear on its face? This would certainly reduce the force of the argument from cost, but not very much. For after all, that still leaves all the cases where the court is today asked to decide a point of statutory construction, and there are enough of those in all conscience. Of course, in some of these cases, the extra cost devoted to a search for parliamentary intention outside the text of the Act might be repaid. Clear signs of intention may be found. But, as Lord Simon also pointed out, the American experience on this is not encouraging. The extra cost is likely to produce rare and dubious benefits.

But the second argument is also important. A statute is, and is intended to be, a formal expression of Parliament's will. Statutes are not drafted hastily, nor are they passed lightly or easily, at least in Britain. A great deal of effort goes into the drafting, and the par-liamentary scrutiny of important bills is no formality. The whole pur-

pose of this procedure is to present to the public and to the legal
profession a document which is designed to be read as a formal document. It is not an argumentative document, nor a discursive document.
It rarely states reasons. It is assumed in the British parliamentary
process that the arguments and the reasons are to be discussed first
by those officials responsible for preparing the bill, and second, in
Parliament itself. Once the bill is passed it is intended to be treated as a
formal piece of law.

Now whether these arguments are found to be convincing may be a
matter on which reasonable persons may differ; it may also be relevant
to inquire into the procedures and practices regarding the drafting and
passing of legislation in different jurisdictions before deciding how
far courts should be permitted to look at extraneous material when
interpreting a statute. But what is surely not open to question is that
these arguments of Lord Simon's for the formal treatment of statutes
are *reasoned* arguments. There are, in other words, *reasons* for treating
formal reasons as overriding or exclusionary reasons, which shut out
other sorts of reasons from consideration.[1]

When we turn to the case of binding precedent we find the situation
is much the same. Here again, to say that a system of precedent involves
an abdication of reason, as Bentham said, seems an absurd exaggeration. There are *reasons* why it seems right to treat questions of law
as having been conclusively settled by earlier decisions—within limits,
of course. These reasons are to some degree the same as those which
apply in the case of statutes. First, it saves time and trouble. Secondly,
it saves us from having to worry about reasons and arguments for a
rule. If the rule has been clearly laid down, then, like a statute, it makes
for greater simplicity and certainty, if we can be confident that future
courts will apply that rule without inquiring too closely into the results,
or into the reasons for its application. But there are, in the case of the
system of precedent, additional reasons for this rather formal approach
which are inapplicable in the case of statutes. In the case of statutes—
at any rate in Britain and other countries where there is no judicial
power over statutes—lawyers do not question the ultimate power of
Parliament to impose on the courts a law which the judges might regard
as contrary to all reason. They have no power to set up their judgment
on controversial questions in opposition to that of Parliament. But
when precedents are in question, it is usually accepted that there are
no final answers to many problems. Policy judgments and value judg-

[1] See Raz, *Practical Reason and Norms*, esp. at p. 36.

ments are involved in much judicial law-making. In the absence of a system of precedent it is difficult to see how finality would ever be achieved if judges were always entitled to decide a case in the way they think it ought to be decided, regardless of prior decisions.

Once again I must beware of appearing to adopt a position about the precise way a system of precedent should work, and about the extent to which judges should accept the call to modernize the law and keep it up to date by jettisoning old and obsolete precedents. All that I am saying is that no system of precedent could work if a judge was entitled to disregard a precedent just because he disagreed with it, merely because he thought it wrong. The concept of a system of precedent is that it constrains judges in some cases to follow decisions they do not agree with. This is no more contrary to reason than it is contrary to reason for a military commander to expect his subordinates to obey orders without asking themselves whether the orders are reasonable or sensible.[1]

Let me now turn to some other illustrations of formal reasoning in the legal system. Consider first, the principles concerning the finality of judgments. If an issue has been properly litigated, and properly decided, and if appeals have been exhausted or are not available, then the judgment is a formal reason for deciding the rights and obligations of the parties. Once that judgment has been rendered, and become final, it shuts out from consideration any further argument on the merits. Even if, in some objective sense, the judgment is fallacious, or based on an incorrect finding of fact, it will no longer avail to adduce contrary arguments of substance. Once again, it is not a matter of the judgment outweighing the substantive arguments; it simply renders them irrelevant. In this connection I should like to refer to two striking decisions of recent years.

The *Ampthill Peerage* case[2] was not strictly a judicial decision of the House of Lords, but was a recommendation of the Committee of Privileges in which the leading opinion was given by Lord Wilberforce. The facts were somewhat unusual, and it is unnecessary to set them out in great detail. The case concerned the legitimacy of Geoffrey Russell, who claimed to be the legitimate son of John Hugo Russell, later third Lord Ampthill. When Geoffrey was born Lord Ampthill denied paternity and indeed petitioned for divorce on the ground of the adultery of his wife. After a long trial a jury found in his favour,

[1] Ibid., p. 38.
[2] [1977] AC 547.

but the decision was reversed by the House of Lords in the case of *Russell* v. *Russell*[1] on the ground that evidence of non-access by the husband was inadmissible to bastardize the son. Following the divorce proceedings a petition for a declaration of legitimacy was brought on behalf of Geoffrey Russell and, there being no evidence against him other than that declared inadmissible in *Russell* v. *Russell*, a declaration was made. Fifty years later, Lord Ampthill died and Geoffrey Russell laid claim to the peerage. The claim was contested and the conclusiveness of the declaration of legitimacy was challenged on a number of grounds, including the legislative reversal of the decision of *Russell* v. *Russell*, and the unwillingness (so it was alleged) of Geoffrey Russell to submit to blood tests. The Committee of Privileges upheld the finality of the legitimacy declaration even though, as Lord Wilberforce conceded, this might be said, in a sense, to prefer justice to truth. Perhaps the truth was, in some objective sense, that Geoffrey Russell was not the legitimate son and heir of Lord Ampthill. Nevertheless, insisted the House of Lords, there was no adequate ground for going behind the declaration of legitimacy issued by a competent court so many years before. They stressed the fact that the parties must have relied upon the declaration and planned their lives accordingly.

So here we have, in rather striking circumstances, an affirmation of the value of finality in judicial proceedings. The declaration granted by a competent court was treated as a formal and conclusive reason for acknowledging Geoffrey's right to the peerage. Contrary arguments of substance, from which reasonable persons might have inferred that Geoffrey was not legitimate, were not considered and rejected: they were simply shut out from consideration. The judgment was final. In this case we find yet further justifications for upholding the formal nature of a reason. In addition to arguments about cost—relevant of course, but not stressed here—there were arguments about reliance, and about the need for peace and repose and security in human affairs.

The second decision I want to mention in this context is the Privy Council decision in *Chokolingo* v. *Attorney General of Trinidad and Tobago*.[2] This was an appeal from Trinidad and Tobago which has a written constitution incorporating an American style provision against deprivation of liberty without due process of law. The appellant was convicted of contempt of court and sentenced to 21 days in prison. He did not appeal and served his sentence; but two and a half years later

---

[1] [1924] AC 687.
[2] [1981] 1 All ER 244.

he sought to challenge his sentence as a deprivation of liberty without due process of law on the ground that the alleged contempt had been based on a publication itself protected as a fundamental freedom under the constitution. This was thus the kind of collateral attack which is familiar under the American system of federal *habeas corpus* but the Privy Council found the whole concept of such attack utterly irrational and subversive of the rule of law. The guarantee of due process of law, said the Privy Council, is a guarantee of a proper trial before a court of competent jurisdiction. If no appeal is brought against such a conviction, or if appeal is brought and dismissed, then the accused has had due process of law, and no further attack on the decision can be launched. Here, then, is another striking affirmation of the importance of finality in judicial decisions, all the more striking for involving such a decisive rejection of a large body of American jurisprudence. It is, moreover, an excellent illustration of the importance and indeed justifiability of formal reasoning in the law. For of course the Privy Council decision was reached without any inquiry into the merits of the original conviction. The judgment of the original court was not just one reason for the decision, to be weighed against other reasons. It was a conclusive or overriding reason—a formal reason in my sense.

As I have indicated, the law makes a great deal of use of such formal reasoning in its own procedures and processes. Apart from the cases I have already mentioned, there are many other types of case in which formal reasons are or may be conclusive reasons which exclude substantive reasons from consideration. To mention just a few, there are rules of jurisdiction—so that application to the wrong court or tribunal must be dismissed irrespective of the merits; there are rules of procedure and pleading under which courts may in the last resort (and I accept of course that this often is a last resort) dismiss a claim or a defence without any consideration of the merits.

Particularly relevant for my purposes is the fact that, in criminal procedure, a plea of guilty is normally regarded as a formal and conclusive reason for recording a conviction against the accused. In the common law adversarial procedure we do not investigate at the trial level a criminal case in which the defendant pleads guilty, though such investigation may of course take place at the police level where an admission of guilt does not have the same formal consequences. But at the trial level we do not proceed any further. We do not look for corroborative evidence, nor for evidence which casts doubt on the guilty plea. Of the many possible reasons for this, I need only mention two—

reasons sufficiently obvious and compelling to require little elaboration. The first is that we are unlikely to go far wrong if we treat guilty pleas as conclusive. Very rarely this may result in the wrongful conviction of an innocent person; but if we required independent proof in all cases in which a guilty plea is today accepted as conclusive, it is almost certain that we should go wrong far more frequently in the opposite direction— that is, we should acquit many more guilty persons than the number of innocent persons wrongly convicted today. The second reason, of course, is the question of cost. Contested trials cost money. At present over 90 per cent of criminal trials in England are resolved by pleas of guilty. The cost of administering the criminal justice system would obviously be magnified manifold if all these cases were tried out. And delay—itself, of course, a source of further costs—would also become a far more serious problem.

Of course, there are limits on the formal effect—on the con- clusiveness—of a plea of guilty, as there are limits on the conclusiveness of all, or nearly all, formal reasons. If there are any indications that the accused is unfit to plead, or does not understand the charge, or if he pleads guilty and then adds qualifying words which cast doubt on the plea, it may be rejected, and further inquiry made; or perhaps a plea of not guilty may be entered. But until very recently it has been uniformly held in England that an unequivocal plea of guilty by a sane adult defendant who understands the charge and the plea, is a conclusive reason for a conviction. Indeed, until the decision in 1984 of *R.* v. *Lee*[1] it was always held that a plea of guilty in such cir- cumstances also precludes appeal. But in that case, for the first time, it was held that an appeal could be entertained and evidence admitted, even where the accused had been convicted on a plea of guilty. This was a remarkable case in which the accused had pleaded guilty to eleven counts of arson and manslaughter, and a subsequent newspaper investigation had revealed facts from which it was manifest that some of these crimes simply could not have been committed by the accused. Yet it was accepted on all hands that the accused was fit to plead, knew what he was doing, intended to make the pleas he did, and pleaded guilty without equivocation after receiving proper advice. One feels, as the Court of Appeal clearly felt, that the case was somehow aberrant. Criminal procedure is based on the assumption that normal sane adults do not plead guilty to crimes which they have not committed. Yet here, it seemed, was manifest proof that this had actually happened. I shall

[1] [1984] 1 All ER 1080.

return to this case later because it seems to me not irrelevant to the remarks I want to make about contract law.

2. Formal Reasoning: the Example of Marriage

I turn from these examples of formal reasoning in the judicial process to consider the same phenomena in private law. But again I defer the subject of contract because I want first to look at an area which seems to raise very analogous problems—namely, matrimonial law. The analogy of marriage may help to illustrate and make more plausible some of the suggestions to be made later about contract.

Now marriage is, of course, a legal status which can only be created in most sophisticated legal systems by actually going through certain formal procedures. But I want to focus not on the forms required to create the status of marriage but rather on the sense in which marriage is itself a formal reason for making many decisions. In order to understand this point, it is only necessary to ask what would happen if the legal institution of marriage were abolished—a proposal which has been seriously canvassed in certain quarters.[1] Plainly this would not prevent or perhaps even discourage men and women from living together just as they do now, in a variety of ways, and for varying lengths of time. Some periods of cohabitation would no doubt be lifelong; others, very short. But why, it is asked, do we need the formality of treating some cohabiting partners in the special way signified by marriage? It is, after all, no longer possible to answer that the purpose of marriage is to indicate to the world that the partners have committed themselves to a lifelong union, when we know and they know that the law permits them fairly easy and painless ways of escape. Those who advocate the total elimination of the marriage status as an unnecessary legal formality do not deny that decisions will have to be made about property rights and maintenance obligations on separation and divorce or death. But, they urge, since these decisions already have to be made, especially on separation and divorce, by having regard to all the circumstances of the case—the length of the marriage, the relative income and behaviour of the parties, the number and ages of any children, and so on—it really makes very little difference whether the formal status of marriage is acknowledged or not. The argument, it will be seen, is tantamount to asserting that marriage is no longer a good formal reason for recognizing obligations of the cohabiting partners, whether

[1] See E. M. Clive, 'Marriage: An Unnecessary Legal Concept?', in *Marriage and Cohabitation in Contemporary Society*, ed. Eekelaar and Katz (1980).

in regard to the continuance of the cohabitation or to what happens after it ends. These questions, it is implied, can only be settled by looking at reasons of substance, and not at purely formal (and hence, within limits, conclusive) reasons.

Challenging and unfamiliar though this argument may seem to the typical conservative lawyer, it has a certain plausibility, particularly in relation to property rights and questions of maintenance such as arise on separation and divorce, where it is now the practice, in England at least, to treat the answers as depending very much on the general weighing of substantive reasons. But there are, as it seems to me, many other legal questions, questions involving both public and private law, which would not be so easily disposed of if we eliminated the formal status of marriage. What about, for instance, rights of action under the Fatal Accidents Acts and similar legislation? No problem, say the supporters of this proposal. We can simply base such rights on *de facto* dependency, not on the legal tie. Well, that might work for dependency claims, but of course many countries have other types of legal rights to sue on the death of a spouse, where some compensation is payable by way of solatium for the bereavement itself. It is not so easy to see how such compensation could be paid if there were no formal reason like marriage to justify it. At the least one might find it necessary to inquire into whether the cohabitation was successful or not if one was going to award a solatium to a bereaved cohabitant. But we will let that pass and go on to ask what would happen on intestacy. Here again, it is said, the law could work on the basis of cohabitation rather than the formal marriage status. How would this work? I suppose we could draw up a tariff under which, say, twenty years of cohabitation would entitle a surviving co-habitant to maximum rights of succession on intestacy, and benefits would be reduced proportionately for shorter periods of cohabitation. But that does not seem quite right. Suppose one cohabitant dies after a very short period of cohabitation, the other partner would then receive very little on intestate succession. Surely, it might be argued, the *intentions* of the parties ought to count for something. Casual cohabitation, not intended to involve a permanent or long-term commitment, ought surely to be distinguished from serious cohabitation, planned and entered upon as a lifetime commitment? Indeed, if marriage were abolished, it seems that we should have to recognize the rights of the cohabitants to express their intentions in some other way which could be taken account of by the law. But, say the proponents, such methods already exist. A cohabitant has only to make a will to give effect to intentions of such a character. The trouble with that, of course, is that it fails to take into account the simple fact that getting married enables one to avoid having to make a will if one does not wish to do so, or postpones doing so until it is too late, as so many people do, without producing totally unacceptable results on intestacy.

But then, it may be objected, what about the relationship of co-habitants to other parties, to the state, for example, or to employers' pension funds. Social security laws commonly want to know if someone entitled to benefits has a spouse, though it is true that a *de facto* dependant may sometimes have similar rights. Pension funds could, I suppose, be taken care of by appropriate declarations of intention. But then there are yet other problems, including that of trying to define what *is* cohabitation.[1] Suppose a man and a woman live in different houses but spend their weekends together? Suppose they do this for ten years? Suppose they live under one roof but do not have normal sex relations? How is the law to decide whether such parties ought to be treated as cohabitants for this or that purpose? One answer, of course, is to enable them to make some appropriate declaration whereby they should be treated as cohabitants for all legal purposes. But then we have, in effect, restored the status of marriage and it might be simpler not to abolish it in the first place.

The purpose of this discussion should now be clear. Marriage is surely an excellent illustration of a formal reason for making many decisions. So many different questions arise about how we are to treat two parties in some sort of relationship that it is exceedingly convenient and cost-effective to make the answers turn uniformly on one simple formal proposition. Are they married or are they not? Marriage thus becomes, within limits, a conclusive formal reason, for instance, in defining social security entitlements or intestate succession rights. We could, of course, abolish marriage as a legal institution, and answer all these questions by looking behind the formal tie for substantive reasons. Indeed, in some circumstances we do already do this; in particular, we tend to do it as regards property and maintenance rights on divorce. But to do the same thing for all the other circumstances in which we wish to have special rules for long-term cohabitants and also for *intending* long term cohabitants would be an immensely costly and troublesome business. Formal reasoning thus has great advantages.

[1] See S. M. Cretney, 'The Law Relating to Unmarried Partners From the Perspective of A Law Reform Agency', in Eekelaar and Katz (ed)., op. cit., ch. 36.

3. Formal Reasoning: the Case of Contract

It is time to turn to the case of contract, and its relationship to the distinction between formal and substantive reasoning. We can start by considering the place of formal reasons in the relatively straightforward case where a contract is required to be, or to be evidenced, in writing. Consider, for instance, those contracts declared to be unenforceable by the Statute of Frauds if they are not evidenced in writing. What is the function of writing in such a case? We must note, first, that in this situation, the absence of writing is a formal and conclusive reason for deciding *against* (rather than in favour of) the creation of a legal obligation. As with other cases of formal reasons, we do not in principle weigh up the reasons in favour of recognizing the obligation,[1] and balance them against the lack of writing. If there is no writing, the case for recognizing a legal duty is simply excluded from consideration. It does not arise at all. But there is no distinction in principle between a formal reason for excluding a liability, and one for recognizing a liability. So we would expect the reasons for the recognition of such a formal rule here to be similar to those we have already identified, such as the saving of cost, and the minimization of the risk of error. In the particular case of the Statute of Frauds there may be grounds for doubting whether these reasons are today adequate except in the case of the requirements relating to the transfer of interests in land. These reasons—the saving of cost and the minimization of error—may well have been more powerful when the Statute of Frauds was first passed in 1677 than they are now. But even in 1825 Bentham protested at the effect of the statute. If, he said, there are grounds for suspecting that the alleged contract is fraudulent, or untrue, or fabricated, then the statute is unnecessary. A fabricated contract obviously ought to be found to be fabricated and will give rise to no legal rights. If, on the other hand, there are no such grounds for suspicion, went on Bentham, it is simply unjust to treat the contract as unenforceable.[2]

This became the standard argument against the Statute of Frauds and the argument largely carried the day in England in 1954. But the argument is mistaken. It fails to take account of one of the principal purposes of formal reasons in the law. It is easy enough to deal with cases where the facts are known, or indisputably point to the contract

---

[1] Though it is true that part performance or reliance is increasingly recognized as a substantive reason for liability, and to that extent reliance is or may be allowed to *outweigh* the absence of writing.

[2] Bentham, *Treatise on Judicial Evidence* (1825), p. 121; 'The Rationale of Judicial Evidence' in *Works* (Bowring edn., vol. vi, 1843), ch. XXV.

either having been made, or not having been made. But one of the main points of formal reasons is that they are designed to save the time and trouble, and to minimize the risk of errors involved in, discovering the truth. So to require certain contracts to be in writing saves us from having to investigate whether an alleged oral contract was ever truly made or not; and because it saves us that trouble, it eliminates the risk that we may find a contract existed when none was in fact made. Of course it only does this at the price of excluding the possibility of an oral contract when there was indeed such a contract. Consequently we have to make up our minds which of these two errors seems more likely. The fact that in England we repealed most of the relevant provisions of the Statute of Frauds in 1954 for the wrong reasons, does not mean that the result was not correct from a policy point of view.[1]

Let me now consider another aspect of formal reasoning in contract law. Ever since the decision in *L'Estrange* v. *Graucob*,[2] it has been accepted that, within certain limits, a signature on a contractual document is a conclusive reason for holding the party who has signed to the terms of the document. Subject to proof of fraud, misrepresentation, or *non est factum*, the signature is conclusive. Some ten years ago, Mr J. R. Spencer, in an interesting article in the *Cambridge Law Journal*,[3] challenged this result as in conflict with the fundamental theory of contract law. Contracts, he said, are supposed to be based on agreement; but the rule in *L'Estrange* v. *Graucob* may bind a person who has not agreed to (because he has not read or not understood) the document which he has signed. Mr Spencer certainly put his finger on an important and interesting question. *Why* do we treat signatures as conclusive? Surely it is because a signature is a formal reason of the kind I have been discussing. A signature is, and is widely recognized even by the general public as, a formal device, and its value would be greatly reduced if it could not be treated as a conclusive ground of contractual liability at least in all ordinary circumstances. As in the other cases, we do not pause to examine the underlying reasons of substance, nor do we weigh the substantive reasons against the fact that the document has been signed. The signature is, at any rate within

---

[1] However, this assumes that it is desired to create liability for purely executory contracts—which is what the statute was designed to prevent as regards contracts within its scope. I have argued elsewhere that in 1954 the tide was running against such liabilities, so that repeal at that date was almost anachronistic: see my *Freedom of Contract*, p. 691.

[2] [1934] 2 KB 394.

[3] 'Signature, Consent and the Rule in *L'Estrange* v. *Graucob*', [1973] 32 *Cambridge L. Journal* 104.

limits, a conclusive reason, a formal reason, for treating the party who has signed as bound by the document. However, what is, I think, less clear, is what is the underlying reason of substance in this kind of situation. The usual explanation for holding a signature to be conclusively binding is that it must be taken to show that the party signing has agreed to the contents of the document; but another possible explanation is that the other party can be treated as having relied upon the signature. It thus may be a mistake to ask, as H. L. A. Hart once asked, whether the signature is merely conclusive evidence of agreement, or whether it is itself a criterion of agreement.[1] But this is something we can leave aside as it does not affect the distinction between formal and substantive reasons.

There was another problem which worried Mr Spencer. The objective rules of interpretation may lead the courts to construe a contract in a way which does not comply with the actual understandings or intentions of either party. This offends Mr Spencer. 'It may be acceptable', he says, 'for the law occasionally to force upon *one* of the parties an agreement he did not want; but surely there is something wrong with a theory which forces upon *both* of the parties an agreement which *neither* of them wants.'[2] I cannot myself see anything very wrong with this result so long as we remember that the law is not so much forcing the parties into a relationship—although it may sometimes do even that—but determining their obligations in a relationship which they have chosen to enter. Indeed, if the parties are in dispute as to what their obligations are, it seems to me a priori much more likely that the reasonable and just view is somewhere between the two parties' contentions, than that one or other party is wholly in the right. Thus it is perfectly natural, indeed commonplace, for the court to hold that the contract imposes obligations on the parties which are not exactly what either of them intended.

The point was made with his usual clarity and vigour by Holmes.

Nothing [he says] is more certain than that the parties may be bound by a

---

[1] See H. L. A. Hart, 'The Ascription of Responsibility and Rights', (1948-9) *Proc. Arist. Soc.* NS 171.

[2] See 32 *Cambridge L. Journal* at p. 113. Spencer, indeed, contends that this particular version of the 'objective' rule of interpretation is not followed by the English courts except for Lord Denning. Certainly the theory of the law may be doubtful (and clearly if one party knew what the other meant, the latter's intentions may govern—see Essay 9) but it seems to me that in construing written contracts English courts habitually follow this version of the objective method of construction. See also, Howarth,'The Meaning of Objectivity in Contract', 100 *Law Q. Rev.* 65 (1984).

contract to things which neither of them intended, and when one does not know of the other's assent. Suppose a contract is executed in due form and in writing to deliver a lecture, mentioning no time. One of the parties thinks that the promise will be construed to mean, at once, within a week. The other thinks that it means, when he is ready. The court says that it means, within a reasonable time. The parties are bound by the contract as it is interpreted by the court, yet neither of them meant what the court declares that they have said.[1]

The point next to be made was also once touched on by Holmes, though on this occasion with less than his accustomed clarity.

I think [he wrote in a letter in 1896] that in enlightened theory, which we now are ready for, all contracts are formal . . . I do not merely mean that the consideration of the simple contract is as much a form as a seal, but that in the nature of a sound system of law (which deals mainly with externals) the making of a contract must be a question of form, even if the details of our law should be changed.[2]

I confess that I am not entirely sure what Holmes meant by saying that 'the making of a contract must be a question of form', but there is one way in which these remarks can be understood. Just as, in the case of marriage, I distinguished between the formalities used to create the marriage tie, and the marriage status itself which also constitutes a formal reason for making various decisions, so also we can distinguish between the formalities (if any) used for the creation of a contract and the contract itself as a formal source of obligation. It is formal in the sense that the mere making of a promise, or even an agreement, the mere act of reaching agreement, the mere act of expressing intention, seems by itself hardly to reach the level of a substantive reason for doing anything. I have argued elsewhere[3] that contractual obligation rarely rests on the bare intention of the parties. In the great majority of cases, I have suggested, a party who is held liable on a contract has received a benefit from the other party, or has induced the other to rely upon him to his detriment. But the receipt of benefits from another is not only a source of contractual liability; it can also give rise to liability even in the absence of an agreement or promise. The law of restitution, or unjust enrichment, deals with these unpromised benefits. Contract law, supposedly, deals with promised benefits; but I have suggested

---

[1] 'The Path of the Law', 10 *Harv. Law Rev.* 457, at 463-4.
[2] Letter to E. A. Harriman of Northwestern University Law School, cited in M. DeW. Howe, *Justice Oliver Wendell Holmes* (1963), vol. ii, 233. See also p. 67 above.
[3] See Essay 2 in this collection.

that it is not obvious why we need to draw a line between contract and unjust enrichment in the way that traditional theory teaches.

So too liability through induced reliance is not confined to the area of contract. In tort, and with the aid of estoppel in all its varied forms, reasonable reliance is itself often a justifiable ground for complaint in law, even where a promise has not been given.[1] So in most cases contractual liability arises out of something—in part at least—which lies behind the actual agreement or intention of the parties. Just as in the case of marriage it is sometimes necessary to see how the parties have behaved, how long the relationship has lasted, and so on, rather than confine attention to the formal status itself, so also in the case of contract it is sometimes relevant to see why the promise was made, or what has actually happened following the making of the agreement. Indeed, it could be said that these are the real reasons of substance for the enforcement of most contractual obligations. It is a good reason for making A pay £100 to B that A has received goods from B worth approximately £100 under a contract of sale. The fact that A promised or agreed to pay that precise sum, £100, is perhaps a purely formal reason for arriving at the same conclusion. It shuts out of consideration the substantive reasons. We do not pause to ask, anyhow within certain limits, whether the goods were indeed worth £100. Similarly, where a person is induced to rely on another's promise, we do not ask whether his reliance was reasonable or justifiable. That question is largely ruled out as irrelevant by the express promise. It is conclusively determined by the promise—it is reasonable to rely upon a promise.

Because these formal or exclusionary reasons only operate within certain limits, and because today these limits seem to be narrowing so that courts often seem to be more willing then they were formerly to open up for examination the value of benefits received, or the justifiability of reliance on a promise, I have argued on a previous occasion that a promise or agreement operates rather like a presumption which is sometimes irrebuttable, but sometimes rebuttable.[2] That a person agrees to pay £100 for this item is, I suggested, good evidence that it is indeed worth £100; and the fact that a person made a promise to another is at least prima-facie evidence of the justifiability of the promisee's actions in reliance on the promise. It has been objected by Professor Eisenberg that my account is faulty because in fact such

---

[1] See *The Hannah Blumenthal* [1983] 1 All ER 34, 49; see also Barry Reiter, in Reiter and Swan, ed., *Studies in Contract Law* (Butterworth, Canada), Study No. 8.

[2] See *Promises, Morals and Law*, ch. 7.

evidence is not treated as rebuttable. Apart from established defences, no evidence is admissible to show that the price agreed was too high or too low. The agreed price is treated as conclusive. And similarly, as Professor Birks has argued, it may be said that because the law requires payment of the price, neither more nor less, the remedy which the law gives must be in a sense 'contractual' and cannot be restitutionary.[1] Of course, as a matter of black-letter law this is correct, though it is not clear why we should brush aside established defences like fraud and misrepresentation as irrelevant to the issue. They do, in a sense, define precisely the limits within which the agreed price is to be regarded as conclusive. But apart from that, the objection to my way of putting the matter simply fails to understand the way in which formal or conclusory reasons work in the law. The fact that a presumption is irrebuttable is often treated as demonstrating that the so-called presumption is really a rule of law, and not a presumption at all. But this is a mistake. The effect of an irrebuttable preumption is of course the same as the effect of a rule of law. But the reason for it may be entirely different. If it is the case, as I have argued, that contractual obligations ultimately derive, at least in the normal case, from benefits received, or acts of detrimental reliance, then it is still possible to explain why we generally treat promises and agreements as formal and conclusive reasons for the establishment and delimitation of those obligations. As is the case with other formal reasons, the obvious reasons for treating them as conclusive are that this saves the cost of more detailed investigation and that it minimizes the risk of error.

It will be helpful at this stage to give a couple of simple illustrations to show how very powerful these reasons can be, so that to call them formal reasons should not be regarded as in any way denigrating their significance. Let me take first of all an illustration of the importance of treating promises and agreements as conclusive on the matter of reasonable reliance. Time was, when, in building contracts, the builder was expected to consult the contract documents, study the site, and then decide how much he would tender for the contract. Contract documents customarily provided quite expressly that the builder had no right to rely upon any information given to him by the client but was to make his own examinations and studies, and rely upon these rather than upon the other party to the contract. For a very long time this has been regarded as conclusive of the respective rights and duties

[1] See Eisenberg, 'The Bargain Principle and its Limits', 95 *Harv. Law Rev.* 741, 785 n. 121 (1982), and for Professor Birks's point, see Essay 2, above.

of the parties.[1] However, following the *Hedley Byrne*[2] decision, and suggestions that a tort duty of reasonable care might arise even between contracting parties, it came to be asked whether a builder might not be able to sue the client for negligence if the client had failed to disclose this or that piece of information to the builder. Such an allegation implies, of course, that the builder did reasonably rely on the owner, rather than on his own inquiries, even though the contract told him quite clearly that he was not to do so. One might have thought, therefore, that the contract ought to be treated as a conclusive reason for refusing to inquire into the possibility of reasonable reliance by the builder in such circumstances. The contract, it might be said, simply defines in advance what sort of reliance ought to be regarded as reasonable, and there is no room for any factual inquiry in the particular case. Yet in 1972 the High Court of Australia held that this was not the case, and that a duty of care might arise between the parties in such a relationship;[3] but of course the existence of such a duty could only be shown by a careful and detailed examination of all the facts. Following that case, another Australian case, *Dillingham Construction Pty Ltd* v. *Downs*,[4] actually proceeded to try out such an issue in a negligence claim. The result was a lengthy trial in which all the facts had to be minutely investigated; what knowledge did the client have about the special conditions of the site, whether that knowledge could reasonably have been collected and sifted and made available to the builder, what knowledge the builder had, who reasonably relied on who, and so on. In the result no liability was established, but the fact that the builder's reliance on the client was not reasonable or justifiable (if indeed there was any reliance at all) was only established at enormous cost. If the traditional view of the effect of a contract on this relationship had been upheld, all these costs could have been saved by treating the contract as a conclusive reason for shutting out these facts as irrelevant. I am not saying that the procedure adopted in this case was unjustified, or even undesirable. I am merely pointing out how costly it was. Broadly speaking treating matters as settled conclusively by agreement is cheap and simple; determining them by the standards of reasonableness is neither cheap nor simple. Still, sometimes this is necessary and the price must be paid. Justice is often an expensive commodity.

[1] See *Thorn* v. *London Corpn.* (1876) 1 App. Cas. 120.
[2] [1964] AC 465.
[3] *Morrison-Knudson International* v. *Commonwealth* (1972) 46 ALJR 265.
[4] [1972] NSWR 49.

Let me now observe that exactly the same thing can happen with regard to benefits. The whole law of restitution or unjust enrichment stands testimony to the difficulty of establishing, in many circumstances, whether one person has benefited from an act of another. I shall offer just one particularly striking illustration of the extra costs which come from disregarding contractual provisions. It comes from a group of late nineteenth and early twentieth century English cases on the *ultra vires* doctrine. After it was finally established that a company could not validly enter into a contract outside the scope of the powers conferred by the memorandum of association, a number of cases came before the courts in which companies had borrowed money under *ultra vires* transactions. The courts were naturally reluctant to see such companies retain the benefit of moneys thus borrowed without having any obligation to repay or restore it, so they resorted to various shifts and devices to overcome this result. If, they held, a company borrowed money under an *ultra vires* contract, but the money was used to pay off debts owed by the company to a third party, then the lender might be able to claim repayment of the money to the extent that this had actually benefited the borrowing company.[1] In so far as the money had actually been used to discharge valid debts of the borrowing company, it was an easy conclusion that a benefit had thereby been conferred. Unfortunately, there were some circumstances in which this conclusion was not so simple as it seemed. How could anyone be sure that the company had really benefited by the money received under the *ultra vires* loan? Suppose, for instance, that the money had been paid into one bank account with the company's own money, and some paid out to third party creditors, while some was used for other purposes? Who could say whether the company had actually been benefited, or was, in the actual result, better off because of the receipt of the *ultra vires* loan?[2] More generally, it will be seen how arguments that a person has been benefited by something that happened in the past involve an inquiry into what would have happened, if he had not received that particular benefit; such inquiries involve hypothetical explorations into what would have happened if the course of events had been different from what it actually was. Like the analogous inquiries which sometimes have to be made in personal injury actions in tort when collateral benefits have to be probed, these hypothetical inquiries are very trouble-

---

[1] See *Re Cork & Youghal Rly. Co.* (1869) LR 4 Ch. App. 748; *Re National Permanent Benefit Building Society* (1869) LR 5 Ch. App. 309.
[2] See e.g. *Bannatyne* v. *D. C. MacIver* [1906] 1 KB 103.

some indeed. Consider how much simpler these cases would have been if the contracts in question had not been *ultra vires*. Then the companies borrowing the money would have been liable to repay the loans without any questions arising as to whether they had benefited from the loans or not. The gain in simplification and the saving of cost would be immense. Once again, it should be made clear that we cannot always avoid these inquiries as to whether a person has been benefited by the actions of another. All I am concerned to point out is that allowing people to decide whether something done for them is indeed a benefit which they should be required to pay for leads to a great simplification and improvement in cost effectiveness in the law. Here again, therefore, the arguments in favour of treating the formal reason as conclusive, and not allowing any inquiry into the underlying reasons of substance, are very strong; even though, on some occasion, justice may require that we disregard them.

4. The Decline of Formal Reasoning

It would not be difficult to multiply examples of the great advantages which derive from the fact that contract law normally treats many of the matters lying behind the contract as irrelevant to the obligations of the parties. At the same time, everyone must be aware of the fact that the power of formal reasons in contract law and, indeed, perhaps in all of the law, has been declining in recent years. More and more often the courts seem willing to unpick the transaction, to open it up, as it were, and go behind the formal reasons, and look at the substantive reasons for the creation or negativing of obligations. In some instances, these developments in the law might seem to amount to a mere narrowing of the limits within which formal reasons are treated as conclusive. But in other cases it is hard to avoid the conclusion that the formal reasons themselves have been jettisoned, and the issues treated as though they were completely at large. The virtual disappearance in modern English law of the parol evidence rule seems one clear example of the emas-culation of a formal reason in contract cases. When it is argued that a written contract is not conclusive of the obligations of the parties, the courts seem simply to balance the arguments for and against imposing an orally derived obligation on a party, rather than treat the writing as conclusive, even within the narrowest limits. Similarly, the statutory discretions now conferred on the courts by the Unfair Contract Terms Act 1977 and other similar enactments, involve the elimination of the conclusionary or formal effect of various contractual clauses. Such a clause does not become irrelevant, but whether it is to be treated as effective depends on a balancing of the substantive arguments for and against the clause.

This movement away from the use of formal reasons in the law seems to me to be evident in many areas besides contract law. I have already referred to the case of *R. v. Lee*,[1] in which the Court of Appeal admitted an appeal from a plea of guilty, as another remarkable example of the abandonment of a formal type of reason in criminal procedure. So too the modern English Limitation Act,[2] which gives the court a complete discretion to override the time limits in a personal injury action, is another illustration of the abandonment of a formal reason for disposing of a case. Today, time limits and other reasons of substance have to be weighed together in deciding whether to allow such an action to proceed after the normal time limit has expired. In other countries, and especially the United States, it seems to me that formal reasons have been waning in scope and conclusiveness for many years; for example, the doctrine of collateral attack in American federal criminal procedure is an extraordinary illustration of the destruction of the formal weight attached to the finality of judgments of state courts.

Why has this been happening? In order to answer this question we must, I think, go back a little, and renew our inquiry into the purposes and reasons underlying the use of formal reasons. In this essay I have attempted to identify a number of different purposes or reasons. I have laid stress on cost, and on the minimization of the risks of error as the two most important reasons of a general character. But these are by no means the only reasons. Thus I have suggested that in some cases a variety of other factors underly the use of formal reasons. In contract law, especially, there is the value judgment that the parties to a contract are the most appropriate persons to decide what the benefits are worth, and that the courts should not prevent parties making their own decisions on such matters. This differs from the argument that it would be very costly for the courts to investigate whether a person has benefited from a contract, and if so, by how much. Then other reasons apply to other cases. For instance, some formal reasons concern the appropriate person to make a decision—matters of jurisdiction arise here—*when* a decision should be made, and by what procedure a question should be raised. Then also there is the value of repose and finality and security in human affairs. The search for justice is important to all

---

[1] [1984] 1 All ER 1080.
[2] See the Limitation Act 1980, s. 33.

lawyers, as well as the public of course; but even that search must be brought to a halt in particular cases when we have eventually done the best we can. Many of these reasons, of course, will overlap in various circumstances.

Now the widespread use of formal reasons for decisions seems to me to presuppose that substantive reasons either will be, or have been, or at least could have been, more appropriately and satisfactorily dealt with another time, or in some other manner or by some other person. When we bar an action under the limitation period, for example, we do so in the belief that the action could and should have been brought within the proper period, and then adjudicated upon on its merits. If that assumption is unfounded, for example, because the statutes of limitation may bar an action before the plaintiff could possibly have been aware that he even had a cause of action,[1] then something is very wrong indeed. Or again, when an action is dismissed for want of jurisdiction, the normal presumption is that someone else will have jurisdiction. Even if no other court or tribunal can hear the case, so that the applicant remains remediless, automatic dismissal for want of jurisdiction presupposes that the matter could at least receive the attention of the legislature. But here too, if the question at issue could not be considered by any other court, and if there were reasons for supposing that the legislature would never deal with the matter, the formal jurisdictional reason for a decision would come to look thin and eventually perhaps, quite unacceptable. No doubt this is one of the main reasons that led the American Supreme Court eventually to intervene in the apportionment cases when it was evident that the legislatures would not right the matter themselves.

Or again, literal, that is formal, interpretation of a statute, ignoring the result and perhaps even the intentions of Parliament, is more likely to be justifiable if it can be assumed, first, that statutes are drafted and enacted with care, so that the presumption that the literal meaning correctly represents the intentions of Parliament is a strong one; and secondly, if it can be assumed that Parliament is likely to act reasonably promptly to remedy any deficiencies in the law caused by such a decision. If the drafting of statutes was constantly done with appalling ineptitude and obscurity, and if Parliament refused ever to do anything about it, it is certain that the courts would no longer try to interpret statutes in such a formal and literal manner. It is, after all, only since the

---

[1] See *Cartledge* v. *Jopling & Son Ltd.* [1963] AC 758 which led to immediate legislative reversal, see now Limitation Act 1980.

present manner of drafting and enacting legislation became standard practice in England, that the present methods of interpretation were adopted. Similarly again, the principle of finality of judgments, still adhered to pretty rigidly in England, is only justifiable if we can generally assume that most judgments are carefully considered, and rendered with competence and integrity, and that opportunities for appeal are available. If these conditions did not obtain—if, for instance, appellate courts could not trust lower courts to observe the law with reasonable competence and integrity—and if, for some reason, there were obstacles in the way of bringing appeals against such decisions, it is hard to believe that the finality of judgments we so much prize today would not become undermined.

To make a decision by reference to a formal reason, after all, is to refuse to consider the reasons of substance bearing on the issue. But if these issues of substance are never to be considered at all, still more, if there never has been an opportunity to consider them, then to make the decision by purely formal reasoning is to shut out the possibility of that decision ever being based on the factors most directly relevant to it. Rational institutions, and a rational legal system, demand that we do not do this if we can avoid it. Now it seems to me that one of the reasons why formal reasons are today less favoured in contract law may stem from increasing doubts as to whether the reasons of substance which bear most directly on the result have ever been properly weighed by anyone. If parties have not in fact anticipated the events which have occurred, it is unsatisfactory to claim that the literal words of the contract can be stretched to cover these events, because that is to use a formal reason where the reasons of substance have not been and will not be considered by the parties or by anybody else. Perhaps, too, increasing doubts about how far consumers read or understand printed contracts is one of the principal reasons underlying the introduction of statutory discretions to deal with unfair exclusion clauses. Here again, to give effect to the clause is to dispose of the case with a formal reason when the reasons of substance have perhaps never been considered at all, and of course cannot now be considered because it is too late.

No doubt, in the area of contract and perhaps also elsewhere, there are factors of this kind which help explain why so many formal reasons of the sort I have been discussing have recently been abandoned or whittled down in the law. Without necessarily condemning all manifestations of these trends, this process seems to me one against which we should be on our guard. Formalism, of course, has a bad name;

and to make a decision for formal reasons requires a degree of self-discipline; it requires that we should admit that some other person, some other time, some other place, some other procedure, may be the right one for this decision. But that is often true of decisions in a legal system in which, by and large, everyone can be trusted to play his proper part. When it is true, we should not be afraid to recognize that to decide a case for formal reasons is to decide it for good reasons.

6

The Liberal Theory of Contract

The liberal theory of contract is close to, if not indeed wholly identical with what I have termed the classical theory of contract, but classical theory was a historical fact whereas liberal theory is largely normative, and there can, therefore, be more than one version of liberal theory. In describing classical contract theory in Essay 2 (and elsewhere), I have largely concentrated on the role of contract law as part of the law of obligations, and on the relationship between contract law and *laissez-faire* ideology. But there is one version of the liberal theory of contract, closely associated with certain philosophical theories, which has only been lightly touched on in Essay 2 and elsewhere in my previous writings, and it deserves a fuller treatment which this essay accordingly attempts to supply.

Strangely enough, it is only in recent times, with the publication in 1981 of Professor Charles Fried's *Contract as Promise, A Theory of Contractual Obligation*, that an attempt has been made to state and defend a version of the liberal theory of contract. But Fried's purpose in this book is not purely, or even primarily, normative; he is not just telling us what sort of theory he thinks contract law ought to be based on; he also seeks to demonstrate that the common law of contract is largely justified by a liberal theory. He seeks to defend the main structure and doctrines of traditional contract law (with qualifications noted below) by reference to the 'promise principle'. He thus aims to demonstrate that the law of contract can be seen as an instrument for the implementation of a basic moral principle that is itself a key feature of liberal theories of justice—the principle that autonomous individuals can choose to impose obligations on themselves by an exercise of free will which the state and its courts are bound to respect. In this essay I shall consider the version of the liberal theory of contract which Professor Fried defends, though I shall also note some of the respects in which it departs from the classical theory described by myself in Essay 2 and elsewhere.

A liberal theory of contract like Fried's starts with the basic principle

of a liberal society—as he puts it, 'that we be secure in what is ours'.
The liberal ideal requires respect for the person, property, and choices
of others, but our purposes frequently make co-operation necessary. A
crucial moral discovery came when free men learned that they could
secure such co-operation, without losing their freedom, through trust
and promises. A promise, unlike a lie or a mere statement of intention,
imports the idea of a commitment, and an initial problem is to explain
how a person can, by promising, become morally obligated to do
something that is not morally required absent the promise. One answer
to this (and it is Fried's answer, as well as that of many others before
him) is to invoke the concept of convention: the moral obligation arises
because a promisor intentionally invokes a convention whose function
is to give moral grounds for another to expect the promised performance. From this point on, then, liberal theory accepts that there is
a moral obligation to perform a promise, and seeks to explain and
justify the law of contract on the basis of promissory obligation. In this
essay I shall not further probe into the moral theory of promising itself.
For present purposes I shall assume, with the liberal theorist, that there
is a moral obligation to perform a promise; and I shall attempt to see
how far the modern law of contract can be justified on the basis of that
obligation.

It is worth beginning by sketching a brief version of the fundamentals of contract law as perceived by the liberal. The liberal
theorist argues that, by and large, contract law provides for the
enforcement of promises, or the payment of damages in lieu. So the
first two questions must concern the doctrine of consideration (which
seems to limit the promises which will be enforced) and the law of
damages which—critics of liberal theory may urge—is not primarily
designed to provide for the recovery of the value of the promised
performance, but for reliance damages. Questions next arise about
doctrines of fraud, duress, and unconscionability. These doctrines,
in various guises, may excuse performance of a promise: can that be
justified on a liberal theory? Similarly, there are problems with the
doctrines of mistake, impossibility, and frustration: are these based,
in some sense, on the fleshing out of what the parties had truly
intended or willed? Or do they reflect policy choices involving the
imposition of judicial, or collective, values on the parties in the
events which have happened? The same dilemma arises with regard
to the function of interpretation of contracts, and the implication of
terms: can these be performed by a judiciary resolved to steer a

wholly neutral course, or do they require policy choices, derived from collective values? Other similar questions could arise with regard to public policy and illegality: here too it must be questioned whether the refusal to enforce certain kinds of promises can be justified by reference to some moral-liberal theory. The question thus resolves itself ultimately into whether it is possible to construct a morally neutral system of contract law, and whether the law of contract does in fact reflect a system of that kind, once the basic principles of liberal theory are accepted. Does everything flow logically and inexorably, once liberal theory is accepted, or are there, on the contrary, constant and massive infusions of collective values into the law of contract?

Paradoxically, the right place to start must be the end: we must begin with the central and crucial problem of damages. The liberal finds the entitlement of the promisee to the full value of the promised performance—the right to expectation damages—to be a natural corollary of basing the law on the promise principle. But this conclusion has in recent years been subjected to much criticism. Because the critics of classical theory have found so many circumstances in which the law awards damages on a reliance or a restitutionary principle, they have been able to argue that the basis of contractual liability may not be the promise itself.[1] Indeed, in the classic article by Fuller and Perdue[2] it is urged that the main function of damages in contract law seems in fact to be the protection of reliance; expectation damages—though apparently required as a general principle of the law—are in truth (they suggest) awarded largely as a surrogate for reliance damages, because reliance itself is often difficult to prove, and because the quantification of reliance damages (which in many cases would approximate the expectation loss) would also be costly and difficult.

Thus, it is now widely accepted that, outside the standard commercial contract, reliance damages are often more appropriate and more likely to be awarded than expectation damages. Indeed, in many of these situations—for instance consumer contracts or family transactions—it will often be found that there is unlikely to be any liability at all (any recognition of a binding contract) before there has been some element of reliance. And even in the ordinary commercial contract, the doctrine

---

[1] It should be said that there are many more of these cases recognized in America than in England, although that may only reflect the greater volume of litigation, and the fact that English law may achieve the same result through different legal techniques.

[2] 'The Reliance Interest in Contract Damages', 46 *Yale LJ* 52, 373 (1936).

of mitigation, as well as commercial practices, make it doubtful whether the 'general rule' of the law in fact governs the generality of instances. Furthermore, if the law was really based on the theory of the moral obligation to perform a promise, then surely specific performance would be the more obvious and primary remedy of the law. Similarly, in a contract of sale of goods, surely, if enforcement of promises was the goal of the law, one would expect to find the seller entitled to sue the buyer for the price whenever the buyer repudiates even an executory contract of sale. Yet in practice, the seller's right to sue for the price is extremely limited in the case of executory contracts, and he is normally confined to damages for non-acceptance. Given the law's reluctance to live up to its apparent theory, then, there must be doubts whether it is indeed the *promise* that creates the duty to perform.

Of all weaknesses in the liberal position with regard to the expectation damages principle, the greatest perhaps concerns that arising from the doctrine of mitigation. For the law does not 'enforce' a promise at all, but instead gives a remedy in damages for its non-performance, and the doctrine of mitigation means that large numbers of contracts are regularly breached for which promisees are unable to obtain any damages at all. A simple example would be the case of a seller who fails to deliver goods where equivalent goods are available in the market at or below the contract price.

The effect of the mitigation rule, therefore, is that the damages which the breaching party pays will not be what he has promised to pay. Even in the simplest situation where the damages are readily calculable as a result of a clear change in market prices, it thus becomes difficult to explain the ultimate outcome of an action for damages as the recognition of a promissory liability; in complex cases, it becomes still more difficult to attribute the ultimate outcome to the intentions of the promisor. An adequate explanation of the mitigation rule is thus an essential part of the argument of the liberal theorist when it is suggested that the expectation damages rule follows as a natural corollary from the promise principle. But in fact explanations of the mitigation principle tend to be pragmatic or efficiency-based. A moral justification for the mitigation principle (such as that made for instance by Fried) must explain the duty to mitigate as a 'kind of altruistic duty . . . the more altruistic that it is directed to a partner in the wrong'.[1] Considering the otherwise limited role of altruism in the liberal theory of contract, it does seem remarkable that one of its chief functions is to shield the

[1] See *Contract as Promise*, p. 131.

promise-breaker from the full consequences of his wrong. But the explanation for this result, it may be argued, is that the duty is one without cost, since at least in theory the victim of the breach is never worse off for having mitigated than he would be in the absence of the duty.

Many will find this argument less than compelling. In practice, the duty to mitigate often places the innocent party in a dilemma. If he fails to mitigate, his damages will be cut, and if he does mitigate, he may find that his only recoverable damages are trivial reliance costs not worth pursuing. The obvious explanation of these rules is that the expectations of the promisee, in so far as they rest on the promise alone, are often not as worthy of protection as liberal theory and the promise principle have claimed. The mitigation rule has the practical result of *pro tanto* (and often entirely) eliminating the binding nature of the promise. Without going as far as Holmes, who denied that a promise created any legal duty of performance at all, the position of the liberal critic does maintain that the duty to perform an unpaid-for and unrelied-upon promise is often weak, and that one purpose of the mitigation rule is to recognize this fact.

The liberal theorist may next argue that he is willing and able to justify exceptions to the expectation damages rule. Exceptions are, of course, recognized by the law when the expectation loss cannot adequately be computed or when reliance losses exceed the expectation value of the promise. Moreover, even unbargained-for reliance is protected by law in some circumstances, most vividly illustrated by the famous American case of *Hoffman* v. *Red Owl Stores, Inc.*,[1] where a plaintiff was held entitled to recover some (relatively small) reliance losses when a protracted bargaining process was abruptly terminated by the defendants, after they had persuaded the plaintiff time and again to act on the assurance that a deal was forthcoming. Although English law has perhaps not quite reached the point at which a remedy could safely be expected in such circumstances (given especially the finding that the defendants did not act in bad faith), it is certainly not far from this position.[2] The law of promissory estoppel and the law of negligence are developing fast in the direction of protecting a plaintiff who has relied in the way that Mr Hoffman relied.

How can this protection be justified on the promise principle? Classical theorists—mostly in America—wrestled with cases of this kind,

[1] 133 NW 2d 267 (1965).
[2] See especially *Box* v. *Midland Bank* [1979] 2 Lloyd's Rep. 391.

trying to force them into the 'implied promise' category. But this classification failed when it was found that only reliance damages could be recovered in these cases; and it is hard to see how imposing obligations in such cases can be justified by liberal theory if it is confined to enforcing promises. One possible liberal answer—which is that of Professor Fried—is that of course it cannot be so justified and that classical contract lawyers who made the attempt were placing too much weight on the promise principle. This does not mean, however, that unbargained-for reliance cannot be protected on some other moral basis, consistent with liberal theory. Principles of tort law can be invoked to support the result in *Hoffman*. Analogous arguments apply to cases in which the law protects restitution interests. I shall return later to this attempt to bolster up liberal theory by invoking other principles to supplement the promise principle itself.

Even the liberal theorist who rests on the moral obligatoriness of a promise may have twinges of anxiety over cases where the promisor has genuinely changed his mind and regrets the promise because he regrets the value judgment that led him to make it. Might there not be a case here for confining the damages to the promisee's reliance losses? Could not the promisor make a reasoned case for asking to be excused from further performance, on tendering the promisee's reliance losses? It is not so self-evident in this situation that the promisee is trying to welsh on a value-maximizing exchange,[1] though there would, of course, be real problems in determining the sincerity of a promisor who tried to make this sort of defence. But even if we could get over the difficulties of proof, the liberal theorist may object that change of mind should not be a permissible defence to a claim for expectation damages because it would show disrespect for contracting parties by not taking their initial choices seriously. This, at least, is Professor Fried's preferred explanation for rejecting change of mind as a permissible argument, even as to the kind of damages which should be recoverable. But is it persuasive? There seems no compelling reason why respect for another's autonomy requires us to accord conclusive weight to a prior choice rather than a present choice. Consider the analogous case of marriage, or even promises to marry. In this field, respect for autonomy seems to mean respect for present and not past choices. Modern divorce laws—usually characterized as 'liberal'—and abolition in many jurisdictions of the

[1] See Essay 7.

action for breach of promise of marriage, appear to be based on this belief in the autonomy of the individual.

I turn next to the doctrine of consideration. The liberal theorist must have grave difficulties with consideration, because he does not, like myself and other critics of classical law, see a valuable role for the doctrine of consideration in emphasizing the links between promissory liability and reliance and restitutionary liability, and in reminding us always of the substantive grounds of liability behind the formal one of the promise or agreement or signature. For the liberal the doctrine of consideration is incoherent because it requires the law to affirm the desirability of enforcing promises and yet at the same time to deny parties the freedom to make enforceable one-sided promises. In enforcing bargained exchanges, the law permits the parties total freedom to decide on the adequacy of what each receives from the other. Once it is conceded that adequacy is entirely for the promisor, it is illogical, the liberal may say, to balk at the final step of allowing the promisor to commit himself to an obligation for what others might regard as inadequate or no consideration.

The most widely held 'theory' to explain the doctrine of consideration is the bargain theory, but this theory is manifestly inconsistent with a mass of case law.[1] In any event, the courts sometimes treat the existence of a bargain as a question of form only, and thus in practice do recognize the promise principle, as for instance when they enforce a promise given for nominal consideration; in other cases the courts require something more than a formal bargain, and therefore fail to give full effect to the promise principle. Hence, to the liberal theorist the doctrine of consideration in the present law is incoherent, as indeed Professor Fried at least concludes. Whatever its normative power, therefore, liberal theory must here concede that the present law involves paternalist values antithetical to the autonomy of the individual which a pure promising theory of contract could justify. Even Professor Raz's alternative version of liberal contract theory—which bases the law on the desirability of securing voluntary co-operation, rather than on the promise principle—must, it seems, run into trouble here. Although Raz's version of liberalism may well explain why the law is only concerned with exchanges (or anyhow relied-upon promises) and not with wholly one-sided promises, it surely cannot escape the charge

---

[1] For a demonstration of this point, see Essay 8, and my *Introduction to the Law of Contract*, 3rd edn. (Oxford, 1981), pp. 119-22.

of paternalism. Professor Raz may wish to argue that there are good reasons why the area of legal and moral obligation should not be coterminous, so that the law may, in this respect, be justifiably paternalist, while the promise principle continues to recognize totally gratuitous and one-sided promissory obligation, as a matter of moral principle. But this still fails to explain why the law should differ in this vital respect (and it surely is a moral respect) from morality itself. Why should the law of contract embody this fundamentally paternalist principle of consideration, if paternalism is, in principle, morally objectionable? I return again to the subject of paternalism later in this essay.

Is there any sign that the doctrine of consideration is likely to wither away, or be replaced by a more coherent body of law, more clearly based on liberal principles? I am bound to say that this seems to me in the highest degree unlikely. Although it is perhaps not impossible to envisage a statutory reform which made written promises enforceable even without consideration (though enforceable to what extent?) the whole trend of the law in the past fifty or even hundred years has been towards greater protection for those who make rash and ill-considered promises. Requirements of writing, 'cooling-off' periods for certain consumer constracts, expansion of protective legislation, expanding doctrines of duress and undue influence, expanding liability for negligence between negotiating parties, all seem to make it unlikely that we are going to move in the near future to a regime of absolutely binding promises, irrespective of consideration. Whatever its normative power as a matter of philosophical or political argument, therefore, liberal theory seems unlikely to carry the day in a democratic society.

Can liberal theory be more successful with the doctrines of fraud, good faith, duress, and unconscionability? Although these may not all be recognized as textbook 'doctrines' of English law, they are sufficiently recognizable in some shape or form to require attention when questions of theory are under consideration. Fraud and duress are certainly known to English law. Good faith is not openly recognized as a principle of English contract law, but it can hardly be disputed that the general idea of good faith permeates various principles, such as methods of interpretation of contracts, and the rule that a person cannot snap up an offer when he knows that the offeror made a mistake in expressing the offer.[1] Unconscionability is

---

[1] See *Hartog* v. *Colin & Shields* [1939] 3 All ER 566.

known in some cases, for instance cases concerning penalty clauses and some cases of undue influence. It is, furthermore, entrenched in some important statutory provisions such as those of the Consumer Credit Act 1974 dealing with consumer loans, and in the Unfair Contract Terms Act 1977. And although the liberal theorist may wish to avoid discussing statutory provisions, insisting that he wishes only to defend the common law, a theory of contract law which has no room for statutes involving such fundamental ideas as these would be gravely deficient.

What then about fraud and duress? Why should these excuse a promisor from performance? Fried contends that these doctrines can be reconciled with a liberal theory of contract. Lying to procure a contract seems an easy case: because lying is morally wrong, the liar should not be allowed to retain any ill-gotten gains and must answer for the losses he causes the promisee. There is no doubt that this seems to have been the doctrine of nineteenth-century classical law, exemplified most clearly in the famous case of *Derry* v. *Peek*.[1] This decision does seem to have been based on the idea that fraud was a moral wrong, and that conduct which was not morally wrongful should not be labelled as fraud. Modern law is, perhaps, less easily squared with these ideas. First, it is clear today that 'moral' wrongdoing, in the sense of an intent to cheat or harm, is not a requisite of an action for deceit.[2] Second, there is the problem that modern law increasingly allows a remedy for non-fraudulent misrepresentation. Negligent misrepresentation is often actionable at common law, or under the Misrepresentation Act 1967, and even innocent misrepresentation allows the remedy of rescission, for which damages may be obtained in lieu. Of course an attempt can be made, along the lines made by Fried, to argue that there is nothing contrary to liberal theory in invoking tort principles to supplement contract law, and thus to defend the expansion of remedies for misrepresentation; but I shall return to this later.

It seems a good deal more difficult for the liberal to explain modern developments such as are exemplified by *Esso Petroleum* v. *Mardon*.[3] This decision acknowledges, not merely a duty to refrain from the misrepresentation of facts—which the liberal may insist can be enforced in a neutral sort of way—but a duty (at least in appropriate cir-

---

[1] (1889) 14 App. Cas. 337.
[2] *Brown Jenkinson & Co. Ltd.* v. *Percy Dalton Ltd.* [1957] 2 QB 621.
[3] [1976] QB 801.

cumstances) on the part of one contracting party to take care in the provision of *advice*, and the making of *forecasts* to the other contracting party. It is hard to see how such a duty can be reconciled with liberal theory, because there is nothing 'neutral' about the imposition of such duties. They are, for a start, plainly distributive in intent,[1] since they require one contracting party to share with the other knowledge which 'belongs' to the first, as a condition of being permitted to deal with him. And secondly they plainly involve a use of values not based on individual autonomy because they require the court to decide when one party *ought* to make such disclosures to the other party.

Passively allowing the promisor to deceive himself is also a difficult case for the liberal, though this is a case in which English law has been reluctant to give relief. Still, there are certainly some cases in which relief will be available, through doctrines like mistake or negligence. Some of these cases can perhaps be defended by the liberal theorist on the ground that they are in effect mistake or 'gap' cases, and must be filled by invoking other (non-promissory) principles, a point dealt with again later in this essay. Other cases may perhaps be justified by reference to the conventions on which parties have relied.

Duress is perhaps one of the most difficult cases for the liberal. Classical theory tried to obscure the value judgments involved in using a law of duress by treating duress as a question of fact, dependent on proof that the promisor's will was 'overborne' by the promisee. On this view a coerced promise was not truly a voluntary act of the promisor's will, and so not really a promise at all. But modern law has come to recognize that this theory rested on an unacceptable psychological basis, and that a coerced promisor still intends to make his promise.[2] To release him from his promise, therefore, requires some additional justification: the coerced promisor does intend to promise, so why should his promise not be binding? Modern law increasingly answers this by saying that some forms of coercion or duress are 'legitimate' and some are 'illegitimate'.[3] Illegitimate coercion invalidates a consent or promise, even though it was intended by the promisor to be a serious promise. Of course, once the language of 'legitimacy' comes to be used

---

[1] Whether they are distributive in result is, of course, more problematic, since once such decisions become known, they may be allowed for in the prices at which such parties deal with each other.

[2] See my Note, 'Economic Duress and the "Overborne Will" ', 98 *Law Q. Rev.* 197 (1982).

[3] See now the dicta in *Universe Tankship of Monrovia* v. *ITWF* [1983] 1 AC 366, at 384 (Lord Diplock) and 400 (Lord Scarman).

in connection with threats, it is hard to continue to proclaim that the law is being 'neutral'. To select between legitimate and illegitimate threats means that the law is being used to favour those able to make certain kinds of threats, and to discriminate against those not permitted to make other kinds of threats. On this view, it may even be arguable that the law discriminates in favour of the intelligent and strong, because threats of violence are not 'legitimate', whereas the use of skill in bargaining is permissible. Of course the liberal, like Fried, would insist that this sort of discrimination is permissible, because it merely recognizes that each autonomous individual is entitled to the fruits of his labour, no more, no less. This traditional liberal argument is doubtless still powerful but, as we shall see later, it does raise some questions about the liberal's right to argue against redistributive laws.

Furthermore, modern duress doctrine means that the ownership of property, in the widest sense, becomes a condition of being able to bargain effectively, because only property owners may sell (or 'threaten' not to sell) their property. This, however, only makes explicit what has all along been clear enough in liberal theory, but it does raise problems where there is doubt about the acceptability of the origins of the existing pattern of wealth distribution in a society, and about the arbitrariness of rules of property law.

The liberal theorist may be able to argue that an 'illegitimate' threat is a moral wrong, that the proponent threatens something he has no right to threaten, and that 'illegitimacy' is not therefore just a value concept which can be filled with any content at will. And he may concede that property rights do in truth lie at the root of the distinction between coerced and fair promises, but property rights (he will urge) can themselves be defended by liberal theory. For they also, he may insist, like the promise principle, rest on moral foundations arising out of respect for individual autonomy. There are, however, serious difficulties with this position. There are, in particular, recurrent types of contractual bargaining situations (for instance, in industrial disputes) in which the kinds of threats which the parties are entitled to make are almost wholly conventional and arbitrary (ruling out threats of actual violence and other such illegalities). Liberal theory simply cannot tell us whether trade unionists should be permitted to threaten to boycott third parties, or black ships which use cheap Third World labour. And yet the law must decide whether such threats are or are not legitimate before it can decide whether contracts resulting from them are to be enforced. Here, therefore, liberal theory seems especially vulnerable.

Unconscionability is perhaps the acid test of any version of liberal contract theory. Can the liberal justify overriding the result of a deal or bargain voluntarily agreed by sane adults? One approach—and it is likely to seem particularly appropriate to the modern liberal—is to separate out from the question of substantive unfairness all issues concerning cognitive flaws in the transaction. These, it may be insisted, concern procedural unconscionability, and in so far as they raise pleas requiring relief, they can be dealt with as cases of mistake or good faith, or at any rate, with expanded doctrines of mistake and good faith. Next, the liberal may insist that doctrines of substantive unconscionability limit the free choice of contracting parties, who are (we must now assume) wholly aware of what they want to do and fully appreciate the risks and prospects. To limit this freedom requires justification, and there is none which the liberal can recognize. To limit freedom of contract in this way is to redistribute part of the gains made by one contracting party to the other, and redistribution is a job for the legislature through taxation, not for the law of contract. However— and here the unconscionability doctrine may make some sense even to the liberal—this assumes a well-functioning market, when in reality cartels, high entry barriers, and informational problems may limit the proper functioning of the market. Moreover, classical liberal theory does not exclude a duty to be concerned about and to assist others. In rare and random situations of market failure or breakdown of the social order, the courts may justifiably refuse to assist the bad Samaritan to retain his ill-gotten gains, even where they are reluctant to impose a requirement to act as a good Samaritan.

To what extent does this approach to ideas of unconscionability stand up? I postpone for the moment the argument that substantive and procedural unconscionability can be wholly separated: this issue is discussed further in Essay 11 where I indicate my view that, in the last analysis, the distinction does not stand up to scrutiny. Here I will confine myself to two other points. First, there is the question whether overriding freedom of contract by use of doctrines like unconscionability is redistributive anyhow; and secondly, there is the question whether, even if unconscionability is redistributive, it is wrong for contract law to attempt some modest element of redistribution.

The first argument—that unconscionability doctrines are redistributive—in turn gives rise to two possible answers. First, there is the *tu quoque* argument: *all* contract law is distributive, the liberal critic may urge, and there is therefore no reason why adopting any particular set of contract law doctrines should be rejected on this ground. No matter what the rules of contract law may be, the result is, in a sense, redistributive. Of course the true liberal will deny this: contract law is 'neutral', once given the capacities and individual abilities of contracting parties, to which they are morally entitled under liberal theory, and once given the existing distribution of wealth and entitlements, to which (though with some nagging anxieties about how these occurred in the past) the liberal must also eventually give his allegiance.

But it seems doubtful whether this argument is ultimately satisfying, given the present rules of contract law. In particular, a fundamental difficulty with reading all redistributive notions out of the law of contract is that the enforcement of executory contracts itself presupposes an initial distribution of entitlements that is part of the very structure of contract law—and I am *not* referring to the distribution of property entitlements, in the ordinary sense. Like the classical theorists, modern liberal theorists such as Fried leap easily over the gulf between laws that intervene to prohibit parties from making a present exchange and laws that intervene in the already interventionist process of enforcing executory contracts. Because the making of a present exchange, if free and voluntary, is so obviously a Pareto-optimal move, it is assumed that the same holds true of agreements to make a future exchange. This is fallacious. People can and do change their minds. Indeed, one obvious reason why parties sometimes fail to perform contracts is that they have changed their minds on the relative value of the benefits to be exchanged. Fried recognizes this possibility, only to dismiss it on the ground that respect for the autonomy of agents requires us to treat their first choices as determinative. I have already given my reasons for rejecting this argument.

The truth is, it seems to me, that the enforcement of executory contracts is only justifiable on the assumption that we have already distributed a property-like entitlement to the promisee: the promisee is entitled to the benefit of the promise, and the promisor is not entitled to change his mind. Without that initial distribution of entitlements, there is no case for enforcing executory contracts. But although this entitlement is like property in the purely definitional sense that allowing a promisee to hold a promisor to his promises analytically requires us to presuppose that the promisee has this entitlement, it differs from more conventional forms of property in that there is in no way in which liberal theory can justify this distribution of entitlements by invoking Lockean Natural Law, or indeed any other moral principle. It seems, indeed, impossible to explain why the promisee has this entitlement except by begging the very questions at issue.

The law may distribute entitlements as it does for good social or economic reasons but the fact that the law of contract, like the Ritz Hotel, is open to all, does not mean that the distribution is fair to all alike. It is only too obvious that this distribution of entitlements is of most benefit to those who are best at planning, whether their advantage lies in material resources, skill, foresight, or temperament. Nor is it enough to say, as the modern liberal might wish to say, that liberalism starts from the basis that each of us is entitled to his own skills and talents and to the fruits thereof. At this point in the argument, the whole question is whether a promisee is entitled to the *additional* advantages that will accrue to him from a law for the enforcement of executory contracts. The upshot is that the enforcement of such contracts cannot be regarded as a distributively neutral exercise.

The second argument against the modern liberal takes his own concessions and stands them on their head. The liberal (like Fried) who concedes that unconscionability doctrine may be justified in rare situations of random market failure or in conditions of virtual breakdown of the social order may not appreciate how large this concession may turn out to be. Market failure is, after all, common enough—indeed almost totally ubiquitous, if one takes 'market' to be a perfect market. But even if one takes a much narrower concept of market failure than this, it should be appreciated how frequently conditions like monopoly can occur in a limited context. Economists are not generally interested in small-scale monopoly—what can perhaps be called micro-monopoly, as opposed to macro-monopoly. But micro-monopolies are very common, and often cause problems in the legal context. For instance, A owns a piece of land, which B needs for special purposes: no other piece of land will do as well. In this situation A has all the advantages of monopoly, and although we generally accept that, in modern societies, A is entitled to hold out for what price he can extract from B, it is not clear that we would be happy to see A reap the advantages of that monopoly in all circumstances, as for instance where B is a public body which needs the land, or where B only needs a temporary right of way over A's land to repair his own buildings.[1]

---

[1] See e.g. *Bradford Corpn* v. *Pickles* [1895] AC 587, (although this was not a case where the corporation wanted to *buy* the land, but rather a case where Pickles wanted to *sell*.) See also *Woollerton & Wilson Ltd.* v. *Costain* [1970] 1 All ER 483 and *John Ternberth* v. *National Westminster Bank* (1979) 39 P and CR 104.

Then again, many contracts are made between parties who are already locked into a legal relationship of bilateral monopoly, so that the contract is not negotiated in an ordinary market context. This is, for instance, true of all variations to existing contracts, and the fact that the law has traditionally been uneasy about the validity of such variations (on grounds of lack of consideration, or duress) seems to show some intuitive understanding of the problem. But other cases of bilateral monopoly have perhaps been less often recognized, such as, for instance, a settlement of a personal injury claim. Similarly although a concession that relief for unconscionability may be legitimately granted where there is a situation of social breakdown may seem very narrow (confined perhaps to war or the like), purely temporary situations of 'social breakdown' may be far more common. Indeed, the inability to obtain from the law adequate protection of one's rights in sufficient time for that protection to be meaningful—which is one of the standard grounds on which economic duress has been recognized by the courts—may well be seen as a situation of micro-breakdown of the social order in the relevant sense. And perhaps inability to obtain independent advice is in like case. But if the liberal's concession to the legitimacy of modern doctrines of economic duress goes as far as this, it seems unlikely that there are going to be many (if indeed any) circumstances in which the liberal and his critic will disagree, at least about the principles to be applied in cases of alleged unconscionability. No doubt reasonable people will always differ about their application in marginal cases, but that is of no relevance to the issue of principle.

The liberal's second argument against use of unconscionability doctrines is that they involve a kind of redistribution which is best left to the legislature, and is inappropriate for contract law. And it must be said that this argument seems to appeal to the English judiciary at the present day. There have been strong hints from the judges that, since the passing of the Unfair Contract Terms Act and similar legislation, the protection of contracting parties against unfair contracts should not be done by the expansion of doctrines like that of 'inequality of bargaining power'.[1] It is not at all clear whether this has any claim to be regarded as a *moral* argument, however cogent it may be as a practical argument about the selection of the most appropriate instrument of law reform. For the argument can only be turned into a

---

[1] See, for instance, some of the dicta in *Photo Productions Ltd.* v. *Securicor* [1980] AC 827, 843 and 850-1 and *National Westminster Bank plc* v. *Morgan* [1985] 2 WLR 588, 600.

moral argument by adopting a particular theory of the appropriate role of the judicial and legislative branches of government, a theory which appears to be much more widely held in America than in England. If it is assumed that the search for objective and fair principles of distribution is a complete chimera, and that the function of the legislative process is not to do this, but simply to provide a forum in which competing political groups strive for temporary and limited victory on this or that issue, then it is understandable why the legislative process seems to be not merely a more appropriate one for redistributive activity, but why it seems *morally* better that this kind of activity should be confined to the legislature. It is the elective and representative nature of the legislature that, on this view, legitimates redistributive legislative activity. The judicial role, having no such democratic legitimacy, must therefore be more limited—and hence judges should eschew redistributive decisions.

It must be said, however, that this view of the legislative role does not represent the political theory of the political process itself: in England neither politicians, nor the public, nor judges and lawyers would in general accept the argument that there is no way (at any rate in limited and selected spheres) of identifying a 'neutral' and objectively fair public interest which it is appropriate to adopt. And if that is the basis on which English political institutions function, then it is not at all apparent that judges should refrain from all redistributive activity. Of course I make no attempt here to argue out the whole question whether indeed there are any such neutral and objective principles of fairness, which is, needless to say, one of the largest, most difficult, and most hotly disputed questions of political theory. I am merely concerned to make the narrow point that the correct judicial role as to these redistributive issues is inextricably tied to one's whole perception of the political theory underlying all democratic and political institutions.

But there is a still narrower point which deserves to be made. Given that the legislature is hard-pressed, and that the legislative process these days often proceeds in a patchy way, eschewing broad general principle, is there any good reason why judges should not take their cue from the legislature itself, and (for instance) extend by analogy some provisions of the Unfair Contract Terms Act to other kinds of transactions which slip through the legislative net? Here again the modern liberal political theorist has a ready answer. This also, he urges, is illegitimate, because to act in this way may be unwittingly to upset some legislative compromise by which the competing views of different interests were reconciled, and thus obtained the stamp of democratic legitimacy. Here at least practical experience of the English political process suggests that this is a very unsatisfying answer. Although no doubt this is occasionally how legislative enactments are produced in England, this view of the political process as one involving the balancing and compromising of various political interests against each other, is fundamentally American, and reflects the nature of the American democratic process. By and large it does not reflect the nature of the English democratic process. In Britain, governments do not generally have to resort to fudge and compromise to pass their legislation. Governments are usually strong enough to decide what they want in their legislative programme, and they have sufficient control of the legislature to see that their legislation is passed.[1] Given that this is the reality of the English political system, it is not at all clear that there are really any sound reasons why judges should not borrow values and ideas from the legislature in order to make contract law redistributive—apart from its inherent distributiveness—if that seems right.[2]

Of course all this says nothing about the desirability on non-moral grounds of using contract law as a redistributive device. Undoubtedly there are grounds for caution here: redistributive decisions may backfire, and make worse off those whom they are designed to protect. But this argument must not be pressed too far, first because there are often hidden cognitive weaknesses in contracting, and second, because there may well be market conditions under which—at any rate in the short term—there will be no such backfiring, and those who are benefited by redistributive decisions will be able to retain their benefits. There are also, of course, pure matters of legal technique to be considered: sometimes legal change is more suited to the legislative method, and any massive use of contract law for redistributive purposes (such as sometimes seems to be envisaged by members of the Critical Legal Studies Movement[3]) could well be thought, in the English legal system, to be undesirable for these reasons alone. But unconscionability is a well-tried concept in the history of English contract law and—even

---

[1] This subject will be dealt with at some length in the forthcoming book by the present author and Professor R. S. Summers, at present tentatively entitled, *Form and Substance in Anglo-American Law*.

[2] See my 'Common Law and Statute Law', 48 *Mod. Law Rev.* 1 (1985).

[3] See Kennedy, 'Distributive and Paternalist Motives in Contract and Tort with Special reference to Compulsory Terms and Unequal Bargaining Power', 41 *Maryland L. Rev.* 563 (1982).

leaving aside the doubts expressed in Essay 11 about the whole distinction between substantive and procedural unconscionability—it seems certain that English judges could be trusted to use the doctrine with care and caution in circumstances where its use would be fully justifiable.

It is in considering the doctrines of mistake, impossibility, and frustration that the modern liberal (such as Fried) may be most willing to make substantial concessions to the critics of classical theory. Classical theorists insisted that contract law and the promise principle were the exclusive sources of the rights and duties of the parties to a contract. This, Fried admits, is manifestly wrong. Since the basis of the promise principle is the will of the promisor to bind himself, an obligation not founded on that will cannot derive from the principle. But the parties do not provide for all contingencies, and there is a gap in the contract when some event occurs or some fact exists to which they have not directed their wills. If such gaps cannot be filled by the promise principle, they can be filled by other moral and legal principles, and that is indeed what the law does. Two such alternatives are a fairness principle based on the encouragement of due care and an administrative principle based on the application of the rule that is least likely to involve court error. But gap-filling is one thing; overturning deliberate agreements on the ground that they are in some sense 'unfair' is quite another, and cannot be justified, except to the limited extent suggested above in dealing with unconscionability.

As to good faith in performance, traditional ideas of 'reasonable interpretation' can be invoked to justify non-enforcement of the literal terms of a promise. Parties often, perhaps usually, have a general or vague intention regarding certain risks, one which the courts must flesh out, but in doing this they must and can still display 'loyalty to the promise'. These concessions enable the modern liberal to avoid—indeed to criticize—many of the familiar weaknesses of classical contract law and many of the decisions, widely regarded as unjust, that are associated with those weaknesses. It thus becomes possible to reconcile much of post-classical contract law with this new version of the promise principle. With respect to the protection of unbargained-for reliance when appropriate, the reading of conditions and promises against a background of good faith conventions, generous use of restitutionary principles, the filling of gaps by tort and other non-promissory doctrines, and even the limited use of rules of substantive unconscionability, the modern liberal is, as it were, on the side of the angels.

As a matter of positive law, there is little difference between this liberal theory and that of most post-classical theorists. The critic might have doubts about the limits which it would place on the use of unconscionability; he might wonder about the role of the massive amount of statutory interference with freedom of contract; and he might take issue with the liberal, even when the outcome is agreed, on the reasons for which contractual liability is imposed. But even on this last point, the modern liberal may be willing to make substantial concessions; Fried, for instance, admits that 'the law itself imposes contractual liability on the basis of a complex of moral, political, and social judgments'.[1] I do not suppose that even the most vehement opponent of liberal theory would dispute that the intention of contracting parties is at least one relevant factor in this complex judgment. Indeed, intention is often a significant factor in the imposition or non-imposition of tort liability as well.[2] Thus, if the law imposes liability for a complex of reasons and the intentions of the parties concerned are a subset of those reasons, there might seem little here with which any modern contract theorist would need to quarrel. On this view, even the line between contractual and non-contractual liability seems to melt away, as the 'death of contract' theorists have argued.

Presumably, however, most modern liberals would not go this far. The distinction between promissory and non-promissory obligation, they are likely to insist, is marked by sharp discontinuities. In so far as contract law reflects the promissory principle, the same sharp discontinuities ought therefore to arise between contractual and non-contractual obligations. If this is not the case, it must be because contract law now uses many moral principles besides the promissory principle. If the liberal admits this much, then what can be justified by the promise principle is only a very small part of contract law. In order to identify the promise principle as the basis of contract law, it becomes necessary to reclassify large parts of contract law as tort, restitution, or some other subject. Let us consider what gets left out.

In the first place, liability for truly unintended consequences—consequences that cannot be fairly imputed to the promisor after all implications and background conventions are taken into account—cannot be justified on the promise principle. For my part I am prepared to

[1] See *Contract as Promise*, p. 69.
[2] See Essay 10, pp. 280–6, below.

agree that liability for truly unintended consequences is a very different matter from liability for intended consequences, and, indeed, I argue in Essay 7 that perhaps expectation damages should not generally be awarded in the case of unintended consequences. Perhaps such cases should be treated more like tort cases. But this is certainly not the law at the moment, so this argument can only be normative, and does not explain the present use made by the law of the promissory idea. Similar issues arise with many cases of mistake, impossibility, and frustration which may have to be treated as gap-filling cases, with the gaps being filled from other moral and legal sources. Once these concessions are made, however, they call into question how often judicial decisions in contractual disputes can be attributed to the promise principle. Indeed, it surely becomes clear that, pushed to its logical conclusion, this view would reduce contract law to a very small role—it would come to deal only with intentional acts, intentional risk-allocations and intentional consequences. Liability in contract would then parallel liability for 'intentional' torts, and would cover only a very small part of what is now known as contract law. Although I am not wholly unsympathetic to such a possibility (for reasons discussed at length in Essay 7), it must be appreciated what an upheaval it would involve for the existing law; and it is not at all evident that many liberals would really want to go this far.

Much of the trouble stems from the fact that most liberals appear to take as the paradigmatic case of contract the situation in which two individuals are face to face and make a bargain of the very simplest character—my cow Rose for your $80. Even that type of bargain can raise issues that cannot adequately be dealt with by this version of liberal theory. How much more is this the case with many standard consumer contracts that are only imperfectly understood by one party and understood scarcely at all, except in essentials, by the other. Even commercial contracts between corporations frequently incorporate all manner of standard printed terms whose effect is only in the most general way 'intended' by the parties. It has never been clear to me whether a signature at the foot of a multipage printed contract indicates the kind of intention to commit oneself to all its contents that Fried— or any other liberal—would think sufficient to invoke the promise principle. Strictly, this ought to be a strong case for the invocation of the notion used by Fried of a generalized intent that can be fleshed out by the court. But if generalized intent goes this far, we are back with the worst absurdities of classical fictitious intent. On the other hand, if these are not cases of intent at all, then the promise principle covers no more than a small fraction of the disputes with which contract law deals.

I have mentioned above that the liberal seems to take a very simple factual case as the paradigm of contractual and promissory obligation. In particular, he seems to assume that it is usually easy to identify the bargain—the set of mutual promises involving intentional commitment on both sides. In these respects the modern liberal has departed little from the classical tradition. But some contract lawyers today would doubt the reality of many of the 'promises' on which contractual obligations are founded. When one lives in a culture and works in a professional tradition in which it is taken for granted that people who do or say certain things ought to come under certain obligations, it is very easy to convince oneself that these obligations have been voluntarily undertaken, impliedly or even expressly. But can we so readily assume that transactions that lead to remedies devised by lawyers must be promise-based? Consider an example of a unilateral contract: a homeowner asks an estate agent to find a buyer for him and agrees to the rate of commission charged by the agent. How does one decide by the light of nature, or of the promise principle, what the owner has promised to do? In English law it is clear that the owner is only bound to pay the commission if a sale eventually takes place. If the owner changes his mind and decides not to sell, he is not liable.[1] So what kind of 'deal' did the parties make at the outset? Were any promises made at all? The 'death of contract' theorist would argue that the court, based on its judgment of policy and social values, is creating and imposing legal rights and duties on the parties.[2] The promises of the parties are legal constructs that cannot be identified until we have decided what the parties ought to do. Obligation comes first, promise afterwards.

Presumably the modern liberal would accept this analysis as correct only where there is a real gap to be filled, and even then he might object to justifying the obligation by 'implying' a promise. But I suspect we differ on the empirical issue of how often such gaps arise. The greater the proportion of cases in which legal duties are imposed by gap-filling, the smaller the role of traditional contract law and the promise principle as seen by this version of liberal theory. Perhaps the liberal would ultimately say that this empirical question is a minor matter since his aims are, after all, philosophical and not sociological. Even if he has to

[1] See *Luxor (Eastbourne) Ltd.* v. *Cooper* [1941] AC 108.
[2] See p.24 and Essay 8, pp. 203–6 below, where this is discussed at length.

surrender the major part of contract law to tort or restitution, he may claim that he is justifying the residue by reference to the promise principle. Although I would not dispute that in principle such an exercise could be valuable, the empirical question still seems important for two reasons.

First, our views of what is morally and legally right are often determined by our vision of a paradigmatic case, and I am quite sure that the paradigm of a contract used by most liberals differs from mine. Indeed, I doubt, for reasons given in Essays 1 and 2, whether it is appropriate to think in terms of a single such paradigm. Second, the larger the number of gaps that the courts have to fill in by use of principles other than the promise principle, the greater will be the number of borderline cases involving a choice between dramatically different principles. This surely must cause trouble for the liberal who wishes to stress that the promise principle produces sharp discontinuities of result, because this means that on his view, very different results may turn on whether we are still in the realm of contract law based on the promise principle or have bridged the gulf that separates promising from other principles.

There is also a serious question as to the true basis of contractual liability even where gaps do not actually eventuate. This is because even standard commercial transactions are full of *potential* gaps. There are all manner of events which *might* overtake a contract, and for which it does not expressly or by implication provide, and if any of these *mights* actually occurs, the law must provide an answer. But when we take our stand at the moment the contract is made, and ask what legal regime binds the parties as a result of their contract, we will not as yet know which of these *mights* is going to occur; and we must therefore admit that all the *mights* are actually a part of the contract, and the legal answers to these *mights* are already in a sense part of the legal obligations (contingent of course) which the contract creates. This being so, it seems clear that the total size of the non-promissory component of any contract must greatly outweigh the truly promissory component.

Because this modern liberal theory rejects so many of the extreme conclusions of classical contract law, it conforms more to modern ideas of justice, and, as I have already indicated in addressing the gap-filling problem, it seems in some respects more theoretically defensible than classical law. But there are, I believe, respects in which it is less coherent than classical law and in which the modern liberal may give the appearance of trying to ride two horses travelling in different directions.

In classical law it was clear that the promise principle was not merely an affirmative principle of liability, but also an exclusionary principle of no liability. In general, if you promised, you were liable, but if you did *not* promise, then conversely you were *not* liable. One might, of course, be held liable under tort law, but that was generally confined to dealing with matters of property, force, and fraud. Laws designed to protect property aud prohibit force had their own justification. Laws against fraud were the weak point of classical theory, but they were also the weak point of classical law. The argument of a modern liberal like Fried that, when the promise principle leaves something to be desired, we can make good its deficiencies by invoking other moral and legal principles, was utterly rejected by classical lawyers. In particular, classical theorists would have denied that liability for unbargained-for reliance or for the unpromised restitution of benefits should be widely imposed when no promissory liability could be found.

If one starts from the position that a promise is an intentional commitment to assume an obligation, the natural inference is that a person who makes no promise is refraining from assuming any commitment. If another party chooses to rely upon him and suffers loss as a result, how then can that other party justifiably demand that the non-promisor be made to pay? Fried makes this argument when he discusses the distinction between a promise and a mere statement of intent. As long as I refrain from promising, he insists, I am not bound; I may foresee and even invite reliance, and yet remain free to change my mind. But Fried leaves here a loophole of which he makes full use later: although I am not bound if I make no promise, I must not mislead you; I must not harm you by my carelessness. It is with the aid of this principle that Fried supports the result in *Hoffman*: 'Red Owl was held liable not in order to force it to perform a promise, which it had never made, but rather to compensate Hoffman for losses he had suffered through Red Owl's inconsiderate and temporizing assurances.'[1]

The difficulty, however, is that Fried does not adequately explain any theory of causation that entitles him to attribute Hoffman's losses to Red Owl. In classical contract law, you were justified in relying on a promise, but you were not generally justified in relying on anything short of a promise. In so far as a person suffered losses through reliance on another's non-promissory conduct, those losses were attributable to his own voluntary conduct and not to the other party. Nor was this exclusionary function of promising purely the result of formalism or of

[1] *Contract as Promise*, p. 24.

limited vision. It reflected an ideological commitment to the respect for individual autonomy that is precisely the basis of Fried's own version of the promise principle. Respect for the autonomy of individuals would have led classical lawyers to reject Hoffman's claim. They would have insisted that his own choices, his own autonomous decisions, led him to rely on the vague assurances of Red Owl. The purpose of giving a promise, they would have said, is to mark the point at which I choose to accept responsibility for your acts of reliance; if I have given no promise, you act at your peril, not mine.

Decisions like *Hoffman* completely reject the exclusionary aspect of the promise principle and are intelligible only if one assumes that, in *some* circumstances, each of us is his brother's keeper. And this goes not only for *Hoffman* but also for large parts of the field of unbargained-for reliance, promissory estoppel, implied warranty, misrepresentation, strict products liability, and other developments of post-classical law. All of these impose liability for losses that would not occur but for the free choice of the plaintiff in acting in reliance on the defendant's language or conduct. In classical law, free choice would often have been decisive in rejecting the claim. Professor Fried respects that choice but accepts its consequences only for the affirmative aspect of the promising principle.

Much the same difficulty faces Fried's attempts to use restitutionary principles to fill in other deficiencies of the promise principle. In classical law, there was little room for a law of restitution except where claims could be said to be quasi-proprietary. In general, classical law imposed an obligation to pay for benefits received only when the recipient promised to pay for those benefits. Again, this arose largely from respect for the autonomy of the individual: each person was entitled to decide for himself whether something was a benefit and how much it was worth. If he did promise to pay for a benefit, he was of course liable, but if he did not, then he was not liable. Here too the promise principle was exclusionary in effect and in purpose.

Consider the American case of *Jacob & Youngs* v. *Kent*,[1] the Reading pipes case. In this case, a building contractor was bound by the contract to use 'Reading' pipes in the construction of a house, but he had instead used some other pipes of similar design and quality. The owner argued that as a result of this breach he should not have to pay the contract price, although the house (being built on his land) was his to keep. Fried stigmatizes as 'absurd' the owner's claim that he could keep the

[1] 129 NE 889 (1921).

house without paying for it.[1] Even at the height of classical times, some might have agreed with Fried, though there is certainly evidence that others, including Baron Bramwell, would not. Faced with such a case, Bramwell might well have argued that he had no means of knowing whether the house as built was worth its price, or worth anything, to the owner.[2] The buyer has decided what the house is worth with the Reading pipes. The court has no power to force him to pay for a house with different pipes. To do so would be to show disrespect for the buyer's autonomy, his free choice. I do not see anything illogical or absurd about such an argument. If it would seem unreasonable to most people today, that is surely because we no longer have quite the same respect for individual autonomy and free choice. We are prepared to overrule the owner's defence in such a case because we feel that the loss to the builder would be too great, and we are prepared to judge for ourselves (through our courts) whether the change in pipes has in fact diminished the value of the house.

But it is much less clear to me that Fried can, consistently with his basic position, defend a verdict for the plaintiff in *Jacob & Youngs*. It is, he claims, just an application of the restitution principle that, if the owner does not retain the benefit under the contract, he need not pay for it. The fact that the owner cannot return the house only means that he cannot avail himself of this principle. All he can do is to claim the next best thing, which is that he should have to pay not the contract price but only the fair value. But this conclusion just does not seem to follow. If the owner cannot return the house (and after all, the cause of that is the builder's breach of contract—*his* free choice), why should he not be entitled to keep the house without payment? As with unbargained-for reliance, the reality surely is that values have changed about such matters; the extreme individualism and subjectivism of classical theory have few followers today. But when it is agreed that benefits ought to be paid for in the *Jacob & Youngs* situation, it must be the case that autonomy is being rejected in favour of other values.

The heart of the conflict between all versions of liberal contract

---

[1] *Contract as Promise*, p. 123. In fact the disputed amount was only $3,483 out of a total price of over $77,000. No realist would think that the defendant's argument would have been treated nearly so respectfully if he had refused to pay any part of the contract price.

[2] In *Boulton* v. *Jones* 2 H and N 564, 566 (1857), Bramwell made no bones about exempting the defendant from liability for paying for goods that he had consumed, and elsewhere Bramwell made it quite clear that he thought a man's obligation to pay for benefits supplied to him rested on contract or nothing. See my *Freedom of Contract*, at p. 376.

theory, including Fried's, and post-classical theories is the extent to which respect for the promise principle, as a matter of morality or law, requires us to recognize as binding and to 'enforce' the free choices of sane adult individuals. The earlier classical theorists, drawing upon utilitarian economic theory and resting heavily upon a subjective theory of value, insisted that every person was the best judge of his own interests. A modern liberal like Professor Fried, while apparently unwilling to rely upon so crude an empirical proposition, prefers to rest his version of liberal theory on the moral argument that to refuse to recognize, or to interfere with, a person's free choice is to refuse him the respect of treating him as an autonomous moral agent. The result is the same.

No modern contract scholar would deny that respect for individual free choice remains an important value of Western societies, but I suspect most of these scholars would argue that the law must also accommodate countervailing values deriving from the pursuit of collective goals and from the paternalistic belief that collective judgments about the best interests of individuals are sometimes more likely to be correct than the individual's own judgment. I have myself argued at length elsewhere that, ever since the reign of Elizabeth I, the common law of contract has, to varying degrees, recognized collective and paternalistic as well as individual values. No doubt it is still open to the liberal to contend that normatively all this is undesirable; but he must then face up to the fact that the movement of Western societies in the last hundred years has uniformly been towards a greater recognition of collective and paternalistic goals. Of course this is no argument from a normative viewpoint. But it should at least make us pause. Judges and lawyers, in all countries, and for many years, faced with practical problems arising from human relationships, have concluded that pure autonomy, extreme liberal freedom of contract, is often unjust and ought not to pursued at the expense of all other values. All these judges and lawyers may have been wrong: perhaps they just reflected the wishes of collective groups who wanted to grab as much of the social product as they could. But then again, perhaps not. I have also pointed out that the pursuit of collective goals by legislative means, even where it is avowedly redistributive, cannot be condemned as illegitimate except by denying the legitimacy of the democratic process in virtually all Western societies. Yet the only way in which the liberal can defend such legislative activity is by invoking a theory of the political process which is based on conditions in, and (by and large) only accepted in, the United States.

But there is another type of collective activity that impinges on contract law—activity in pursuit of egalitarian, but not necessarily redistributive, goals. For it is wrong to assume that the use of egalitarian values in a contractual setting is always in pursuit of redistributive goals. Courts may rely on egalitarian values not in order to redistribute wealth between plaintiff and defendant, but to insist, for instance, that the defendant should treat this plaintiff in the same way he has treated other contracting parties. In this respect, egalitarianism carries none of the suspect redistributive connotations of majoritarianism but is based on traditional notions of equality before the law. If, for example, a person refuses to make with a black man a contract that he would have been willing to make with a white man, the law may condemn this refusal on egalitarian, but not necessarily redistributive, grounds. Fried sees nothing inconsistent with his views in supporting laws of this kind because, he says, this discrimination is 'without reason' and therefore morally wrong.[1] Whether or not this can be reconciled with the subjective theory of value which also underlies the liberal theory, a more difficult question arises when a party does contract, say, with a black man, but only on terms more advantageous to himself than he would have exacted from a white man. Intervention here overrides the consent of both parties in the pursuit of egalitarian values. Perhaps it could still be discrimination, but there are more difficult cases yet. For instance, the take-over rules enforced in the City of London (without any statutory backing) compel a take-over bidder to treat all shareholders equally; if he buys shares from one seller at so much a share and later, in pursuit of the same take-over bid, acquires shares from another seller at a higher price per share, he is obliged to pay the first seller the difference.[2] Considering the source of these rules, it is hardly possible to write them off as socialist nonsense, yet observe how the first seller is entitled to reopen his contract, voluntarily and freely made, because it is felt that equality of treatment of the shareholders in a take-over bid is an overriding value.

I turn finally to the paternalistic grounds for overriding the promise principle in limited circumstances. Professor Fried likens this to holding out a helping hand to the person who has bought a lottery ticket and failed to win a prize, even though he would do the same again. No

[1] *Contract as Promise*, p. 103 n. *.
[2] See A. Johnston, *The City Take-Over Code* (1980), pp. 202-5.

sympathy, it seems, need be wasted on this gambler. But all surely depends on the ability of the person in question to judge his own future state of mind, as well as more obvious matters like the true nature and extent of the risk. In fact, all democratic Western societies have massive bodies of law—retirement pension laws, compulsory medical insurance, compulsory liability insurance laws, and so forth—that demonstrate our considerable sympathy for one who wrongly calculates, or otherwise foolishly takes, a risk. The proposition that a person is always the best judge of his own interests is a good starting-point for laws and institutional arrangements, but as an infallible empirical proposition it is an outrage to human experience. The parallel moral argument, that to prevent a person, even in his own interests, from binding himself is to show disrespect for his moral autonomy, can ring very hollow when used to defend a grossly unfair contract secured at the expense of a person of little understanding or bargaining skill. If a smart operator makes a highly advantageous deal with a person of low intelligence or skill, does the former really show 'respect' for the latter's moral autonomy by exploiting his advantage in this way?

Surely it makes more sense to treat the promise principle as presumptive rather than conclusive. By and large, this is what the law does. Promises ought to be treated as prima facie binding rather than absolutely and conclusively binding. Exchanges of benefits are likely to be in the interests of those who make them, and there is therefore a strong prima-facie case for upholding them. Promises are likely to be relied upon and those who rely would suffer loss from breach: these too are prima facie good reasons for upholding the binding nature of a promise.[1]

On the other hand, to say that such results are likely to follow is not to say that they are certain to follow; the presumption must be rebuttable. Even classical law recognized some circumstances—fraud, coercion, and the like—that would rebut the presumption. Today, there are rather more circumstances in which the presumption is rebuttable, especially if we take account of legislation. The liberal theorist would say that we take a great leap when we move from cognitive failures to substantive unfairness as a ground for allowing the binding nature of a contractual promise to be rebutted. But even if this is true in some

---

[1] It is interesting that Fried, who rejects the notion that promises are binding because of reliance, is constantly drawn to justify the promise principle itself in terms of 'trust', which is virtually a synonym for reliance. See *Contract as Promise*, pp. 8, 16, 65, 78, 83, 85.

conceptual sense (and reasons are given in Essay 11 for doubting it), in practice the leap is not usually obvious. The reason is that those who rely upon fraud, misrepresentation, and other cognitive weaknesses as grounds for upsetting contracts are usually complaining that the contract was substantively unfair. But even if we agree with the liberal on the quantum nature of the leap, we take it because we recognize that the law must reflect diverse and conflicting values. Given this diversity, there is no hope of reducing the whole body of contract, or even its main outlines, to a single principle.

7

Executory Contracts, Expectation Damages, and the Economic Analysis of Contract

In this essay I propose to discuss a number of very difficult questions which arise if my views on the theory of contract have any validity. I have argued in Essay 2 and elsewhere that bare consent, a bare promise, is a much less powerful source of obligation than induced reliance or actual benefits rendered. Indeed, I have suggested there that it is far from clear to what degree bare consent or promises ought to be held binding at all. On the other hand, in Essay 5 I have given reasons for thinking that to treat contracts as at least prima facie absolutely binding is, in a broad and general way, a highly efficient tool of legal administration. It is so much simpler to treat contracts, or the consent of the parties, as conclusively disposing of all sorts of issues which would otherwise have to be resolved by some kind of judicial arbitrament. At the same time, nothing that I said in Essay 5 denies the importance of the substantive reasons which lie behind the formal reasons, and which, from time to time, it does become necessary to look at. What I need to do now is to see if we can discover whether the present law of contract strikes the right balance between formal and substantive reasons. In so far as current law actually does hold actual promises or bare consent to be conclusively binding (apart from reliance and benefits rendered) is it hitting a reasonable balance?

Closely related to the degree to which we ought to accord conclusive force to a promise or an assent is the question of expectation damages. Indeed, in the case of a wholly executory contract, these two questions are but different sides of the same coin: for if such a contract is binding, the only kind of damages we can award are damages for loss of expectation, since, by hypothesis, there will be no reliance and no benefit which can form the basis of the damages. But once the discussion of executory contracts becomes linked in this way with the question of expectation damages, we get dragged into the further question, how far should expectation damages be awarded even in cases where there is some element of reliance or some element of benefit, but not a full performance?

1. Is Contract Law Efficient?

The right place to begin seems to be to look at some of the modern law-and-economics literature which seeks to demonstrate that contract law, and indeed the whole common law, is, in some sense of the term, economically efficient as it is. One of the most curious phenomena of the law-and-economics theorists represented especially by Richard Posner (but with many followers) is the way in which they are so often able to demonstrate that 'the common law' is efficient in its result, though its reasoning may be awry. Generally speaking the only occasions on which the common law went wrong (it seems) was in the (rare) adoption of paternalistic rules which restricted freedom of contract, for example the rules against penalties. The monotonous regularity with which judges untrained in economics have come up with solutions which are thus said to be economically optimal has, not surprisingly, come in for a good deal of scepticism, not to say derision. (If judges are such good economists, perhaps they ought to be advising the Treasury, rather than judging.) Given the ideological stand of Richard Posner and his followers, one is naturally tempted to suppose that their preference for 'the common law' is a part of their dislike of 'intervention'. If the common law is efficient, it obviously follows that legislation which interferes with the common law (and what legislation does not?) must be inefficient. Could it be that the desirability of demonstrating this conclusion has something to do with the theory itself? One could try to challenge the theory by arguing over the efficiency of particular rules of law analysed by the economists. But there do seem to be more fundamental problems which are worth raising.

The first, of course, is what do these economists mean by 'the common law'? There is not *one* body of common law doctrine. The common law has been developing for hundreds of years. It was one thing in 1800, another in 1900, and it will be yet another in 1990. Even in modern times, it varies, as courts develop doctrines in this or that direction, and overrule older decisions. Was the doctrine of fundamental breach part of 'the common law'? Was *Chandler* v. *Webster*[1] a part of 'the common law'? Richard Posner is prepared to argue in defence of that much maligned, and later overruled case.[2] But if it were

---

[1] [1904] 1 KB 493.
[2] See *The Economics of Contract Law*, ed. A. T. Kronman and R. A. Posner (1979), p. 137 n. 38.

right then presumably the *Fibrosa*[1] case was wrong to overturn it. The Statute of Frauds, apparently, is defensible,[2] so it seems that old enough statutes can be given the same support as the common law. (That is something of a relief: it would be unfortunate to discover at this late day that *Quia Emptores* was a mistake.) Then there is the problem that the common law varies in place as well as in time. The common law is not the same throughout the United States; it is certainly not the same in England as it is in (say) California. As one reads more of these economic studies, it gradually becomes apparent that what these writers see as the efficient part of the common law is (roughly) the common law as it was in the fairly recent past. Modern judges are apt to go whoring off after false gods such as consumer protection and doctrines of unconscionability.

Now if we concentrate on some of the most basic parts of the common law—the very core rules protecting innocent parties from violence, robbery, theft, and (perhaps) breach of contract—it would not be very surprising to discover that these rules are reasonably efficient. Obviously these are the first rules which must be established in any sort of society, and as the common law was the first part of the law to be established, it is hardly surprising to find that the common law devised rules for the prohibition of murder and theft. Most lawyers would be willing to agree that such rules are likely to enhance the general welfare, and that they are therefore efficient as well as morally desirable. Moreover, as we move from very early times into more modern periods, we know that many of the most basic rules of the common law were profoundly influenced by political and economic ideologies. I have argued myself at some length that the economic ideological belief in freedom of contract was closely associated with the development of contract theory in 1770-1870 or thereabouts.[3] So it would not be surprising to discover that the common law around 1870 or perhaps (especially in America which was about fifty years behind England in these matters) even around 1920, was efficient in some rough and ready sense. Of course this proposition becomes more dubious if a more precise concept of efficiency is used, but all is well with the argument so long as one accepts an appropriate definition of efficiency. Now Richard Posner's definition of efficiency is that which maximizes wealth, but wealth depends on value, and value depends on free choice (willingness

[1] [1943] AC 32.
[2] *The Economics of Contract Law*, pp. 253-4.
[3] *Freedom of Contract*, Part II.

to pay). If you maximize free choice, therefore, it is hardly surprising that you maximize wealth; you can hardly do otherwise because the one follows the other by a process of definition.

Little has so far been said by economists about the explanation for this curious tendency for (older) judges to come up with efficient solutions to legal disputes. But there is one explanation which has gained some currency, and that is that a competitive or evolutionary process has helped efficient rules to survive. The argument, in a nutshell, is that contracting parties will always unerringly go for the efficient solution (an argument assumed to be more plausible than the corresponding argument about judges because contracting parties are at least motivated by self-interest); if the rules of the law are inefficient, therefore, parties will contract round them, that is, exclude the inefficient rules from their contracts. They will gradually perish through lack of use; the efficient rules will survive.

There is, of course, an element of truth in all this—indeed, a necessary element, since an appropriate definition of efficiency will inevitably lead to this result. If, for instance, we assume that free and voluntary exchanges are always efficient (ignoring or overlooking third party effects) and if we assume that some rules of law restrict the making of such exchanges, but others enable the exchanges to be made, it is a pure truism that parties who contrive to make their exchange will succeed in producing an efficient result. In this sense we might argue (for example) that the discovery of the hire-purchase contract in the late nineteenth century was efficient because it enabled consumers of modest means to buy goods on credit, using the goods as security, and thus to circumvent the Bills of Sale Acts which paternalistically tried to prevent parties from doing this, or anyhow tried to regulate the terms on which it could be done. The virtual obsolescence of the Bills of Sale Acts could then be taken as confirmation of this economic thesis, that efficient rules or processes drive out the inefficient. There are, however, problems with this thesis. First, of course, there is the problem of third-party effects, which means that we cannot be sure that the new solution is efficient until we have taken account of them. But secondly, this example itself demonstrates that the apparently efficient solution may only enjoy short run success.

Let us actually put this argument to the test by considering the historical development of the law of hire-purchase. When the hire-purchase contract was first invented it is reasonable to suppose that at common law the contract prima facie contained various implied terms of merchantability and so on, analogous to those in a contract of sale. But, as is well known, hire purchase contracts in fact always contained the most extensive and rigorous exclusion clauses which stripped the hirer of these common law rights. The Posner thesis requires us, therefore, to deduce that the common law rules were a mistake: they were inefficient as was demonstrated by the fact that the parties always contracted round them. But what happened next? Did the inefficient rule gradually perish? Far from it, of course. It was the contracting-out which was increasingly frowned upon by the law, and eventually prohibited. Perhaps that is an example of legislative inefficiency; but it is hard to believe that the common law would not have achieved the same solution as the legislature if left to itself. Indeed, the doctrines of fundamental breach in England, and unconscionability in America, were formulated largely for this very purpose. So the idea that the 'inefficient' rules would have perished and been supplanted by the efficient contracting-out process looks somewhat unconvincing.

Other examples could easily be put where inefficient contract rules have persisted because of social custom, moral ideals, or the sheer weight of legal tradition. I have, for instance, referred elsewhere to the English agricultural tenancy contract which, in the nineteenth century, did not adopt the apparently efficient 'share-cropping' contract. Instead, the almost universal custom was for the tenant to farm the land under an annual lease. It was at the time widely argued that this was inefficient economically speaking.[1] Tenants lacked an adequate incentive to invest in their farms because of their lack of tenure. The economic theorists would argue (indeed have argued)[2] that no legislative intervention was needed because farmers and landowners ought to have realized that annual leases were inefficient, and begun to contract for longer leases. Perhaps they ought to have done so; but the stark fact is they did not. Only with the coming of the Agricultural Holdings Acts in the late nineteenth century did tenant farmers begin to acquire security of tenure (or the right to compensation for investment). Since then English agriculture has benefited from massive investment and is widely thought to be the most efficient in Europe. One final example of an absurdly inefficient common law rule, which shows no sign of withering away,[3] or even of being abolished by legislation,[4]

---

[1] *Freedom of Contract*, p. 636.

[2] See R. Turvey, *The Economics of Real Property* (1957), ch. VIII.

[3] See *La Pintada* [1984] 3 WLR 10.

[4] Despite the excellent Law Commission *Report on Interest* (Cmnd. 7229) proposing abolition of the old rule, there seems to be no prospect of implementation.

is the rule that a creditor cannot claim interest on an overdue debt.

The above discussion leads on to a wider criticism which the English lawyer may feel impelled to make against much of the theorizing of the kind to be found in the law-and-economics literature. Much of it seems over-simplified to the point of unreality. The empirical assumptions made seem often absurdly unreal or just contradicted by experience. Take, for instance, the very fundamental question whether contracting parties are the best judges of their own interests. No doubt this is a reasonable working assumption—indeed, the only possible assumption in a society which is to have any respect for human freedom and dignity; but it is surely to fly in the face of all human experience to treat it as a universal truth. Even reasonably intelligent people like law or economics professors must often find it very difficult to know whether major personal decisions are likely to be in their long-run interests (for example to take a new job, buy a new house); but university professors have IQs somewhat above average. For every professor, there must be someone in the population with an IQ below average. When these people come to make important decisions, the chances that they will act in their own long-term interest are often quite low.

But this fact is quite overlooked in the facile way in which some law-and-economics writers reject the need for paternalism (in the form of the doctrine of unconscionability) for the poor, the unemployed, those on welfare, or members of racially disadvantaged groups. There is no case (for instance), says Professor Epstein,[1] for protecting these groups because 'it is difficult, if not impossible, to assert that the persons who fall into any of these classes are not in general competent to fend for themselves in most market situations. They are not infants, impressionable heirs, or gullible prisoners of war.' He then attempts to bolster this proposition by suggesting that such people tend to buy simple standard goods, not investments in trusts or other things difficult to value. But this overlooks the facts that such people often 'buy' credit, which is very difficult to value unless one has some knowledge of methods of calculating interest; and that they also 'buy' contract terms, which are also very difficult to value unless one has some knowledge of law. These sweeping propositions are too often made the basis for important legal conclusions.

A similar problem arises with Trebilcock's attack[2] on the doctrine of unconscionability as applied by the House of Lords in *Macaulay* v.

[1] *The Economics of Contract Law*, p. 95.
[2] 26 *Un. Tor. L. Rev.* 359 (1976).

Schroeder.[1] He argues that the concept of substantive unconscionability, meaning that there is a significant non-equivalence between the two sides to a contract, presents real conceptual difficulty
unless one assumes either that there is abnormal market power, such
as monopoly, or alternatively that there has been some aberration in
the process of contract formation. If these factors are not present, he
argues, then 'almost by definition the outcome of such a process cannot
be unfair'. In one sense, of course, this is *all* a matter of definition, but
the fact is that otherwise normal rational people do sometimes (indeed
quite often) sign contracts which are significantly unfair, in the sense
that one party gets a much better deal than the other. Consider, for
instance, the separated wife in *Backhouse* v. *Backhouse*,[2] who signed
away her half share in the matrimonial home in return for an indemnity
against her liabilities on the mortgage. Mrs Backhouse was not stupid
(the judge in fact referred to her as 'an intelligent woman') and there
was no evidence that she was pressurized or unduly influenced by her
husband's solicitors in signing the contract. But from her point of view
the signing of the contract was obviously 'irrational' in the sense that
any legal adviser would have at once advised her most strongly on no
account to sign. If this sort of irrationality is to be treated as conclusive
evidence of 'an aberration in the process of contract formation', then
of course all is well with Trebilcock's argument. But why must it be
assumed that rational people never do irrational things? Is it not one
of the commonest things in the world for perfectly rational normal
people to behave in ways which are manifestly contrary to their own
interest? Why people behave in this way is a matter for psychologists
rather than lawyers to explain. (Lawyers of course have great fun
with such people in the witness box, because lawyers often share the
economists' assumption that all behaviour must be rational, but in
practice they know prefectly well that people often do things against
their own interest for reasons which are unable to explain.)

A related weakness which is to be found in much economic writing
about contract law is the over-facile and casual assumptions about how
legal rules work in practice. Professor Kronman's well-known article
on specific performance, for example,[3] appears to be largely vitiated by
the fact that, in discussing the concept of 'uniqueness', he concentrates
almost entirely on contracts for the sale of chattels. This enables him

---

[1] [1974] 1 WLR 1308.
[2] [1978] 1 WLR 243.
[3] 45 *Un. Chi. L. Rev.* 351 (1978).

to suggest that there is little 'market' for such goods, that they are often very difficult to value, and that the promisor usually has every intention of performing his promise because he does not expect to receive other offers. Well, of course, we all know that a contract to sell a Rembrandt may be specifically enforceable, but I am willing to wager that nine out of ten decrees for specific performance in England concern contracts for the sale or lease of houses or other buildings. So far as I can see, the empirical assumptions so casually made about contracts for unique goods are just inapplicable to contracts for the sale of houses for which there is an extensive market and (usually) a reasonably ascertainable market price—or at least a range within which the market price can be ascertained to fall. Moreover, the suggestion that a contract to sell a house is specifically enforceable because the vendor does not expect to receive other offers looks preposterous: surely it is just the reverse. Kronman also assumes rather casually that decrees of specific performance involve more legal costs of enforcement because of supervision problems and the like. This again is just wrong. In England, at least, it is usually simpler, quicker, and cheaper to obtain a decree of specific performance of a contract for the sale of a house than to obtain damages for breach of a contract to sell goods.

There are far too many of these sweeping empirical or legal assumptions which seem highly debatable to the English lawyer. Others not so far mentioned, which can be identified in the pages of *The Economics of Contract Law*, include for instance the suggestion by Priest (p. 174) that it is less costly for consumer buyers than for merchants to reject goods for breach of contract (but what happens if the buyer has started to use the goods?); Posner's suggestion that finders of lost property are more likely to return it if a reward is offered (but since the value of the property is likely to exceed that of any reward by an order of magnitude, why should anyone tempted to keep the goods be swayed by the prospect of a reward?); the suggestion (pp. 125-6) that well-drillers who fail to complete a well because they strike rock will be more careful next time if they are held strictly liable (rather than simply write in an exclusion clause); and the truly remarkable suggestion that if a person who knows that he has a lower than average expectation of life takes a job without telling his employer, his estate may be liable for damages for not performing his work in the event of his death (p. 125).

The economic analysis made by writers on damages also often seems to suffer from the over-ready assumption that breach of contract is a one-off affair, and that the purpose of the law is to provide a sufficient incentive to encourage the potential contract breaker not to breach if, by doing so, he would cause a loss *in the particular case* which can be more cheaply avoided by not breaching. Economists who have written about the criminal law have been quick to observe that only a small proportion of criminals are usually charged and convicted; they argue, therefore (as Bentham did), that the punishment must be multiplied by the probability of being convicted if it is to be an effective deterrent. Surely there are many contract situations where similar considerations apply. A manufacturer of a drug (say) puts on the market a dangerous or defective product. Many consumers suffer losses as a result, but probably only a small minority will sue or claim damages (either directly, where permissible, or through the retailer where the doctrines of privity so require). In such cases it would seem that the general levels of expectation and reliance damages are quite inadequate to encourage the manufacturer to spend sufficient on safety to minimize the aggregate social costs. So perhaps exemplary damages (or conceivably, in appropriate circumstances, restitutionary recovery) would be more economically efficient for some such cases. *Jarvis* v. *Swan Tours*[1] is perhaps a case which could be explained along these lines, although, of course, the theory of English law denies exemplary damages in most such cases.

2. Is the Expectation Damages Rule Efficient?

This last point leads to a further issue which we now need to look at with some care. It is clear that much of the theory being drawn upon by writers on economic issues in contract law appears to be utilized to bolster up the sagging structure of clasical contract theory. Now one of the key points in the causes of the decline of classical contract theory has been the difficulty of justifying the enforcement of the wholly executory contract under the terms of that theory; and, equally, the difficulty of justifying the award of expectation rather than reliance damages as a general rule, and more particularly, where there has been no reliance suffered or benefit conferred. It might therefore have been hoped that some serious attempt would be made to see if economic analysis can offer any better explanation of legal doctrine on these points. Unfortunately, little has so far been written specifically on these questions.

[1] [1973] QB 233. But for a different explanation of this case (that the law protects the 'consumer surplus' of the plaintiff) see Harris, Ogus, and Phillips, 'Contract Remedies and the Consumer Surplus', 95 *Law Q. Rev.* 581 (1979).

General attempts to justify the award of expectation damages for breach of contract by law-and-economics writers do not appear to have been so far very successful. Posner, for instance, says in a very brief discussion,[1] that expectation damages are necessary because an award of pure reliance losses would not be sufficient to deter the promisor from breaching his contract in cases where it would be inefficient to do so. But the (hypothetical) example he gives is palpably weak.

Suppose [writes Posner] A contracts to sell B for $100,000 a machine that is worth $110,000 to B, i.e., that would yield him a profit of $10,000. Before delivery C comes to A and offers him $109,000 for the machine promised B. A would be tempted to breach were he not liable to B for B's loss of expected profit. Given that measure of damages, C will not be able to induce a breach of A's contract with B unless he offers A more than $110,000, thereby indicating that the machine really is worth more to him than to B. The expectation rule thus assures that the machine ends up where it is most valuable.

But since in this example B has contracted to pay $100,000 for the machine expecting to make $10,000 profit out of it, it seems reasonable to assume that when C offers $109,000 for the machine he expects to make a similar profit. And if he does, then of course the machine is worth more to C than to B; yet the expectation damages rule means that A has an incentive to deliver the machine to B, so C will not get the machine.

In any event, this discussion, and also that of Barton in a well-known article,[2] appear (so far as I understand them) to assume, as their starting-point, that the promisee's full expectations deserve protection. Once this assumption is made, they then try to demonstrate that the expectation damages rule (plus the mitigation rule and other qualifications of it) produce the right degree of incentive on the promisor: he will perform, or breach and pay damages, according to whichever is the most efficient. But these writings do not assist in helping us to determine whether the basic assumption of the law—that the plaintiff's full expectations should be protected—is itself sound.

Much economic writing in this area takes as its basic assumption the view that free and voluntary exchange must be to the advantage of the parties, absent third party effects. If two parties here and now want to make a simultaneous exchange, if S wants to exchange his orange for

---

[1] *Economic Analysis of Law* (2nd edn. 1977), p. 90; compare Polinsky, *An Introduction to Law and Economics* (1983) who argues that the expectation damages rule is sometimes efficient and sometimes not.

[2] 'The Economic Basis of Damages for Breach of Contract', 1 *J. Leg. St.* 277 (1972).

10p, and B wants to exchange his 10p for S's orange, the argument that both parties gain from the exchange seems self-evident. This was what the classical economists had in mind when they talked of 'freedom of contract'. They assumed and vigorously argued that the law should not *prohibit* people from making free and voluntary exchanges because such a prohibition would manifestly prevent them from maximizing their utility. It was this same belief in freedom of contract which was taken over and developed by the lawyers in the first half or three quarters of the nineteenth century. But modern contract law has very little to do with simultaneous exchanges. Indeed, contracts are traditionally defined by lawyers in terms of agreements or mutual promises, and not in terms of exchange at all. To the contract lawyer, the typical contract, or at least the conceptual paradigm of contract (as we saw in Essay 2), appears to be the wholly executory contract, entered into by mutual promises, for future performance. I have argued elsewhere that this paradigm is itself the heritage of nineteenth-century ideas about the will as the source of human obligations, and of classical economic theory in so far as that theory stressed the importance of free choice in maximizing utility. What I propose to do now is to look at the enforcement of executory contracts to see whether the economic arguments relating to simultaneous exchange continue to hold good.

One simple argument needs to be considered first, perhaps, because its correctness is taken for granted by most economists writing in this area. The argument is that since the law permits but does not require anyone to make executory contracts, it must be assumed that when anyone chooses to make such a contract he is necessarily better off. If he did not think he would be better off, he would, of course, refrain from making any such commitment but would arrange his affairs in some other way, for example, he would make a non-binding agreement, or he would simply wait until the time comes, and then make a simultaneous exchange. Conversely, if the law did not permit people to make binding executory contracts, this would restrict the choices open to them and bias their decisions in favour of simultaneous exchanges, when they would perhaps prefer to make future commitments. Nobody is, it seems, made worse off by a law which permits the making of executory contracts: nobody has to make such contracts, while those who wish to do so are afforded the facility. Thus when the law makes provision for binding executory contracts this seems a perfect (and rare) example of a Pareto-optimal move. Executory contracts are highly efficient.

Unfortunately, there are problems with this argument, powerful as it seems at first sight. First of all, it will be observed how efficiency is simply defined (as elsewhere in economics) as a maximization of free choice. The more choices we have, the more efficient our society, even if the choice is (for instance) a choice to smoke, take drugs, become an alcoholic, or blow all our capital by eating the seed corn. Presumably, on this view, even the choice to enter into a contract of slavery might be binding if it was truly voluntary, as would a Faustian bargain to sell one's soul to the devil. The slavery example might be met by attempting to argue that to become a slave one has to abandon one's right to exercise free choice in the future, and therefore slavery would not maximize freedom of choice in the long run. But this will not do, because the abandonment of the right to choose in the future is exactly paralleled by the results of entering into any future commitment. A contract, once made, prevents the promisor from making choices which are inconsistent with that contract in the future. The difference between slavery and other contracts is purely a matter of degree. If we assume that a rational person is able to decide now what he is likely to want in the future, and whether a present price offered to him now is worth the future commitment, then there is no reason why we should distinguish between any ordinary contract and a contract of slavery.

The truth is that this argument from free choice just will not work. It will not work because it assumes that choices and preferences remain the same. As we saw in Essay 6, there seems no reason why any person who believes in maximizing free choice should not wish to respect the choice of a contracting party to withdraw from a contract after he has made it, rather than to insist that his original choice to enter into the contract remains binding on him. So even a person who believes that efficiency means the maximization of free choice need not support a legal regime which enables someone to deprive himself of choice by exercising a choice.

Let us try a slightly different tack. Suppose that efficiency is taken to mean, not the maximization of free choice, but something like the maximization of wealth, as Posner seems to assume it to mean. I will not inquire too closely into what this 'wealth' means, and for present purposes we can rest content woith Posner's idea that, roughly speaking, efficiency requires that property should end up in the hands of those who value it most, that is, who would be willing to pay most for it.[1] Can it now be demonstrated that a law of executory contract is

[1] See Posner, *The Economics of Justice*, chs. 3-4 (1981). Compare Dworkin, 'Is Wealth a Value?', 9 *J. Leg. St.* 191 (1980).

efficient? The answer to this question will require a fairly extended analysis.

I will take a simple case, where S contracts to sell an orange to B for 10p, and B contracts to buy it at that price. The agreement is that the contract is to be performed on both sides tomorrow. Because this is a free and voluntary agreement we can assume that S values the orange at less than 10p, otherwise he would not sell it for that price. Let us assume he values it at 8p, which means that he would be willing to sell it at any price exceeding that sum. B, on the other hand, must obviously value it at more than 10p otherwise he would not pay 10p for it. Let us assume that B values it at 12p. Clearly a simultaneous exchange now will improve the position of both parties. S gets 10p instead of an orange which is worth only 8p to him, and B gets an orange worth 12p to him, for only 10p.

Let us now assume that when the time for performance arrives, S refuses to deliver the orange. Why does he do this? There are several possible reasons, but one very common reason for such a refusal would be that S now feels the orange is worth a different amount from the value he originally placed upon it. This may be due partly, or entirely, to a change of taste, of valuation on S's own part; but it may also be due to a change in the market price for oranges, which makes S feel that he is letting the orange go too cheaply at 10p. For present purposes, it is immaterial which of these is the explanation. We need now to consider a number of different possibilities.

No Transaction Costs
1. Assume that, at the time for performance, S thinks the orange is worth to him 11p. The efficient solution to the case is still that an exchange should be made, because B values the orange at 12p, thus more highly than S. Assume, first, that S is legally liable on the contract he has made. The result is that S is faced with a choice. He can deliver the orange (now worth 11p to him) and receive the price of 10p, thus losing 1p overall. Alternatively he can refuse to deliver, and pay damages in lieu. Damages, according to normal principles, will reflect the value of B's lost expectations. Since he valued the orange at 12p and contracted to buy it for 10p, his expected profit was 2p. Thus he should recover 2p damages. So if S has to pay damages, he will have to pay more than he loses if he performs the contract. S will, therefore, deliver the orange, which is the efficient result. So the result here seems to

favour the imposition of legal liability on the assumption that there are no transaction costs involved.

2. Suppose, however, that there is no legal liability for breach of an executory contract, retaining for the moment our other assumption of no transaction costs. Obviously, S will, in the first instance, refuse to deliver the orange, because he values it more highly than the contract price. However, as B still values the orange more highly than S does (12p against 11p), the chances are that B will raise his offer, and that a bargain can still be struck somewhere between 12p and 11p. It is still profitable to both parties to carry through the exchange (for instance) at 11½p. The orange will therefore end up with B, and the efficient solution is again arrived at.

3. We now need to vary our factual assumptions somewhat, while still retaining our other assumption of no transaction costs. Suppose that S refuses to deliver the orange to B because he has revalued it at 13p, that is, S values the orange even more highly than B at the date fixed for performance of the contract. If there is liability for breach of the executory contract, S is faced with the same choice as before. To breach involves paying 2p in damages to B; but S will retain an orange worth now 13p, so that his net assets after paying damages will be 11p. If, however, he performs, he delivers an orange and receives the price of only 10p. Plainly, he will breach. Equally plainly this is the efficient result because it means the orange remains in the hands of the person who values it most.

4. If there is no liability for breach of an executory contract, the result will be the same. S clearly will not deliver the orange, and in this situation B will not raise his price; or at least, he cannot raise it high enough to enable a new bargain to be struck. So again, the orange will remain with S, and this again is the efficient result.

Transaction Costs Considered

We now need to consider what happens to these examples when the real world of transaction costs is taken into account.

1. I return first to the case where S has revalued the orange to 11p, which is above the contract price, but below the value placed upon it by B. If there is legal liability for breach of an executory contract, then, as we saw before, the efficient result is that A should deliver the orange, which is what would happen absent transaction costs. What transaction costs are likely to be involved? We may assume that there are no transaction costs in the actual performance by S of his duty to deliver.

(Of course, there will normally be performance costs, but these are already taken account of in the price fixed for the exchange.) There will, however, be legal costs if S breaches and B has to resort to litigation, or the threat of litigation, in order to extract from S his damages. Unfortunately it is impossible to say, in the abstract, what the effect of those legal costs will be in the case under discussion, because these costs will tend to weight the result of S's choice both for and against the efficient solution. On the one hand, if S is sued and loses, he will have to pay both the damages and heavy legal costs, doubly heavy because these costs, under the English system, will be his own plus a large proportion of B's costs as well.[1] Fear of this result will naturally bias S's decision towards performance, which is the efficient solution. But legal transaction costs are more complex than this. Going to law is rarely a simple matter. Proving the facts and securing a legal verdict usually involve uncertainties. In addition, even if B wins and is awarded costs against S, this award will not normally cover all his legal expenses, but only a proportion of them—commonly about two-thirds. If B's lost profit is less than the third of the likely costs which will be irrecoverable, B will have no incentive to sue at all. S and B will both know this. One result will be to bias B towards writing off his lost profit, rather than going to law at all. Another result will be that S will be more likely to refuse to perform, calculating correctly that B will not sue because of the uncertainties, and also the rules as to costs.

The net result therefore is nothing like as determinate as it should be according to legal theory. There is no way of knowing whether in the abstract, given the uncertainties and costs of litigation, to what extent a legal remedy for breach of an executory contract actually forwards the efficient solution in this sort of case.

2. Suppose, next, that there is no rule of legal liability for breach of an executory contract, and S refuses to deliver because he has revalued the orange at 11p. As we saw earlier, the efficient solution, if B values the orange at 12p, is still for the orange to end up in B's hands, and absent transaction costs, that would probably happen. But transaction

---

[1] I leave out of account small claims which have to be dealt with by arbitration, under the County Court Rules, where costs are not normally awarded at all. But it must be borne in mind that if no costs are awarded (and this is the normal American practice) the law provides no direct incentive whatever to perform a contract, after the other side has performed. As Leff once said, 'Under the American law of contracts, after the other party has fully performed his obligations it is absolutely irrational for you fully to perform yours.' (*The Economics of Contract Law*, p. 175.) It should be added that the purpose of this remark was probably to make a point about the economists' use of the word 'rational'.

costs in this case will make the efficient solution less probable. If there is no liability rule, B can only attempt to persuade S to sell by raising his offer. There may be high transaction costs here, especially if this is a bilateral monopoly situation which it may well be. S and B may fail to strike a new bargain, with consequent loss to both. But suppose there is legal liability, the result will be the same as in the previous case (1), that is, fear of being sued may bias S towards performance (the efficient solution) but uncertainty and costs may deter B from suing, and as S will know of this possibility, will bias S against performance. One cannot be sure in advance which way the bias will work in any particular case.

Can it be argued that legal liability will at least make it more likely that the parties will be able to strike a new bargain for which there is room on our present figures? In practice, of course, a breach of contract is likely to lead to renegotiation and compromise far more frequently than it is likely to lead to actual litigation. Perhaps if there were no legal liability, the parties would be less likely to renegotiate. But once again, this is purely speculative. In the absence of legal liability, it is much more likely that S will be willing to explain clearly to B why he refuses to deliver, namely that he thinks the price too low, and will only sell for above 11p. If S is willing to be frank about this, a new bargain can readily be struck at $11\frac{1}{2}$p.[1] Where S is under the threat of legal liability he is, *per contra*, likely to conceal the reason for his breach, and invent other possible reasons which might be tenable as defences in a legal suit. Such pretence would make renegotiation more difficult. It is therefore impossible to argue in advance that legal liability in such a case forwards the efficient solution. Whether it does so or not will depend on the circumstances of the particular case.

3. Let us now reconsider the case where S revalues the orange to 13p and inject transaction costs into the example. As we have seen, the efficient solution here is that S should retain the orange. If there is legal liability then, absent transaction costs, S will retain the orange and pay damages of 2p. But given transaction costs, what will happen? The

---

[1] It will be noted that this is very much what happens in transactions for the sale of houses where the seller 'gazumps' after the initial, non-binding, agreement is made; that is, the seller, having perceived that the value of his house is greater than he originally thought, usually offers to continue with the transaction if the buyer is prepared to increase his price. Despite the bad name which gazumping has, it is far from evident that this result is less efficient than if the parties were already legally bound. The real problem with present procedures is that the seller is free to gazump even after the buyer has incurred substantial reliance costs.

answer is again unclear. If there is no uncertainty, it would obviously be in S's interest to pay the 2p on demand, and not wait to be sued; and that would be an efficient solution. But fear of being sued, the uncertainty of the law, and S's own ignorance of the law may well cause him to deliver the orange in lieu of paying the 2p. That would be irrational if S knew exactly what the position was, but litigation and the threat of it are rarely conducted in a wholly rational manner. In practice, it may be quite unclear what B's claim for damages really amounts to; he may start by claiming either the orange or some huge sum in damages, and S may have little means of knowing whether B's claim is justified or not. Thus there may be an over-incentive for S to deliver the orange—the inefficient solution.

Moreover, in this particular instance, the moral effect of the law almost certainly adds its force to the less efficient solution. Businessmen may be indifferent between performance and paying (or receiving) damages—though even that seems exceedingly implausible in practice—but lawyers and judges do not generally reason in this sort of way. They tend to regard it as morally wrong to breach a contract; they bring morality into play perhaps as an additional way of securing compliance with the legal norms. But that tends to produce additional pressure to perform, rather than to pay damages in lieu.

4. The last case concerns the same fact situation as the previous once, but assumes no legal liability. Transaction costs seem to make no difference to this situation. Whatever costs there may be, the result will be efficient. S will simply refuse to deliver, and he cannot be sued for his refusal. The result is efficient because he keeps the orange which he now values more highly than B.

Thus of these four possible cases in which transaction costs are taken into account—and these are, in the end, the only ones that matter—the only case in which it is quite clear that the efficient solution will always be arrived at is the fourth, where S has revalued the goods above the value placed upon them by B, and no legal liability exists. In the other three cases the conclusion is indeterminate. To impose legal liability for breach of an executory contract thus seems to give us a rule the efficiency of which is quite uncertain, while to abolish legal liability for breach of such contracts would give us a rule which clearly produces an efficient result at least in some cases, and whose effect in the other cases remains uncertain.

3. A Right to Change one's Mind?

All this seems a pretty flimsy foundation for the belief that economics provides solid arguments for the moral and legal rules underlying executory contracts. But the argument does not end there, because the above analysis can be extended to show that the binding force of executory contracts is not even required as a matter of fairness, at any rate on the ground that it is fair to protect reasonable expectations. That may seem strongly counter-intuitive. In the above example, B has agreed to buy an orange for 10p and S refuses to deliver because he now thinks the orange is worth 11p. In order to get the orange (worth 12p to B) he will have to raise his price to 11½p. Most people brought up on the conventional moral and legal view of the binding nature of 'deals' would find the result offensive. Of course, as economists insist, that is irrelevant to the question of efficiency, but it may be suggested that even the unfairness of the result is arguable. The result is really only unfair if one first assumes that S has no right to change his mind after making the deal. If S has this right, then B's expectations should have been discounted to take account of the possibility that S might change his mind. If B correctly calculates the proportion of sellers who will change their minds between making a deal and performing it, and is able also to calculate correctly the amount by which these sellers will revalue the goods they are selling, the discounted expectations which he eventually arrives at ought to match exactly the ½p profit which he now expects to make on his exchange with S. So what is unjust about the result? B's expectations are still fully realized.

Or again, B has agreed to buy the orange for 10p but S refuses to deliver, having now made up his mind that it is worth 13p. As B thinks the orange is worth 12p at most, he will not be able to persuade S to sell at all; and in the absence of any legal liability on A, B will get neither the orange nor damages. Is this unfair? It seems so at first sight; because B's expectations have been disappointed, and it seems that he ought to have some remedy for that. But if S had the right to change his mind, B ought not to entertain the expectation that S would perform without allowing some discount for the fact that people do exercise their right to change their minds. If B correctly calculates the appropriate discount, then his expectations (at least averaged over his transactions) will not be disappointed. So the notion that it is morally wrong to break an executory contract, and that the promisee has a moral right to be recouped for his disappointed expectations seems to be based on virtually the same fallacy as the economic argument. Both sets of arguments start by assuming that a person who makes a deal has no right to change his mind. If he did have such a right, his contract or promise would have to be read as conditional, as subject to the possible exercise of the right, and neither economic nor fairness arguments seem to require that the right be given up.

The result will stick in many throats. If so, it may be that this is because most of us have intuitively made the value judgment (or the decision as to the allocation of a right to change one's mind) that changing one's mind after a deal is somehow not a 'good thing'. But this intuition may be faulty. Changing your mind imposes costs on other people, and these are the costs which the normal moral and legal views about binding agreements are designed to avoid. But not being able to change your mind imposes costs too; and these costs are habitually ignored by moral and legal views about binding agreements. Of course some people are much better at planning (their lives or their businesses) than others and therefore at making decisions which they are unlikely to want to change; other people are not very good at this, and constantly make decisions which they later regret. A moral or legal code which recognizes the prima facie binding force of an executory contract thus favours the first group at the expense of the second. It is, in effect, an 'entitlement' decision, of very much the same kind as decisions about the allocation of property entitlements. Modern laws and commercial and social practices which allow consumers the right to extricate themselves from what would otherwise be binding executory contracts are thus of a redistributive character. They are redistributing these property-like entitlements from those who are good at planning to those who are less good at planning.

Of course, it will immediately be argued that imposing costs on other people is one thing, imposing costs on oneself is another. The legal and moral systems ought to discourage the former, but have no need to discourage the latter. But there are two answers to this. The first is that the nature of the costs may differ in the two cases. In the very simple example I have been discussing, I have assumed that B has not suffered any reliance cost or any opportunity cost as a result of S's change of mind—or rather I have simply not taken account of this possibility. I propose to continue to leave that possibility out of account. If B had suffered a cost through passing by an opportunity of buying oranges from someone else because he expected S to perform his contract, and if B can now no longer obtain oranges from that source of supply, then S has indeed caused a loss to B, and such a possibility might change the entire picture. I do not propose to discuss that possibility, and I confine myself in this essay entirely to the case of the executory contract, where nothing has happened between the making and the date for the performance of the contract, except that S has changed his mind about the value of the orange. B had 10p when the contract was made and he still has 10p after it is breached. His complaint is that he had expected to have an orange worth (to him) 12p. His grievance is that his expectations have been disappointed. S, however, actually has in his possession an orange which he now values at 13p. If he delivers it, he receives in exchange 10p. His loss will be an actual loss of utility or value. There is surely a case for saying that his actual loss is more serious than the expectation loss of which B is complaining. Of course, to compare an actual loss and an expectation loss in this way seems to violate that most serious of all economic taboos—it requires us to make an interpersonal comparison of utility. But the award of damages always requires us to do that anyhow. Any holding that damages should be awarded for breach of contract rests on the supposition that we do not do more harm to the utility of the defendant by taking the damages from him, than the value of the utility which will be obtained by the plaintiff: if this were not the case we could never be sure that the award of damages would not impose social costs in excess of any benefits it may serve.

But the second answer to this point is equally important. It is wrong to say that S, by changing his mind, has imposed the loss (or cost, if cost it is) on B, while S has only himself to blame for the cost which he has imposed on himself. For the truth is that each of these costs is the result of a combination of factors—S's change of mind on the one hand, plus B's expectations on the other. And if we were to contemplate abolition of the binding force of executory contracts, this would be still more apparent. For in that case it would surely be clear that the loss or cost to B would not be due to S's acts (certainly not to S's 'fault') but to B's own over-sanguine expectations.

The conclusion is that the economic or fairness arguments I have been considering simply cannot justify the binding force of executory contracts. The usual assumptions that are made about the efficiency of executory contracts (in so far as they are distinguished from partly performed or partly relied-upon contracts) depend upon the belief that executory contracts are made to allocate the risks of changes in events between the making and the performance of the contract. No doubt this is often the case with business contracts, and perhaps there are adequate arguments in such a case for supposing these to be efficient, where the whole purpose of the contract is to allocate these risks. In this situation, there may be sufficient ground to suppose that the person who acquires the 'bad' risks is better able to distribute them, or eliminate them altogether; and the distribution or elimination of such risks may itself eliminate uncertainty, and thus be of real social value.

But in the example I have been discussing this is not the situation, and there is absolutely no reason to assume it always is the situation. Parties who make contracts today for performance tomorrow may not be doing so in order to allocate risks at all. They may be doing so because they cannot perform today, although they would if they could. In my example, perhaps S does not have his orange available, or B does not have his money available today. Even commercial contracts that have to be performed over a time span because of their inherent nature are not necesarily entered into in order to allocate these risks. A contract by which a customer opens a current bank account must be performed over a period of time, but it is absurd to suggest that it is made in order to allocate the risks of changes in events, or change of mind, between making and performance. Indeed, contracts of this kind which are both simultaneous exchange contracts and contracts for future performance are often terminable at will, or on reasonable notice, and are thus not regarded as binding as to the future unperformed part. It seems that lawyers assume far too readily that contracts made for future performance must be designed to allocate risks, but this is not necessarily the case at all. And even if we do assume that in these cases the parties make the contract in order to allocate the risk of change of mind, it is hard to see how or why it is efficient to hold the parties to their allocation if there should in fact be a change of mind *before* any reliance or performance occurs.

4. Abolition of the Executory Contract?
It might seem, then, that the case for the binding force of executory contracts is very dubious; and we may need to consider seriously whether it should be abolished, except (at any rate) for those cases which clearly are genuine risk-allocation devices. What would happen if we did abolish it? The first question which would immediately arise would be whether we should at the same time abolish the right to claim expectation damages for breach of a relied-upon or partly performed contract. If we did not do this, then the result would be that a trivial act of reliance (or some trivial benefit rendered in part performance) would have the very drastic result of entitling the aggrieved party to

full expectation damages if a breach thereafter occurred; whereas until that moment, no liability at all would exist. Clearly, this would be an uncomfortable result, and might well lead to all sorts of inefficiencies—parties would be impelled to invent, or go through, unnecessary and perhaps even fictitious acts of reliance or part performance where they really did want to bind each other by a full commitment.

But there are two other possible reasons against any general abolition of the executory contract which need to be adverted to. First, proof of reliance will often be very difficult, especially where it is of a negative character, for example where the promisee claims that he could have bought (or sold) elsewhere if he had not been relying on a promise of performance by the promisor. Second, an additional problem arises from the fact that one of the commonest ways in which a promisee relies on a promise is by entering into further contracts with third parties—who may, of course, also rely on *these* contracts by entering into contracts with fourth parties, and so on. If only relied-upon contracts were enforceable it would not be easy to know what to do with cases of this nature. If the third party has not relied on the second contract, then he would presumably be unable to hold *that* contract to be binding; that in turn would mean that entering into the second contract would not create any reliance losses which could be recovered under the first contract. But the result of that would be that nobody would know whether the first contract is really 'binding' without examining whether the third party has relied on the second contract; and that in turn might require investigation of a third contract and so on. It can hardly be denied that all this would be exceedingly inconvenient and, in a common-sense sort of way, highly inefficient.

However, both of these practical difficulties would largely be met by throwing onto the promisor a heavy onus of proof: the law could simply require him to disprove all reliance as a condition for escaping from liability on his contract. We are still left, therefore, with no apparent reason for enforcing executory contracts—except in clear risk-allocation cases. Perhaps there are other good reasons which at present escape me, for recognizing the binding force of executory contracts (and awarding expectation damages) in many ordinary cases of breach of commercial contracts, though I confess I am still searching for an adequate theoretical justification for doing so, not just for its own sake, but in order that we should be able more clearly to separate out those cases where it is appropriate to do so, from those cases where it is not appropriate.

I do not think we can just assume that businessmen expect the law to protect their full expectation interests when they enter into contracts. The empirical researches of Stewart Macaulay in America,[1] and of Hugh Beale and Tony Dugdale in England,[2] found considerable evidence that, at least in manufacturing industry, businessmen do not generally count on getting expectation damages in the event of cancellation. I know of no hard evidence to rebut this research, though I am willing to believe that there are some commercial contexts in which a belief in expectation damages is the norm. Those who deal on commodity markets—or stock or currency markets—certainly know the law and assume they are entitled to have their expectations realized. But these markets are rather a special case in which the reliance measure and the expectation measure of damages would normally be identical anyhow.

For reasons which should be apparent from Essay 2 I am not nearly so enamoured of expectation damages as most contract lawyers, and there certainly are many cases in my view in which expectation damages are quite inappropriate. It is, for instance, very doubtful to me whether there is any real case for awarding expectation damages in many cases where the defendant made a serious mistake as to the transaction, even if the mistake is not such as would or should acquit him of all liability. To hold a person liable for damages in this situation cannot be justified on the ground that the transaction is prima facie a value-maximizing transaction, as even Posner acknowledges.[3] It can only be justified—as Posner does justify it—on the ground that a person who induces another to enter into a contract in such circumstances is misleading the other, and ought to be liable as though he had committed a tort. This is thus to equate the actions of a party who mistakenly induces another to contract on terms which he did not intend, with the liability of a misrepresentor. But of course, if this liability is to be treated as a liability in tort, the damages ought not to be expectation damages— or, at any rate, a completely new case needs to be made for expectation damages in such circumstances, just as it does whenever such damages are claimed in tort.

An excellent example of this problem is provided by a recent Court of Appeal decision of great general interest, *Centrovincial Estates plc* v.

---

[1] 'Non-contractual Relations in Business: A Preliminary Study', 28 *Am. Soc. Rev.* 55 (1963).

[2] 'Contracts between Businessmen: Planning and the Use of Contractual remedies', 2 *Br. J. of Law and Soc.* 45 (1975).

[3] *Economic Analysis of Law*, pp 71-2.

Merchant Investors Assurance Co. Ltd.[1] The plaintiffs in this case were landlords of an office building, let to the defendants, at a yearly rent of some £68,000, subject to review from 25 December 1982. The rent review clause provided for the new rent to be fixed by reference to the current market rental value, but the minimum rent was to be the original figure of £68,000 odd. On 22 June 1982, the plaintiffs' agents sent to the defendants a letter proposing a new current market rental value of £65,000 which, as the court said, seemed somewhat surprising as that figure was less than the minimum stipulated in the lease. The next day the defendants' agent wrote a letter to the plaintiffs in which they accepted this offer, but immediately on receipt of this letter the plaintiffs told the defendants that the figure of £65,000 was a mistake. The plaintiffs sought a declaration that no binding agreement had been made by this exchange of letters. It was common ground that if the defendants knew or ought to have known of the mistake, then there was indeed no binding contract. But as the defendants contested this fact, the plaintiffs also contended that even if the defendants had no reason for knowing of the mistake, the contract ought not to be held binding, on the ground that their offer had not been relied upon or acted upon in any way by the defendants.

It will be seen that this case raises in a very neat form the issue discussed above. If the contract was binding from the outset, despite the plaintiffs' mistake, then the defendants expectations were entitled to be fully protected by the law—indeed they would manifestly have obtained a decree of specific performance in such circumstances and have thus actually enjoyed the renewed lease at the rental which they claimed that they had accepted in good faith, or, more strictly, at the minimum rental. The Court of Appeal rejected the plaintiffs' arguments, and held that—if the defendants were indeed in good faith—then they were entitled to enforce the contract despite the mistake, and the fact that they had not relied upon or acted upon the offer was immaterial. The reasoning of the court was very much in the classical tradition: the distinction between an executory and a relied-upon contract was rejected as irrelevant, the doctrine of consideration was treated as a wholly technical requirement, meaning only that the offer had to be accepted by a counter-promise, and apparent intent was wholly equated with actual intent.

This decision appears to me to be difficult to justify, and the difficulty is accentuated if the case is for a moment approached as a tort problem.

[1] (1983) Com LR 158.

The plaintiffs' agent, in making the mistake as to the rent, acted in a way which in all probability was negligent. Suppose the defendants had sued the plaintiffs for their economic loss due to this negligence. There can be no doubt that if the plaintiffs were in principle liable for this negligence, the defendants would nevertheless have obtained no damages because they had not acted upon the misrepresentation. A misrepresentation inducing another party to enter into a contract is a tortious misrepresentation, for all that it is followed by a contract. Why then should it make a difference that the negligence consisted of the making of a contractual offer? An offer can be accepted, and can create a binding contract at once, because (it is assumed) there are fairness or efficiency arguments in favour of this result where the parties have made a genuine deal or bargain. Do these arguments still hold where there was no genuine bargain, but the contract is held binding on the 'objective test' principle? It is hard to see why it should. The plaintiffs never intended to make the contract at the rent which the defendant is now entitled to pay, and their liability cannot be rested upon their will, their intention, their agreement or their promise. It is rested upon the fact that they gave the appearance of agreeing or promising, that is, that they misled the defendant. But then we are back to the point that the real gravamen of the defendants' complaint was that they had been misled by a negligent misrepresentation, upon which they had not acted.

This case can perhaps be contrasted with another recent Court of Appeal decision, *Peyman* v. *Lanjani*,[1] in which the court did very clearly distinguish between apparent and real consent, albeit in a slightly different context. In this case the court held that a party to a contract induced by fraud may either affirm it, with full knowledge of the facts and of his rights, or he may give the other party to believe by his conduct that he is so affirming it. The former (a genuine subjective affirmation) appears to be binding without more; the latter (a kind of objective—tort-like—affirmation) is only binding when acted upon or relied upon by the other party. If people are to be bound by bare consent, then this result does at least ensure that it is a real consent that binds them.

But surely, there are no economic or other grounds which can justify the imposition of a contractual-type liability in the *Centrovincial* case. So this result seems clearly wrong unless it can be adequately explained why the law cannot distinguish cases of genuine mistake from cases in which the defendant wishes to exculpate himself dishonestly by pleading

[1] [1984] 3 All ER 704.

that he made a mistake when he did not, or why it should be thought that the law should make no inquiry into such cases because of the possible cost and complexity of doing so. These arguments are often made in this sort of context, but they are not attractive as arguments of fairness, nor does there seem any way of measuring their economic strength.

As to the fairness point, it is far from clear why we cannot meet the problem by throwing the burden of proof fairly and squarely—and no doubt firmly—on the defendant to prove the mistake to the satisfaction of the court. This is, after all, the sort of burden thrown on the defendant in the comparable case of mistake which is held to justify rectification of a written contract. And as to the economic argument, it can only be said that this is one of those arguments whose weight simply cannot be assessed. How can we possibly tell whether the cost to the legal system, and therefore to society, will be greater by enforcing executory contracts, or the award of expectation damages, in cases where there may have been some sort of mistake, or by allowing such pleas of mistake to be made in cases where there may be no adequate justification for the plea? I do not say the argument has no force; as I have indicated in Essay 5, any such argument is a formal argument and must have force. My difficulty is in trying to evaluate the weight we should allow the argument to have.

It should be appreciated that this argument about mistake may have much wider implications than it seems at first sight. For if the argument is accepted, it would follow that expectation damages should only be awarded where the defendant really did intend to assume liability for what has happened. Wherever events have turned out unexpectedly, or the defendant finds himself saddled with a liability he did not anticipate, he should only be liable for reliance damages, at any rate on these grounds. So (for instance) I now think that it is wrong that breach of an agent's warranty of authority should carry an entitlement to expectation damages except in the rare case where the agent knows that there is doubt as to his authority, and intends to assume the risk, or possibly where the consideration is actually enhanced because of the warranty.[1]

This latter possibility is suggested by examination of another case, the Canadian decision in *Sealand of the Pacific* v. *MacHaffie*.[2] In this case the defendant warranted that some building material would be

[1] See Essay 8, p. 209–10 and Essay 10, pp. 298–9.
[2] 51 DLR (3d) 702 (1974).

suitable to keep afloat the plaintiffs' marine acquarium which was in danger of sinking under its own weight. It turned out that this material was not suitable for the purpose, and that the job could only effectively be done by use of a much more expensive material. The plaintiffs obtained the traditional measure of damages for breach of warranty in this situation—that is the value of the 'promised performance', and thus (in effect) the right to the more expensive material for much below its market price. It is not evident to me that this is an appropriate measure of damages in such a case unless one can assume that the defendant really did promise *that* performance, that is, intended to take the risk that the material he was warranting would not be fit for its purpose. I find it improbable that he did intend to take that risk, because the truth seems to be simply that neither he nor the plaintiffs realized that there was such a risk, neither expected the material to fail of its purpose—and moreover, it was in a sense fortuitous that the only material which would have served the purpose was far more expensive. Hence the charge which the defendant made for his services probably included no 'premium' to cover this risk. So this was again a case in which the defendant's actions amounted to a misrepresentation—he misled the plaintiffs—rather than to an intentional assumption of risk.

I have not here considered the possibility that there may in some circumstances be adequate justification for protecting expectations on totally different grounds—on the sort of grounds that sometimes justify expectation damages in a tort action today. It is possible that there is sometimes sufficient justification for this (as for instance in *Ross* v. *Caunters*[1]) and no doubt a completely integrated account of the law of obligations—embracing tort as well as contract—would need to consider this possibility. But the issues involved are complex indeed, and I cannot pursue them here where my main focus of attention is the traditional justification for expectation damages in contract.

5. Expectation Damages and Specific Performance

I turn now to consider some arguments of a different character. Professor Waddams has argued that the expectation damages rule is appropriate and ought to be retained because of its relationship with the law relating to specific performance.[2] He begins by suggesting that the expectation damages rule lives fairly harmoniously with the remedy of specific performance, and that elimination of the expectation damages

[1] [1980] Ch. 297.
[2] 'The Modern Role of Contract Law', 8 *Can. Bus. LJ* 2 (1983-4).

remedy would introduce new tensions into the law here. Plaintiffs would be more inclined to seek, and perhaps courts would be more inclined to grant, decrees of specific performance if a plaintiff could not be assured of his right to expectation damages.

I do not find this a very persuasive argument. In the first place, specific performance today plays a fairly minor role in contract law and I would not easily be persuaded that the law of damages ought to be fashioned to harmonize with a remedy which is often of no relevance in practice. But I am, in any event, dubious about Professor Waddams's premiss here. Is it really the case that the remedy of specific performance harmonizes with the remedy of expectation damages? The answer surely is that sometimes it does and sometimes it does not. Consider, for instance, the remedies of the seller in a contract of sale of goods against a buyer who refuses to take delivery. The seller's action for the price is the equivalent of a decree of specific performance, but far from 'harmonizing' with the remedy of damages for non-delivery, the two remedies are in fact quite distinct. Indeed the law is caught up here in a severe tension between the two remedies, one of which is more favourable to the seller, and one to the buyer.

Then again, one of the attractions of specific performance to the party entitled to that remedy is that it seemingly enables the plaintiff to bypass the ordinary rules about damages which may be relevant in a particular case, for example rules about mitigation, rules about the date for assessing the damages, rules about penalties, and so on. Thus, far from harmony, here too there already exist major tensions between the two remedies.

Professor Waddams's next argument is that formal promises under seal which serve a useful social purpose in certain situations are already enforceable to the full value of the promise; it would, therefore, be anomalous (he says) if the law of informal contracts were to develop a different rule. Perhaps this would lead to a great increase in the use of seals for ordinary business contracts, thus introducing artificiality and fortuity into the law. But Professor Waddams seems to me to overlook the fact that even under the present law we effectively have two different rules applying to enforceable gratuitous promises. Those under seal are enforceable to their full extent, while those which are enforceable because of reliance will only be enforced to protect that reliance. Thus there is already a measure of coexistence between the expectation and the reliance rules in these cases and I see no reason why such coexistence could not also be workable in appropriate non-gratuitous cases.

6. Conclusion

At the end of the day I remain troubled and uncertain about the extent to which executory contracts should be enforced, and the extent to which the expectation damages measure is appropriate, both in wholly executory contracts (where it is, of course, the same as the rule that such contracts are binding in principle) and in partly performed or relied-upon contracts. I remain uncertain how far it would seriously interfere with the expectations of businesmen if expectation liability was confined to certain kinds of contracts, uncertain about the economic arguments for expectation damages and the binding force of executory contracts, uncertain whether it would make a great deal of difference to the law if unrelied-upon contracts were held not binding, so long only as a firm onus of proof of non-reliance was thrown on the party claiming to be free from liability. On the other hand, I feel convinced that, at least in many cases in which executory contracts are in theory binding today, they should not be so binding (for example against consumers) and that there are also many cases in which the defendant did not intend to undertake the liability which the law presently imposes on him, and in which it would be more appropriate if the liability were treated in the same way as a liability in tort.

8

Consideration: A Restatement

It is a constantly recurring phenomenon in all systems of law that generalizations drawn from antecedent experience become insufficient to do justice in the disputes of new times and become too narrow to explain decisions that are actually being made. We are at first tempted to say that the inconsistent decisions are wrong and that 'the law' is otherwise. But, if these 'wrong' decisions continue to seem just and are themselves followed as precedents, they make 'the law' in exactly the same way that former decisions made the former law. A new and corrected generalization is necessary and a new 'Restatement' of the law is in order. So it will always be.[1]

It is appropriate that this essay should be prefaced with a quotation from Professor Corbin's masterly survey of the law of contract, for the whole essay was originally inspired by Corbin's work, and although today, some fifteen years after it was first written, I wish to qualify my original ideas in some respects, the essay remains thoroughly Corbinian in intent. My chief purpose remains what it was fifteen years ago, to do what Corbin did for American law in the 1930s and to demonstrate that a close analysis of the actual decisions of the courts suggests that English law is in need of fundamental restatement. My theme is the same as Corbin's, namely that the conventional account of the 'doctrine of consideration' no longer accords with the law actually enforced in the courts. A few decisions out of harmony with an established current of otherwise harmonious principle can no doubt be explained away as anomalous, or inconsistent with 'pure' doctrine, or even as wrong; but when decision after decision cannot be reconciled with the traditional orthodox treatment of the law, it is time to take a close look at the orthodox treatment itself. The fact that our most distinguished and orthodox interpreter of the modern law of contract is driven to admit that the courts can 'invent' consideration—and still remain orthodox—itself seems an indication that there is something pretty strange going on.[2]

---

[1] Corbin on *Contracts* (revised edn., 1963), i. 533.

[2] See Professor G. H. Treitel's critique of my original Essay, 'Consideration: A Critical Analysis of Professor Atiyah's Fundamental Restatement', 50 *Australian LJ* 439 (1976), hereafter cited as 'A Critical Analysis'. For the idea of 'invented consideration', see below, p. 183.

1. The Nature and Purposes of Consideration

It is desirable to start by taking a preliminary look at the nature and purposes of the law relating to consideration. Although my principal purpose is to demonstrate by an actual examination of the cases that the conventional account of the law is in need of restatement, it is necessary to begin with a more general discussion. The purpose of this is simply to try to persuade the reader to examine the evidence set out below with an open mind and without preconceived ideas. This is particularly necessary in this area because the need for a restatement arises principally from the fact that for a very long time common lawyers have approached the law of consideration in the belief that there is a 'doctrine of consideration' which can be reduced to a set of fixed rules, and that these rules were arrived at by the courts over a period of time culminating in some sort of 'final' form or version towards the end of the nineteenth century.[1] Closely allied with this seems to be the assumption that the doctrine of consideration serves no rational or justifiable purposes, and that it consists simply of a series of highly technical and totally purposeless rules which must be applied blindly without asking what they are for. It really is essential to rid oneself of these two presuppositions. On the one hand, it is clear that the law has never had a 'final' or definitive version. It has, on the contrary, been continually developing up to the present day, and will no doubt go on developing in the future, in so far as it lies in the power of the courts to mould and adapt the law to changing circumstances and moral values. And on the other hand, even though the doctrine of consideration may sometimes seem to work unfairly, it does it injustice to regard the whole doctrine as irrational and purposeless.

The conventional statement of the doctrine of consideration is not perhaps as easily reduced to a simple set of rules as it is often assumed, but few would disagree with the following propositions. Firstly, a promise is not enforceable (if not under seal),[2] unless the promisor obtains some benefit or the promisee incurs some detriment in return for the promise. A subsidiary proposition, whose claim to be regarded as a part of the orthodox doctrine is perhaps less certain, is sometimes put forward,[3] namely that consideration must be of economic value. Secondly, in a bilateral contract the consideration for a promise is

---

[1] See, e.g., Holdsworth, *History of English Law*, viii. 34-48.

[2] Throughout this essay I ignore promises under seal.

[3] See e.g. Treitel, *Law of Contract*, 6th edn. (hereafter cited as Treitel, *Contract*), p. 66.

a counter-promise, and in a unilateral contract consideration is the performance of the act specified by the promisor. Thirdly, the law of contract only enforces bargains; the consideration must, in short, be (and perhaps even be regarded by the parties as) the 'price' of the promise. Fourthly, past consideration is not sufficient consideration. Fifthly, consideration must move from the promisee. Sixthly (and this is regarded as following from the first three propositions), the law does not enforce gratuitous promises. Seventhly, a limited exception to these propositions is recognized by the *High Trees*[1] principle which, however, only enables certain promises without consideration to be set up by way of defence.

More generally, it would, I think, be commonly agreed that there is such a concept as a 'doctrine of consideration'. This very phrase carries certain implications. In particular it implies that there is *one* doctrine, and *one* concept. The word 'consideration' is invariably used in the singular. Lawyers do not today inquire what are *the considerations* which lead a court to enforce a promise, but whether *there is* consideration. The word 'doctrine' also appears to carry certain implications. In this particular area of the law, it seems to carry the implication that the 'doctrine' is 'artificial', and has no rational foundation except possibly in so far as it may be argued that gratuitous promises should not necessarily be enforceable.

It is my purpose to suggest that the conventional account of the law is unsatisfactory, and that scarcely one of the propositions set out above accurately represents the law. But it is necessary to start by suggesting that one of the principal reasons for the present divergence between the conventional account of the law and its actual operation arises from the more general beliefs about the existence of a set of artificial and irrational rules termed the doctrine of consideration. The truth is that the courts have never set out to create a doctrine of consideration. They have been concerned with the much more practical problem of deciding in the course of litigation whether a particular promise in a particular case should be enforced. Since it is unthinkable that any legal system could enforce *all* promises it has always been necessary for the courts to decide which promises they would enforce. When the courts found a sufficient reason for enforcing a promise they enforced it; and when they found that for one reason or another it was undesirable to enforce a promise, they did not enforce it. It seems highly probable that when the courts first used the word 'consideration' they meant no more than

[1] [1947] KB 130.

that there was a 'reason' for the enforcement of a promise. If the consideration was 'good', this meant that the court found sufficient reason for enforcing the promise. All this is not to suggest that the law was ever unprincipled, or that judges ever decided cases according to personal or idiosyncratic views of what promises it was desirable to enforce. As always in the common law, it was the collective view of the judges, based largely on the conditions and moral values of the community, which prevailed over a period of time. The doctrine of precedent, then as now, was always available as an aid to the courts in deciding what promises to enforce.

The notion that consideration means a reason for the enforcement of a promise was largely borrowed in my original essay from Corbin, and although Professor Treitel has objected to this,[1] and insisted that it cannot just be asserted that this is what consideration means, it seems clear to me that it is both a historical and an analytical truth. I will not inquire further into the historical use of the term here,[2] but at least it must be admitted that in modern law the presence of consideration is a necessary condition for the enforceability of a promise, leaving aside promissory estoppel and other 'non-contractual' means of enforcement. To translate that into saying that consideration means a *reason* for the enforcement of a promise only requires us to make the assumption that the law is a rational enterprise. To assert that the law 'will not do A unless B' surely entails, if law is purposive in its nature, that the presence of B is a *reason* for doing A—unless (which can hardly be suggested here) it is merely a condition for the doing of A. Of course this does not carry the implication that the *reason* is always a good one; nor that sometimes the reason ought not to be outweighed by other reasons. But unless the presence of consideration is regarded, in general terms, as a reason for the enforcement of promises, the whole doctrine would have to be treated as mumbo-jumbo. Doubtless the law is sometimes irrational, but to treat a whole doctrine of the law as irrational implies both an extraordinary lack of faith in the intelligence of former judges, and an astonishing perversity in the erection of a system of precedent which requires that their decisions should be followed. I decline to make either of these assumptions.

Professor Treitel's critique of my original essay (and his textbook on

[1] See Treitel, 'A Critical Analysis'.

[2] See A.W.B. Simpson, *A History of the Common Law of Contract*, pp. 316-488 (1975); J. H. Baker, 'Origins of the "Doctrine" of Consideration', in *On the Laws and Customs of England: Essays in Honour of Samuel E. Thorne* ed. M. S. Arnold, T. A. Green and others (1981).

the *Law of Contract*) insists that the courts have power to 'invent' consideration, and that this ability is an important phenomenon which I have overlooked and which explains many otherwise puzzling things about the doctrine. I find this a difficult concept to grasp. Is an 'invented' consideration something different from a 'real' consideration or is it the same thing? If it is the same thing, then it is hard to see in what sense it is invented; and if it is not the same thing, then it either violates the rules of law, or it modifies them. Presumably Professor Treitel does not mean to suggest that when judges invent consideration they are defying the law and violating their judicial oaths, but if an invented consideration modifies the rules governing ordinary consideration, then an invented consideration becomes again an ordinary consideration, though the legal significance of the doctrine has now changed. The only other possibility that occurs to me is that the courts might use the concept of 'invented consideration' rather like an equitable or merciful dispensation from the ordinary law, but it is unthinkable that judges should behave in this way. They have no power to invent a consideration in one case and refuse to do so in a relevantly identical case. Thus an invented consideration must in the end be the same thing as an ordinary consideration. I fear that Professor Treitel has himself invented the concept of an invented consideration because he finds it the only way in which he is able to reconcile many decisions with what he takes to be the 'true' or 'real' doctrine. This is, of course, exactly the sort of process against which Corbin warned us, and I give my full allegiance to Corbin on this point.

Nevertheless, I would today wish to qualify the suggestion that consideration 'means' a reason for the enforcement of a promise. It now seems to me to be more accurate to suggest that consideration really was and is a reason for the recognition of an obligation, rather than a reason for the enforcement of a promise. Given that (as argued in Essay 2) reliance and benefit are often themselves good reasons for the recognition of obligations in the law—that we have many non-promissory cases in which the obligation is based upon an element of detrimental reliance or an element of benefit rendered or obtained— and given also that many cases in contract law are based on implied promises which seem more or less fictitious, the wider formulation of the function of consideration seems more accurate. But for the purposes of this essay, I do not think that it matters much whether I proceed on the narrower or wider understanding of what is the general purpose of the doctrine of consideration.

At a relatively early date it was established that the courts would enforce a promise if another promise or an act was given in return for it; and also that they would not normally enforce a promise if it was merely intended as a gift with no return of any kind. In the first class of case it came therefore to be said that there was good consideration; there were good reasons for enforcing the promise. In the second class there was no such reason, and therefore no consideration. But it also became clear from a very early time that the whole law could not be reduced to such very simple terms. There were some cases in which a promise was given in return for another promise or an act, in which for one reason or another it was felt unjust or inexpedient that the promise should be enforced. Such cases could be, and sometimes were explained by saying that there was no consideration for the promise; but as the nineteenth century wore on, an alternative approach began to manifest itself. This was to say that there was good consideration (though perhaps the word 'good' would more usually be omitted) but that nevertheless the promise was unenforceable for other reasons, for example, because it had been extorted by duress, or fraud, or because it was illegal. The last type of case was often dealt with by saying that the consideration was unlawful; a judge who formulated his reasons in this way would perhaps, if pressed, have said that there was no 'good' consideration.

More recently still, this alternative approach has hardened so that courts now find nothing inconsistent in holding that there is consideration for a promise, but nevertheless refusing to enforce it because the transaction is illegal. This approach also manifests itself in the relatively modern device of refusing to enforce a promise on the ground that the promisor did not 'intend' to create legal relations by his promise. Where this is done (as it usually is) in a case where there is no express disavowal of the intent to create legal relations, it appears to be merely a legal justification for refusing to enforce a promise which the courts think, for one reason or another, it is unjust or impolitic to enforce. There seems no doubt that a hundred years ago the courts would have dealt with these problems in terms of consideration. Indeed, the comparison between *Shadwell* v. *Shadwell*[1] and *Jones* v. *Padavatton*[2] is striking. In the former case, where an uncle promised to pay his nephew an allowance on his marriage, the whole discussion was in terms of consideration. In *Jones* v. *Padavatton*, where a mother promised her

[1] (1860) 9 CBNS 159.
[2] [1969] 1 WLR 328.

daughter an allowance while she studied for the bar, the whole discussion was in terms of the intent to create legal relations.

This change of approach is symptomatic of the change which has developed in the way lawyers think about consideration. It is no longer thought that consideration is a compendious word simply indicating whether there are good reasons for enforcing a promise; it is widely assumed that consideration is a technical requirement of the law which has little or nothing to do with the justice or desirability of enforcing a promise. Modern lawyers thus see nothing incongruous in asserting that a promise made for good consideration should nevertheless not be enforced.

Exactly the same development has taken place with regard to those promises which are not normally enforced, that is the promise to make a gift with no return of any kind. Since the courts first decided that such promises were not enforceable, it came to be asserted that gratuitous promises were promises given without consideration. But in course of time, occasions arose when the courts found that there were sometimes very good reasons for enforcing gratuitous promises in certain cases, and they accordingly enforced them. When cases of this kind arose during the first part of the nineteenth century the natural approach of the courts was to say that there *was* consideration—which at that time seems merely to have meant that there were good reasons for enforcing the promise. But here again, as lawyers began to treat consideration as a 'doctrine' whose content was a set of fixed and rigid rules tailored to the typical case, these cases came to seem anomalous. It therefore became fashionable to deny that there was consideration; and yet such promises were and still are quite often enforced. Modern lawyers are thus forced to say that some promises may be enforceable even though there is no consideration for them.

However, this last proposition is one which lawyers have been much more reluctant to accept than the one previously discussed, that is that even promises supported by consideration may sometimes be unenforceable. There has seemed to be something almost akin to heresy in admitting that a promise may be enforced without consideration. This is fully borne out by the initial reactions to the *High Trees*[1] case which was originally looked on with great scepticism by the legal profession as an instance of Lord Denning's advanced and 'unsound' views.[2] But this is by no means the only instance of gratuitous promises

[1] [1947] KB 130.
[2] See e.g. Bennion, 'Want of Consideration' (1953), 16 *Mod. L. Rev.* 441; Gordon [1963] *Camb. LJ*. 222.

being enforced by the courts. As will be seen below, many gratuitous promises are enforced by the courts, if the word 'gratuitous' is understood to mean a promise to make a gift, but the difference between most of these instances and the *High Trees* decision is that in the older cases it was traditionally asserted that there was in fact consideration. To the orthodox lawyer there seems a contradiction in terms in asserting that a gratuitous promise may in fact be supported by consideration, and he has therefore generally adopted the consoling and face-saving device of acknowledging the existence of these cases, but denying that they involve gratuitous promises; or if he is driven to admit that they involve gratuitous promises, he is reduced to the still more desperate expedient of 'explaining' such cases as being anomalous and inconsistent with the 'pure' doctrine of consideration, though he will also admit that they are due to the desire of the judges to do justice in the particular circumstances of the case.

As will be apparent from the above discussion, there has gradually been a hardening of the attitude of the English common lawyer to the whole notion of consideration. From being merely a reason for the enforcement of a promise (or possibly a reason for the creation or recognition of an obligation), it has come to be regarded as a technical doctrine which has little to do with the justice or desirability of enforcing a promise, or recognizing obligations. Thus a promise for consideration may be unenforceable; and a promise without consideration may be enforceable. Interwoven with this development has been another which has also played a large part in leading to the conventional view of the law at the present day. This has been the persistent and apparently compulsive desire of lawyers to concentrate on the typical contractual promise and to draw conclusions of universal validity from that typical case. Thus, because it is often (or indeed usually) a good reason for enforcing a promise that the promisor has received a counter-promise in return, lawyers appear to have convinced themselves that a wholly executory contract should always be enforceable, and that a counter-promise is necessarily a benefit or a detriment, even before any performance or reliance. Because most contracts are bargains, lawyers have steadfastly refused to recognize the evidence under their very eyes, that courts often enforce promises which are not bargains, and that they do so for reasons of justice and good policy. Because a promise to make a gift is not usually recognized as a sufficient reason for its enforcement, lawyers have refused to acknowledge that in some circumstances it is particularly desirable to enforce a gratuitous promise and that the courts in fact do so. Because in most circumstances the consideration must in practice be supplied by the promisee, it was deduced (and even on one occasion stated by the House of Lords) that consideration must always move from the promisee; yet the courts in fact sometimes enforce promises in which the real ground for enforcing the promise is something done by a third party. Much of this hardening of the arteries is, it seems to me, due to the great power of the classical theory of contract, as I have already suggested in Essay 2.

As we shall see below, the restatement of the law which the actual decisions compel us to adopt differs from the conventional view principally in recognizing the importance of the untypical and marginal cases. It is not, however, merely a question of recognizing that there are exceptions to the ordinary rules to which adequate attention has not always been paid. If that were all, there would be little need, or justification, for a fundamental restatement of the law. A restatement will require rather more than that; it will require in particular that lawyers start to think of consideration once again in terms of reasons for enforcing a promise; it will require lawyers to recognize that the presence of factors like benefit, detriment, and bargain is taken into account not because they fit some preconceived plan or definition, but because they are often very material factors in determining whether it is just or desirable to enforce a promise; and this necessarily involves recognition that these are not the only factors to which attention must be, and is in practice paid by the courts.

2. Benefit and Detriment

The conventional and classic statements of the law (such as the famous dictum of Lush J. in *Currie* v. *Misa*[1]) declare that consideration consists of a benefit to the promisor or a detriment to the promisee. There is some doubt about the relative importance of the two. It is universally agreed that detriment to the promisee is sufficient even though there is no benefit to the promisor; the ordinary promise of a surety or a guarantor is a sufficient illustration of a promise which is commonly given without benefit to the promisor, but is nevertheless clearly enforceable in law. On the other hand it is less certain whether a benefit to the promisor without any corresponding detriment to the promisee will suffice. The reason for this doubt is principally the rule, or supposed rule, that consideration must move from the promisee. If the promisee

[1] (1875) LR 10 Ex. 153, 162.

must in fact supply the consideration to the promisor, and if the promisor must benefit by the consideration, there must be few cases indeed in which the promise will be enforceable without detriment to the promisee. But I propose below to suggest that the rule that consideration must move from the promisee is in fact not enforced by the courts. There are, moreover, some cases in which it is possible for a benefit to be conferred on the promisor by the promisee without any detriment to the promisee himself,[1] and it may therefore be possible for a benefit to be a sufficient consideration without any detriment, even on the orthodox view of the law.

Now I do not doubt for one moment that one of the most common reasons for enforcing a promise, and for thinking it just to enforce a promise, is that the promisor has obtained a benefit in return for his promise, or the promisee has suffered some detriment in reliance on the promise. Indeed, one could go further and assert that the combination of benefit and detriment makes a very much stronger case for the enforcement of a promise than either benefit or detriment taken by itself. That the courts have often felt uneasy about enforcing promises where there is detriment to promisee but no benefit to promisor is illustrated by the extraordinary shifts and devices invented by nineteenth-century judges for relieving a surety of his liability in a great variety of situations.[2] But it is sufficient to accept that benefit or detriment is normally a good reason for enforcing a promise. It does not in the least follow that the presence of benefit or detriment is always a sufficient reason for enforcing a promise; nor does it follow that there may not be other very good reasons for enforcing a promise. It is in fact quite plain on the authorities that the presence of a benefit or a detriment is neither a *sufficient* nor a *necessary* condition for the enforcement of a promise, and that therefore a definition of consideration in terms of benefit and detriment is simply inaccurate. This assertion needs to be justified.

Benefit or detriment are not sufficient

The presence of a benefit or a detriment or both does not by itself render a promise enforceable. Is it possible to doubt this statement?

---

[1] *Bolton* v. *Madden* (1873) LR 9 QB 55 is cited by Treitel, *Contract*, p. 52, as an illustration of such a case, and other cases may be imagined, as for instance where one person wishes to give something away in order to get rid of it, and yet that thing may have value to another (for instance an unwanted pet).

[2] See e.g. Chitty on *Contracts*, 25th edn., vol. ii, §§ 4434-54.

Plainly all sorts of reasons may render a promise unenforceable at common law even though the promisor receives a benefit, or the promisee incurs a detriment. The promise may be contrary to public policy; it may have been extorted by duress or undue influence; by fraud or misrepresentation; the promisor may be held not to have 'intended' to create legal relations; and so on. To the orthodox lawyer these cases involve no inconsistency with the traditional doctrine because they involve legal rules which in some sense are drawn from outside the law of consideration altogether. But the distinction between a rule 'within' and a rule 'outside' the doctrine of consideration is a purely conceptual distinction. The rules are all part of the law; they all go to determine what promises should be enforceable, and they are all in the last resort applied by judges in the attempt to do what is just, bearing in mind that respect for the doctrine of precedent is itself one aspect of doing justice. So when the courts declared (for instance) that a collective bargaining agreement between trade unions and employers was not a legal contract at common law, and that promises contained therein were not legally enforceable, they were giving effect to what they thought was required by justice or policy.[1] The fact that they did so under some other head of the law of contract does not alter the fact that in this situation the presence of benefit and detriment is not treated as sufficient reason by itself for the enforcement of the promises. It is neither bad English nor bad law to say that the courts do not think that the *considerations* for the enforcement of such promises outweigh the arguments against enforcement. Would it not be more rational therefore to say that the promises are unenforceable because they lack *good consideration*, rather than to say, as the orthodox doctrine would have us say, that there is good consideration but that the promises will none the less not be enforced?

But it is, in any event, unnecessary for me to place my entire case on this point on the arguments set out above: for even if attention is confined to cases which have been argued and discussed within the framework of the law of consideration, it is perfectly plain that there are instances in which the presence of benefit or detriment in fact has

---

[1] See *Ford Motor Co.* v. *AEU* [1969] 2 QB 303. In saying this I do not suggest that Geoffrey Lane J. decided this case according to what he personally thought the desirable rule to be; in fact he did not even pause (in his judgment) to consider what that rule might be. But there are other facets to policy besides giving effect to the most desirable rule. In view of the acute political controversy surrounding the legal enforceability of such agreements it may well have been an act of policy for a puisne judge not to upset the generally accepted view of the law.

not been treated as a sufficient ground for the enforcement of a promise. One need scarcely look further than *Foakes* v. *Beer*,[1] where it will be recalled that Lord Blackburn came close to dissenting on the very ground that commercial men regularly accept part payment of a debt as something more valuable than the right to the whole debt. On this point I cannot do better than quote the words of Corbin:[2]

It is error of fact to suppose that one gets no benefit when he gets only that to which he had an existing right. A bird in the hand is worth much more than a bird in the bush; and that is why the promisor bargains to pay more in order to get it.[3] It is likewise error of fact to suppose that performance of duty is no detriment to the promisee. If this performance is the payment of money, it is money that he might have paid to other persons with greater advantage to himself (and even without doing any legal wrong whatever); if it is the rendition of service, it is the spending of time and effort that might more advantageously have been spent elsewhere. It is true that failure to render the performance would have left the promisee liable in damages for breach of his duty; but it should be obvious that the damages that he could be compelled to pay would have no definite relation to the extent of the advantage that he might have derived from using his time and money otherwise.

One has only to think of the case of a debtor who may labour for years to pay off part of a large debt when he has the choice of filing a bankruptcy petition and ridding himself of the whole debt with comparative ease, to appreciate the force of these remarks.

In order to keep this essay within reasonable bounds I forbear from going on to consider in detail other cases in which the presence of benefit or detriment has not been held—or at any rate has not been held without difficulty and argument—to be a sufficient consideration for the enforcement of a promise. It is enough for me to refer to the well-known problems concerning the promise of payment in return for the performance, or a promise of performance, of an existing legal or contractual duty. It is, I suggest, plain that doubts about the enforceability of promises in such cases have not arisen from doubts about whether there is benefit or detriment in fact, nor from doubts about whether there is technically some 'consideration' which complies with the rules of some preconceived definition. The difficulties have arisen because there have been doubts (perhaps often unfounded) as to

---

[1] (1884) 9 App. Cas. 605.

[2] Op. cit., vol. i, § 172.

[3] Corbin is here considering the case of a promise to pay additional remuneration for the performance of an existing duty, rather than the case of acceptance of part payment in full satisfaction, but his reasoning is applicable to both cases.

whether there are sound policy reasons for not enforcing promises in such cases, and therefore as to whether there are *good* considerations for their enforcement. Nevertheless, I have to concede that the doctrine of consideration remains to this day so hardened in its arteries, that we have the curious result that a variation of a contract procured by duress may now be held to have been obtained for 'good consideration', while yet the variation may be set aside because of the duress.[1] This again illustrates the way in which the doctrine of consideration has been cut loose from the reasons underlying it, so that it almost necessarily becomes a technical and purposeless set of arbitrary rules.

Benefit or detriment is not necessary
Here again I need hardly stress that many promises are given in order to obtain some reciprocal benefit; and that a detriment incurred by a promisee in reliance on the promise is often a very good reason for enforcing a promise. But it seems incorrect to assert that the presence of benefit or detriment is always a necessary prerequisite for the enforcement of a contract. In the first place, an executory bilateral contract is and has for centuries been enforceable by the courts, although neither benefit nor detriment usually arises until the contract has been at least partly performed. It is of course true that once the law has begun to enforce bilateral executory contracts, the mere giving and receipt of the promises may be said to involve a benefit and detriment because they are legally enforceable. But enforceability comes first, and benefit and detriment afterwards; it is purely circular to assert that the presence of benefit and detriment can be a ground for the enforcement of such contracts. It is also true that if an executory bilateral contract is in due course performed the promisor may receive a benefit and the promisee may incur a detriment. But where the promisee sues for damages for breach of an executory bilateral contract the promisor has in fact received no benefit, and the promisee has not necessarily incurred any detriment.

It is common for lawyers to apply the benefit–detriment analysis even to bilateral executory contracts; the inquiry then takes the form of asking if performance of the promise will be, or would have been beneficial to the promisor or detrimental to the promisee. The fact that the answer may be in the negative may well be a factor which leads the court to decide that there is no reason (or consideration) for enforcing

[1] *The Atlantic Baron* [1979] QB 705.

the promise. But the fact that the answer is in the affirmative does not and cannot demonstrate that the promise is being enforced because of a factual benefit or detriment, unless that is, it is possible to argue that a promise may be a benefit or a detriment irrespective of its legal enforceability. In the original essay I assumed perhaps too easily that this could not be so, but Professor Treitel argues cogently that promises can be beneficial or detrimental even if they are not legally enforceable;[1] and if we assume a society in which promises are generally performed, and in which their non-performance carries a certain odium, then I am prepared to admit that this may be the case. Nevertheless, there is an element of unreality in treating bilateral executory contracts in this way. Counter-promises are treated by the courts as beneficial (or detrimental) unless it can be demonstrated that there is or was no possibility of any benefit or detriment being derived from the promise. A counter-promise is thus treated more like a formal reason for the enforcement of a promise than a reason of substance, and in most actions for breach of an executory bilateral contract, there is no possibility of the promisor obtaining any benefit, or the promisee suffering any detriment by the time the case comes for trial.

The truth seems to be that bilateral executory contracts are enforced for other reasons (or considerations) than the existence of benefit or detriment. Quite what those other reasons are, whether they are adequate reasons, and whether they extend to all cases of bilateral executory contracts, are all very difficult questions, as is apparent from some of the other essays in this collection, especially Essay 7. In the original version of the present essay I assumed far too readily (again largely under the influence of Corbin) that bilateral executory contracts are enforced because in modern societies business could scarcely be carried on if they were not enforced. Professor Treitel challenges my reasoning here with some justification; though it is a little ironical that he should do so, given that he has no apparent doubts that bilateral executory contracts *should* be enforced, while I have a great many such doubts.

If we leave aside the problem of bilateral executory contracts, it must be admitted that it is not easy to find many instances of promises being enforced despite the absence of benefit and detriment. There are two reasons for this. Firstly, most contracts which the courts find worthy of enforcement do in fact involve benefit or detriment or both. And secondly, promises are not usually given for no reason at all; the promisor, it may safely be asserted, always has some reason for making a

[1] 'A Critical Analysis', p. 442.

promise; a promise made totally without reason would seem an insane gesture, and it is hard to imagine such a promise ever being sued upon or enforced. In theory, the promisor's reasons are merely a motive, and motive does not itself constitute good consideration. But it is not difficult for a court to treat the motive as a consideration where the court thinks it is in the circumstances just to enforce the promise. Alternatively, the court may find some very indirect benefit accruing to the promisor from his promise, though in fact this benefit may itself be nothing more than the motive. This may be illustrated by the decision of the House of Lords in *Chappell & Co. Ltd.* v. *Nestle Co. Ltd.*,[1] the well-known case in which chocolate wrappers were sent to the defendants together with some payment, as the price of gramophone records, offered in the modern fashion as a sales-boosting or advertising device. The actual wrappers in this case were plainly worthless and were thrown away on receipt, and it would be ridiculous to assert that the sending or the receipt of the wrappers necessarily involved an actual detriment to the sender or a benefit to the defendants. But it is also plain that the defendants did not make their offer to the public out of pure generosity; the defendants, like all business concerns, were operating with a view to profit; and they decided, whether rightly or wrongly, that they would derive some indirect benefit in the form of enhanced sales from the whole campaign. But this indirect benefit did not derive from the actual receipt of the wrappers; it was in truth the motive which inspired the promise. The case itself was not, of course, an action for breach of contract, but the decision of the House plainly implies that had it been such an action (and even if there had been no cash payment in addition to the wrappers) the action would have succeeded. This seems, therefore, to be an instance of a promise which is enforceable despite the absence of benefit to the promisee in the sense in which the word 'benefit' is normally used in the orthodox doctrine.

But leaving aside cases such as this in which there may be argued to be some very indirect benefit, there are other promises which are undoubtedly enforceable even where there is (as I would submit) plainly no actual benefit or detriment. The promise for nominal consideration seems an obvious instance. A promise in return for a peppercorn is enforceable, but it is surely clear that the reason why such a promise is enforced is not because the promisee incurs a detriment in delivering a peppercorn, nor because the promisor derives a benefit by receiving a peppercorn. 'A peppercorn does not cease to be good consideration if

[1] [1960] AC 87.

it is established that the promisee does not like pepper and will throw away the corn.'[1] It is surely obvious that in such a case the reasons (or considerations) which lead to the promise being enforced must be found elsewhere. One possible reason is that a promise for nominal consideration is just about the clearest possible indication that the promisor intended his promise seriously and intended to give the promisee a legally enforceable right. In the absence of some countervailing consideration (such as illegality and so on), this appears to the courts to be a good reason (or consideration) for the enforcement of the promise. I do not think the correctness of this suggestion is rebutted merely because the courts have not drawn the general conclusion that prima facie *any* promise clearly intended to give the promisee a legally enforceable right is enforceable. The fact that the courts have not done this is no doubt a result of the strength of orthodox doctrine (in this instance at variance with classical theory) though it is hardly a tribute to its logical coherence.

Professor Treitel objects to my argument from nominal consideration by suggesting that I have overlooked or paid inadequate weight to the principle that adequacy of consideration is immaterial. The rule as to nominal consideration 'follows logically', he asserts,[2] from the rules about adequacy. This, however, seems to me a plain mistake. The sufficiency in law of nominal consideration is a distinct question from that of adequacy, as is demonstrated by the fact that in America, the adequacy principle is followed, whereas the nominal consideration rule is not generally observed.[3] I do not therefore see how it can be asserted that the one follows logically from the other. I must admit that I am today less sure why nominal consideration has been treated by English law as a sufficient consideration, and incline now rather to think that it is because of the strength of the formal reasoning to which English courts have always been attracted.[4] So although I do not think the nominal consideration rule 'follows logically' from the adequacy principle, I can understand why a court wedded to formal reasoning may choose to accept nominal consideration as sufficient in law without further inquiry. Still, this hardly detracts from my point that nominal consideration cases show that factual benefit and detriment is not always required by the law. If the courts are so formal in their reasoning

---

[1] *Per* Lord Somervell in *Chappell & Co. Ltd.* v. *Nestle Co. Ltd.* [1960] AC at 114.

[2] 'A Critical Analysis', p. 442.

[3] See e.g. Restatement (Second) of Contract, § 79, notes *c* and *d*.

[4] See Essay 5 on the nature of formal reasoning in general and in contract law in particular.

that they do not inquire into underlying facts, like benefit and detriment, but rest content with appearances, then it is dangerous to state the law in terms of benefits and detriments without qualification.

There are still other instances in which promises appear to be enforceable in law despite the absence of benefit to promisor or detriment to promisee. In particular, there are promises in return for a forbearance where the promisor derives no benefit and the promisee incurs no detriment. An uncle promises his nephew $5,000 if the nephew does not smoke until he is 21. The nephew plainly incurs no detriment in fact by forbearing from smoking (indeed, quite the reverse) and it is hard to see that the uncle derives any benefit from the forbearance. Yet such a promise has been held enforceable in America,[1] and it is generally thought that it would also be enforceable in England. It may, of course, be argued that in such a case there is some indirect benefit to the uncle. No doubt he has reasons for wishing the nephew not to smoke or he would not have made the promise; and no doubt he will be gratified if in fact the nephew forbears for the stated period. But here again, this seems to be a matter of motive rather than benefit. If this were a benefit in the sense in which that word is used in the orthodox doctrine, it would seem that many gratuitous promises would become enforceable simply because the promisor derives a sense of satisfaction from his generosity or from the recognition of it by the promisee or the public. Profesor Treitel objects that the plaintiff in this case gave up a right;[2] but in a unilateral contract the plaintiff gives up no right except by his behaviour. He just acts in reliance on the promise; and the reward cases suggest that the promise does not have to be a necessary condition for this 'action in reliance'. A promise of a reward to the winner of a race is generally believed to be legally enforceable even if the winner would still have run just as effectively absent the promise. It is hard to see that there is anything here which can sensibly be called a 'detriment'. The truth appears to be once again that a promise of this kind may be enforced because, if the promisee is induced to act on it, it may appear to the courts to be just to enforce it. Although a detrimental change of position is the usual reason for thinking it would be just to enforce the promise, the absence of detriment does not by itself seem fatal.

Nevertheless, in most cases there will be no difficulty in concluding that some element of detriment to the promisee must be shown, though the term itself may be misleading. It is not so much the act itself which

[1] *Hamer* v. *Sidway* (1891) 27 NE 256. Many English authorities were relied on.
[2] 'A Critical Analysis'.

must be shown to be detrimental, but the change of position; it is the fact that, as a result of the promise, the promisee has acted *irrevocably* which seems critical. In this situation it is the detriment *which would arise* if the promise were not performed which is the critical factor.[1] But even this formula is not wide enough to explain the reward cases where there is some action in reliance—of a kind—but no real detriment.

It must now be observed that, although the presence of benefit or detriment may be the commonest reason for enforcing a promise, other sorts of consideration may well be more relevant in cases where consideration seems to perform the wider function of supporting the recognition of an obligation of a non-promissory character. In most societies it is accepted that obligations derive from other sources than benefits and detriments. Typically, such other obligations arise in the family context. A person may owe obligations to his wife (or former wife) or children, for example, or even other relatives in less usual circumstances. A promise to discharge such an existing obligation seems in a sense to be a promise for which there is good consideration (a good reason). In many nineteenth-century cases concerning promises in consideration of marriage, for instance, the promise would have been regarded as given in discharge of family or social obligations. Such a promise, it may well be thought, needs less to support it in the way of induced or detrimental reliance, which may explain why in these cases it was so rarely questioned (*Shadwell* v. *Shadwell*[2] being a notable exception) whether the promisee would have contracted the marriage even in the absence of the promise. In other cases, where the obligation behind the promise may be weaker, a stronger element of causally induced reliance may well be necessary.

Need the Benefit or Detriment be of Economic Value?

If I am right in what I have so far said, it is clear that actual benefit and detriment in an ordinary factual sense are not always necessary for the enforcement of promises, and it must therefore follow that it is not always necessary to show a benefit or detriment of economic value. Moreover, if actual benefit and detriment are not always required, it

---

[1] As also in the wholly analogous case of promissory estoppel, see e.g. *The Post Chaser* [1982] 1 All ER 19, where the promisee had acted in a way which could have been detrimental, but the action was easily reversed, and the (implied) promise was held not binding.

[2] See above, p. 184.

would be extraordinary if, where benefit or detriment is present, the law were to require it to be of economic value. In fact, there are many cases inconsistent with the supposed rule that consideration must always be of economic value. Perhaps the most striking instance is that of mutual promises to marry which at common law were held enforceable for centuries (although this is no longer so) without any inquiry into the economic state of the parties. Indeed, until quite recently, marriage would normally have been regarded as an economic burden to the husband, and yet the great majority of actions for breach of promise were, of course, brought by the lady concerned.

Other instances of promises which have long been held enforceable despite the absence of any benefit or detriment of economic value are to be found in many separation agreements. For instance, a wife's promise not to 'molest' her husband, or to live a chaste and sober life,[1] or to keep their children 'happy',[2] was accepted as sufficient to justify the enforcement of the husband's promise to pay the wife maintenance. Here again, of course, it would be entirely unreal to regard the benefit derived by the husband as the reason for the enforcement of such a promise. The real reason is doubtless to be found in social policy. Until very recently it accorded with the moral values of our society that a husband should maintain his wife if they separated unless in some very extreme case the wife was regarded as having forfeited her claims on her husband. It is therefore not surprising that the courts were formerly very ready to enforce an actual promise by a husband to pay his wife maintenance. In recent years it is clear that a change has been taking place in the moral values of our society in relation to the husband's obligations to a separated wife. Where there are no dependent children, and where the marriage has not lasted for very long, and, more particularly, where the wife is capable of earning as much as the husband, it is very doubtful whether a husband would today be regarded as under any moral obligation to maintain a separated wife. It is therefore not surprising if the courts today are less inclined to find sufficient reasons for enforcing such promises.[3]

Legal benefit and detriment

I sense at this stage a growing impatience in the reader. He may be quite willing to concede that I have made out my case that benefit and

---

[1] *Dunton* v. *Dunton* (1892) 18 VR 114.
[2] *Ward* v. *Byham* [1956] 1 WLR 496.
[3] See the discussion of *Combe* v. *Combe* [1951] 2 KB 215, pp. 231–3, below.

detriment are not necessary or sufficient prerequisites to the enforcement of a promise. But he is likely to respond that I have underestimated the subtlety of the doctrine of consideration. It is not, he may assert, benefit or detriment *in fact* which the law is concerned with, but benefit or detriment *in law*. These, he may insist, are both necessary and sufficient for the enforcement of promises. Even if there is a factual benefit or detriment, there must also be a legal benefit or detriment before the promise will be enforced; and equally if there is a legal benefit or detriment, the promise will always be enforced despite the absence of factual benefit or detriment. This is, I believe, a statement of the orthodox doctrine, and there are undoubtedly many references in the Law Reports and the books to consideration 'in the eye of the law'. But as a rational argument this will not pass muster. Once again I cannot put the point more clearly than by quoting the words of Corbin:[1]

Such statements not only abandon the requirement of actual detriment; they tell us nothing at all as to the nature of this 'detriment' that is said to be required. To say that it must be a 'legal detriment' says no more than that the detriment must be one that the law recognizes as sufficient, a prime illustration of begging the question. What kind of consideration will make a promise binding? Why, it must be a consideration that is legally sufficient. Obviously, a true statement; also, obviously, one that gives not the slightest help in determining whether a consideration that is before us is a sufficient one. . . . The very common statement that consideration must be a 'legal detriment', or that it must have 'value in the eye of the law' was induced by the discovery that courts were holding considerations to be sufficient even though they were not 'detriments' in fact and had no 'value' in the market place, and were holding other considerations to be insufficient even though they were such detriments and had such value. We must abandon the term 'legal detriment' because it does not serve the desired purpose; we must separate the good from the bad considerations on some basis other than 'detriment' or 'market place value'.

These arguments appear to me to be irrefutable. When a court refuses to enforce a promise despite actual benefit or detriment on the ground that there is no benefit or detriment 'in the eye of the law', it is merely asserting that there are other reasons for refusing to enforce the promise. A restatement of the law must make it its business to try to find out what those other reasons are. Equally, when a court does enforce a promise despite the absence of factual benefit or detriment, on the

---

[1] Op. cit., i, pp. 530-1. Corbin writes of detriment only because he takes the orthodox version to be that which regards detriment as the crucial factor.

ground that there is a benefit or detriment, 'in the eye of the law', the court is plainly enforcing the promise for some other reasons. Again a search for these other reasons must be a necessary part of a restatement of the law.

3. Unilateral Contracts and Consideration

I suggested above that the second proposition of the orthodox doctrine is that in a bilateral contract the promises are consideration for each other, while in a unilateral contract the performance of the acts specified (or on some versions, requested)[1] by the promisor is the consideration. I have nothing to add here to what I said in the previous section concerning consideration in bilateral contracts. But I wish to examine one aspect of the orthodox position with regard to unilateral contracts.

The problem I wish to examine is usually discussed in the books under some such heading as 'Revocation of offers in unilateral contracts', and it concerns the famous and age-old problem whether a promisor can revoke his promise (or withdraw his offer) after the promisee has commenced performance of the act but before he has completed performance of it. Orthodoxy tells us that this case presents a difficult problem. It is said that the usual principle is that the complete performance of the act specified is necessary to 'conclude' the contract; that until the act is completed there is, therefore, no consideration (there being of course no return promise), and that it therefore appears logically to follow that the promisor can revoke his offer at any time before completion. It is acknowledged that this might seem unjust in some cases, and that it might therefore be desirable to 'circumvent' the ordinary results of the doctrine, and two possible methods of circumvention are offered. According to the first, a distinction should be drawn between the acceptance of the offer and the performance of the act. Commencement of performance is said to be the acceptance of the offer, though the whole act must be completed before the promisee can claim enforcement of the promise.[2] The second method of escape is said to lie in the possible implication of a subsidiary promise by the promisor not to revoke his primary offer once the promisee has commenced performance; the consideration for this promise would be the commencement of the performance, though the consideration for the primary promise would remain the complete performance. This solution is usually criticized because of its artificiality. As to authority,

---

[1] As to this, see p. 213, below.
[2] See e.g. Treitel, *Contract*, p. 31.

the cases have not generally been very helpful, although the Court of Appeal has recently endorsed, *obiter*, the possibility of using the second of these ways of escape.[1] Apart from this case, and earlier inconclusive dicta, there is only the authority of Denning L.J. in *Errington* v. *Errington*.[2] And (without intending any disrespect to Lord Denning) orthodoxy tends to look askance at his dicta in view of his well-known radical and unorthodox views.

It is my contention that the orthodox position here is just about as wrong as it could be. The theoretical foundation of the orthodox position is hopelessly confused, and for many years the discussion on authority has unaccountably failed to notice that the whole of this question was discussed with great care by the House of Lords in a case well known in another branch of the law, namely, *Luxor, Ltd.* v. *Cooper*.[3] Let us look at the theory of the matter first.

I must start by observing that the orthodox position here (as so often elsewhere) begins by begging the whole question. It is assumed that there is somewhere a definition of the doctrine of consideration from which it logically follows that, in a unilateral contract, the consideration for the promise must be the complete performance of the acts specified by the promisee. Yet this assumption is found to be consistent with the fact there is no actual authority which says that this is always the case. If we refuse to beg the question, we must begin by asking whether complete performance must always be treated as the consideration. And bearing in mind what I have already said earlier, what this means is whether there are ever any good reasons for preventing a promisor from revoking his promise even though performance of the act is not completed.

The second fallacy in the orthodox position is to assume that the two methods proposed for circumventing the supposed normal rule are alternatives. This is not so. The first method (as we saw above) suggests that the commencement of the performance should be treated as ac-

---

[1] *Daulia Ltd.* v. *Four Millbank Nominees Ltd.* [1978] Ch. 231.

[2] [1952] 1 KB 290, 295.

[3] [1941] AC 108. Smith and Thomas's *Casebook on Contract* first drew attention to this case in this context. So too, Mr Reynolds in Bowstead on *Agency*, 13th edn., pp. 184-5, was one of the earliest writers to suggest that this case was hardly consistent with orthodox discussions of consideration, and that some restatement might be needed. Professor Treitel, ' A Critical Analysis', p. 443 (and *Contract*, p. 33), continues to regard the decision as irrelevant to this point, because he thinks the case turned on the construction of the contract, and not the fact that the contract was unilateral. But this fails to appreciate that the construction adopted required that the contract *should be treated* as unilateral.

ceptance of the offer; but even if this can be so, it will not help the promisee if he is unable to complete the act specified by the promisor.[1] The reason for this is not logical necessity but consistency with other parts of the law of contract. Prima facie the promisee cannot enforce the promise until he has completed the act requested because it is only upon completion that the promisor has promised to pay anything. Now if the promisor revokes his offer, he may in a sense be said to have waived the need for completion of the performance; and it would be perfectly possible for a rational legal system to take the view that in such a case the promise should become enforceable although the performance has never been completed. But this is not the solution adopted by English law of most analogous problems. A promisee may be entitled to claim damages where the promisor waives performance on his part, but he is not entitled to sue for the sum promised. Such an action is a claim for the price promised, and it is very well established that the price is not claimable unless performance is completed. Accordingly, the promisee's commencement of performance may be a good reason (or consideration) for enforcing some promise (if any) other than the principal promise to pay on completion. The question therefore arises whether there is any other promise which the promisee can enforce. Plainly, if there is any express promise not to revoke the offer, that promise would, on ordinary principles, become enforceable when the promisee has acted on it by commencing performance; equally, if it is possible to imply such a promise, that promise could be enforced. But if the promisor has made no such express promise, and if there is no sufficient reason for implying a promise, the position is simply that the promisor has reserved his freedom of action. The promisee may have acted on the promise by commencing performance but he has simply taken the risk that the promisor may revoke before performance is completed.

In saying that a subsidiary promise by the promisor not to revoke his primary promise may be implied in a suitable case, it must be appreciated, of course, that normal principles of 'implication' hold good. Since these principles permit the court to read into a contract any term which it thinks 'necessary' for business efficacy—and 'necessary' here seems a fairly flexible term—what this means is that the court may read in a subsidiary implied promise wherever it feels that the

---

[1] It is true that this analysis might work where the promisee is able to complete the act without the promisor's concurrence; but then difficulties are encountered in connection with the rule in *White & Carter* v. *McGregor* [1962] AC 413.

justice of the case demands it with sufficient force.[1] The question therefore must always be whether revocation of the primary promise prior
to the completion of the act specified would be seriously unjust. If that
seems too vague, one way of giving it more precision—though it may
be a rather spurious precision—is to say that the revocability of the
primary promise depends on the intention of the parties, which must
be looked at in the light of customary practices and all the surrounding
circumstances. But more realistically, it could be suggested that the
implication of a promise here depends on showing that the act of part
performance was a sufficiently weighty act of reliance to justify the
imposition of some liability on the promisor, though not necessarily a
liability to pay the whole of the original sum promised. The liability
thus falls into place, alongside many others, as one for reliance damages
where a complete contract has not been concluded, but nevertheless
sufficient steps have been taken along the way to give the aggrieved
party some entitlement to recompense.[2]

It will be seen, therefore, that the first method of circumventing the
supposed rule is insufficient by itself. Unless the promisor has promised
not to revoke his promise, or unless he can be treated as having made
such a promise, there is no obligation on the promisor which the
promisee can enforce despite his 'acceptance' of the offer. Or to put the
point another way, to treat the promisee as being entitled to accept the
offer before full performance of the act requested, raises serious difficulty about the remedy which that acceptance ought to give the
promisee—in particular, it seems wrong that he should thereby be
entitled to claim the full price promised, or expectation damages for
breach.[3] But equally the second method of circumvention cannot stand
by itself, for it suggests that the way out of the difficulty is to imply a
promise that the offer will not be revoked, and that the commencement
of performance will be a consideration for that promise. But this also
begs many questions. It appears to assume that the commencement of
performance is always a good reason for preventing revocation, and
therefore for implying a promise not to revoke. But this is not necess-

---

[1] See *Liverpool City Council* v. *Irwin* [1977] AC 239. This case may seem to re-establish
the need to show actual 'necessity' before a term can be implied, but it is clear enough
from the whole judgment that 'necessity' here was taken to mean 'reasonable necessity'.
It can hardly mean anything else.

[2] See my *Introduction to the Law of Contract*, 3rd edn., pp. 61-5, 'The Relationship of
Negotiating Parties'.

[3] Professor Treitel's preference for this solution presumably stems from his preference
for the remedy of expectation damages over reliance damages.

arily the case. There may well be situations in which the promisee customarily takes the risk of revocation before completion of performance. Business practices often require risks of this kind to be assumed, and where this is the case the commencement of performance is not a good reason or consideration for implying and enforcing a promise.

I turn now to an examination of the decision in *Luxor, Ltd.* v. *Cooper*.[1] The facts were simple. The defendants wished to sell some properties and they engaged an estate agent to find them a purchaser. They promised to pay the agent a commission of £10,000 on the completion of the sale if he found a purchaser for at least £185,000. The agent found a purchaser willing to complete the sale but the defendants changed their minds and eventually disposed of the properties by a method which did not involve their sale.

The question at issue was whether the defendants did anything wrong, whether they violated an obligation, in not proceeding with the sale. In order to decide that question, it was necessary to ask, first, what exactly the defendants had obliged *themselves* to do, and secondly, whether there any good reasons for *imposing* an obligation on the defendants which they had not voluntarily assumed. These inquiries led first to another question, namely whether the contract alleged was unilateral or bilateral, because if it had been an ordinary bilateral contract—promise for promise—the normal construction would have been that the defendants had *promised* to pay the commission, subject to the sale being completed, and that they had no right to frustrate the completion of the sale by withdrawing the property or selling it in any other way. It might have been thought that such a contract would be bilateral, the consideration being a promise by the estate agent to use his best endeavours to find a purchaser, but the House of Lords decided that it was a unilateral promise in which the agent himself undertook to do nothing. The promise was a promise to pay on the occurrence of the specified event, namely, completion of the sale at not less than the price specified. In so construing the promise it is thought that their lordships were being realistic. It may be true that the understanding in such a transaction is that the agent will use his best endeavours to sell the property, but such an understanding may well arise because it is naturally assumed that the agent will be anxious to earn his commission. It does not necessarily follow that he is promising to do anything. Moreover, a promise by an agent to use his best endeavours

[1] [1941] AC 108.

to find a purchaser would be of exceedingly little value to the client, which is why he does not normally promise to pay the agent merely for use of his best endeavours, but only in the event of those endeavours being successful. A client would find it very hard to sue an agent for breach of any such promise, and perhaps harder still to prove any damage resulting therefrom.

Since the promise was therefore a promise in return for an act, the application of the orthodox rules about consideration would seem to suggest that the client could have revoked his promise at any time before completion of the act, and this is indeed what the House of Lords held that the client was entitled to do. But the important thing is not the result itself but the reasoning by which that result was reached. The House did not arrive at their conclusion by any mechanical application of the supposed rules about consideration. Indeed, consideration was not discussed at all, which no doubt explains why the case has not generally figured in conventional accounts of the law of consideration. The whole case turned on the possibility of implying a promise by the clients that they would not do anything to prevent the agent earning his commission—which seems to be identical in effect with an implied term not to revoke the offer. The Court of Appeal, applying earlier decisions of its own, had held that such a promise could be implied, but had also treated the contract as bilateral and not unilateral. The House of Lords held that such a promise should not be implied, but the reasons for not implying such a promise were all firmly based on sound considerations of policy. It was first pointed out, most clearly by Lord Wright, that the agent's acts in finding a purchaser and introducing him to the defendants could not be treated as completion of the act requested by the defendants so as to entitle them to their commission. The defendants had promised to pay on completion of the sale and they were not bound to pay unless the sale was completed.

There remained, however, the question whether the agent was entitled to claim, not the agreed commission, but damages for breach. The approach of their lordships was to stress that a claim for damages must be based on a breach of a promise by the defendants; the fact that the defendants had changed their minds was no ground for awarding damages against them unless they had promised not to do so. There was certainly no express promise. Was it right to imply a promise? An alternative way of putting it—in my view a clearer way—would have been to ask, first, whether the defendants had assumed an obligation to pay in the events which occurred, and if not, then to ask whether there was any reason to impose an obligation on them. But the two methods of formulating the issues do not greatly differ when the real nature of 'implied promises' is appreciated.

In the event, the House held that whatever promises had been given had not been broken, and no additional promises should be implied. Briefly, their reasons seem to have been three. First, the transaction was for a sale of real property. In such a case the vendor is not normally legally committed until the exchange of contracts; accordingly it would be undesirable to treat the vendor as committed to the estate agent before he becomes committed to the purchaser. The vendor usually understands that he is free to change his mind *vis-à-vis* the purchaser until contracts are exchanged; and he would normally expect to be free to change his mind without commitment to the estate agent before that time. Secondly, the estate agent takes many risks in his business. He normally takes the risk that he may find no purchaser at all, or that the purchaser may resile before he is legally bound, or even after he is legally bound. There is, therefore, little reason why he should not be required to carry the additional risk that the vendor may change his mind; this risk is a small one compared to the others, for the vendor has himself approached the agent, and may be assumed to be desirous of selling. Thirdly, and this is very much tied up with the second reason, the agent expects to earn a very substantial remuneration in the event of success. He is paid by commission, and not by the hour, or for the value of his actual labour. In this case the agent's commission was no less than £10,000. As Lord Russell pointed out,[1] this was, at that time, the equivalent of the remuneration for a year's work by a Lord Chancellor for work done within a period of eight or nine days, and was 'well worth a risk'.

It will be seen, therefore, that the reasons for the decision were firmly grounded on their lordships' views of the justice of the case—and they are very convincing reasons. There is not the slightest suggestion in the judgments that there was any technical difficulty about consideration; had the House felt that it was just to imply a promise such as was contended for by the plaintiff, there is no reason to doubt that it would have been implied, and enforced. It is true that their lordships suggested that such promises should rarely be implied in unilateral contracts, but this is a perfectly natural view when contracts of a recognized commercial character are under consideration. In such contracts the absence of any express promise (or perhaps custom) to pay remuneration

[1] [1941] AC at p. 126.

except on completion of the act specified is itself a strong indication that the promisee takes the risk of the promisor changing his mind before completion. Both in bilateral and unilateral contracts there are many types of case in which commercial custom requires one party to bear the risks, which may be substantial, of incurring costs before any binding commitment is entered into. For instance, an ordinary purchaser of a house often incurs mortgage costs, legal costs, and survey costs, before he has any legal protection against a change of mind by the vendor; a businessman tendering for a large contract may incur very substantial costs in preparing his tender, and these too are irrecoverable if the other party decides not to proceed. All these are well-understood risks, even though the acts leading to the costs may, in a sense, be done in reliance, or at the invitation of the other party. They are acts of reasonable reliance, but are still at the risk of the party relying.

But it does not at all follow that in special circumstances—particularly outside the commercial sphere—there may not be very good reasons for protecting the relying party, and therefore for implying and enforcing a subsidiary promise not to revoke the primary promise before the promisee has had a chance to complete the acts specified by the promisor. *Errington* v. *Errington*[1] seems to have been just such a case. Here a man bought a house for his son and daughter-in-law, gave them possession, and told them that the house would be theirs if they paid all the mortgage instalments. A majority of the Court of Appeal held that the son and daughter-in-law had not promised to pay the instalments, which seems to have been clearly right; yet it was held that the father's promise was enforceable in the sense that the son and daughter-in-law were entitled to remain in possession, and would be entitled to the house on payment of the mortgage instalments. Clearly there was in this case a very good reason for implying a promise not to revoke the offer; it would have been unreasonable to say that the son and daughter-in-law 'took the risk' of the father changing his mind, and surely contrary to the intentions of all concerned. There was therefore a sufficient reason (or consideration) for imposing an obligation on the father, and if that could only be doctrinally justified by implying a promise, then there was sufficient reason (or consideration) for implying and enforcing that promise.

4. Consideration and Bargains
The third proposition which I suggested above forms a central part of

[1] [1952] 1 KB 290.

the orthodox doctrine is that the law enforces only bargains; that all contracts are bargains;[1] that consideration is not an artificial or accidental requirement of the law, but merely a recognition of the law's concern with bargains;[2] and that accordingly nothing can be consideration which is not regarded as such by the parties;[3] consideration, in short, is the 'price' of the promise.[4] It is my contention that this part of the orthodox doctrine, like the ones already considered, simply does not represent the law.

Before I consider the validity of the orthodox view it seems necessary to devote some consideration to an examination of what precisely is meant by a bargain. English writers and judges who make frequent reference to the concept of a bargain always appear to assume that the meaning of the concept is self-evident. I cannot recollect ever having seen any discussion in English legal literature of what precisely is meant by the concept. The American Restatement, Second (§3) defines a bargain as 'an agreement to exchange promises or to exchange a promise for a performance or to exchange performances', but Corbin adopts a narrower definition for the purposes of his great work. He regards a bargain as involving not merely an exchange, but an exchange of equivalents.[5] I think that Corbin's definition is nearer to the meaning of the term in ordinary usage, but whichever definition is adopted, I suggest that there are many contracts recognized and enforced by the courts which do not involve a bargain in either of these senses. I will refer to the Restatement's definition as the wider sense, and Corbin's as the narrower sense of the term. Both agree that the essential element of a bargain is that there should be an *exchange* of promise for promise, or promise for act. The consideration must be given *in return for* the promise. Now it cannot be doubted that most contracts are bargains, both in the narrow sense and the wide sense; but once again one sees here the apparent compulsion to generalize from the typical case. Because bargains are the most common form of contract, it is simply assumed, without examination of the evidence, that all contracts are

[1] See e.g. Cheshire and Fifoot, *Law of Contract* (10th edn. by M. P. Furmston, 1981), pp. 60-1, though revealing serious doubts by the new editor.
[2] See Hamson's well-known article in 54 *Law Q. Rev.* 233.
[3] A proposition stated by Holmes, *The Common Law*, p. 292 (see Essay 3) and frequently cited by modern writers; see e.g. Odgers, 86 *Law Q. Rev.* 69, 79. Perhaps it goes too far to regard this as having been received as part of the orthodox doctrine; it never seems to have been applied by the courts, and Professor Treitel rejects it.
[4] Pollock's definition, adopted by Lord Dunedin in *Dunlop* v. *Selfridge* [1915] AC at p. 855.
[5] Op. cit., vol. i § 10.

bargains. Let us now examine the evidence, which in this context consists of the actual decisions of the courts. Naturally, there are more cases which do not fit the narrower sense than the wider sense.

Nominal consideration

A promise given for nominal consideration is perhaps a bargain in the wide sense, but not in the narrow sense. I doubt if the ordinary person would call such a contract a bargain which is one reason why the narrow definition of the term seems more accurate.

Collateral contracts

A collateral contract is sometimes a bargain in the wide sense, and perhaps arguably even in the narrow sense. For example, if a car dealer says to a prospective buyer, 'If you enter into a hire-purchase agreement to acquire this car from the X Finance Co., I promise to repair the brakes', or 'I warrant that the brakes are in good order', this is arguably a bargain even in the narrow sense. But even here it seems to stretch the meaning of the term to say that here is an exchange of *equivalents*, and I would prefer to regard this as a bargain only in the wider sense. But it must be recognized that there are a large number of collateral contracts which cannot possibly be regarded as bargains in either the narrow or the wide sense. An auctioneer promises to sell goods without reserve; this promise is enforceable by the highest bidder, his bid being treated as a sufficient consideration for the promise.[1] There is clearly no bargain here in any sense of the word; the auctioneer does not *exchange* his promise for the bid; the bid merely follows the promise in natural reliance thereon. Orthodox lawyers have indeed looked askance at the decision holding the auctioneer's promise binding,[2] but if we rid ourselves of the preconceived assumption that all considerations must fall within some predetermined pattern, is there any reason for doubting the decision? Orthodoxy finds difficulty in the decision because the consideration found in that case does not fit the typical pattern. But let us rephrase the issue facing the court in that case, and ask: Is there a sufficient reason for enforcing the auctioneer's promise? Can there be any doubt that the court's answer was correct?

Another well-known instance of the collateral contract, and the first to emerge historically, is the agent's warranty of authority. The con-

[1] *Warlow* v. *Harrison* (1859) 1 E. and E. 309.
[2] See Slade, 68 *Law Q. Rev.* 238; cf. Gower, ibid., 457, and Slade's reply, 69 *Law Q. Rev.* 21.

sideration for this warranty is the mere act of entering into the transaction (which is otherwise void) by the promisee.[1] Here again there is
plainly no bargain in any sense of the word. There is an implied promise
or representation followed by natural reliance thereon. The agent does
not *exchange* his promise for the promisee's conduct, or at least he does
not do so as a rule. Doubtless, such a promise could form part of a
genuine exchange, for instance where the third party is sceptical of the
agent's authority, and a warranty is held out as an inducement to
overcome the third party's doubts. But in most circumstances, this is
plainly not the case, the warranty being 'implied' to protect what seems
to be the reasonable reliance of the third party. This is still more true
of recent extensions of the implied warranty of authority such as may
be found in *V/O Rasnoimport* v. *Guthrie & Co. Ltd.*[2] In this case a
shipping company's agents were held liable for a false statement in a
bill of lading acknowledging the receipt of more goods than were in
fact shipped. The plaintiffs were endorsees for value of the bill, and the
consideration was found in the mere fact that they relied on the statements in the bill of lading in accordance with normal commercial
practice. Any attempt to spell a bargain out of this situation is clearly
doomed to failure.

It is sometimes argued that cases of implied warranty are not 'really'
contractual at all; such cases are in fact actions for misrepresentation
and would have been brought in tort if the law of torts had been more
willing to recognize liability for misrepresentation at an earlier date.
There is a germ of truth in this inasmuch as the 'promise' in many
actions of this kind is plainly a fiction; the desired result is to impose
liability on the agent and this is done by implying a promise. But the
explanation is nevertheless not wholly acceptable. For one thing, the
liability of the agent is strict; he is liable as for a warranty, and not
merely for negligence.[3] Secondly, the measure of damages awarded in
these cases is plainly the measure appropriate to contract and not tort;
for instance, the plaintiff can recover for loss of his profit in the *Collen*
v. *Wright* situation.[4] I now think that these two rules (certainly the
second) are mistaken deductions from the assumption that the cause

---

[1] *Collen* v. *Wright* (1857) 8 E. and B. 647. Another line of cases on the agent's warranty
of authority which is exemplified by *Starkey* v. *Bank of England* [1903] AC 114 is arguably
reconcilable with the notion of bargain in the wide sense, but certainly not in the narrow
sense. See further on these cases, Essay 10.

[2] [1966] 1 Lloyd's Rep. 1.

[3] *Yonge* v. *Toynbee* [1910] 1 KB 215.

[4] See *Re National Coffee Palace Co.* (1883) 24 Ch. D. 367, 374-5.

of action ought to be treated as contractual, rather than as tortious,[1] but all this only goes to show how expansive the concept of contract is, and what uses it has been put to. If contract can be usefully used to enforce a tortious liability, then it is not surprising if difficulty is found in squeezing all contracts into the concept of bargain.

Bailments without reward

A asks B to lend him a chattel for purposes of his own; B complies. A expressly or impliedly promises to return the chattel. This promise is undoubtedly enforceable, and a sufficient consideration (or reason) for enforcing the promise is the mere fact that B has voluntarily handed over his property to A for A's benefit.[2] There is plainly no bargain. Here again, it is sometimes argued that such cases are not 'genuinely' contractual. If the bailee damages the goods he is liable in tort, and therefore there is no need to invoke the law of contracts. This is true, but there may sometimes be situations where it is necessary to rely on the bailee's promise. For example, the bailee may promise to return the chattel on a specified date, and may return it late. No action would lie in tort for this, but it can hardly be doubted that an action would lie on the promise, and that there is good reason (or consideration) for such an action.

Conditional gift promises

A whole range of cases in which promises are enforced though there is no bargain is to be found in those cases in which the courts have enforced conditional gift promises. This group of cases may come as a surprise to the orthodox lawyer because orthodoxy insists that a promise to make a gift is not enforceable as a contract at all. The fact that the promise is conditional does not, according to orthodox doctrine, render the promise enforceable; and it is in fact necessary to distinguish very carefully between a conditional gift promise and a contractual promise. Nevertheless, the fact is that many such contracts have been enforced; or have been refused enforcement only on other grounds than absence of consideration.

One type of case in which a conditional gift promise may be enforced is exemplified by *Wyatt* v. *Kreglinger*.[3] The plaintiff retires from the

---

[1] See Essay 7 on the award of expectation damages where no risk allocation is intended by the parties.

[2] *Bainbridge* v. *Firmstone* (1838) 8 Ad. and E. 743.

[3] [1933] 1 KB 793. The position is of course different where the pension arrangements were part of the original employment terms, and so part of the bargain, as e.g. in *Bull* v. *Pitney-Bowes* [1963] 3 All ER 384.

defendant's employment and the defendant promises to pay him a pension in consideration of a promise by the plaintiff not to compete or otherwise damage the defendant's interests. These promises are exchanged, but they are certainly not exchanged as equivalents; there is therefore a bargain in the wide sense, but none in the narrow sense. It is true that in this particular case there was considerable doubt about the enforceability of the contract, and the decision indeed went against the plaintiff on the ground (which was later much criticized) that the consideration was in restraint of trade. But this is not surprising. By 1933 orthodoxy had acquired such strength with regard to the doctrine of consideration that even the judges sometimes found difficulty in enforcing a promise in flat defiance of orthodox doctrine. It is of course pretty plain that the real reason (or consideration) for enforcing such a promise is the plaintiff's past services but it is also part of the orthodox doctrine that past consideration is bad.

In other similar cases, orthodoxy seems to have been defied by the courts with less difficulty. For example, there are cases in which a person has desired to make a gift of a house to another, and has persuaded the donee to enter into a contract to buy the property from a third party on the strength of a definite promise that he will himself pay the price. Such promises have been enforced,[1] though they are plainly gift promises, and there is equally plainly no bargain in any sense of the term. Perhaps the courts have felt less difficulty about such a case because the promisee clearly incurs a detriment in reliance on the promise by entering into the contract to purchase and pay for the property. Orthodoxy thereby seems to be complied with in so far as detriment is present; but orthodoxy is not complied with inasmuch as no bargain is involved.

Then there is the well-known line of cases beginning with *Dillwyn* v. *Llewellyn*,[2] and continuing up to the present day through *Inwards* v. *Baker*[3] to *Pascoe* v. *Turner*[4] and many similar cases, in which a person promises another to give him some land, and allows the promisee to

<hr/>

[1] *Crosbie* v. *M'Doual* (1806) 13 Ves. Jr. 148; *Skidmore* v. *Bradford* (1869) LR 8 Eq. 134; *Coles* v. *Pilkington* (1874) LR 19 Eq. 174; *Hohler* v. *Aston* [1920] 2 Ch. 420.

[2] (1862) 4 De GF and J. 517; *Ramsden* v. *Dyson* (1866) LR 1 HL 129; *Plimmer* v. *Mayor of Wellington* (1884) 9 App. Cas. 699; *Chalmers* v. *Pardoe* [1963] 1 WLR 677.

[3] [1965] 2 QB 29.

[4] [1979] 1 WLR 431.

build a property on the land in reliance on the promise.[1] Here again (need one repeat it?) there is plainly no bargain. It is true that here also orthodoxy has caused the courts and commentators some uncomfortable moments. The promise in such a case is so obviously a promise to make a gift that the orthodox lawyer is unwilling to believe the evidence in front of him when he sees that the courts actually enforce such promises. Explanations are therefore put forward to show that the cases are not really contractual. Perhaps they are based on some 'equity';[2] perhaps they are based on estoppel of some kind or another;[3] perhaps the promise was not really enforced, but the courts were merely concerned to prevent unjust enrichment[4] (though this does not explain why—at least in some cases—the promisee gets the land as well as the house). Thus, for instance, we find Professor Allan criticizing Lord Westbury for not making it clear in his judgment in *Dillwyn* v. *Llewellyn* 'whether the right of the plaintiff was contractual in nature or whether it was a right bestowed *ex aequo et bono* by the court to compel completion of a gift'.[5] This criticism would have been unintelligible to Lord Westbury, who would probably have replied that of course the plaintiff's right was both. It was the right to enforce a promise (and to that extent contractual) because in the particular circumstances there was good reason (or consideration—and Lord Westbury uses this word in his judgment) to enforce the promise although it was a promise to make a gift. Professor Allan's criticism is only intelligible to the modern lawyer because orthodoxy appears to require a distinction to be drawn between a contractual promise and a promise to make a gift.

Another similar case—though admittedly an isolated decision—is *Re Soames*,[6] where a promise to make a gift to a school was enforced on the ground that the school governors had entered into various commitments in reliance on her promise, which the promisor must have anticipated. Once again, an enforceable promise though no bargain.

---

[1] See the analysis by S. Moriarty, 'Licences and Land Law: Legal Principles and Public Policy', 100 *Law Q. Rev.* 376 (1984) with much of which I am in full agreement. Moriarty finds many of these cases inspired by a desire to protect a person who has detrimentally relied upon an oral assurance that he would be granted an interest in land—often by way of gift.

[2] Lord Denning in *Inwards* v. *Baker*, at p. 37.

[3] Maudsley, 81 *Law Q. Rev.* 183 (1965).

[4] Treitel, *Contract*, pp. 105-8, though conceding that this cannot be the sole explanation.

[5] 79 *Law Q. Rev.* 238, 241 (1963).

[6] (1897) 13 TLR 439; cf. *Re Hudson* (1885) 54 LJ Ch. 811 which is to more orthodox tastes.

Finally, mention may be made of two modern decisions which show that the courts are still not deterred by orthodoxy from enforcing promises where there is no bargain. In *Alder* v. *Moore*[1] the defendant, a professional footballer, was insured by his union against disablement from playing professional football. He suffered an injury for which the insurers paid him £500, but extracted from him (as they were entitled under the policy) a promise to repay the money if he should ever play professional football again. This promise was held enforceable, though there was plainly no bargain in the narrow sense, and probably no bargain in the wide sense either. The promise to repay was in truth a condition of the payment by the insurers; it was not *exchanged* for the payment. The second case is *Gore* v. *Van Der Lann*[2] in which the plaintiff was issued with a free pass to ride on the Liverpool Corporation's buses. She signed a written application for the pass which stated that in consideration of her being granted the pass she would undertake and agree that the pass should be subject to certain conditions—in particular that she would not hold the corporation or their servants liable for personal injury. Clearly the plaintiff's promise was not *exchanged* for the pass, and, predictably, the decision has been criticized on this very ground. The 'pure doctrine is, or should be that of Holmes',[3] we are told; in other words, nothing should be treated as consideration if it is not regarded as such. The belief that all contracts are bargains has been unconscionably long in dying—indeed, it may be premature to say that it is dying even now, but it is certainly time that it was buried.

The need for a request in unilateral contracts

Associated with the belief that all contracts are bargains is the argument sometimes put forward that a promise for an act is not enforceable unless the performance of the act has been expressly or impliedly *requested* by the promisor.[4] Naturally if there is a genuine bargain, the act will be requested. The whole notion of an exchange of promise for promise or for act involves that the promisor has requested the counter-promise or act in exchange for his promise. But it will be seen that the need for a request could be reconciled with the fact that not all

---

[1] [1961] 2 QB 57.
[2] [1967] 2 QB 31.
[3] Odgers, 86 *Law Q. Rev.* 69, 79 (1970). The veneration accorded Holmes's views by some English writers would surprise lawyers in America where his views on the common law have long been subjected to very severe criticism, see Essay 3.
[4] See Smith, 69 *Law Q. Rev.* 99 (1953); Goodhart, ibid., 106.

contracts are bargains. Even if an exchange, or a bargain, is not a requirement of an enforceable contract, it might be argued that the consideration must still be requested by the promisor, and it must be admitted that in some cases the courts have used the absence of a request as a ground for not enforcing the promise, as in *Combe* v. *Combe*.[1] I shall return to this and other relevant cases later. For the moment I wish merely to inquire what rational purpose is served by the supposed rule that the promisor must request (and not merely specify) the act to be performed. Request as a part of a requirement of a bargain would make sense, but once the requirement of bargain is abandoned I cannot see any virtue in the element of request standing by itself. The only distinction between the case where the promisor requests the consideration, and the case where he merely specifies it, appears to be that in the former case it is more likely that the promisor will derive some benefit from the consideration, and, indeed, a request could perfectly sensibly be treated as evidence of such benefit. But now that I have (I hope) demonstrated that benefit is also not a prerequisite for the enforcement of a promise, this distinction does not appear to be of crucial significance.[2] Accordingly I would expect a court to enforce a promise for a specified act even though it is clear that performance of the act is not requested by the promisor. But I would only expect this to be so where the act is performed in reliance on the promise. I have not here considered the case where the act performed by the promisee is not specified at all. This is precisely the point which (according to orthodoxy) marks the frontier between consideration and quasi or promissory estoppel. If the promisee acts on the promise (or perhaps if he acts to his detriment) then the promise will not be treated as supported by consideration where the act is not specified by the promisor; but it may none the less be enforceable to the limited extent recognized by promissory estoppel. I return to this question later.

Past consideration

Orthodoxy asserts that 'past consideration is no consideration'. Apart from the case of the bill of exchange, now embodied in statute, it is generally thought that there is no real exception to this rule. The ap-

---

[1] [1951] 2 KB 215, see below, p. 231.

[2] Naturally it is of *some* significance in that an act which benefits the promisor is more likely to make it just to enforce the promise. It also seems that the element of 'request' is more important in cases of representation rather than promise, see Essay 10. And as Moriarty argues (see p. 212, n. 1, above) enforcement by way of expectation remedies may well be more justified where there is a request, because that does suggest benefit.

parent exception recognized in *Lampleigh* v. *Braithwait*[1] is explained along the lines suggested in *Re Casey;*[2] if the promisee has rendered some service for which payment was expected and could have been enforced on an implied promise, then the express promise of the promisor to pay for those services is enforceable. This merely fixes the amount of the reasonable remuneration which the promisor was already bound to pay. Otherwise no exceptions to the rule are recognized.

Clearly, there is an association between this rule and the belief that all contracts are bargains. If it were indeed true that all contracts were bargains it would logically follow that something done before the promise and without reference to it could not constitute consideration. But now that it is (I hope) clear that not all contracts are bargains, a less rigid rule might be more appropriate. There are, as I have shown, cases in which a promise has been held enforceable because in the particular circumstances some act or promise by the promisee has been thought to be a good reason (or consideration) for its enforcement even though there is no bargain. It would, therefore, be strange and illogical if the fact that the act or promise was past was by itself sufficient to prevent the promise being enforced. In fact this does not seem to be the case. Although orthodoxy here seems a good deal stronger than in the areas previously discussed, I believe that even the rule about past consideration is too strongly stated. The true position seems to be that something done or promised before the promise sued on is not by itself treated as a sufficient reason for the enforcement of the promise. But in particular circumstances it may be held sufficient. It is, however, a tribute to the strength of orthodox doctrine that the particular circumstances recognized as sufficient to justify the enforcement of a promise given for some past act or promise are relatively few in number. Perhaps the law here would have developed further if some other exceptions recognized by the common law to the rule about past consideration had not been taken over or reversed by statute. I have already mentioned the case of bills of exchange. Two other cases recognized by the common law were the enforceability of a promise to pay a statute-barred debt, and the enforceability of a promise to carry out a promise previously given for a consideration during infancy. The former has been superseded by the provisions of the Limitation Acts, while the latter rule was reversed by the Infants Relief Act 1874. As these cases disappeared from the common law, the rule itself appeared to

[1] (1615) Hob. 105.
[2] [1892] 1 Ch. 104.

acquire a greater generality of application; and this may partly explain why there seems to have been such reluctance to recognize circumstances in which a past service or promise may be a very good reason for the enforcement of a promise. As it is, the courts have recognized few such circumstances. I can think of only three such situations.

First, a promise given by an employer to an employee in respect of past services may be enforceable if the employee gives some undertaking in respect of his future conduct, for example that he will not compete with or damage his employer's interests. I have mentioned the case of *Wyatt* v. *Kreglinger*, which exemplifies such a case, though it is a weak authority, for reasons already given. Of course orthodoxy is satisfied in this sort of case because the promisee has given a counter-promise, and this means that the courts do not have to acknowledge openly that the promise is enforceable though given for a past consideration. But it seems clear that in fact 'golden handshakes' are not given *in exchange* for promises not to compete, and so on. They are given in recognition of past services; the promise not to compete is a condition of the continued payment of the pension, not a return for it. Parliament certainly took this realistic view because it used to tax golden handshakes as earned income, so long as a distinction was maintained between earned and unearned income in these matters.[1] A similar case is *Bell* v. *Lever Bros.*,[2] though this question was not there discussed. In this famous case the defendant gave up his position as manager of the plaintiff company in return for a very handsome golden handshake. There was no doubt that a substantial part of this promise was intended as a reward for past services, because the amount promised (and paid) substantially exceeded the total income which the defendant would have earned even if he had served out his whole contract. Here again, of course, orthodoxy is well satisfied by the fact that the defendant gave up something of value in that his contract had still some period to run.

Secondly, in contracts of suretyship it has often been held that a promise to pay some existing debt is enforceable provided that the promisee renders or promises to render some future performance as well.[3] This proviso, of course, derives from the orthodox requirement, but it seems that in some cases it is merely a case of paying lip service

---

[1] Income and Corporation Taxes Act 1970, s. 580. For an unusual case of this kind, see *Higgs* v. *Olivier* [1952] Ch. 311 where there clearly was a bargain in both senses.

[2] [1932] AC 161.

[3] See Chitty on *Contracts*, 25th edn., vol. ii, § 4412.

to orthodoxy. Where, for instance, the services rendered or promised *after* the promise are trifling in comparison with the size of the existing debt shouldered by the surety, there is an element of unreality in treating the former as a good consideration, and dismissing the latter as no consideration for the enforcement of the promise. At least it may be said that one reason (or consideration) for enforcing the *whole* promise must be the pre-existing debt.

Thirdly, the rule relating to the enforcement of compromises, or forbearance to sue, means that past consideration may be sufficient not merely (as orthodoxy would say) where the promisee was already entitled to sue for some remuneration in respect of the past service, but also where he honestly thinks he is so entitled. For instance X finds some lost property and returns it to the owner Y who promises X a reward. If X honestly thinks that a finder is entitled by law to a reward (although he plainly is not in the absence of express promise), it seems that X may be able to sue Y on his promise, though given *after* the service is rendered. That this seems to be the law may be inferred from *Horton* v. *Horton*,[1] where a husband promised in a separation agreement to pay his wife £30 a month and later signed an amending agreement in which he promised to pay her £30 a month tax free. This was held to be enforceable despite the absence of any fresh consideration. The court paid lip-service to orthodoxy by holding that there was some doubt as to what the parties had intended in the original agreement, and that the wife might have applied for rectification of it, though with uncertain result. That the wife forbore so to apply was therefore a good new consideration. Doubtless, this sort of reasoning will continue so long as there are laws and lawyers, but it is exceedingly artificial. The substance of the case was that the husband first promised to pay his wife £30 after tax, and later promised to pay her £30 tax free. The consideration in both cases was the same—namely the social desirability (as it was then thought) of a husband maintaining his wife after they are separated.

More recently, the Privy Council seems to have taken this point a stage further in *Pao On* v. *Lau Yiu*,[2] where the defendant's promise was held enforceable, even though the plaintiff had actually already received a consideration for his own performance from a third party. The case resembles the *Horton* case in one way, because the plaintiff did not receive what he was reasonably entitled to receive (in a com-

[1] [1961] 1 QB 215.
[2] [1980] AC 614.

mercial sense) from the earlier agreement. It may, therefore, be possible to treat these two cases as illustrating a wider exception to the past consideration rule, though this was not itself recognized in the Privy Council's decision.

It will be apparent from the above discussion that orthodoxy in this area has been stronger than elsewhere. There are no clear examples of actual decisions which cannot be reconciled with orthodox reasoning. It is therefore not surprising that the law here seems capable of producing greater injustice than elsewhere. Much of the difficulty about past consideration can be traced back to *Eastwood* v. *Kenyon*[1] which seems to modern eyes to be an extraordinarily perverse and unjust decision. But I doubt whether the judges who decided that case thought that the result was impolitic though they may have thought it unjust. The plaintiff in this case was the executor of one Sutcliffe who had left some cottages and a daughter, Sarah, not adequately provided for. The plaintiff had laid out money (borrowed from one Blackburn) in expenditure on Sutcliffe's cottages and in maintaining Sarah. When she came of age Sarah herself promised the plaintiff to pay off Blackburn, and on her marriage, her husband did likewise. The husband's promise was held unenforceable because the consideration was past. I do not think that it is unreasonable to deduce that the court felt that there were policy reasons against enforcing the promise, thought it may not be easy today to understand precisely what they were. But the court seems to have been concerned at the conduct of the plaintiff in borrowing money to spend on Sarah and the cottages. Thus Lord Denman CJ said:[2]

The enforcement of such promises by law, however plausibly reconciled by the desire to effect all conscientious engagements, might be attended with mischievous consequences to society; one of which would be the frequent preference of voluntary undertakings to claims for just debts. Suits would thereby be multiplied, and voluntary undertakings would also be multiplied, to the prejudice of real creditors. The temptations of executors would be much increased by the prevalence of such a doctrine, and the faithful discharge of their duty be rendered more difficult.

It is, unfortunately, only too common that the policy reasons underlying decisions are forgotten, and that the decisions themselves come to be treated as authority in entirely different circumstances. Good cases, as well as hard cases, can make bad law.

[1] (1840) 11 Ad. and E. 438.
[2] At pp. 450-1.

6. Consideration Must Move From the Promisee

No rule is more often repeated as a part of orthodox doctrine than that the consideration must move from the promisee. Yet the actual decisions of the courts seem to be quite inconsistent with this rule, and not a single satisfactory modern illustration of this supposed rule has ever been cited by those who give it allegiance. Again, of course, I must stress that in the great majority of contracts, the consideration will move from the promisee; again, the fact that the promisee has himself supplied the consideration is often a very good reason for enforcing the promise. But again, there is often very good reason in justice and policy for enforcing a promise even where the promisor has received some return from a third party.

The history of this part of the doctrine of consideration is a strange one. The rule that consideration must move from the promisee was first clearly stated in *Tweddle* v. *Atkinson*,[1] but this case has ever since been explained by the courts as the *fons et origo* of the modern rule of privity, and not as depending on the rule about consideration. In *West Yorkshire Darracq Agency Ltd.* v. *Coleridge*,[2] in 1911, a puisne judge was able to brush aside the rule that consideration must move from the promisee, and distinguish *Tweddle* v. *Atkinson* on the ground that in that case the plaintiff was no party to the contract. In the very next case in the King's Bench volume of the Law Reports, *Hirachand Punamchand* v. *Temple*,[3] the Court of Appeal also declined to apply the supposed rule. In this case X owed money to Y. X's father paid part of the debt and Y (in the view of the court) promised that he would not sue X for the balance. This promise was held to be a good defence to X in an action for the balance of the debt. The case certainly caused the court some difficulty because not only had X not supplied the consideration; he was not even a party to the promise. Yet by one means or another the promise was held enforceable by X.

The rule that consideration must move from the promisee was restated by the House of Lords in *Dunlop* v. *Selfridge*,[4] and is arguably part of the ratio of that case. Yet, the courts have continued to treat *Tweddle* v. *Atkinson*, and now *Dunlop* v. *Selfridge* itself, as based on

---

[1] (1861) 1 B. and S. 393.

[2] [1911] 2 KB 326.

[3] [1911] 2 KB 330. There is also a long line of cases (whose relationship to privity and consideration has been ignored) holding that a promise to release a joint tortfeasor may be relied on by another tortfeasor if it was intended for his benefit too: see my *Vicarious Liability* (1967), p. 405.

[4] [1915] AC 847.

privity, and not on the rule about consideration. In both *Scruttons, Ltd.* v. *Midland Silicones, Ltd.*,[1] and *Beswick* v. *Beswick*,[2] the House of Lords appears to have ignored the supposed rule that consideration must move from the promisee: the whole discussion was in terms of privity. In recent times the suggestion has been made,[3] and has gained powerful converts,[4] that there is no distinction between the rule that consideration must move from the promisee, and the rule of privity of contract. The assertion is made that these two rules are merely different facets of the same question. I do not agree with this argument, and it is necessary to digress a little in order to consider this point.

Let it first be noted that in point of *fact* it is possible for a person to be a promisee (that is for a promise to be made *to* him), and yet for the consideration for that promise to be supplied by some other person. A promises B and C that he will pay £100 to B if C renders him some service. B is in point of fact a promisee; the consideration (or reason) for enforcing this promise (if sufficient) is supplied by C. It is argued that it is erroneous to regard B as a party to this contract at all; but the whole argument seems to be based on circular reasoning. It starts by assuming that only a person who supplies consideration can properly be treated as a party to the contract; it is then deduced (correctly, if the premisses are sound) that therefore B cannot be treated as party to the contract because he supplies no consideration. The circularity of the reasoning is evident. In point of fact, as I have stressed, B is a promisee. Moreover, the policy and justice of the two situations are not necessarily the same. A person who supplies no consideration for a promise has a better claim for enforcing the promise if he was at least a promisee. As a matter of logic, therefore, it appears that there are here two distinct questions. Examination of the actual cases also suggests that the two questions are distinct, because although the privity rule is still a firmly established part of the law,[5] promises are in fact often enforced by the courts at the hands of a promisee who has supplied no consideration.[6]

---

[1] [1962] AC 446.

[2] [1968] AC 58.

[3] Furmston (1960) 23 *Mod. L. Rev.* at pp. 383-4.

[4] Cheshire and Fifoot, op. cit., p. 67.

[5] Though it may be wondered how often the privity rule is applied, given the number and width of the exceptions to it.

[6] But it must be admitted that sometimes the two rules are still treated as though only one was in question, as in *Snelling* v. *John G. Snelling Ltd.* [1973] 1 QB 87.

I have already referred to the *Darracq Agency* case,[1] and to *Hirachand Punamchand* v. *Temple*. Similar to these cases is the well-established rule that a composition with creditors is binding and enforceable even at the hands of the debtor. Orthodox lawyers naturally find this a hard case to explain. Yet it is perfectly evident that there are very good reasons (or considerations) for the enforcement of the promise by the debtor even though he himself gives up nothing of value.[2] There are other cases too.

Joint promisees

A makes a promise to B and C jointly in return for an act or a promise by B alone. There seems no doubt that C can enforce A's promise. Lord Atkin said so in *McEvoy* v. *Belfast Banking Corporation*.[3] Predictably, this dictum has been criticized as a departure from orthodoxy.[4] But more recently a similar view was also taken by the High Court of Australia. In *Coulls* v. *Bagot's Executor & Trustee Co.*,[5] the whole court seems to have taken the view that the promise is enforceable in such a case though only a minority found that the plaintiff actually was a promisee. Barwick CJ and Windeyer J. put the point quite explicitly.[6] In the case of a promise to joint promisees it is necessary that the consideration must be supplied by the promisees jointly, but the promisor is not concerned in how the promisees provide the consideration as between themselves. This new formulation may satisfy even orthodox opinion since it continues to affirm the principle that consideration must move from the promisee as a matter of theory while disregarding it in practice.

My original citation of these two cases was criticised by Professor Treitel on the ground that I failed to distinguish between *joint* promises (which was what *Coulls*' case was about) and *joint and several promises*, to which Lord Atkin's dictum related.[7] The distinction was said to be

---

[1] Anyone wishing to argue that this case was impliedly overruled by *Dunlop* v. *Selfridge* must explain why it was cited without disapproval in *Re William Porter* [1937] 2 All ER 361 by Simonds J., a judge not noted for unorthodox views.

[2] Corbin, however, is prepared to argue that the debtor does in fact give up the opportunity of treating his creditors unequally; op. cit., vol. ii, § 190.

[3] [1935] AC 24, 43, 52.

[4] 51 *Law Q. Rev.* 419; Treitel, *Contract*, pp. 452-3.

[5] (1967) 119 CLR 460.

[6] At pp. 478-9 and 493 respectively; the majority opinion also concurs on this point, at p. 486. See also the judgment of Windeyer J. in *Olsson* v. *Dyson* (1969) 43 ALJR 77, at pp. 86-7, where he points out that many cases of novation are inconsistent with the rule that consideration must move from the promisee.

[7] 'A Critical Analysis'.

crucial because, in the case of joint promises, both promisees had to sue together (except after the death of one), while a joint and several promisee may sue alone: hence if such a promisee can sue, a real exception to the rule about consideration moving from the promisee is involved, whereas no such exception is involved in the case of joint promisees. I must plead guilty (in company with Lord Atkin) to having overlooked this ancient technicality of English law; but Lord Atkin and I appear to have been retrospectively vindicated by modern procedural developments. Although at common law it was usually necessary for joint promisees to sue together, it has for a long time been permissible for one joint promisee to sue as sole plaintiff provided that he joins the other joint promisee as defendant, but even this is now no longer strictly necessary as a matter of law. Under the modern Rules of the Supreme Court,[1] it is clear that this distinction between joint promises, and joint and several promises, has been all but abolished; certainly it has come to be treated as a mere rule of procedure. In all cases the plaintiff may now sue such one or more defendants as he chooses; application may then be made to the court that other defendants should be joined as parties, but the court has a substantial discretion as to the outcome of any such application. For all practical purposes, therefore, my original point must stand. A joint promisee who provides no consideration will often be able to enforce a liability against the promisor.

Bankers' commercial credits

Every first-year law student knows that there is something mysterious about bankers' commercial credits and the law of consideration. A bank promises to open a credit in favour of a seller of goods; on the presentation of shipping documents the credit must be honoured by the bank. Nobody doubts that once the documents have been presented to the bank, there is sufficient consideration (in the form of detrimental reliance), but it is questioned whether the promise is binding in the absence of reliance. Yet in practice it is unthinkable that a court could declare such a promise to be unenforceable in modern times, even before reliance. Millions of pounds' worth of business depend on the smooth operation of bankers' credits every year, and an adverse judicial decision could only result in immediate legislative reversal.[2] Although

[1] See Ord. 15, rule 6(2) (*b*).

[2] As argued in Essay 7 it is possible that a presumption of reliance, with a heavy onus of disproof on the bank, might not in practice cause much difficulty; yet I am doubtful that the business community would be content with that result.

no appellate court has had to pronounce on the enforceability of these promises there are certainly dicta which appear to put the law beyond doubt.[1] It is said that if these promises are enforceable without action in reliance by the promisee, this is a clear exception to the doctrine of consideration.[2] It is (with respect) no such thing. There is excellent consideration for the enforcement of the promise, but it is supplied by a third party. It is the buyer who instructs the bank to open the credit in favour of the seller, and the buyer who will have to pay the bank's charges for this facility. Since the buyer does so in fulfilment of his contractual obligations to the seller, there are very good reasons why the promise should be enforceable by the seller.

The Motor Insurers' Bureau agreement

In *Gurtner* v. *Circuit*,[3] there are dicta by the Court of Appeal suggesting that the relevant minister could obtain an order for specific performance to compel the performance of the agreement between him and the Motor Insurers' Bureau. There appears to be no consideration moving from the minister for this agreement, though perhaps this is immaterial in view of the fact that the agreement is under seal. But it is to be noted that the equitable remedy of specific performance is traditionally said not to be available if there is no consideration, even for contracts under seal, so these dicta appear difficult to reconcile with the orthodox view.

Cases where a fictitious consideration by the promisee has been found

There are a number of cases in which the promisor expects to receive a substantial and real consideration from a third party, and yet the promise has been held enforceable by the promisee on the ground that he has supplied some fictitious consideration. *Charnock* v. *Liverpool Corporation*[4] is a striking instance of such a case. Here the plaintiff took his damaged car to the defendants' garage for repair. It was understood and agreed that the bill would be paid by the insurers who promised the defendants to do just this. The court held that the plaintiff was entitled to enforce an implied promise that the work would be done within a reasonable time. Clearly the real consideration was supplied by the insurers, and not by the plaintiff. But it was said that the mere fact of the plaintiff's leaving his car with the defendants was a sufficient

---

[1] *Hamzeh Malas & Sons* v. *British Imex Industries* [1958] 2 QB 127, 129.
[2] Treitel, *Contract*, p. 116.
[3] [1968] 2 QB 587.
[4] [1968] 1 WLR 1498.

consideration. This attempt to conform with orthodoxy seems even thinner than usual, for it would suggest that the plaintiff would still have been entitled to succeed even if the garage had promised to do the repairs without any reward at all. This seems wrong; although I have suggested above that a promise by a gratuitous bailee will be enforceable where the bailment confers a benefit on him, it seems unlikely that the courts would go so far as to enforce such a promise where the only beneficiary is the bailor. If, however, they are prepared to go thus far, then one must recognize another instance of a gratuitous promise being enforced by way of contract. Professor Treitel, of course, sees in this case an example of the court 'inventing' a consideration,[1] and on this point I agree with him. Where I disagree is in thinking that this is a sufficient explanation of the law, because if the court feels justified in disregarding a rule by 'inventing' a consideration in one case, it seems clear that the rule is in fact being modified, and what is being done in one case can be done in others.

Somewhat similar to this case are those in which a person is treated or examined by a medical practitioner engaged and paid by some third party. In *Gladwell* v. *Steggal*,[2] in 1839, it was said that the mere submission to treatment by the infant plaintiff was a sufficient consideration for the defendant's undertaking to treat her with all due care and skill. Yet if the facts are looked at realistically, it is plain that the real consideration moved from the plaintiff's father who engaged the doctor and would have had to pay him. Certainly, the only *bargain* was between the father and the doctor. The same point was taken by Scrutton LJ in *Everett* v. *Griffiths*.[3] In more modern times it has been found unnecessary to construct a contract between the patient and the doctor in this sort of case, because a sufficient foundation for liability has been found in the tort of negligence. Conceivably, however, the question could still arise in a practical form. Suppose, for instance, that a patient is treated by a doctor who is not paid by him, and that the patient is (let us say) inoculated with some drug which turns out to be unfit for use. If the doctor is not negligent, it is nevertheless arguable that an action for breach of warranty could lie, provided that some contractual relationship can be established in the first place.[4] Perhaps, too, this

---

[1] 'A Critical Analysis', p. 446.

[2] (1839) 5 Bing. NC 733.

[3] [1920] 3 KB 163, 193; affirmed [1921] 1 AC 631.

[4] I cannot argue this out fully in a footnote, but the lawyer who wishes to challenge or bypass *Roe* v. *Minister of Health* [1954] 2 QB 66 will find ammunition in *Dodd* v. *Wilson* [1946] 2 All ER 691, and *Young & Marten Ltd.* v. *McManus Childs Ltd.* [1969] 1 AC 454.

expansive approach to consideration might meet the difficulties which are commonly believed to arise when a person orders a meal in a restaurant and it is evident that he is the guest of another.[1] In such a situation it has usually been assumed that no warranty can be implied in favour of the plaintiff because he supplies no consideration though he seems to be plainly (if impliedly) a promisee. Surely, also, there can be no doubt that a person who stays in a hotel, or travels by train or air, is in a contractual relationship with the hotel or the transport concern, even though he is on company business, the arrangements have all been made for him by his company, and the company has told the hotel or other concern to bill it directly.[2] In all these cases, it may be stressed, the real difficulty does not arise from the doctrine of privity but from the supposed rule that consideration must move from the promisee. In all of them it is fairly evident that the plaintiff is, at least impliedly, a promisee; and it is also evident that a genuine consideration is supplied by some third party.

I arrive accordingly at the conclusion that the supposed rule that consideration must move from the promisee is not in practice observed by the courts. Indeed, I have been unable to find a single modern case in which a court has refused to enforce a promise at the suit of the promisee on this ground except for *Dunlop* v. *Selfridge* itself. And in that case, of course, the plaintiff was not in fact the promisee though the House of Lords was prepared to assume that he was an undisclosed principal of the promisee. Orthodox lawyers may find it difficult to believe that a decision of the House of Lords has been so persistently ignored or defied over so long a period, but it is so. To those who may seek some face-saving consolation in this desperate situation I can only offer the following suggestion. The ratio of a case is not what the court deciding the case thinks but what later courts hold the ratio to be. It seems to me indubitable that all later cases treat the ratio of *Dunlop* v. *Selfridge* as concerned with the privity rule and not the consideration rule. It will be seen that my conclusions here lend weight to my preliminary observations about the nature of the rules relating to consideration. If, as I suggest, these rules are merely guides which are used by the courts to help them in deciding whether it is just and politic to enforce a promise, no surprise need be occasioned by this conclusion.

---

[1] *Lockett* v. *A. & M. Charles Ltd.* [1938] 4 All ER 170.

[2] Nor will it do to say that the company supplies the consideration as agent, because that would imply that it has a right of indemnity for the cost—which it plainly does not have.

If a promisor receives a real and substantial consideration from a third party, this is itself a perfectly good reason, in most cases, for enforcing the promise at the suit of the promisee. And so the courts hold.

7. The Enforcement of Gratuitous Promises

It is, of course, an integral part of the orthodox doctrine that gratuitous promises are not enforced by the courts except when they are under seal. So long as a 'gratuitous promise' is defined as meaning a promise without any consideration (as that word is in practice understood by the courts), then this conclusion is not merely sound but self-evident. But if the term 'gratuitous promise' means what it means in ordinary speech, namely a promise to make a gift, then the proposition is not sound. No promise is enforced by the courts unless there is some good reason (or consideration) for its enforcement; and the mere desire to make a gift is not a sufficient reason standing alone. Nor, according to the traditional view of the law, is it a sufficient reason that a man may be morally obliged to keep his word. But all this is just as true of commercial promises as it is of gratuitous promises. In both cases some good reason (or consideration) for enforcement must be shown, though it hardly need be stated that such reasons (or considerations) are more commonly found in the former than in the latter case.

I have already discussed one group of gratuitous promises which are regularly enforced by the courts, namely those cases in which the promisee has performed some act in reliance on the promise which makes it just to enforce the promise. I must now go on to consider the area of promissory estoppel.

The frontier between promissory estoppel and unilateral contracts

Orthodox theory draws a firm line between a promise given for consideration, and a promise enforceable on the ground of promissory estoppel. In the case of a promise for an act, the distinction comes down to a very fine point. If the act is stated or specified (or possibly if it is requested) by the promisor, then the promise is enforceable in the ordinary way; the performance of the act is a good consideration. If the act is done by the promisee in reliance on the promise, but it has not been requested or stated or specified by the promisor, then orthodoxy asserts that there is no consideration, though there is a sufficient reason for giving the promise the limited validity recognized by promissory estoppel. It may help to see this distinction in perspective if the following possible fact situations are differentiated:

1. The promisor requests and desires the act, and the act confers a benefit on him, for example A promises commission to an estate agent if the agent introduces a purchaser who buys A's house. This promise is enforceable once the act is done.

2. The promisor requests and desires the act, but it confers no direct benefit on him, though it involves a factual detriment to the promisee, for example A promises to give B the price of a house if B enters into a contract to purchase it from a third party. This promise is enforceable once the act is done.[1]

3. The promisor requests and desires the act though it confers no direct benefit on him and involves no factual detriment to the promisee, for example A promises a reward to the winner of a race. This promise is enforceable by the winner of the race once he has complied with the condition.[2]

4. The promisor states the act to be performed by the promisee, but does not request or desire it; it confers no benefit on him though it might involve a factual detriment to the promisee, for example a father promises to give an allowance to his daughter if she should decide to leave her husband. This promise is, I submit, enforceable if the promisee acts on it.[3]

5. The promisor does not state any act which is to be performed by the promisee but it is reasonably implicit that such an act is requested or desired by him, for example A promises additional payment to his creditor without stating that he asks for more time to pay, but it is reasonably implicit in the circumstances that this is what he wants. This promise is enforceable once some reasonable time has been given.[4] (It would of course be enforceable at the outset if the creditor expressly or impliedly *promised* to give some reasonable time.)

6. The promisor does not state any act which is to be performed by the promisee but the promisee does act in reliance on the promise in a way which was the natural and foreseeable result of the promise. This promise is said to be not enforceable as a contract, but enforceable to the limited extent recognized by promissory estoppel.

7. The promisor states the act to be performed by the promisee, and the promisee performs some other act which is a necessary step towards

---

[1] *Crosbie* v. *M'Doual* and *Skidmore* v. *Bradford*, p. 211, n. 2, above.

[2] *Hamer* v. *Sidway*, p. 195, n. 1, above.

[3] This was Goodhart's view (67 *Law Q. Rev.* 456 (1951) and 69 *Law Q. Rev.* 106 (1953)). See also *Davies* v. *Rhondda U.D.C.* (1918) 87 LJKB 166.

[4] *Alliance Bank* v. *Broom* (1864) 2 Dr. and Sm. 289. Most collateral contracts also fall into this category.

the performance of the act stated by the promisor, but he does not perform the act stated. The promisee cannot enforce the principal promise but may in some circumstances be able to enforce an implied subsidiary promise.[1]

8. The promisor does not state any act which is to be performed by the promisee, but the promisee acts in reliance on the promise in a way which the promisor had no reason to anticipate.

9. The promisee does not act on the promise at all.

I do not suggest that the above list is an exhaustive statement of the possibilities; indeed, there are plainly other permutations and combinations, but this list will suffice for my purposes. The crucial cases are 6, 7, and 8. Few, I think, would contend that Case 9 is enforceable in the present state of the law, either as a contract or even as a case of promissory estoppel.[2] Certainly *some* factor must be present in this case beyond the bare fact of the promise, if the promise is to be given any recognition, and none is stated in the facts assumed. Case 8 is not a case which has been much discussed. It is, at any rate, clear that orthodoxy would not allow Case 8 to be enforced as a binding contractual promise. The case I wish to concentrate on is Case 6. This is the case of promissory estoppel, but what I want to examine here is not why this case should be enforceable (to a limited extent) as a case of promissory estoppel, but why it should not be enforced as a case of consideration.

The factual difficulty of defining the frontier

If the law of consideration had been recognized for what I suggest it to be, namely a set of guides for deciding whether there is good reason for the enforcement of a promise, the answer would surely have been clear. There is no natural frontier between Case 5 and Case 6. Indeed, there are frequently great difficulties in drawing the factual distinction between Case 5 and Case 6. *Combe* v. *Combe* is one well-known case in which the act was not stated and the court refused ·to imply a statement (or request, as it was there put). On the other hand, in the collateral contract cases, the act to be performed by the promisee would rarely be expressly stated, though it would normally be implicit. The man who deals with another by professing to be an agent is clearly impliedly requesting the other to deal with him. The car dealer who

---

[1] *Luxor, Ltd.* v. *Cooper*, and *Errington* v. *Errington*, above, pp. 203-6.

[2] As to whether the promisee must act to his 'detriment' and in what sense, see pp. 195-6.

gives a collateral promise to a prospective hire-purchaser usually makes it fairly clear what is the act to be done by the promisee. But it is to be observed that the *precise* act need not be stated or specified for a collateral promise to be enforceable. In *Wells* v. *Buckland Sand*,[1] a collateral promise was enforced where the act was the purchase of chrysanthemum sand from a third party who himself acquired the sand from the defendant. It was held that a collateral warranty is enforceable 'notwithstanding that no specific main contract is discussed at the time it is given', although it must be shown that it was contemplated that some such contract would be entered into. No particular contract of sale or hire-purchase thus needs to be identified as the one into which the promisee must enter to make the promise enforceable. But it will be seen that the less precise is the nature of the act stated by the promisor, the closer does Case 5 get to Case 6.

Next, it is to be noted that Case 6 is, or may be, very close to Case 7. In Case 7 the promisee may be given some enforceable contractual right although he has not actually performed the act stated by the promisor—though we have seen that this will only be so in somewhat rare cases.[2] On the other hand in Case 6 the promisee also performs some act other than the act stated, being an act which is the natural result of the promise. The fineness of this distinction in fact is illustrated by the situation in *Hohler* v. *Aston*.[3] In this case the defendant, Mrs A, promised to give a London house to Mr and Mrs R, her niece and husband. She contracted to acquire the property and Mr and Mrs R gave up the lease of their country property and moved into the London house. The defendant then died before the property had been transferred to her or to Mr and Mrs R. Sargant J. was able to decide the case in favour of the plaintiffs without having to consider whether the facts already stated were sufficient to enable Mr and Mrs R to enforce the aunt's promise. But he expressed the view that the promise would probably not have been enforceable, although he acknowledged the hardship which this would have entailed for Mr and Mrs R. If they had given up their country house at Mrs A's request, this would have rendered the promise enforceable, but because this was not actually stated as an act to be performed by them, the promise was (he thought) unenforceable. This distinction is exactly the orthodox doctrine, but the distinction seems so fine as to be virtually unintelligible. It seems

[1] [1965] 2 QB 170.
[2] As shown by the discussion of *Luxor, Ltd.* v. *Cooper*, above.
[3] [1920] 2 Ch. 420.

most undesirable to decide a case of this kind on such a point because the whole issue would turn on oral evidence as to whether the aunt ever said to Mr and Mrs R that they must give up their country property and come and live in the London house. It is probable that recollection of oral discussions to this degree of accuracy would be impossible, and that the decision would actually turn on findings of fact which are bound to be unreliable. Perhaps if the decision had actually turned on this issue Sargant J. would have been prepared to imply a request. It could not be said that this was a *necessary* implication of the defendant's conduct; doubtless Mr and Mrs R could have retained the lease of their country house while going to live in the London house. But the possibility of implying a request where the court feels it necessary to do justice is another confirmation of the unreality of the factual distinction between Case 5 and Case 6.

Policy arguments for maintaining the frontier
But even if these arguments are not felt to be convincing, it remains to inquire whether there can be any rational ground for distinguishing between Case 5 and Case 6. I have already indicated that this seems to me an impossible line to maintain. So long as it is believed that all contracts are bargains, there is some rational ground for requiring that the act to be performed by the promisee must be stated, if not actually requested, by the promisor; but once it is agreed that many promises are enforced though they are not bargains, it is hard to see what rational purpose is intended to be served by the insistence that the act must be stated. The natural place to draw a line in the above listed cases is not between Case 5 and Case 6 but between Case 7 and Case 8. The difference between an act done by the promisee which is impliedly stated by the promisor, and an act done in natural and foreseeable reliance on the promise seems much less substantial than the distinction between the latter case and an act in reliance which could not have been anticipated by the promisor. That is not to say that even this last case may not, in certain circumstances, be thought to be a promise worthy of enforcement.

The authorities
I turn, now, to inquire whether the orthodox distinction between Case 5 and Case 6 is in fact supported by the actual decisions of the courts. And here we find a somewhat paradoxical situation. By the time of the *High Trees* decision in 1946, orthodox opinion had become so hardened

in the view that gratuitous promises were never enforceable and that only bargains could constitute contracts, that orthodox lawyers could not believe that the dicta of Denning J. in that case could be sound law. When the issue came up again in *Combe* v. *Combe*, even Denning LJ (as he had then become) resiled from the view that a *High Trees* type of promise could be fully enforceable as a contractual promise. *Combe* v. *Combe*, it will be recalled, involved the enforceability of a promise by a husband to pay his wife £100 per annum on their separation. The wife did not apply for maintenance to the court, nor did she make any attempt to enforce the husband's promise for a period of some six years. She then sued the husband for £600. At first instance Byrne J. applied the dictum of Denning J. in the *High Trees* case and gave judgment for the wife. The judgment of Byrne J. gives no hint that the learned judge thought that he was doing anything very radical or unprecedented in enforcing the husband's promise. Perhaps he thought that the husband had impliedly requested that the wife should forbear from applying for maintenance. But even if he had thought that there was no such implied request, his decision would have been perfectly explicable in terms of the existing case-law. As we have already seen, a forbearance (or an act) which naturally and foreseeably follows a promise had been previously held to be a good consideration for the enforcement of a promise in a number of situations.

When *Combe* v. *Combe* came before the Court of Appeal, however, that decision was reversed. The court first held that there was no implied request by the husband that the wife should forbear; and even if they were wrong in thinking that a request (as opposed to a statement of the act or forbearance) was necessary, the absence of an implied request must have also led to the view that there was no implied statement in that case. Perhaps the court should have implied a request, as Professor Goodhart cogently argued.[1] Certainly they *could* have done so without doing the least violence to the facts. Why then did they not do so? I submit that they did not do so because they did not feel that the justice of the case required it. Denning LJ himself made no secret of his views as to the merits of the case: 'The doctrine of consideration is sometimes said to work injustice, but I see none in this case . . . I do not think it would be right for this wife, who is better off than her husband, to take no action for six or seven years and then come down on him for the whole £600.'[2] With this statement I find myself in complete sympathy.

[1] 67 *Law Q. Rev.* 456 (1951), 69 *Law Q. Rev.* 106 (1953).
[2] [1951] 2 KB at p. 222.

In recent times it has become clear that the changing moral values of our society mean that a man is not necessarily regarded as under any obligation to maintain a separated wife—especially if she has an income as large as his own. It is true that the addition of an express promise may suffice to create such an obligation but in this situation the length of time which had elapsed since the promise was made had completely altered the nature of the promise which the wife was trying to enforce. What the husband promised was an income of £100 per annum, a matter of £2 per week. What the wife was trying to enforce was payment of a lump sum of £600. While I would freely admit that two views may be possible as to the merits of the case, I find it hard to believe that the Court of Appeal did not regard the merits as with the husband. Had they wished to find in favour of the wife it would have been so easy to imply a requested forbearance that it is hard to believe they did in fact wish to do so.

If we pause here for a moment, what did *Combe* v. *Combe* actually decide? The common (and now orthodox) interpretation of the case is that it decides this: that action by a promisee in reliance on a promise (where the action is not requested or stated) is not directly enforceable by the promisee, but may be set up by him as a defence to proceedings by the promisor. Once again I feel obliged to depart from orthodox doctrine. I would suggest that, on the contrary, the case decided nothing more than this: that an act (or forbearance) which naturally and foreseeably follows from and in reliance on a promise is not a consideration for the enforcement of the promise *where the justice of the case does not require that it should be.* So viewed the decision is perfectly in line with older cases. Among these cases are the ones to which I have already made reference, namely *Dillwyn* v. *Llewellyn*, and the line of authorities following it. There is no doubt that the principle stated in these cases is flatly inconsistent with orthodox doctrine; for these cases stand for the principle that if a man promises to give another some land, and permits the other to build a property on his land, then even though he has not requested or stated that such building is the act on which his promise becomes enforceable, the promise will be enforceable. As I have already pointed out, the judges who decided these cases did not find anything inconsistent between the notion of requiring a consideration for the enforcement of a promise, and yet enforcing the promises in these cases. I have also pointed out that attempts have been made by orthodox lawyers to 'explain' away these decisions, but the need for such 'explanations' only arises because of the conviction that they are inconsistent with some 'doctrine' for which there was (in this respect) no contrary authority.

Today, it must be admitted, the *High Trees* case has itself become the new orthodoxy; or at least it has become the new orthodoxy as orthodoxy interprets *Combe* v. *Combe*. Here is a paradox indeed. The *High Trees* principle, as cut down by the generally accepted interpretation placed on *Combe* v. *Combe*, was not the radical and forward-looking innovation that it was thought by orthodoxy to be. It was, on the contrary, a reactionary step. It did not create new defences to actions which would previously have found the defendant helpless. On the contrary, it refused to recognize as a consideration what earlier courts were willing to recognize as consideration.

I do not rely solely on *Dillwyn* v. *Llewellyn* and the cases following it for my view that an act done in reliance on a promise may be a good consideration even though it is not stated or requested by the promisor as an act to be performed by the promisee. These particular cases may be explained away as anomalous or exceptional. I therefore turn to an examination of the House of Lords' decision in *Jorden* v. *Money*,[1] which lies at the heart of this whole question. The treatment of this case by lawyers during the past fifty years is one of the most extraordinary chapters in the whole law of consideration,[2] and must make one wonder whether lawyers actually read the cases which form the pillars of orthodoxy.

The facts in *Jorden* v. *Money* were as follows. The plaintiff M had executed a bond for £1,200 in favour of one C, and on C's death the bond had passed to the defendant, Miss M, now Mrs J. The defendant had frequently stated to M and others that the debt was gone, and that she would never enforce it; she repeated these statements at a time when M was contemplating marriage. In reliance thereon M did marry; subsequently the defendant married and then demanded payment on the bond. The plaintiff therefore brought a suit in equity asking for an order that the bond be given up and cancelled. It was held that the suit should be dismissed. Now, what did this case decide? The commonly accepted view is that the case decided that a representation of intention cannot be the foundation for an estoppel; estoppel can only arise from a statement of fact. Therefore, although the plaintiff relied on Mrs J's

---

[1] (1854) 5 HL Cas. 185.
[2] See, for a typical example, Jackson, 81 *Law Q. Rev.* pp. 87-95 (1965). This treatment of *Jorden* v. *Money* is also to be found in the Sixth Interim Report of the Law Revision Committee in 1937, para. 40, but I have not attempted to trace it back further.

representations of intention by marrying, he could not plead estoppel. Naturally this causes great difficulty to the new orthodoxy which recognizes the defence of promissory estoppel based on a representation of intention. How can this be reconciled with *Jorden* v. *Money*? One suggestion is that that case was a decision at common law, while promissory estoppel is an equitable development.[1] But this will not do; *Jorden* v. *Money* was a decision in equity on appeal from the Chancery Court of Appeal. Another explanation is that *Jorden* v. *Money* does not lay down an absolute rule; exceptions to it may be justified.[2] Another suggestion is that Mrs J did not intend to be legally bound by her promises,[3] and there are remarks by Lord Cranworth which would support this,[4] though the suggestion is difficult to reconcile with some of the evidence, and it would anyhow involve rejection of most of the speeches as erroneous dicta.[5] Another suggestion is that promissory estoppel is not really estoppel at all.[6] Another is that the new promissory estoppel has a more limited effect than a 'real' estoppel,[7] and another is that the decision was wrong.[8]

The truth is that there is a very much simpler explanation of *Jorden* v. *Money* which seems to stare in the face anyone who actually reads the report.[9] Discussions of the case all start with the assumption that the plaintiff could not enforce the defendant's promise in contract because he could show no consideration; and it is for this reason that (it is assumed) the plaintiff relied on estoppel. The truth is precisely the opposite. The plaintiff could have proved a good contract; in fact—it

[1] This explanation was hinted at in earlier editions of Cheshire and Fifoot, op. cit., p. 207 above (e.g. 6th edn., p. 83), but see now 10th edn., p. 89, suggesting that the effect of promissory estoppel is suspensory only.

[2] Anson on *Contracts*, 26th edn. (1984), p. 102.

[3] Lord Denning in *High Trees* [1947] KB 130, 134.

[4] Although the defendant repeatedly said that she would not enforce the bond she refused to give it up physically; the difficulty was to draw the correct inference from this fact. Lord Cranworth thought that it showed she did not mean to be bound in law but in honour only (5 HL Cas. 221-2) but another explanation which the defendant herself gave was that she hoped one day to enforce the bond against the plaintiff's co-obligor (who was, however, bankrupt at the time).

[5] Not to mention many other cases in which *Jorden* v. *Money* has been followed, see e.g. *Maddison* v. *Alderson* (1883) 8 App. Cas. 467; *Nippon Menkwa* v. *Dawson's Bank* (1935) 51 Ll. L. R. 146.

[6] This explanation was offered in earlier editions of Treitel, *Contract* (e.g. 3rd edn., p. 98), but see now 6th edn., p. 101 for a similar view to that of Cheshire and Fifoot.

[7] Wilson, 67 *Law Q. Rev.* 330 (1951).

[8] Jackson, 81 *Law Q. Rev.* 84 (1965).

[9] See also J. H. Baker, 'From Sanctity of Contract to Reasonable Expectation', [1979] *Cur. Leg. Prob.* 17 which substantially supports my interpretation of *Jorden* v. *Money*.

is scarcely too much to say—he *did* show a good contract, and that is precisely why he failed. To understand this paradoxical statement it must be recalled that the Statute of Frauds required at this time that a promise in consideration of marriage must be proved in writing. The only act in reliance on the promise which the plaintiff could show was his marriage; *but he had no written note or memorandum signed by the defendant.* His counsel, therefore, deliberately refrained from arguing his case in contract but relied on estoppel. The whole point of the case (at all events as it developed in the House of Lords) was whether the plaintiff was entitled to do this. Could he evade the Statute of Frauds by calling his cause of action estoppel instead of contract? Had this stratagem succeeded, a blow would have been dealt to the Statute of Frauds greater than anything that had gone before; for it would have meant that any plaintiff who could show that he had altered his position in reliance on the defendant's promise could ignore the statute and rely on estoppel.[1] And since at this time the distinction between estoppel as a cause of action and as a ground of defence was not established, the threatened evasion of the statute would have seemed even wider than it might today. Had *Jorden* v. *Money* gone the other way, the result might well have been to confine the Statute of Frauds to executory contracts. It is, therefore, quite understandable that the House of Lords should not have sanctioned the plaintiff's claim.

That this is the true explanation of the case seems to me borne out by the whole of the report, but as this explanation appears to run counter to everything said about the case since, I must justify my assertion by detailed reference to the report itself. I look first at the arguments and there I find that the plaintiff's counsel, Mr Roundell Palmer (afterwards Lord Chancellor Selborne), argues that the Statute of Frauds does not apply:[2]

MR PALMER: The first question on this point is, whether this is a case in which the Statute of Frauds applies at all. The respondent relies on two grounds of equity;[3] first, that there having been an assurance of the creditor that the bond should not be enforced, a marriage took place on the faith of that assurance. The Statute of Frauds cannot apply to such a case.

THE LORD CHANCELLOR: It does not apply if the party was led into the marriage

---

[1] Viewed in this light, it will also be seen that the plaintiff's case was in a sense based on his 'part-performance' (i.e. the detrimental act which formed the basis of the alleged estoppel) and the decision was therefore a forerunner of *Maddison* v. *Alderson*.

[2] 5 HL Cas. at 206-7.

[3] The second point was an attempt to set up a wholly independent consideration (which did not move from the promisee) but which failed on the evidence.

by a misrepresentation of fact; but the question is, whether, when the creditor says, 'I have abandoned' (supposing her to have said so), she means more than 'I will not enforce'; and then the further question is, whether that is not a contract to which the Statute is applicable.

MR PALMER: It is not: the statute says, 'nor upon any agreement made upon consideration of marriage'. This was not so made: it is a promise with reference to a marriage, a promise of a creditor not to enforce a claim; but it is not a promise the consideration of which, in the legal sense of the words, is a marriage.

The real issue in the case could hardly be more clearly put. Palmer is arguing that a representation of intention followed by marriage in reliance thereon differs from a promise supported by the consideration of the marriage. Lord Cranworth disagrees.

In his judgment Lord Cranworth maintains this opinion:

I think that that doctrine [estoppel] does not apply to a case where the representation is not a representation of a fact, but a statement of something which the party intends or does not intend to do. In the former case it is a contract, in the latter it is not; what is here contended for, is this, that Mrs. Jorden, then Miss Marnell, over and over again represented that she abandoned the debt. Clothe that in any words you please, it means no more than this, that she would never enforce the debt; she does not mean, in saying that she had abandoned it, to say that she had executed a release of the debt so as to preclude her legal right to sue. All that she could mean, was that she positively promised that she never would enforce it. My opinion is, that if all the evidence had come up to the mark, which, for reasons I shall presently state, I do not think it did, that if upon the very eve of the marriage she had said, 'William Money, I never will enforce the bond against you' that would not bring it within these cases. *It might be, if all statutable requisites, so far as there are statutable requisites, had been complied with, that it would have been a very good contract whereby she might have bound herself not to enforce the payment. That, however, is not the way in which it is put here; in short, it could not have been, because it must have been a contract reduced into writing and signed; but that is not the way in which this case is put; it is put entirely upon the ground of representation.* Now my Lords, I think that the not adhering to this statement call it contract or call it representation, is no more fraud[1] than it would be not adhering to her engagement if she had said, 'Mr William Money, you may marry; do not be in fear, you will not be in want; I promise to settle £10,000 Consols upon you.' *If she does not perform that promise, she is guilty of a breach of contract, in respect of which she may be sued, if it is put into a*

---

[1] Had there been fraud of course the Statute of Frauds could have been bypassed because it was already well established that the statute was not to be used as an instrument of fraud.

valid form, but not otherwise; so if she had said, as she did to William Money, 'I mean to give you everything I am worth in the world; I promise to do so', her not doing so, is no fraud in the sense in which these cases speak of fraud; it is no misrepresentation of a fact which the party is afterwards held bound to make good as true; it seems to me that the distinction is founded upon perfectly good sense, and that in truth in the case of what is something future, there is no reason for the application of the rule, because the parties have only to say, 'Enter into a contract,' and then all difficulty is removed.[1]

I do not see how the point could be more clearly put. Estoppel is a necessary part of the law where the misrepresentation is one of fact because that cannot be enforced as a promise.[2] It is unnecessary where the misrepresentation is one of intention because there is no difference between such a misrepresentation followed by reliance and a promise given for consideration.[3] Lord Brougham, the concurring judge, does not expressly deal with the Statute of Frauds but he also makes it plain that in his opinion the defendant *promised* that she would not enforce the bond.[4] I have no doubt that Lord Brougham, like Lord Cranworth, would have regarded that promise as made for consideration and enforceable if it had not been for the Statute of Frauds, subject perhaps to the argument that Mrs Jorden intended to be bound in honour only. The dissenting judge, Lord St Leonards, thought that the principle of estoppel could be applied to a representation of intention. But he too makes it clear that he is not treating promissory estoppel as a doctrine which can only be used when there is no contract, but as a doctrine which may legitimately be used by the courts even where there is a contract which is unenforceable under the Statute of Frauds.

Your lordships are asked to consider that a representation of an intention is not a binding contract, and that you cannot misrepresent what you intend to do. But if you declare your intention with reference, for example, to a marriage, not to enforce a given right, and the marriage takes place on that declaration, I submit that, in point of law, that is a binding undertaking.[5]

I cannot quote here the whole of Lord St Leonards's judgment but

---

[1] 5 HL Cas. at pp. 214-17. The italics are mine.

[2] Lord Cranworth was not to know that such misrepresentations were very soon to become enforceable as implied promises in a wide variety of cases.

[3] This is also confirmed by Lord Cranworth's speech only a few months before *Jorden* v. *Money* in *Maunsell* v. *Hedges* (1854) 4 HL Cas. 1039, at pp. 1055-6, in which he explicitly states that there is no difference between a promise intended to be and in fact acted upon, and a contract: 'they are identical'.

[4] 5 HL Cas. at p. 227.

[5] Ibid., at pp. 251-2.

anyone who cares to read it for himself will see that the question to which he adverts throughout is whether the misrepresentation of intention can be sued on despite the Statute of Frauds.[1]

The true view: an unnecessary frontier

It will be seen, therefore, that virtually all modern academic (and much judicial) discussion of promissory estoppel has been entirely beside the point. This discussion invariably takes as its starting point the assumption that the performance of an act in reliance on a promise, not requested or stated by the promisor, cannot be a good consideration. If this assumption is unfounded then there is not, and never was, any need for promissory estoppel.[2] *Jorden* v. *Money*, far from being (as the new orthodoxy would have it) a difficult obstacle in the way of recognition of promissory estoppel, is a clear indication that promissory estoppel was never necessary at all. The facts of *Jorden* v. *Money* are the clearest possible example of my Case 6 that I have been able to find. The plaintiff undoubtedly married in reliance on the defendant's promise but the defendant never requested the marriage nor did she promise to release the debt if and when the plaintiff married. Her promise was, indeed, originally made before any question of marriage was in contemplation; it was repeated time and again and the plaintiff acted upon it by his marriage. I have myself no doubt that, as the law was then understood, this was a good consideration for the enforcement of the promise which would (apart from the Statute of Frauds) have been enforced by the House of Lords in 1854.

I do not, of course, mean to say that nineteenth-century courts would have held that a promise always becomes enforceable whenever the promisee acts in reliance on it (even though the act is not requested or stated by the promisor). But what I suggest is that the courts were at that time prepared to enforce such a promise where they felt that the justice of the case required it. If this was so, then there was good reason

---

[1] Lord St Leonards also argued that estoppel based on a statement of fact was itself invented partly in order to evade the Statute of Frauds and that there was therefore no reason why the courts should be afraid to use statements of intention in the same way. Support for this is to be found in *Pickard* v. *Sears* (1837) 6 Ad. and E. 469, 474. If this is right, it seems that the doctrine of estoppel by misrepresentation may have had its origins in the attempts to evade the Statute of Frauds, and that, without the statute, cases of estoppel might from the beginning have been treated as contractual misrepresentations. For further analysis of the distinction (if any) between estoppel and warranty, see Essay 10.

[2] It might, of course, be argued that estoppel is a useful device in *limiting* the enforceability of promises, but needless to say it has never been put forward as such.

(or consideration) for enforcement in the promisee's actions in reliance on the promise.[1] Alas, the new orthodoxy has now itself grown so strong and vigorous that it seems too late for the courts to recognize what they have actually done. In *Crabb* v. *Arun District Council*[2] the Court of Appeal actually 'enforced' (by appropriate equitable decrees) an arrangement (to use a neutral term) in a case where one judge insisted that the whole question was whether there was an agreement between the parties. But this 'agreement' though 'enforced' by court decrees was not regarded as a contract, but merely as a set of representations of intention which were enforceable because they had been relied upon to the plaintiff's prejudice. When I protested that if there was an agreement and it was enforced, this must have been a contract,[3] I was rebuked[4] for failing to understand that contracts are designed to enforce agreements, while estoppel is designed to protect reliance. The reader will (I trust) by now know enough of my views to appreciate that I do not assume that because there was (as I think) a 'contract' in this case, it should have been enforceable without any reliance by the plaintiff. I merely protest at the absurdity of a conceptual analysis which states that the agreement in *Crabb* v. *Arun District Council* was not enforceable because the detrimental reliance was not requested, and therefore failed to comply with the requirements of consideration; and then proceeds to add that the 'agreement' was nevertheless enforceable because the element of reliance did satisfy the doctrine of promissory estoppel. Surely, it would be simpler and more sensible if the law made up its mind what kind of detrimental reliance was sufficient to justify the imposition of some kind of obligation without regard to whether the case should be classified as involving consideration or promissory estoppel.

The present position—what I have called the new orthodoxy—might be more defensible if estoppel, or promissory estoppel, was only called upon to protect reliance, and therefore was confined to cases in which expectations should not be protected. Whether or not these cases should be called 'contracts' therefore would be settled by arbitrary fiat: cases

---

[1] This is, of course, the position taken by the American Restatement of Contracts (first and second), §90. It is well known that Corbin wanted to see 'action in reliance' treated as 'consideration', but in the result the Restatement treated such promises as enforceable contracts without consideration.

[2] [1976] Ch. 179.

[3] 'When is an Enforceable Agreement Not a Contract? Answer: When it is an Equity', 92 *Law Q. Rev.* 174 (1976).

[4] '*Crabb* v. *Arun District Council*—A Riposte', ibid., p. 342.

where only reliance interests are to be protected would not be entitled to be called contracts. But the new orthodoxy is far more complex than this. In *Crabb* v. *Arun District Council* (and many similar cases), plaintiffs have had their expectation interests protected by use of promissory (or as it is now called in these cases, proprietary) estoppel, and there are, of course, many genuine contracts in which only reliance interests are protected. Thus the line between promissory estoppel and consideration does not parallel the line between reliance protection and expectation protection.

The present orthodoxy therefore seems to me unnecessarily cumbrous. It would be a great deal simpler if the courts were willing to treat action in reliance which suffices for estoppel as also sufficient to satisfy the requirements of consideration; but it would at the same time be necessary, of course, for the courts to become more sophisticated about when expectation protection is, and when it is not, justified. If American experience is anything to go by, it may well be necessary to retain considerable flexibility as to when to confine contractual redress to the protection of reliance, and when to go further; it is unwise to try to draw this line by fastening on the absurdly narrow and unreal distinction between an action in reliance which is requested, and one which is not requested, but merely foreseeable. Fortunately, in practice it is so easy for a court to 'imply' a request when it wishes to do so, that no court which wishes directly to enforce a promise in this sort of case need find any difficulty in doing so. And I may illustrate that this can and still does happen by referring again to *V/O Rasnoimport* v. *Guthrie & Co. Ltd.* The consideration for the enforcement of the promisor's implied warranty of authority in this case was held to be the act of the plaintiffs in taking up the bill of lading in due course of business. It seems to strain the meaning of words to say that the defendants requested anyone to take up the bill of lading; it even strains the meaning of words to say that the defendants promised that they had authority to sign the bill of lading and impliedly stated to the world that the promise was to take effect on the taking up of the bill of lading. It is much more in accordance with reality to say that the defendants impliedly warranted their authority and that in the ordinary course of business the plaintiffs relied on this statement by taking up the bill of lading.

8. Reform of the Law of Consideration

This is already a long essay and I have not space here to develop fully my ideas about the reform of the law of consideration. But there are, I suggest, important conclusions to be drawn from what I have tried to demonstrate. The first is that to talk of abolition of the doctrine of consideration is nonsensical. Consideration means a reason for the enforcement of a promise, or, even more broadly, a reason for the recognition of an obligation. If the broader sense is right, then, of course, talk of abolition is quite absurd. But even if one takes only the narrower sense, it is hard to take seriously talk of abolition. Nobody can seriously propose that all promises should become enforceable; to abolish the doctrine of consideration, therefore, is simply to require the courts to begin all over again the task of deciding what promises are to be enforceable. They will, of course, have to use new technical justifications for this task, and the obvious one that lies to hand is the 'intent to create legal relations'. No doubt there is something to be said for beginning this task all over again, and for using a new technique for the purpose. Changes in social and commercial conditions, and changes in the moral values of the community, mean that the courts will not always find the same reasons for the enforcement of promises to be good today as their forbears did; equally, it is likely that they will often find good reasons for the enforcement of promises where their predecessors did not. Moreover, I think there is less likelihood of the 'intent to create legal relations' formula ossifying into a 'doctrine'; though there is the converse danger that its application may create uncertainty as to what promises will be enforceable. But I question whether the 'intent to create legal relations' formula will in the long run work any better than the rules of consideration.

In particular, I believe that the problems arising from the enforcement of gratuitous promises are too complex to be adequately dealt with by either the rules of consideration or the 'intent to create legal relations' formula. For a start, the 'intent' formula can only be squared with the importance of detrimental reliance by repeated use of fictions. And if it should be suggested that the law should be more willing to enforce gratuitous promises, I believe that it will be necessary to start by asking more about the concept of a 'gratuitous' promise. To be legally enforceable, gratuitous promises will presumably need to be sensible, rational activities. But surely we then need to ask more about the kind of circumstances in which people do rationally make gratuitous promises, and we may need to distinguish various classes of cases. For instance, there are promises made in a commercial context which may appear gratuitous, but where the promisor expects some return in a rather more indirect way than the present doctrine of consideration recognizes. There is a lot to be said for the view that such promises are really bargain promises, and should be fully enforceable, even while executory, to the same extent as ordinary contracts. (But there is also a lot to be said for achieving this result by modification of the present rather rigid view of what kind of benefit constitutes a sufficient consideration.) Then there are gratuitous charitable promises, gratuitous family promises, and so on. Above all, of course, there is the distinction between gratuitous relied-upon and unrelied-upon promises.

Whether unrelied-upon gratuitous promises should ever be rendered enforceable seems to me a very dubious proposition, and even if the principle is conceded, such promises are difficult to generalize about in advance, because so much depends on the context out of which they arise. It may conceivably be found desirable to enforce gratuitous promises in a much wider range of circumstances than exists at the moment, but not to the same extent as ordinary commercial promises. For instance, it may be found wise to render some gratuitous promises enforceable in principle against the promisor, but not necessarily against his executors. Whether this would be just may well depend on his family obligations, and the solvency of his estate. It may be wise to provide for a much wider defence of frustration in the case of gratuitous promises, if they are to become enforceable while yet unrelied upon. A man promises his son an allowance while the latter is at the university; it may be just and equitable to enforce this promise, but would it remain just and equitable if the promisor became incapacitated and lost his job? Perhaps, too, a wider latitude should be allowed to some form of defence based on mistake. Perhaps we need to consider the possibility of the conduct of the promisee depriving him of the right to enforce a gratuitous promise. Perhaps we need to consider a shorter limitation period. And perhaps after all some gratuitous promises may be better treated as merely giving rise to a defence rather than a cause of action.[1] Certainly we shall need to consider whether the same rules will be appropriate for all kinds of gratuitous promises. A promise to render gratuitous services is not necessarily in like case with a promise to make a cash gift; and a promise of money to a charity is not necessarily the

---

[1] So perhaps after all the modern orthodoxy may have something to be said for it. But the distinction between enforcing a promise as a sword and not just as a shield must be based on some more rational ground than the wholly artificial distinction recognized by the new orthodoxy.

same as a promise made to a member of the family. In short we must look to the reasons (or considerations) which make it just or desirable to enforce promises, and also to the extent to which it is just to enforce them.

9

Judicial Techniques and the Law of Contract

1. Introduction

The purpose of this essay is to explore a number of problems and cases in the law of contract with a view to illustrating the way in which the same problems can be, and indeed have been, dealt with by use of differing legal techniques, to suggest that some of the academic controversies of recent times are in reality arguments about the use of these techniques, and to consider the respective merits and demerits of some of the principal techniques in current use.

A large part of the law of contract is concerned with allocating the risks of untoward events between the parties, using this term in the broadest sense to include events or facts existing at the time when the contract is made, and events occurring only subsequently. In many contracts there are certain obvious risks which are allocated by the very nature of the contract, and, leaving aside such external factors as fraud, lack of capacity, or illegality, there is no room for argument about the outcome of a case concerned solely with such risks. The buyer in a contract of sale takes the risk that the market price of the goods may fall, the insurer in a life insurance contract takes the risk that the insured may be run over by a bus the day after the policy is issued, the surety takes the risk of the principal debtor failing to pay, and so forth. To be sure, there is nothing in the law of nature which prescribes these results. A buyer may contract on terms that he is only to pay the market price of the goods prevailing on delivery, a life insurance contract could be entered into which does not cover accidental death, a surety could guarantee the ability but not the willingness of the principal debtor to pay.[1] But the point is that, however unusual the contract, however circumscribed the liabilities of the parties, there will almost always be some obvious risks which are allocated by the contract, and which the parties probably realize they are assuming by the very act of entering

[1] Cf. *Gerrard* v. *James* [1925] Ch. 616, concerning the liability of the guarantor of an *ultra vires* debt, where the court regarded the question as turning on whether the guarantor had assumed the risk of non-payment by the company on grounds of legal incapacity as well as on grounds of financial inability.

into the contract—though (as I have argued in Essays 2 and 7) it does not follow that the parties subjectively *intend* to assume these risks.

The difficulties in the allocation of risks begin to emerge when the risks which eventuate are unlikely to have been contemplated by the parties, or perhaps one of the parties. Lawyers tend to assume that this is only the case when the risks are somewhat out of the normal, although I think it likely that, as a matter of strict fact, parties frequently do not actually advert to all sorts of possibilities which are not really unusual. For present purposes, however, I will continue to talk of 'unusual risks' as signifying risks 'unlikely to have been contemplated'. It is in these circumstances that disputes are likely to arise, each party feeling it unjust that he should bear a risk which he did not contemplate. In resolving these conflicts, the traditional approach of the English lawyer has been, in the first instance, to conceptualize the problem. Is there a contract at all? Is it void or voidable? Is this a question of mistake, misrepresentation, duty of disclosure, frustration, or construction? Indeed, the ability to classify the problem into its 'correct' legal category is regarded as one of the most important skills to be inculcated into the English law student. But what is crucially important—and this is the aspect of the matter which has perhaps been insufficiently discussed in English legal literature—is to appreciate that what is involved in this process of conceptualization is largely the selection of a particular technique. It is well known that the 'true' basis of the doctrine of frustration has given rise to considerable academic controversy in which even the judiciary has shared.[1] And the arguments over the 'correct' classification of problems of mistake have given rise to a voluminous literature (in which the present writer has taken part) which is so well known that it is unnecessary to cite again here. But these controversies now appear to me to be largely, though not necessarily exclusively, about the use of techniques: they tell us nothing about the actual solution of the problems from which they spring. When, for example, there is controversy over whether a problem of common mistake is 'truly' a problem about the construction of the contract, or whether there is an independent rule of law avoiding a contract for common fundamental mistake, this tells us nothing about when in fact a contract will be held 'void' and the risks allocated in a particular

---

[1] See e.g. Treitel, *Law of Contract*, 6th edn., pp. 694-7; Cheshire and Fifoot, *Law of Contract*, 10th edn., pp. 512-16; *British Movietonews Ltd.* v. *London & District Cinemas Ltd.* [1952] AC 166; *Davies Contractors Ltd.* v. *Fareham Urban District Council* [1956] AC 696.

manner. Similarly, arguments about the 'true' foundation of the doctrine of frustration do not by themselves tell us when a court will hold
a contract to be frustrated.

This is not to say that the use of legal techniques is not important,
nor even that the outcome of a case may not sometimes be determined
by the selection of one technique rather than another. The proper use
of legal technique is, in some contexts, of vital importance. For the
practising barrister the correct use of legal techniques means, after all,
that he must talk the kind of language which the court understands.
Even the merest tyro will soon learn, for instance, that it is not much
use arguing against a particular construction of a written contract on
the ground that it would produce unjust or inconvenient results for his
client; but he will equally soon learn that it is perfectly permissible to
present the same argument in the form that 'the parties could not have
intended' the contract to bear the meaning argued against because of
the results which would follow. This is an illustration of the fairly
harmless foible of ascribing the 'true construction' of a written instrument to the intention of the person who made it—harmless because
in most cases it is perfectly clear what is being done. But in other cases
what is being done may not always be so apparent, and may indeed be
disguised by the skilful use of certain techniques. In such cases, the
selection of one technique rather than another by careful pleading and
advocacy may be essential to success.

I do not, of course, deny that some of these controversies about
correct legal technique sometimes echo controversies of a more ideological character about the very foundations of contractual liability.
Indeed, disguising what is actually being done by skilful use of technique is often itself due to a desire to appear to comply with one
theoretical basis of contractual liability rather than another. English
judges who constantly refer everything to the 'intention of the parties'
are, whether they appreciate it or not, placing themselves in the line of
direct descent from classical contract theory. Judges who profess
greater candour and admit that they are sometimes engaged in 'imposing' a solution on the parties, are departing from that theory.[1]
However, what I wish to suggest is that disagreements among the judges
as to the formulation of the legal principles to be applied rarely reflect

---

[1] See e.g. Lord Wilberforce in *National Carriers Ltd.* v. *Panalpina (Northern) Ltd.*
[1981] AC 675 at 696. But cf. Lord Scarman in *Tai Hing Cotton Ltd.* v. *Liu Chong Hing
Bank Ltd.* [1985] 2 All ER 947, 955 where the language of 'imposition' is expressly
rejected in favour of that of 'implication'.

fundamental disagreements about ideology or basic theory or values. The ideology of the English judiciary at any one time displays an astonishing uniformity in most areas of law, although there have been wide variations in ideology over the centuries. These disagreements today tend to display, rather, variations in the level of sophistication about the true nature of judicial reasoning. So although these controversies about technique often echo more fundamental disagreements about values, they tend in practice not to be about these fundamental controversies themselves, but about the matters of technique and little else. In the remainder of this article I propose to examine a number of problems connected with mistake and with duties of disclosure with a view to illustrating the way in which these problems are now usually dealt with by the use of one particular technique—the construction technique. I hasten to add that I do not wish to review here any of the well-worn controversies about mistake, and I propose to confine my attention largely to a small group of cases in most of which no mention was made of mistake at all.

2. Common Fundamental Mistake and Construction

The decision of the Court of Appeal in *Financings, Ltd.* v. *Stimson*[1] is a case of such interest to the theme of this essay that it will be worth setting out the facts in some detail, for it will be necessary to return to the case repeatedly. On 16 March the defendant called at a car dealer's garage, inspected a car, and indicated that he wanted to buy it on hire-purchase terms. The dealer gave him the usual finance company proposal forms which the defendant duly completed, and which were thereupon dispatched by the dealer to the plaintiff finance company. The forms stated that the agreement was only to become binding on signature on behalf of the plaintiffs, and also contained a declaration that the hirer had examined the goods and satisfied himself that they were in good condition. The dealer would not allow the defendant possession of the car without production of a comprehensive insurance certificate. Two days later the defendant again called on the dealer with the certificate, and asked to be allowed to drive the car away. The dealer communicated by telephone with the plaintiffs who agreed to the car being delivered to the defendant. Accordingly, the defendant drove it off and used it for two days, but he was so dissatisfied with it that he returned it to the dealer, told him that he did not want to go on

[1] [1962] 3 All ER 386.

with the agreement, and even offered to forfeit his initial payment of some £70 rather than remain bound by the agreement, as he thought he was. He also cancelled his insurance coverage. The dealer failed to inform the plaintiffs what had happened, and on the night of 24-25 March the car was stolen from the dealer's garage and was only re-covered in a damaged condition some days later. It was estimated that the damage would have cost about £44 to repair. On the following day, both parties being in ignorance of what had happened, the plaintiffs signed the proposal form and returned a copy to the defendant. When the defendant repudiated the agreement, the plaintiffs resold the car at a loss and sued the defendant for damages for the breach.

The defendant took two points, on both of which he succeeded. First, he argued that he had revoked his offer to enter into the hire-purchase agreement by returning the car to the dealer, and the dealer must be treated as the plaintiffs' agent to receive notice of revocation; second, he argued that his offer to enter into the agreement was subject to an implied condition that the car was, at the time of the acceptance, in substantially the same condition as at the date of the offer itself. The first point is of no special interest for the purposes of this essay, but the second gives rise to some interesting questions.

It will be observed, in the first place, that the condition which the court was prepared to imply was not a condition of the contract, but a condition in the offer, the whole effect of which, indeed, was that there never was a contract because the condition was not satisfied, and the offer became therefore incapable of acceptance. It is, in fact, probable that no condition as to the state of the car could have been implied in the contract itself, because the contract almost certainly contained the wide exemption clause invariably found in such contracts before the Hire-Purchase Act, 1964.[1] But the court evidently found no in-consistency between implying a term in the offer and the terms set out in the proposal form. Indeed, the declaration that the hirer had exam-ined the car and found it in good condition was used by the court to justify the inference that there must be an implied condition in the offer. Of this declaration, Pearson LJ said: 'The obvious intention is this, that both the proposed hire-purchaser and the finance company will be able to rely on the condition of the car as it appears to the proposed hire-purchaser when he made his offer . . .' .[2] As an application of the

---

[1] The Reports do not tell us whether there was such an exemption clause, but it would have been a remarkable contract had there not been one.
[2] [1962] 3 All ER 392.

normal principles of construction, this is impeccable; as a statement of fact of what the parties' 'obvious intentions' were, it is almost certainly false. Declarations of this kind are inserted in hire-purchase proposal forms by finance companies for their own protection. The idea that the finance company really intended by this declaration to confer rights on the hirer is so far-fetched as to be laughable; and it is most improbable that the hirer himself read it or gave it a thought. But this is by the way. The interest of the case lies in the technique adopted by the court for the solution of the case, and the effects of that technique.

Since the contract was held to be void, neither hirer nor finance company was under any liability. The court did not hold that the finance company was obliged to deliver the car to the hirer in the same condition that it was in when he made his offer, though in the particular circumstances of the case this would have been immaterial. The result was that the risk of this event was held to be not fully on either party to the purported contract. It should be noted, in this connection, that holding a contract to be void or frustrated does not necessarily mean that the risk of the events giving rise to the holding are placed on neither party (though I must admit that I have sometimes assumed this in earlier writings). In practice such a holding divides the risks, placing some on one party and some on the other, though it is true that such a result may mean that it is no longer possible to speak of 'the risks' of this or that event falling exclusively on one party.

Now the particular condition which the court implied in this case was, of course, of rather an unusual kind. Since it related to facts which occurred between the date of the offer and the date of the acceptance, it could only lead to one of two possible results. Either the condition was fulfilled, in which case the contract came into existence on acceptance and operated normally thereafter, or the condition was not fulfilled, in which case the offer could not be accepted at all, and there never was a contract. In short, the condition was a condition precedent, but a condition precedent of a special kind. In the more usual case a condition precedent does not prevent the formation of a contract, but only goes to its operation.[1] However, having said this, it does not in the least follow that an implied condition in an offer is something radically different from an implied condition in a contract. The contract textbooks have treated the case as illustrating the notion of a conditional offer,[2] as though this somehow differs from the kind of offer

---

[1] See e.g. the hypothetical case put by Lord Reid in *William Cory & Son Ltd.* v. *Inland Revenue Commissioners* [1965] AC at 1107-8.

[2] See e.g. Treitel, op. cit., p. 245 above, pp. 47-50.

which results in a conditional contract. But the truth, of course, is that, whenever a conditional contract is made, whenever a contract is subject to a condition precedent, the condition must have been 'in' the offer. Since an offer must be accepted precisely as it stands, it follows logically that no condition can be implied in a contract unless it was first implied in the offer.

It is at this stage that the implications of the technique adopted by the court in this case can be fully appreciated. It will, of course, be recalled that many lawyers (including myself) have argued that problems relating to 'common mistake' are essentially problems of construction, and that when a court declares a contract to be void for common mistake, it is, in effect, implying a condition precedent in the contract.[1] Thus it is nowadays generally agreed that the decision in *Couturier* v. *Hastie*[2] is explicable on the ground that there was an implied condition precedent that the cargo which was the subject of the sale was in existence at the time when the contract was made. But it has frequently been argued that a contract can never be held void on such grounds unless the case relates to non-existent goods, and this argument is still to be found in the current edition of Cheshire and Fifoot's *Law of Contract*.[3] Yet in the *Stimson* case, the contract was held to be 'void' on just such grounds despite the fact that the 'mistake' did not relate to the existence of the goods. Of course, because the court chose to use the construction technique, no reference to 'mistake' is to be found in the judgments, and students have sometimes been puzzled at the suggestion that there was a mistake in that case.[4] But the mistake is plain enough: both parties mistakenly thought the car was in the same condition at the date of the acceptance as it was at the date of the offer.

I have already stressed that in the *Stimson* case the change in the condition of the goods occurred between the date of the offer and the date of the acceptance, whereas in *Couturier* v. *Hastie* the goods had perished before the offer was ever made. But it is hard to believe that this was a material factor in the latter decision, or that the language of

---

[1] See e.g. Slade, 'The Myth of Mistake in the English Law of Contract', 70 *Law Q. Rev.* 385 (1954); Atiyah, '*Couturier* v. *Hastie* and the Sale of Non-Existent Goods', 73 *Law Q. Rev.* 340 (1957); and the famous case of *McRae* v. *Commonwealth Disposals Commission* (1951) 84 CLR 377.

[2] (1854) 5 HL Cas 673.

[3] 10th edn., p. 210.

[4] So also are the contract textbooks, none of which seem to see any connection between this case and the law of mistake.

the court would have been different had the cargo perished between the date of the offer and the date of the acceptance. It becomes plain, then, that the *Stimson* case is a decision holding a contract to be 'void' by the use of the construction technique, in circumstances in which the use of a different technique—the mistake technique—might easily have been adopted. But this itself demonstrates the crucial importance of technique, for no one can be sure what the result of the case would have been if counsel for the defendant had pleaded that the contract was void by reason of a common fundamental mistake. It is very probable, I think, that the plea would have received short shrift, for the mistake technique is now so rarely used that the court would probably have shied away from invoking it here, whereas by inviting the court to use the construction technique, counsel was able to achieve the desired result.

There are two other points about this case which ought to be discussed. First, why did the court feel able to invoke the construction technique to decide the case in the way in which it did? Even those who have previously argued that a contract can be declared void on construction in circumstances not involving perished or non-existing goods,[1] have always stressed that such a construction is not one to be lightly adopted, and that it would require some very unusual facts to justify it. Thus I have previously argued that in most circumstances the court will place the risk of untoward events wholly on one party or the other, and that they will only rarely declare that neither party bears the full risk, or (as I would now put it, more accurately, I think) that some of the risks which were formerly placed, or are usually placed, wholly on one party, will now be shared or divided between them.[2] In the *Stimson* case, it seems that this construction was justified by three facts. First, the terms of the declaration in the proposal form, which have already been referred to. Second, the fact that a change took place in the condition of the goods between the date of the offer and the date of the acceptance. Although this fact does not seem to be of critical legal significance in the sense that the same technique could not be used even where no such change has taken place, it is undoubtedly a fact which has a bearing on the construction to be adopted. And third was the fact that the goods were in the possession of neither party to the contract at the time when they were stolen. In these circumstances it

---

[1] See e.g. Slade, loc. cit., at pp. 398-401; Atiyah and Bennion, 'Mistake in the Construction of Contracts', 24 *Mod. L. Rev.* 421, at 432 (1961).

[2] Atiyah and Bennion, loc. cit.

would have been unjust to treat the risk of damage between offer and acceptance as wholly assumed by either party to the contract. This third factor leads naturally on to the next point.

It will be noticed that the condition implied by the court was one of some simplicity, and that on the facts as they actually were, this condition was amply sufficient to dispose of the case. But it needs only a slight adjustment in the facts to make it clear that the condition implied by the court would not have served in different circumstances. Suppose, for example, that the car had been damaged by the negligent driving of the defendant during the two days it was in his possession. It does not seem very likely that the court would still have been content to imply a condition that no substantial change should have taken place between offer and acceptance. Surely the court would have felt obliged to elaborate on the condition by saying that it was only to be implied where the change was not due to the fault of either party. But even this might not have sufficed. If the car had been damaged while in the possession of the defendant, but as a result of negligent driving by a third party, the court would surely have still been reluctant to imply a condition which would have prevented the contract coming into existence. Indeed, given the fact that the defendant was comprehensively insured (and that the dealer would not allow him possession until he was so insured), it seems certain that once again the court would have felt obliged to modify the implied condition. It would then have been, presumably, a condition to the effect that the car should, on acceptance, be in substantially the same condition as it was at the time of the offer, but excluding from consideration any damage done to it while it was in the possession of the defendant (or perhaps either party). It would not be difficult to construct yet further variations in the facts which might have required even more complications to be introduced into the implied condition, for example, if the car were damaged in an accident while being driven by the defendant, but the accident was due to a defect present in the car when delivered to him and not reasonably discoverable by him.

Now the fact that the court did not feel called upon to elaborate on the implied condition beyond what the circumstances of the case actually required is indicative of the fact that the court was here merely using a well-tried technique to achieve justice in the particular circumstances of the case. Given the relatively unusual nature of the facts this was no doubt a perfectly reasonable approach. Unfortunately, this will not always do. Courts cannot disregard their precedent-making powers when they use the construction technique. Although (as will be seen below) the doctrine of precedent is not too strictly applied in dealing with questions of construction, it remains true that in dealing with stereotype contracts and regularly recurring situations, a decision on construction is likely to be regarded as a precedent. In such a case, therefore, it may well be necessary for a court to be more cautious in implying terms. In particular, it will be necessary for the court to be satisfied that the term can be formulated in a manner which will enable it to be applied even with variations in circumstances. It was the great difficulty facing counsel in so formulating the condition which he wanted the court to imply, which was at least one of the reasons for the decision in *Lister* v. *Romford Ice & Cold Storage Co.*[1]

3. Unilateral Mistake and Construction

Generations of law students are familiar with the proposition that a unilateral mistake which is known to the other party may render a contract void if it relates to identity or to the terms of the contract, and not merely to its subject matter. Here again there has been much controversy over the 'theoretical basis' of the law, or (as I would prefer to put it) over the technique best adapted to deal with these problems. After Professor Goodhart's article[2] on the decision in *Sowler* v. *Potter*,[3] the view gained ground that this part of the law could best be treated as depending on the rules of offer and acceptance.[4] From here it is but a short step to saying that this also is a question of construction because before it can be determined whether offer and acceptance coincide, the offer and the acceptance must both be construed. Indeed, Professor Goodhart himself explained the mistake of identity cases in terms of the true construction of the offer, and this view of the matter appears to have been accepted by the majority of the Court of Appeal in *Ingram* v. *Little*.[5]

But here, at least, it is not possible to dismiss the whole question as one of construction without some further explanation, for one of the most crucial and difficult questions in this field concerns the effect of knowledge by the parties of each other's intentions on the 'true' construction of offer and acceptance. And on this point, it appears to

---

[1] [1957] AC 555.

[2] 'Mistake as to Identity in the Law of Contract', 57 *Law Q. Rev.* 228 (1941).

[3] [1940] 1 KB 271.

[4] Slade, loc. cit.; Shatwell, 'The Supposed Doctrine of Mistake in Contract: A Comedy of Errors', 33 *Can. Bar Rev.* 164 (1955).

[5] [1961] 1 QB 31.

me that the view to which the authorities now lead involves an analysis, complex though it may be, which has never been fully articulated in the case law. I believe that the law on this point can now be stated in the form of a number of rules as follows:

1. The true construction of an offer or acceptance, where the meaning intended by one party is not known to the other party (and there is no reason why he should know), is the 'objective' construction arrived at in the normal way, according to all the circumstances of the case. But it is necessary that the recipient should actually believe in this 'objective' construction and (perhaps) act upon that belief.[1]

2. The true construction of an offer or acceptance, where the meaning intended by one party *is or ought to be known* to the other party, is that meaning, so long as the party who knows or ought to know of the other party's intentions has led that party to believe that he accepts that meaning.

3. Where both parties know or ought to know the meaning attributed by each other to the offer or acceptance, and these meanings differ, then the contract is void, unless both parties are content to be bound by the terms of the contract, whatever those terms may be held to mean. In this last case, again, the controverted term will be construed by the courts in the normal objective manner.

As so often happens with the attempt to state the law in the form of a series of rules, however, some further qualification is needed. In particular, with regard to the third of the above 'rules', it needs to be added that whether the parties 'intend' or are content to be bound by the terms of the contract, whatever those terms may be taken to mean, is likely to depend to some degree on the question whether the agreement remains wholly executory or whether some degree of reliance or performance has occurred. In this connection there are two English cases which require examination. In *London County Council* v. *Henry Boot & Sons*,[2] the plaintiffs were building contractors who had entered into a standard form of contract employed by the London County Council for certain construction works. The contract contained a 'rise and fall' clause for increased payment in the event of increases being granted in the 'rates of wages'. The dispute concerned a holiday scheme in the building industry under which employers in this industry purchased holiday credit stamps from a central agency, with a view to ensuring

---

[1] *The Hannah Blumenthal* [1983] 1 All ER 34.
[2] [1959] 1 WLR 133 (CA), reversed, [1959] 1 WLR 1069 (HL).

that all workers had a paid holiday every year even where they had been employed by several different employers through the year. By agreement between associations of employers and trade unions, the holiday entitlement of the workmen was increased from one to two weeks, and the cost of the stamps to the employers was therefore doubled. The question was whether this increase in cost fell within the 'rise and fall' clause of the contract. Now, had there been nothing further in the case, this would of course have been simply a question of 'construction' or, perhaps more accurately, of 'interpretation'. But there had been some correspondence about the meaning of this clause before the contract was entered into. The council had taken the view that the clause did not cover increased costs of the holiday scheme, and had notified the contractors to that effect in connection with a different contract. But the council had also corresponded with the London Master Builders' Association, of which the plaintiffs were members, and had taken the same point with them. The Builders' Association had, however, stated that they could not agree with the interpretation placed on the clause, and although the council wrote back maintaining their view, the matter was allowed to rest there.

In the Court of Appeal it was held that the correspondence was not admissible in evidence on the ground that the plaintiffs were entitled to say: 'We do not agree with that [the construction placed on the clause by the council]; we accept your contract and let the court decide whether you are right or we are.' In the House of Lords the decision was affirmed on the inadmissibility of the correspondence, but the actual decision was reversed on the ground that the objective interpretation of the 'rise and fall' clause clearly led to exclusion of the holiday credits scheme from its purview. This decision was severely criticized by Professor Goodhart,[1] both on the objective construction point (which is of not great moment, and does not concern us) and on the point about the admissibility of the correspondence. The real question which faced the courts, he urged, was this: 'Can an offeree who has been notified by the offeror that he attaches a particular meaning to a phrase in his offer, accept that offer and then ask the court to attach an entirely different meaning to it?' And he cited English and American authorities to suggest that this was not possible.

Professor Goodhart seems to have been clearly right in suggesting that a person who accepts an offer knowing that the offeror places a particular construction on his words is bound by that construction,

[1] Note, 76 *Law Q. Rev.* 32 (1959).

provided that by his acceptance he has led the offeror to think that he does so accept that construction. But the proviso is crucial. In this case, the council had no reason whatever to assume that the plaintiffs accepted their construction of the controverted clause after their correspondence with the Builders' Association. Indeed, when both parties know full well that they hold different views on the construction of the contract, there is no more reason to treat the offeror's construction as conclusive than there would be to treat the offeree's construction as conclusive. The plaintiffs could have made a case no more and no less plausible than the defendants' case for arguing that, since the council knew the construction placed on the clause by the Builders' Association, and nevertheless offered the contract to them on these terms, they were bound by the plaintiffs' construction. But if both parties know then that their intentions differ, how is it possible to find a contract at all? Is this not a classic case of a contract being void because the parties are not *ad idem*? One party means one thing and the other party means another, and what is more, each is aware of the other's intentions. Under these circumstances, indeed, the Restatement, Second, appears unequivocally to opt for the solution of treating the contract as void. Article 20(1) says:

There is no manifestation of mutual assent to an exchange if the parties attach materially different meanings to their manifestations and . . .

(*b*) each party knows or each party has reason to know the meaning attached by the other.

The argument that the contract was void was put to the House of Lords, somewhat half-heartedly it would appear, for no argument was heard on the point from the defendants, and Lord Simonds, who delivered the leading judgment, did not even mention it. It was left to Lord Denning, who delivered the only other speech, to point out that the parties were agreed on the only thing that really mattered, namely the terms that should bind them. It is on this point that the case appears to me principally to break new ground: parties may contract on terms, disagreeing as to the meaning of those terms, and knowing that they disagree, but (in effect) delegating to the court the ultimate decision on their meaning. Where the Restatement seems to have gone wrong is in failing to recognize this possibility, but where the House of Lords may have gone wrong was in failing to note that the result was only appropriate because the parties had proceeded with the performance of the contract. Had either party refused to proceed until they agreed on the correct meaning of the 'rise and fall' clause, it is hard to see how the court could have held that a contract had been fully agreed.

Apart from this point the case seems to be clear support for the view that cases raising problems known to some academic lawyers as problems of unilateral mistake tend to be treated by use of the construction technique. It may be objected that in fact the court was here using another technique altogether, namely the 'evidence' technique, that is, the technique of treating questions of substantive law by reference to the admissibility of evidence. This was, of course, a very common technique in the last century though it has been waning for many years now. But in any event, in this particular type of case, a decision on the admissibility of evidence was itself a decision on the construction of the contract. The real question, as viewed by the courts in this case, was whether the construction of the contract was affected by the actual intentions of the parties, and their knowledge of each other's intentions.

The other decision which is worth examining in this connection is *A. Roberts & Co.* v. *Leicestershire County Council*[1] which was a decision on rectification. In this case the plaintiffs tendered for the construction of a school for the defendants, the tender documents requiring the works to be completed in eighteen months. However, the formal contract prepared by the defendants provided for completion in thirty months, and after the defendants had accepted the plaintiffs' tender, they sent the formal contract for execution without informing the plaintiffs of the change, which was actually in the interests of the defendants rather than the plaintiffs. The plaintiffs executed the contract without noticing the change. The defendants knew all along that the plaintiffs were unaware of the change and had executed the contract in ignorance of it, and it was held that the contract should be rectified by altering the completion time from thirty months to eighteen months. The interesting feature of the case is not so much the actual decision as what is involved in it. For it is necessarily implied in the decision that there was all along a valid contract with an eighteen months' completion time. This was a necessary implication because it is settled law that the court only rectifies written instruments, not obligations themselves. In other words, despite the terms of the formal contract, it was held to mean what the plaintiffs intended to the knowledge of the defendants. Although both parties had different intentions, the contract was thus very far from being void. The decision thus seems to bear out Professor Goodhart's

[1] [1961] Ch. 555.

argument that a person who accepts an offer knowing the real intentions of the offeror is bound to treat that offer as though it correctly stated the offeror's intentions, whatever the objective construction of the offer might be. The distinction between this case and the *Henry Boot* case is that here the defendants' conduct was such as to lead the plaintiffs to believe that the defendants accepted the offer of the plaintiffs in the terms intended by them, whereas in the *Henry Boot* case this was not so.

In the light of these cases it may be interesting to re-examine, very briefly, the celebrated decision in *Smith* v. *Hughes*,[1] for so long the leading authority on unilateral mistake. Stripped to their simplest, the facts disclosed a contract by A to sell a specific parcel of oats to B. A knew that the oats were new and did not intend to warrant them to be old. B thought the oats were old and thought that A was warranting them to be old. Now there seem to be the following possible fact variations in the situation. First, neither party may have known the other's real intentions. Here it seems to me plain that a court would today treat the case as entirely one of construction. On the objective view of what was said and done, and all the surrounding circumstances, was the true construction of the contract that there was a warranty or not?[2] Second, the seller may have known of the buyer's belief that he, the seller, was warranting the oats to be old, and the buyer may not have known of the seller's intention to sell without warranty. Here it seems clear (and the *Roberts* case is an authority for it) that the true construction of the contract would have been that there was a sale with a warranty. Third, the buyer may have known the seller's intentions, and the seller may not have known of the buyer's intentions. This possibility (which could not have been seriously entertained on the evidence) would of course have led to the view that there was a binding contract without a warranty. Fourth, both parties may have known of the other's true intentions. Here, there plainly would have been no contract at all. It would have been as though the seller had written to the buyer offering to sell him 'these oats as they are' and the buyer had written back agreeing to buy the oats 'with warranty that they are old'.

---

[1] LR 6 QB 597 (1871).

[2] There was, in fact, a good deal of evidence as to the 'surrounding circumstances', much of which conflicted. The buyer was (as the seller knew) a racehorse trainer, and his evidence was that trainers never bought new oats, and that the agreed price was very high for new oats. The seller's evidence was that trainers did sometimes buy new oats, and the high price was explicable by the scarcity of oats at that time. On the question whether expectation damages are justifiable in such a case, see the discussion in Essay 7.

Clearly, offer and acceptance would not have coincided. Of course, if the whole contract had been reduced to writing, there might have been room for the possibility adopted in the *Henry Boot* case, that the parties had agreed to contract but disagreed on the meaning of their contract, but this would hardly have been open on the evidence.

It will be noted that, on this view, the knowledge by one party of the intentions of the other, far from being a ground for holding the contract to be void, would be a ground for holding that there was a valid contract in the sense understood by the mistaken party. In *Smith* v. *Hughes* itself, it cannot be asserted that (even on this view of the facts) the court decided that the contract was void, for the decision and most of the judgments are equally explicable on the assumption that there would have been a valid contract for the sale of oats warranted to be old. The warranty being broken, the buyer was entitled to reject the goods.[1]

It has, however, been objected[2] that the offer and acceptance theory does not adequately explain the cases of unilateral mistake for two reasons. First, it is said that it does not explain why there can be verbal correspondence of offer and acceptance, as for example, in *Raffles* v. *Wichelhaus*[3] (the famous *Peerless* case), and yet no contract. But this objection is hardly formidable. Of course, the offer and acceptance 'theory' requires that the court construe the offer and the acceptance and ascertain the 'true' construction. If the court is unable to do this because there are no surrounding circumstances pointing to one construction rather than another (*quod raro accidit*), the contract is simply void for uncertainty. The court can hardly enforce a contract unless it can say what the contract means.

The second objection to the offer and acceptance 'theory' is that 'it makes no allowance for the crucial distinction between mistakes which are fundamental and mistakes which are not'.[4] But this is to underestimate the flexibility of the construction technique. For it is a simple enough matter for the court to construe the offer as only including those matters which it regards as sufficiently fundamental. If, for example, the mistake in *Smith* v. *Hughes* related only to the quality of the oats, and not to the terms of the offer (as, on one view of the facts, it did), the

---

[1] Today, of course, a 'warranty' as opposed to a 'condition' would not justify that result, but the modern terminology had not been settled at that time.

[2] Treitel, op. cit., p. 245 above, pp. 232-3. Professor Treitel's opposition to the 'offer and acceptance' theory seems more muted than in earlier editions of his book.

[3] (1864) 2 H. and C. 906.

[4] Treitel, op. cit., p. 245 above, p. 232.

true construction of the contract would have been that there was simply a contract to buy and sell the oats without warranty. This is not necessarily because the quality of the oats was not fundamental—in one sense it certainly was fundamental to the buyer—but because the court would have felt that the sale was for specific goods as they stood and no warranty was needed to do justice between the parties, the buyer having been given a sample. Similarly, in a mistake of identity case where the identity of the offeree is wholly immaterial (and so the mistake, if any, is not fundamental), the court would naturally construe the offer as being made without reference to the identity of the offeree.

But when all is said and done on this controversial subject, if, as I submit, the 'theoretical basis' is a matter of technique and no more, then the 'correct basis' is not a matter for academic disputation but one for empirical verfication. What techniques are the courts in fact using? In point of fact, it is hard to find a single modern case of sale of goods in which the court has preferred the mistake technique to the construction technique. A typical modern case, which in many ways resembles *Smith* v. *Hughes*, is *Sullivan* v. *Constable*,[1] which was treated throughout as a simple case of construction and nothing more.

4. Mistake in Equity

It will be recalled that, in *Solle* v. *Butcher*,[2] Denning LJ (as he then was) put forward the thesis that even where a contract is not 'void for common mistake' at common law, there is an equitable jurisdiction to set the contract aside where the justice of the case so requires. I do not wish here to rehearse the many criticisms which have been levelled at this idea,[3] but as Lord Denning's view has been applied in one or two English cases, it may be worth devoting some attention to one such decision in the light of the suggestion that the courts are here basically faced with problems of technique. The case in question is *Grist* v. *Bailey*.[4] There, the defendant contracted to sell to the plaintiff a house which was occupied by a weekly tenant. Both parties believed that the tenant had statutory security of tenure, and the price of £850 was based on this assumption. In fact the statutory tenant had died and the house

---

[1] 48 TLR 369 (1932).

[2] [1950] 1 KB 671.

[3] In which I have joined in the past. But for my present views, which would draw a line between wholly executory and relied-upon, or partly performed contracts, see Essay 2, above, and for my doubts about the protection of expectations in cases of mistake, see Essay 7.

[4] [1967] Ch. 532.

was occupied by his son who had no security of tenure. The house was, therefore, worth considerably more (in fact about £2250), as it could be sold in effect with vacant possession. It was held that the contract should be set aside on the ground of common mistake in equity, though the buyer was given the option of resiling from the contract completely or paying the full value. Now the actual decision in this case seems, on any view, almost indefensible. Even on my own view that expectations do not generally deserve protection in face of such mistakes (see Essay 7), it would seem perfectly clear that risks of this sort are regularly imposed by the courts on the parties to a contract for the purchase and sale of a house. Indeed, it is difficult to see how the mistake could have occurred without negligence on the part of the solicitors acting for the seller, who would, in this event, have been liable to the seller for the loss suffered by him. There would thus have been no serious risk of unfairness to the seller if he had been held to his contract.

But this is not to suggest that facts may not occur in which the most fair and reasonable solution might be to release both parties from the contract, subject possibly to the protection of reliance interests. For example, to adapt the facts of the *Stimson* case, suppose that parties have reached agreement for the sale of a house 'subject to contract' and that the house is burned down without fault of the seller after the formal offer and before the acceptance.[1] It might, depending on the circumstances, be fair and reasonable to release both parties from the contract in such a case, subject perhaps to payment of the buyer's reliance costs, or alternatively, to a division of those costs such as that envisaged by the Law Reform (Frustrated Contracts) Act 1943. It is here that difficulties may be encountered with the construction technique, for although there is no logical reason why this technique should not be used in this type of contract, the fact is that implied terms with regard to the physical condition of the property are virtually unknown in contracts for the sale of land. It is thus not surprising that it is in this type of case that the courts still occasionally fall back on the mistake technique, as was done in *Grist* v. *Bailey*.

But there are dangers in this course. If it is the mere unfamiliarity of the construction technique in this context which leads a court to fall back on the mistake technique, the danger is that the mistake technique may be invoked in cases in which there is no real justification for it, as seems to have been the case with *Grist* v. *Bailey* itself. For the construction technique is remarkably flexible (of which more later), and if

[1] See *Hitchcock* v. *Giddings* (1817) 4 Price 135.

the court refuses to imply a term in the contract to deal with the untoward events which have occurred or come to light, this is presumably because the court feels that justice or policy, call it what you will, does not require that result. In this event, it seems almost perverse to achieve the same result by use of a different technique. If, on the other hand, the mistake technique is invoked because there is some positive-law barrier to the use of the construction technique (for example, some binding and indistinguishable authority), then the use of a different technique to achieve the same result is open to other objections. To those who believe in the sanctity of *stare decisis* this process is of course objectionable simply because it amounts to evasion of binding authority. But even those who are not so wedded to *stare decisis* may find objections to this process. For if the binding authority is really unsatisfactory, it is much better that the rules of precedent should be relaxed and the decision overruled rather than that it should be avoided by use of different techniques. There is also the danger that by shifting to a different technique, the underlying policy considerations behind the authority in question may get overlooked. For instance, in contracts for the sale of land, the general refusal of the courts to imply conditions relating to the physical state of the property is not entirely irrational. It may produce injustice in particular circumstances, and may for that reason need relaxing slightly, but in the majority of cases there are obviously good reasons for it, for example, that purchasers normally inspect the property that they buy, that it is desirable that dealings in land should be fully recorded in written documents rather than oral agreement or implication, and so forth. If these policy considerations are sound, it is undesirable that they should be overlooked, as they may well be, simply by the process of shifting to a different technique, and using (say) the 'mistake' doctrine to achieve a result which cannot be achieved by construction.[1] If, on the other hand, these policy considerations are unsound, it would be much better for the courts boldly to modify the existing law by using those techniques which are already most familiar in analogous situations.

5. Duties of Disclosure and Construction

The use of differing techniques to achieve similar results can be pro-

---

[1] Similar objections can be made to a decision refusing to enforce a promise as a contract because it is too uncertain, and then, nevertheless, enforcing the very same promise by way of promissory estoppel: see my note, 'When is an Enforceable Agreement not a Contract?' 92 *Law Q. Rev.* 174 (1976). But it would be perfectly rational to refuse an award of expectation damages while granting reliance damages in such circumstances.

fitably examined by comparing the process of construction with the imposition of—or refusal to impose—duties of disclosure on the parties to a contract. The comparison is a particularly instructive one for it does not seem open to doubt that this is a field in which the courts have largely shifted from one technique to the other over a course of years. And this shift illustrates the dominating part played by the construction technique in the modern law of contract.

It is, of course, well known that according to orthodox theory a party to a contract is under no obligation to disclose facts to the other party unless the contract is *uberrimae fidei*, and in certain other well-defined cases such as where a representation which has been made has become falsified by a change of circumstance, or where a partial disclosure has been made which is misleading standing by itself. Most of the books and the cases are content to state the duty of disclosure, where it exists, as a duty imposed by law, independent of the parties' intentions, though it may of course be modified by express agreement. It is true that there are a number of cases in which the courts have discussed the 'theoretical basis' of the duty to disclose and have sometimes treated it as resting on an implied term in the contract,[1] but these cases were all dictated by specific statutory questions and did not involve any analysis of the rival merits of the two different techniques. Even those who have explained the duty to disclose as resting on an implied term have made it plain that the term must be an implied condition precedent and not a promissory condition, for it has never been suggested that breach of a duty to disclose could give rise to a claim for damages.[2] Still less, of course, is it possible to urge the existence of the duty of disclosure independently of the contract in the sense that a breach of duty might be actionable even if no contract were subsequently entered into.

The result is that for most practical purposes it is a purely academic question whether the duty is treated as resting on an implied condition or not. If a person takes out life assurance without disclosing that he knows he is suffering from a serious heart disease, it is quite immaterial whether the insurer can defend himself by pleading that the assured broke his duty to disclose, or that it was an implied condition precedent that the assured was not, to his knowledge, suffering from the disease. When breach of promise of marriage was still actionable, the courts

---

[1] See e.g. *William Pickersgill & Sons Ltd.* v. *London & Provincial Marine etc. Insurance Co.* [1912] 3 KB 614; but cf. *Merchants & Manufacturing Insurance Co.* v. *Hunt* [1941] 1 KB 295.

[2] See *Blackburn, Low & Co.* v. *Vigors* 17 QBD 553, 563 (1886).

held that it was a defence for the man to prove that the woman had been unchaste,[1] but they never found it necessary to explain whether this was because there was a duty to disclose the facts (though such a contract was not *uberrimae fidei* in the full sense),[2] or whether it was because of an implied condition precedent. Indeed, in strict logic, there is no *necessary* difference between these two things at all. They are merely different ways of saying the same thing, namely that the defendant is not liable. But they do, of course, involve different legal techniques, and once techniques are established, they have a habit of acquiring a cluster of rules about them, so that even where different techniques do not necessarily produce a difference in result, it is quite probable that as a result of positive law they will gradually diverge. Now the law relating to duties of disclosure has in fact acquired three serious limitations over the years which have proved so restrictive that it is not surprsing that the technique has fallen largely into disfavour.

First and foremost, the category of contracts *uberrimae fidei* is closed by authority. Despite some doubts about certain fringe contracts (such as contracts of guarantee),[3] it is clear that it is not open to a court today to recognize an entirely new class of contracts *uberrimae fidei*. Second, the duty of disclosure is limited to a duty to disclose those facts which are known to the party under the duty.[4] And third, as pointed out above, the remedy for breach of the duty is the inflexible remedy of rescission or repudiation. As it happens (and this is obviously no accident), in most cases in which there is a duty to disclose, rescission is the only practical remedy, but there are many other contracts in which greater flexibility in the available remedies is desirable.

Now the construction technique suffers from none of these crippling limitations. There is no closed category of cases in which terms may be implied though (as already seen) there may well be types of cases in which particular authorities decide against the implication of certain kinds of terms. There is also no reason why terms should only be implied with regard to facts known to the parties. Further, it is possible to provide for flexibility in the remedies by varying the kind of term to be implied. A term in the nature of a warranty gives a right to damages,

---

[1] *Beach* v. *Merrick* (1844) 1 C. and K. 463.

[2] *Beachey* v. *Brown* (1858) El. Bl. and El. 796.

[3] See e.g. *London General Omnibus Co.* v. *Holloway* [1912] 2 KB 72; see also, below, p. 266.

[4] See, e.g., *Blackburn, Low & Co.* v. *Vigors* (1887) 12 App. Cas. 531; *Joel* v. *Law Union & Crown Ins. Co.* [1908] 2 KB 863. Of course the duty can be, and commonly is, extended by the terms of the contract itself.

a term in the nature of a promissory condition gives a right to damages or repudiation or both, whereas a term in the nature of a condition precedent releases both parties with no liability in damages.

These differences in the two techniques may be illustrated by contrasting a number of cases on the duty of disclosure with the *Stimson* case which has already been considered at length above. There is a good deal of authority that a party who makes a statement which is true when made but which subsequent facts render untrue to his knowledge is under a duty to disclose the change of circumstances, provided, of course, that they occur before the contract is concluded.[1] But all these authorities formulate the duty as one which only arises when the party who made the statement knows of the change in the circumstances. It needs little imagination to appreciate that it might be very unjust to hold a party liable on a contract when there has been a change in the circumstances occurring during the negotiations even where the other party did not know of the change—the very thing that happened in fact in the *Stimson* case. And here, as has already been seen, the court was able to do justice by implying an appropriate term despite the fact that the finance company was unaware of the change in the condition of the car.

Similarly, the old controversy as to whether there is any duty on a seller of goods to disclose latent defects known to him[2] has been completely bypassed in modern times by the shift to the implied term technique. In the great majority of cases the terms implied in favour of the buyer under the Sale of Goods Act protect him against latent defects whether these are known to the seller or not. Furthermore, the buyer's remedies for breach of these terms are more flexible than would be a bare right of rescission which would not protect against consequential damage. True it is that the buyer will have no remedy under the Sale of Goods Act (in the absence of express warranty or misrepresentation) where the seller is not a dealer in the goods in question, and therefore a buyer from a non-dealer might still try to persuade a court that there is a duty to disclose latent defects known to the seller. Any such holding would, of course, be an evasion, by the use of different techniques, of the provisions of the Sale of Goods Act, but in particular circumstances, the court might be driven to this evasion if the Sale of Goods Act appears to produce a very unjust result.

[1] *Traill* v. *Baring* (1864) 4 De G. J. and S. 318; *With* v. *O'Flanagan* [1936] Ch. 575.
[2] *Horsfall* v. *Thomas* (1862) 1 H. and C. 90, 100; *Smith* v. *Hughes* (1871) LR 6 QB 597, 605.

I do not suggest that knowledge of facts may not, in some cases, be an appropriate ground for invoking or limiting the construction technique, much as knowledge limits the application of the duty of disclosure technique. If, for instance, the duty to disclose in insurance contracts were indeed to be treated as resting on an implied term, it would surely be reasonable to treat the implied term as relating only to facts known to the insured.

The implied term technique, like the duty of disclosure technique, usually requires that it be shown that the other party would have been influenced by the undisclosed facts. But if this is often, or even normally, a necessary condition to the implication of a term, it is certainly not by itself a sufficient condition. In *Percival* v. *Wright*,[1] for example, the director of a company bought some shares from a member of the company, knowing of circumstances which were likely to enhance the value of the shares. It was held that the director was under no duty to disclose these facts to the member. No attempt was, indeed, made to invoke the implied term technique in this case, as the plaintiff's case was based on the argument that the director had abused his fiduciary position, and the court held that the fiduciary duties of a director were owed to the company alone. But even if the plaintiff had tried to persuade the court to imply a term in the contract he would plainly have been faced with formidable difficulties. Even though it may have been reasonably certain that the shareholder would not have sold on the agreed terms had he known the facts, it is hard to believe that the court would have implied a term to protect the shareholder. The problem of formulating a suitable term would have been extremely difficult, a fact which illustrates one of the weaknesses of the construction technique to which I have already drawn attention.

Since this essay was first published, another twist to this shift in techniques has occurred, though it is as yet too early to say how important it will prove. In *Cornish* v. *Midland Bank*,[2] the Court of Appeal shifted, in dealing with problems of non-disclosure, to yet another technique, namely to the tort of negligence. In this case the wife of a debtor joined in a mortgage of the matrimonial home in order to guarantee his debts to their bank, and later complained, when the bank came to enforce the guarantee against the matrimonial home, that she had not realized the guarantee involved a mortgage of the matrimonial home for her husband's business debts, and not just the amount ad-

[1] [1902] 2 Ch. 421.
[2] [1985] 3 All ER 513.

vanced on the house itself. She had, indeed, been misled by active misrepresentation on this point, and was held entitled to damages for that misrepresentation, though the guarantee was enforceable against her. But Kerr, LJ went on *obiter* to suggest that banks might well be liable in tort for negligently failing to disclose unusual circumstances in connection with the guarantee in such a situation. The strange thing about the use of the negligence technique here is that there is already authority holding that contracts of guarantee may require the disclosure, as a matter of contract law, of unusual circumstances known to the creditor but not to the guarantor.[1] There was, thus, no need for this shift from contract to tort; but, as history tells us, once a new technique becomes popular, it will tend to be used even where the old techniques are perfectly adequate for the task. And today nobody can doubt that the tort of negligence is the most favoured technique of all.

6. The Scope of the Construction Technique

It will be apparent from the above discussion that the construction technique has considerable advantages over the duty to disclose technique. But it is not only in this sphere that the construction technique has swept all before it. Apart from the problems raised by mistake, which I have sought to show are now also generally dealt with by use of this technique, it hardly seems to be open to doubt that construction has become by far the most popular technique for the solution of practically all problems in the law of contract which do not depend on unyielding rules of positive law, such as capacity, illegality, and the requirements of consideration. But even with these rules which appear to be the most unyielding of all, the construction technique is continuously making inroads. Although parties cannot agree that their agreement will be binding in the absence of consideration, the existence of consideration may itself depend on the intention of the parties, and from there it is but a short step to saying that it is, in some cases at least, a question of construction. For example, the distinction between a unilateral contract supported by consideration, and a conditional gift, is now usually said to be a question of construction. And although parties cannot by their intentions override all the rules relating to illegal contracts, it is becoming increasingly evident that the question whether a contract is an illegal one at all, may be, in the first instance, a question of construction.[2]

[1] See *London General Omnibus Co.* v. *Holloway* [1912] 2 KB 72.
[2] See *Archbolds (Freightage) Ltd.* v. *Spanglett Ltd.* [1961] 1 QB 374, especially at pp. 391-2.

And although parties cannot by their intentions evade all the un-yielding rules of privity, the court can often enough create a collateral contract by 'construing' a statement as a collateral warranty and finding consideration for it.[1] These developments have assuredly not come to an end. Given the necessary bold spirits on the bench, there is no logical reason why the construction technique should not be used to develop and modify the law in a way which would have seemed utter heresy not long ago, and indeed may still seem so to some. For instance, there is no reason why a court should not impose strict liability on the manufacturer of defective products by holding that a mere ad-vertisement can be construed as 'an offer to the world' and then 'im-plying' warranties in the 'offer' and finding that the parties 'intended' the purchase of the product from a retailer to be the consideration.[2] Indeed, the same result could be achieved in the absence of any reliance on an advertisement by finding that the manufacturer makes an 'implied' offer to the world merely by putting his goods on the market. This is not to suggest that developments such as these (although they have of course largely taken place in the United States) are just around the corner in England or other common law jurisdictions which closely follow English law. It may, indeed, be that they will never come at all as a matter of common law, especially as proposals for statutory change have been in the offing for some years, and the courts may feel it appropriate to defer to Parliament. But what I do suggest is that the construction technique as now used by English courts would be su-fficiently flexible to enable such developments to take place in the absence of legislation if the courts were so minded.

Again, the latest attempts by the English courts to create a new class of unyielding rules, namely the rules relating to 'fundamental breach', have been sternly rebuked, and the rules themselves relegated to the status of rules of construction.[3] And although it is undeniable that, in this sphere at least, the construction technique has weaknesses, every lawyer knows how, prior to the latest legislative reforms, it was possible and frequent for the courts, by the ingenious use of construction, to defeat unreasonably wide exemption clauses.

7. Advantages and Disadvantages of the Construction Technique

It may now be appropriate to take stock, and inquire a little more

---

[1] For a striking example, see *Wells* v. *Buckland Sand* [1965] 2 QB 170.

[2] This is, after all, little more than a combination of *Carlill* v. *Carbolic Smoke Ball Co.* [1893] 1 QB 256 and *Wells* v. *Buckland Sand*, above.

[3] *Suisse Atlantique* case [1967] 1 AC 361; *Photo Productions Ltd.* v. *Securicor Transport Ltd.* [1980] AC 827.

closely into this process of construction. What is it that a court does when it embarks on the process of construction? Why has this particular technique become such a dominating one in the English law of contract? Surprisingly enough, little attention has been devoted to this question. To an English lawyer 'construction' is treated as almost synonymous with 'interpretation' (indeed it is symptomatic that nobody appears to have explored the relationship between these two processes), and this is thought of as a subject to be treated in books on the 'Construction of Documents', rather than in books on the law of contract. None of the standard English textbooks contain separate chapters on 'Construction', and the word is not even to be found in the index of the two leading English textbooks, Cheshire and Fifoot's *Law of Contract* and Treitel's *Law of Contract*. When we do find discussions of the process of construction in connection with particular problems, it is usually brief in the extreme, consisting of little more than the statement that, of course, the 'true' construction of a contract depends on all the circumstances of the case.

Full examination of the intricacies of the construction technique would require an article in itself, and I propose here to content myself with a few generalities. It seems to me undeniable that the attractions of the construction technique lie principally in its extreme flexibility. The familiar formula that the construction of a contract 'depends on all the circumstances of the case' appears to be little more than a device by which (subject to certain limitations) the court is able to achieve what it regards as the most just result in the circumstances of the case. I have already pointed out how, with a little ingenuity directed to the kind of term which may be implied in a contract, the court is able to produce the most appropriate kind of remedy, that is, by implying a warranty, a promissory condition, or a condition precedent. Similarly, the construction technique enables the court to avoid, where necessary, the suffocating grip of the doctrine of precedent. I do not think anyone familiar with the English legal scene over the past two or three decades can have failed to notice the ease with which courts today distinguish cases as 'decisions on questions of fact'.[1] Those who wrestled as students twenty or twenty-five years ago with the problem of reconciling the apparently irreconcilable may be relieved (or, according to temperament, irritated) when a court today cuts the Gordian knot with the simple statement that the cases are decisions on 'questions of fact', but of the increasing tendency to take this way out, I do not believe there

---

[1] See further my inaugural lecture, 'From Principles to Pragmatism' (Oxford, 1978).

can be any doubt. It is, for example, noticeable how nearly all the modern cases of frustration are treated as raising largely questions of fact—or of the application of 'well-settled principles' to the facts, which amounts to much the same thing so far as freedom from the binding force of precedent goes.

Another attractive facet of the construction technique is the immense range of facts which may be taken into consideration by the court in arriving at the 'true construction' of the contract. Everything said or done by the parties and all the 'surrounding circumstances' may be relevant, subject to a number of limitations (such as the parol evidence rule) which seem to be largely formal today. This extends so far that even the knowledge by a party of some fact may be a part of the 'surrounding circumstances' to be taken into account, and the mistake cases show how ignorance of a fact is in like case. A still more striking illustration of the reach of the 'surrounding circumstances' is to be found in *Hollins* v. *J. Davy Ltd.*[1] In this case, which concerned the effect of the doctrine of fundamental breach on an exemption clause in a car-parking contract, the court took into consideration as part of the 'surrounding circumstances' and therefore as bearing on the 'intention of the parties' the fact that many car owners carry comprehensive insurance coverage, and that therefore an exemption clause may well be in the customer's interest as saving him from the extra cost of double insurance. In a jurisdiction where it is more usual to take account frankly of policy considerations, there would be nothing specially note-worthy about this, but in England, where every legal decision is conventionally required to be justified by the use of traditional legal techniques, the case is a remarkable example of the flexibility of the construction technique. Only with the enactment of the Unfair Contract Terms Act has wider recognition been given to the importance of studying the insurance situation in deciding whether effect should be given to exemption clauses.

But, it may be objected, if the use of the construction technique is so widespread in the law of contract, and if it is so flexible as to enable the court to do justice in such a wide variety of circumstances, is there not a danger that the law will become too uncertain? Every law student knows of the need for the law to strike a balance between flexibility and certainty, and if the construction technique is as flexible as I suggest it is, are the scales not being weighted too much in the interests of flexibility and the justice of the case, and is this not likely to make for

[1] [1963] 1 QB 844.

unpredictability, with all that that implies in commercial relations? Of course the danger is undeniable, but it is mitigated by some important factors, in particular, the existence of the 'rules of construction'. However flexible the construction technique may be, it does not involve the use of brushwork on an empty canvas. There is a great deal already on the canvas in the form of prima-facie rules which will normally be applied unless there is some reason not to apply them. In some standard classes of contracts the prima-facie rules are so strong (and I need only cite again the classic example of the conditions implied by the Sale of Goods Act) that their implication is a matter of course in the absence of special circumstances. Furthermore, the kind of factors which are likely to be taken into account by the courts as circumstances displacing the prima-facie rules are, up to a point, discoverable by examination of the precedents. Of course, if flexibility is to remain at all, the relevant factors in any particular situation can never be exhaustively enumerated, and still less can their relative weight be evaluated in advance.

But perhaps it is not too fanciful to suggest that even this element of uncertainty is to some extent mitigated in England by a number of institutional factors, such as the organization of the legal profession. The small number of practising barristers, the fact that judges are all recruited from the bar, and the closeness of bar and bench, all help to make counsel's opinion a prediction which is a good deal better than an informed guess. The sort of factors which may weigh with a judge in deciding whether the prima-facie rules of construction ought to be displaced in a particular situation, even when they are not clearly articulated, are not based on pure hunch or subjective sentiments of the justice of the case. They tend to be based on sentiments likely to be shared by the great majority of at least that branch of the profession which is concerned with the decision making.[1] These, then, seem to be the reasons for thinking that the construction technique is the one which best balances the needs for flexibility and certainty in so many contractual situations, and which explain why it has become such a popular technique in the last fifty years or so.

Of course, there are disadvantages to the construction technique, some of which I have already mentioned. First and most obvious, construction must in the last resort bow to the expressed intention of the parties, and it is hardly necessary to cite examples to show how (for

---

[1] These institutional factors have not yet received the study their importance deserves in this context. They will be dealt with more fully in the forthcoming work on which I am engaged with Professor R. S. Summers.

example, when dealing with exemption clauses) this leads to injustice on occasion. Here one calls to mind the advice to look the problem firmly in the face and then move on. Clearly, there can be no solution to this problem by development of the construction technique. Once construction is allowed to override the expressed intention of the parties, it ceases to be construction. To a considerable extent construction can be, and is, used to modify or qualify the literal terms of a contract on the ground that the parties 'could not really have intended' it to have the effect it appears to have, but it is apparent that this is not a sufficient answer in all cases. One can but note that the answer to this problem lies elsewhere, for example, by development of the doctrine of unconscionability, or by legislation.

Another possible disadvantage of the construction technique which has sometimes bothered lawyers (including myself) is its artificiality. It involves imputing an intention to the parties which in many circumstances is simply not there. I do not, of course, suggest that this is invariably what is being done under the guise of construction. There are undoubtedly many circumstances in which the court genuinely discovers and gives effect to the intention of the parties, and it is one of the misfortunes of the law (though hardly an accidental one) that the term 'construction' is used for two such very different purposes. But I do not believe that it can be denied that in a large number of cases the court is simply filling in gaps, or making law for the parties, when it is engaged in the process of construction, and that it is a pure fiction to treat this as a matter of 'giving effect to the intention of the parties'.

It was no doubt awareness of the artificiality of imputing a fictitious intention to the parties which led the Court of Appeal in *British Movietonews Ltd.* v. *London & District Cinemas Ltd.*[1] to reject the 'implied term' theory of the basis of the doctrine of frustration. And most academic lawyers (including myself) have felt the force of these objections to the 'implied term' or construction theory. But it now seems to me that the objection is largely misconceived. This is not so much because there may be no practical difference in result, whichever theory is adopted (a proposition which is itself highly controversial),[2] but because, as it now seems to me, insufficient attention has been paid to the nature and purposes of judicial techniques. If we consider the three main 'theories' as to the 'basis' of frustration, namely the 'construction' or 'implied term' theory, the 'just solution' theory, and the 'change in

[1] [1951] 1 KB 190.
[2] See Treitel, *Law of Contract*, pp. 697-8.

the fundamental obligation' theory, it is surely clear that they are all in part correct. There is no inconsistency between them because they do not purport to answer the same question.

When academics and even judges have puzzled over the 'true basis' of the doctrine, they have, as it seems to me, paid insufficient attention to the nature of the question they have been trying to answer. There are clearly several distinct questions involved in attempting to analyse the 'basis' of a doctrine. One such question might be, what is the general justification for the doctrine, what goal is the court trying to achieve when it uses the doctrine? Another question might be, what technique do the courts use when deciding these cases? A third such question might be, when will the courts in fact find a contract to be frustrated, what are the circumstances which are regarded as sufficient to justify invocation of the doctrine? These questions are not on the same plane. The 'construction' theory is not a theory at all, but a technique; and whether this technique is used or not is not a matter for academic disputation, but depends on simple facts. Either it is used by the court in its judgment or it is not. The 'just solution' theory is likewise not a theory at all, but it is also not a technique. It is simply the end purpose of the technique which is used, as, indeed, one hopes it is the end purpose—or anyhow one of the end purposes—of all legal techniques. And finally the 'change in the fundamental obligation' theory is not a theory either, nor again is it a technique. It is merely a statement of conditions, though rather a sketchy one, in which the court will use the construction technique in one way rather than another. One could parody this famous and rather futile controversy by asking whether the 'true basis' of contract is 'agreement', or 'offer and acceptance', or 'the just solution.' Is it not perfectly plain that the last is merely the ultimate policy objective, the first indicates the direction in which policy points in any given case, and the second is the technique which we use to arrive at the desired result?

8. Conclusion

None of this essay is likely to seem in the least startling, or perhaps even very original, to lawyers bred in jurisdictions, such as most of the United States, where courts are not afraid to base their decisions frankly and openly on policy considerations. But to lawyers in England and most of the Commonwealth, where the traditional conventions require that policy should be skilfully deployed under the concepts and techniques of the law, it is a matter of vital importance that lawyers should be fully aware of what they are in fact doing when they use legal techniques. This essay has been written in the belief that too little attention has hitherto been paid to what is involved in the technique of construction, a technique which has absorbed almost as much of the law of contract, as negligence has absorbed of the law of torts.

Misrepresentation, Warranty and Estoppel

The law relating to misrepresentation occupies a hazy and undefined area generally thought to lie along the boundaries of tort and contract. Some of the subject—that covered by 'estoppel by representation'—is also thought to have some connections with, or even to be an integral part of, the law of evidence. As is so often the case in the law, the principles and rules themselves give an appearance of order and relative certainty which in practice is only achieved by prejudging many of the crucial issues in the initial classification of the problem. If we once place our fact situation under the heading 'warranty' or 'contract' or 'estoppel' or 'deceit' or 'negligence', the result often appears to be dictated inexorably by the legal principles applicable to that category. So often, however, the real difficulty is to know what determines the initial classification. Consider, for instance, this basic situation, which is to be found in a large number of actual cases:[1]

A misrepresents certain facts to B; relying on this representation, B enters into a contract with C, and later suffers loss through C's failure to perform.

These facts carry no legal classification on their face. And yet the result of any claim made by B against A may well turn on whether this is classified as a contractual situation in which case A may be held to have 'warranted' the facts he has stated, or a tort situation in which A may be liable if he has been fraudulent or negligent, or even as an estoppel situation in which case the law is still more obscure. This being so it seems important that we should try to probe behind these legal labels to see if there are factors which help us in making our initial classification.

In this essay I want, therefore, to analyse the nature of liability for misrepresentation in the modern law in order that the policy issues can be more clearly seen, unobscured by the technical classifications and concepts which, as lawyers, we impose on the factual situations we have to deal with.

[1] This statement of facts is true of the following cases: *Pasley* v. *Freeman* (1789) 3 TR 51 (liability for deceit); *Hedley Byrne* v. *Heller* [1964] AC 465 (negligence); and *Wells* v. *Buckland Sand Ltd.* [1965] 2 QB 170 (warranty).

I. MISREPRESENTATION AND WARRANTY

It is necessary here to distinguish two situations, one of which is familiar to all students, but the second of which covers ground of which discussion is rare.

A. REPRESENTATION INDUCING CONTRACT BETWEEN PARTIES

1. Representation or Warranty: the Nature of the Question

The first situation is the familiar case of a contract between A and B which is preceded by a misrepresentation made by A to B. As every law student knows, the question which arises here has traditionally been whether the representation is a 'warranty' or a 'mere representation'. It is true that since the Misrepresentation Act 1967 the question is much less important than it used to be; but the approach of English lawyers to statutory reforms like this means that the initial common law question will still usually be posed, and will often require to be answered. In the great majority of cases the purpose of asking this question is to determine whether the representor is liable in damages to the representee. At common law, certainly between about 1700 and 1963, the position was that the representor was always liable in damages if he was fraudulent, and was sometimes liable even where he was not fraudulent. If we leave fraud out of account, the difficulty was to distinguish those cases in which the representor was to be held liable from those where he was not. This distinction was expressed by using the notion of 'warranty'. If the representor warranted the truth of the facts he stated then he was liable (even absent fraud); otherwise, not. However, it will be seen that there is an element of circularity in legal reasoning here. The word 'warranty' may be a convenient label to attach to the one fact situation and not the other; to say that 'A warranted the truth of the facts' is a simple shorthand way of expressing the legal conclusion that A is liable in damages if the facts he stated are untrue. But if this is why we use the word 'warranty' it will be seen that we must first decide if there is liability in damages before we can apply the label. There is then a danger that we are reasoning in a circle, that is (1) whether A is liable depends on whether he gave a warranty; but (2) whether the representation was a warranty depends on whether A is liable.

In either event we have so far not even begun to answer the ultimate question. If we start with question (1), the ultimate question is whether the representation is a warranty, while if we start with question (2) the ultimate question is whether A is liable. In fact, as is well known, the courts start with question (1) and ask whether the representation is a warranty. How then is this question to be answered? Again, as is well known, the courts treat this question as depending on the intention of the parties. In *Heilbut, Symons & Co.* v. *Buckleton*,[1] the House of Lords treated it as having been settled by Lord Holt that 'An affirmation at the time of the sale is a warranty, provided it appear on evidence to be so intended'.[2] It has often been pointed out that Lord Holt never said anything of the kind in the decisions to which reference was made in *Heilbut, Symons & Co.* v. *Buckleton*,[3] namely *Crosse* v. *Gardner*[4] and *Medina* v. *Stoughton*.[5] Indeed Lord Holt is reported to have said in both these cases that a buyer could sue a seller of goods upon a 'bare affirmation';[6] and since he reported both decisions himself it is somewhat remarkable that he omitted to mention the requirement of 'intent' if, as the House of Lords thought over 200 years later, Lord Holt regarded this as the essential element of a warranty.

It is, of course, well known that this requirement of 'intent' was a gloss on Holt's own decisions which derives from the judgment of Buller J. in *Pasley* v. *Freeman*.[7] But what has not often been observed is the precise context in which this remark appears. The requirement of 'intent' is mentioned by Buller J. in that part of his judgment in which he is explaining away the old decision in *Harvey* v. *Young*.[8] In that case the plaintiff had bought a lease from the defendant for £150. He later tried to resell the lease and found he could not get even £100 for it. He then sued the seller alleging that the seller had affirmed the lease to be worth £150. The action was dismissed on the ground that this was a 'bare assertion' and that it was the 'plaintiff's folly to give credit to such assertions', but the court added that the defendant would have been liable if he had warranted the lease to be of the value stated.

---

[1] [1913] AC 30.

[2] *Per* Lord Moulton, at 49.

[3] Nor indeed anywhere else so far as is known.

[4] (1689) Holt KB 5; 3 Mod. Rep. 261; 1 Show. 68; Carth. 90; Comb. 142. None of the reports says anything about 'intent'.

[5] (1700) Holt KB 208.

[6] In *Medina* v. *Stoughton*, Holt's own report states (of an action for misrepresentation by a seller of a lottery ticket that he is the owner of the ticket) 'the bare affirming it to be his amounts to a warranty'. In *Crosse* v. *Gardener*, only the report in Carth. 90 contains the reference to 'bare affirmation'.

[7] (1789) 3 TR 51.

[8] (1603) Yelv. 21.

In dealing with this sort of situation it is quite understandable that Buller J. should have used the language of 'intent'. Clearly, assertions by a seller of the value of what he sells are normally disregarded by buyers (and therefore by the courts) as mere 'sales talk'. Even today the decision in *Harvey* v. *Young* does not look at all unreasonable. In this connection it is interesting to note that although representations in contracts of sale of goods are treated as warranties in America, the UCC[1] (as well as the Uniform Sales Act which it replaced[2]) specifically provides that assertions about value are not to be construed as warranties. Nevertheless, it is also clear that in *some* circumstances it might be just to regard an affirmation of value as amounting to a warranty, for example where the seller is an expert and the buyer makes it plain that he regards the seller's statements as binding commitments. This distinction is not unnaturally expressed by saying that in this situation the seller 'intends' his affirmation to be a warranty. But it does not at all follow that representations as to matters of ordinary fact within the peculiar knowledge of the seller should only be treated as 'warranties' if there is positive evidence of an intention to that effect. Nothing that Holt or Buller said could possibly justify such a conclusion.

It is possible that in introducing the requirement of intent into the notion of warranty, Buller J. may also have been influenced by another fact. At the time of Holt's decisions, a claim for breach of warranty was prosecuted in the form of an action on the case in the nature of deceit. In modern parlance this smacked more of tort than contract, and indeed in modern times the action of deceit is a purely tortious remedy. But shortly before *Pasley* v. *Freeman* it had been decided that a claim for breach of warranty could be brought in assumpsit.[3] This meant that warranties had, procedurally at least, shifted over to the law of contract at the time when *Pasley* v. *Freeman* was decided.

This little excursion into history may not be thought of great moment, for modern doctrine is settled clearly enough. And most probably it matters little in any case for 'intent' to warrant is readily found by the courts when a seller makes statements of matters peculiarly within his knowledge. But the slender historical foundation on which the requirement of 'intent' rests is still of interest if only because it

---

[1] UCC 2-313.   [2] Sect. 12.

[3] *Stuart* v. *Wilkins* (1778) 1 Doug. KB 18. Buller J. was a party to this decision which he regarded as merely confirming long-standing practice. Yet at about the same time Blackstone regarded warranties as so similar to representations that he thought there could be no warranty of a future fact; see 3 Bl. Comm. 165.

shows that there is nothing in the law of nature which places 'warranty' in the area of contract rather than tort law.

The question which I now want to pursue is how far liability for breach of warranty is, even today, 'genuinely' contractual—taking that question to mean, how far is it the case that liability for breach of warranty derives from contractual principles or ideas. English lawyers are by now imbued with the idea that a statement of fact inducing a contract may be treated as a warranty and thereby become in a sense 'incorporated in the contract'. But the language of 'incorporation' also has its dangers, for two related reasons. First, because 'incorporation' looks like a factual concept whereas it is in truth a legal concept expressing (like the word 'warranty' itself) a legal conclusion from a factual situation. And secondly because when 'the contract' is in writing there is a tendency to assume that 'incorporation' means physical incorporation in the written document itself. It is needless to dwell on the illogicalities of all this; needless to stress that 'the contract' is not the physical document in which terms are written down, but the rights and duties imposed by the law; needless to point out that the whole treatment of the idea of 'incorporation in the contract' was greatly influenced by the policy of the courts to prefer written to oral evidence. It suffices to point out that the idea of 'incorporating' a representation in a contract states a legal conclusion rather than a fact.

This is not to say that physical incorporation of a representation in a written contract is (or has ever been) irrelevant to the ultimate legal question; quite the reverse, for, as a matter of fact, the representor will almost invariably be held liable as for a warranty in this situation. Thus physical incorporation is usually a sufficient condition of legal incorporation; but it is not a necessary condition. It is in this latter respect that the law has gradually been relaxed, for at one time the combined effect of the Statute of Frauds and the parol evidence rule was almost to elevate physical incorporation into a necessary condition of legal incorporation.

I return then to the question whether liability for breach of warranty is 'truly' contractual. This question is not as meaningless or futile as it may seem at first sight. For if there is something 'truly' contractual about warranties we would have a firm basis for the treatment of all misrepresentations. We would then only need to enquire if a misrepresentation is genuinely contractual in nature in order to decide if it is to be treated as a warranty or relegated to the field of tortious liability.[1] If, however, it should transpire that warranties differ from other forms of contractual liability and are merely *treated as though they were* (while not in fact being) contractual, then this easy approach will be barred.

This method of approach requires us to come perilously close to indulging in the exercise of looking for the 'essence' or 'basis' of 'truly' contractual obligations, as to which I have already said a good deal in the previous essays. But the contrast betwen promises and representations does, I believe, shed a good deal of light on some of these theoretical questions, and I make no apology, therefore, if the present essay goes over some ground already discussed in previous essays—the point of view will be different. For the present, however, I will by-pass these difficulties by taking as a starting-point the assumption that all contractual obligations are either representations or promises, and that the typical or paradigm contractual obligation is a promise. In America it is customary to *define* contracts in terms of promises. In England it is perhaps more usual to define contracts in terms of agreements, but even this sort of definition usually imports that the parties are agreeing about their future behaviour. Parties often agree about a state of facts, but nobody would think of such an agreement as being remotely like a contract. The question, then, is in what respects does a warranty resemble, and in what respects, differ from a promise?

2. The Role of Consent or Agreement as a Basis for Liability

The first and obvious question is whether, and if so to what extent, promises and warranties are based on the consent or will of the parties, or at least of the defendant? At first sight it might seem that both promises and warranties are based on the will or agreement of the parties. So far as ordinary contractual promises are concerned, traditional dogma asserts that liability here is rested on the voluntary assumption of liability, on the free choice of the parties, and in this essay I shall not question this dogma; so far as warranties are concerned, the position seems to be the same since no representation is a warranty unless 'intended' as such. This approach has, however, been strenuously criticized by American lawyers. In 1911 Williston attacked the notion that a warranty comprising a bare representation is contractual, and argued that a representor, unlike a promisor, never intends to impose

---

[1] This assumes that one accepts the basic starting-point that contract-type liability is normally 'strict' while tort-type liability is normally fault based. Much could be written about the desirability of this distinction, but it is unnecessary to pursue this here in view of my conclusions on the question raised in the text.

liability on himself merely by affirming a state of facts to be so.[1] The liability is imposed by the law. Other American academics have generally followed Williston. Prosser,[2] for instance, points out that the imposition of liability on a seller of goods by way of 'implied terms', even where nothing is said, is also confirmation of the fact that the liability is imposed by law and not based on agreement of the parties.

The American position is more easily defensible because the requirement of 'intent' for warranty liability has never struck root there in the way that it has in England. It is normally understood to mean that the representor must have 'intended' to affirm his statement as a fact and not (for instance) merely to have proffered an opinion on facts not known to him, or to have been indulging merely in sales talk.

In order to consider the validity of the American view it now becomes necessary to look more closely at this requirement of 'intent'. What precisely is it that the parties, or the representor, must 'intend'?[3] Buller J.'s formulation which was approved (though attributed to Holt) in *Heilbut, Symons & Co.* v. *Buckleton* is merely that the representation must be 'intended' to be a warranty. Now the result of treating a representation as a warranty is to impose on the representor strict liability for the consequences of the untruth of the statement. To 'intend' a representation to be a warranty therefore must presumably be to 'intend to accept strict liability for the consequences of the statement being untrue'. For instance, if a representor says: 'I will be answerable for the consequences if the representation is untrue', the requisite 'intention' will be present.

It will, however, be seen that in this situation the representor is in fact making a promise, and not merely representing certain facts to be true. Such a promise would more commonly be found over and above a representation, rather than standing alone.[4] Thus the representor may

---

[1] 'Liability for Misrepresentation', (1911) 24 *Harv. L. Rev.* 415. And see also Williston on *Contracts*, 3rd edn., 1970, vol. xii, §1505.

[2] Prosser and Keeton on *Torts*, 5th edn. (1984), at 748-9.

[3] I need not pursue here the additional complication that it is the appearance rather than the reality of intent which matters (see Denning L.J. in *Oscar Chess* v. *Williams* [1957] 1 WLR 375) but this adds to my doubts concerning the protection of expectation interests by use of warranties, see Essay 7, and also below pp. 321-3.

[4] It is possible for a person to promise to be answerable in the event of certain facts turning out to be untrue without representing the truth of these facts. For instance, an agent may induce a third party to contract with him by saying: 'I do not assert that I have my principal's authority; but I will be answerable for the consequences if I have not.' See *Halbot* v. *Lens* [1901] 1 Ch. 344, 351. But although this is possible, a promise to be answerable for the truth of certain facts would more normally be based on a representation that those facts are so.

first make a representation and then promise to be answerable if it is untrue. Corbin, indeed, argues that every warranty is really a promise to indemnify against loss,[1] but this seems to be the legal effect rather than the intent of a warranty. The distinction emerges where the representee does not believe what the representor says: in that case he has no ground of complaint if the representor was merely making a statement of fact, although that statement might otherwise have been treated as a warranty. But if the representor really has promised to be answerable for the consequences, non-belief in the facts is immaterial.[2] Alternatively, perhaps an 'intent' to warrant is more accurately seen as an 'intent' to accept the risk of the warranted facts being untrue, an intent to assume responsibility for the facts. But however this may be, it is at any rate clear that no express promise, or acceptance of risk is required. Even if no such express promise is made, a representation is still often treated as carrying with it such an 'implied promise'. The question now is whether such an 'implied' promise is a genuine implication or a fiction?

It is at this point that the current American view seems to be too simple: the attempt to separate liability for breach of promise as based on agreement from liability for breach of warranty as imposed by law independently of agreement is surely too black and white. The true view surely is that (i) both types of liability are in the last analysis imposed by the law; that (ii) these liabilities are imposed for a variety of reasons; that (iii) one such reason is frequently that the defendant has to some degree consented to or agreed to bear the liability; that (iv) this element of consent or agreement plays a larger role in some cases and a smaller role in other cases; that (v) *typically*, it plays a larger role in liability for promises than liability for representations; but the magnitude of the part played by consent or agreement is dependent on many other factors besides the distinction between promises and warranties. Hence it will certainly be found that there are some cases of breach of warranty which are based on a greater degree of agreement or consent than some cases of breach of promise. I proceed to enlarge on these points.

(i) Both types of liability imposed by law
It is surely unnecessary at this day and age to labour this point. Even in a legal system where full recognition is given to the private autonomy

---

[1] Corbin on *Contracts*, vol. i, §14.
[2] See *Legg* v. *Brown & Dureau Ltd.* (1923) 32 CLR 95.

of parties to make their own contracts, it is the law which creates legal rights and duties.

(*ii*) *Liabilities imposed for a variety of reasons*

Here again, the point hardly needs labouring. Throughout the whole field of civil liability, from tort liability for personal injuries through breach of contract and breach of trust, legal rights and duties are imposed for a complex mixture of reasons.

(*iii*) *Consent or agreement as a relevant factor*

Again, a simple point. That consent or agreement is *one* relevant factor in the imposition (or negation) of civil liability is surely beyond argument.

(*iv*) *Consent or agreement plays a varied role*

It is perhaps here that we begin to approach more difficult terrain. The traditional distinction between contract and tort which is so built into the ways of thought of the modern lawyer is based on the supposition that contractual duties derive from consent while tort duties are imposed by law. I have already discussed this question extensively in earlier essays, and will confine myself here to suggesting that what we have in fact is not a sharp dividing line between voluntarily accepted duties and legally imposed duties, but an enormous variety of circumstances in which consent or agreement plays a more or less prominent part as a ground for ultimate decision. Even in simple contract cases there is, for instance, a considerable chasm between (say) an action to recover an agreed price and an action for damages for breach of contract. In the former case the whole claim is an attempt to compel the defendant to pay what he has promised, though even here the requirement of consideration is a reminder that consent or agreement to be bound is not a sufficient basis for imposing liability without reference to other factors. But an action for damages for breach of contract is to a much less extent based on the agreement or consent of the promisor. A seller of goods promises to deliver the goods; but he does not usually make an express promise to pay damages if the goods are not delivered. But this case also illustrates that the distinction between a genuine 'implied' promise and an obligation imposed by law is similarly a distinction which cannot be maintained by any hard and fast line. Although a seller usually makes no express promise to pay damages for non-delivery it is arguable that a seller in a modern legal system must know that a liability to pay damages is a common result of failure to deliver, and that in a sense he may therefore be taken to 'agree' or 'consent' to this result. Even here it is clear that there will be wide variations in the reality of this consent or agreement. At one extreme there may be a case in which a seller acts in the ordinary course of business and is (perhaps) warned by the buyer that he will be held responsible for non-delivery; here the seller may come very close to promising to pay damages for non-delivery. At the other extreme there may be a case in which a private seller who has no knowledge or understanding of the law is held liable for consequential damage. In such circumstances the agreement or consent of the seller plays little part in the ultimate result. Indeed its role is merely as a factor helping to set the stage, the ultimate result of which is prescribed for reasons of policy and justice independent of agreement or consent. There is little difference between this type of situation and (say) the tortious liability of an occupier of premises to his visitors.

(v) *Typically, consent plays a larger role in imposing liability for promises than for misrepresentations*
Undoubtedly promises differ from misrepresentations in a number of important respects which bear on the reasons for imposing liability, but the distinction cannot be wholly explained in terms of the role played by consent or agreement. I have already shown that the part played by consent or agreement in imposing liability for promises varies enormously from case to case. But the same is also true of liability for misrepresentations. For example, a business seller who makes positive assertions of fact about the goods he sells may well appreciate that such assertions may amount to warranties and therefore know that he is assuming, and be willing to assume, such liability in making the representation. At the other extreme a person may make a relatively casual misrepresentation without appreciating or anticipating that it will have any legal repercussions on any resulting contract.

Moreover, in a typical warranty case—for instance, warranty of quality in contracts of sale of goods—the distinction between warranty and promise often turns merely on whether the sale is of specific or unascertained goods. In a sale of unascertained goods to be acquired by the seller, statements about the quality of the goods can only be part of the promise: the seller promises to deliver goods of a certain quality. In a sale of specific goods, however, the self-same statement may amount to a warranty. It seems strange, therefore, to insist that in the former case the liability is self-imposed while in the latter it is imposed by law.[1] A similar objection arises in other cases from the fact that a seller may be unable to deliver the goods he has promised to sell because of a certain state of facts which he has misrepresented. It seems wholly artificial in such a situation to say that the liability for non-delivery is contractual and arises from consent, while any liability for misrepresentation cannot arise from consent.

So far it may appear that there is little distinction between the role of consent or agreement in liability for promises and for representations. But this would not be the correct conclusion. As I have already suggested, the typical case of breach of promise does differ from the typical case of liability for representations. First, the typical promise *looks like* a binding commitment, and the typical promisor must normally realize that he is undertaking liabilities which may in the last resort be legally enforced against him. But it is much more doubtful whether this can be said of the 'typical representation' or, indeed, whether there is such a thing as a 'typical representation'. This becomes even more obvious when we pass to cases where a representation is made which does not induce any other transaction between representor and representee. After all a representation is merely a statement of fact, and statements of fact are constantly being made by all people in the course of daily conversation without any thought or intention of assuming any legal obligations whatever. And this is even true of many statements in business contexts. Consider, for instance, the familiar action for breach of warranty of authority. In *Cherry and McDougal* v. *Colonial Bank of Australasia*,[2] the defendants were company directors who appointed C as a manager and notified their bankers by letter that C had authority to sign cheques. C overdrew the company's bank account without the authority of the shareholders as required by the company's regulations. Being unable to recover against the company, the bank sued the directors for breach of implied warranty of authority: in notifying the bank of the appointment of C they had represented that C had the authority of the company to borrow. The defendants'

---

[1] I do not assert that there is no relevant distinction between a sale of specific and a sale of unascertained goods. In the former case the buyer may have the opportunity of examining the goods before he buys and therefore a statement as to quality etc. may not always be treated as a warranty, at least according to prevailing English doctrine (though it is probably otherwise in America). But in a sale of unascertained goods the buyer must perforce trust to the seller's statements and therefore statements about quality will be almost inevitably construed as promises.

[2] (1869) LR 3 PC 24.

counsel protested, not unjustly, that they had no intention whatever of incurring any liability to the bank:[1] 'This letter', he said, 'contained no words of contract, it stipulates for no consideration, and shows no intention on either side to make a contract, yet the action brought is founded on a contract, and no contract is proved.' The objection did not prevail,[2] for the court held that the jury were entitled to 'imply a warranty' to the bank, on the part of the defendants, that C had authority to bind the company so as to make them reponsible to the bank for the advances on the cheques.[3]

The same is true of any number of cases of misrepresentation which are enforced by way of estoppel where the representor probably had no intention or thought of binding himself to any legal liability by his representations.

Another reason why a representation is not so often or typically intended as a binding commitment when compared with a promise is that a promise as to the future conduct of the promisor is only one possible way of declaring the intentions of the promisor. A person may intend to conduct himself in a certain way and may declare that intention to another who may rely on that statement of intention; yet the party making the declaration will not be liable if he changes his mind.[4] To say that you intend to do something is not necessarily the same thing as to promise to do it, though doubtless in appropriate circumstances a declaration of intention may reasonably be understood as a promise. But a representation of existing fact differs in this way from a statement as to the future. The former has to do double service within the same linguistic framework; an ordinary statement of existing fact corresponds, in relation to future facts, both with mere statements of intention and with promises. To some extent, no doubt, a statement of fact may be made in the more guarded language of 'opinion', and this perhaps corresponds more closely with mere declarations of intent, while positive assertions of fact correspond more with promises. But it would be unrealistic to assume that in ordinary speech a representor of facts, even when he makes a positive assertion as opposed merely to stating an opinion, intends to take upon himself any sort of commitment; while a person who makes a promise, as opposed to merely declaring his intention, clearly does normally accept a commitment.

[1] Ibid., at 28.

[2] Yet in other cases this sort of argument has been accepted as conclusive that there can be no warranty-type liability, see e.g. *Low* v. *Bouverie* [1891] 3 Ch. 82.

[3] (1869) LR 3 PC, at 31.

[4] See *Maunsell* v. *Hedges* (1854) 4 HLC 1039; *Wells* v. *Matthews* (1914) 18 CLR 440.

3. Other Distinctions between Representations and Promises

It would be misleading to think that the distinction between a statement of fact and a promise turns only on the extent to which any resultant liability is based on the consent or agreement of the defendant. There are other important distinctions which must surely have had some bearing on the differing degrees to which legal liability is in fact imposed in the two cases.

First, and perhaps most importantly, promises usually give rise to expectations while statements of fact are less likely to do so. Allied to this is the fact that promises are more likely to induce conduct in reliance than representations of fact; moreover a promise is usually a better reason for relying on another than a representation. One of the major issues in determining whether the law should give relief for a misrepresentation is whether the representee was entitled to act in reliance on the representation. The problem is often said to be whether the representee acted *reasonably* in reliance on the representation, but I believe this is too simple a view. It is one thing to say a person has acted reasonably in relying on a representation; quite another thing to say that he was *entitled* to rely on it so as to hold the representor liable for the consequences if the representation should be untrue. The difference is perhaps most marked in cases of representations or advice published to the world in the form of advice in newspapers etc., or the certificate of a company's auditors. It is often quite 'reasonable' to rely on such statements, but it does not follow that legal liability is or should be imposed where the statement is untrue. This problem is far less acute in the case of a promise, because a promise virtually invites reliance; indeed, a very common way of making a promise *is* to invite reliance ('You can count on me'). Moreover, the gap between relying on a promise and being entitled to rely on it is shorter than the corresponding gap in cases of misrepresentations, because at the very least a promise (unlike a representation) is a prima-facie admission by the promisor that reliance will be justified.

These factual distinctions have led to important legal distinctions between promises and representations. One of the most significant distinctions is that actions for damages for breach of a promise can be brought on a purely executory transaction. The promisee does not have to show reliance on the promise, though in the absence of such reliance he will have to show consideration in the form of a counter-promise. But an action for a misrepresentation is almost invariably a claim for relief against the consequences of having acted upon the misrepresentation. This raises an issue of considerable theoretical interest. Why should a bare executory promise give rise to liability while an unrelied-upon misrepresentation never does so? As we shall see later, where a misrepresentation is made which does not induce a contract between the parties, the misrepresentation is sometimes treated as a warranty by the courts, and the consideration for this is the very action in reliance which leads to the damage. If it is the expectations generated by the promise which give rise to the obligations of a promisor for liability on an unrelied upon promise (as the law seems to assume), why should not a misrepresentation which gives rise to expectations also be actionable even if it has not been acted upon? I return to this point later.

But if there are important distinctions between representations and promises there are also many similarities. Perhaps the most obvious is that it is unfair and unreasonable to impose liability for either promises or misrepresentations which form part of ordinary social discourse. In the case of promises this is justified by holding that there is no 'intent to create legal relations'. In the case of misrepresentations it is justified by holding that there is no 'intent to warrant' or no 'duty of care'. These differing legal concepts obscure the fact that similar policy issues arise whether a case is classified as contract or tort, as an action for breach of warranty or negligent misrepresentation.

B. REPRESENTATION NOT INDUCING CONTRACT BETWEEN PARTIES THERETO

1. Representation Inducing Contract with Third Party

Where a misrepresentation is made by A to B and no subsequent contract is entered into between these parties the case looks at first sight as though the misrepresentation cannot be treated as a warranty at all. On the face of it, the situation does not look contractual, but (if wrongful at all) tortious. But if this situation had been characterized as tortious rather than contractual it would have followed that, at least until the *Hedley Byrne* case,[1] the representor could rarely be liable unless he were fraudulent. And even since the *Hedley Byrne* case the representor could only be liable if he was held to be negligent. To impose strict liability on the representor it was necessary[2] to treat the

---

[1] [1964] AC 465.

[2] Not of course *logically* necessary, because there is nothing impossible about strict liability in tort. But when it is remembered that liability even for fraudulent misrepresentation (apart from contract) was only recognized in 1789 and for negligent misrepresentation in 1963, the practical possibility of the courts holding a representor strictly liable in tort was and still is remote indeed.

representation as a contractual warranty. But this of course gave rise to many difficulties. A representation standing alone does not look like a contract; it is hard to reconcile the treatment of such a representation as a contractual obligation with the traditional contract analysis of concepts such as offer, acceptance, bargain, and so on. Above all it seems (at least to modern lawyers) difficult to find any consideration for the warranty.

But in fact these difficulties were overcome by the courts. Starting with the great case of *Collen* v. *Wright*[1] the courts first recognized and then developed the possibility of treating a representation as a warranty even where the representation did not induce a subsequent contract between the parties. As we shall see, the eventual developments of this principle enable strict liability to be imposed by the courts for virtually any type of representation where justice and policy seem to demand this result.

In *Collen* v. *Wright* the plaintiff negotiated with the defendant, who was the agent of a third party, for a lease of the third party's property. On the conclusion of the negotiations the plaintiff went into possession but the third party later repudiated the agreement and denied that his agent had any authority to make it. The plaintiff sued the third party for specific performance but lost his suit because of the agent's lack of authority. He then claimed damages from the agent. It was not denied that the agent bona fide believed himself to have authority. In substance the claim was for damages on the ground that the agent had held himself out to be, or represented himself to be, agent of the third party with authority to enter into the agreement. But an action in tort for an innocent misrepresentation would have stood scant chance of success in 1857. The plaintiff therefore alleged that the defendant's representation was a 'warranty'. And this claim was upheld by the Court of Exchequer Chamber.

It is not surprising that strict liability for representations standing alone should have first been recognized in the *Collen* v. *Wright* situation, because this situation is very close to the traditional type of warranty. The representation did in fact lead to the making of a contract between the representor and representee and to that extent fell squarely within

---

[1] (1857) 8 E. and B. 647. There were already at this date some very strong dicta which favoured a wide view of warranty in *Maunsell* v. *Hedges* (1854) 4 HLC 1039, 1055 and 1059-60, though these seem to have been largely forgotten. In this case Lord St Leonards even found a 'general principle' that 'a representation which is made as an inducement for another to act upon it, and is followed by his acting upon it, will, especially in such a case as marriage, be deemed to be a contract'.

the older cases holding representations by sellers of goods to be warranties. There were, of course, two new factors in the case which caused problems: firstly, the agreement for the lease was void, and secondly, the representor only entered into that agreement as agent. These factors caused some doctrinal difficulty, particularly in relation to consideration. But they did not seriously trouble the court, it simply being asserted that the plaintiff's entry into the main transaction was a sufficient consideration for the agent's warranty of authority.

What did trouble the court more seriously was whether the plaintiff was justified in relying on the defendant's representation of authority. Having regard to the general common law attitude of *caveat emptor* it could be (and indeed was) argued that the plaintiff should have inquired of the defendant's principal whether the defendant had the necessary authority, and that since he made no such inquiry he simply accepted the risk of absence of authority. This argument was accepted by Cockburn CJ, but he found himself in a minority of one;[1] the majority took the more realistic view that the plaintiff was entitled to rely on the defendant's representation of authority, since the defendant of all people should have known the extent of his authority.

Collen v. *Wright* has fathered a considerable progeny. Amongst its descendants can be numbered many cases of collateral contracts. A makes a representation to B. B, in reliance thereon, enters into a contract not with A but with C. B can sue A for breach of warranty so long as he can show an 'intent' to give a warranty or an *animus contrahendi*.[2] But the two major developments in the principle of *Collen* v. *Wright* occurred in the early years of this century. In the first, the principle of the agent's warranty of authority was extended to cases where the representee was induced to act otherwise than by making a contract with the agent. And in the second, the whole doctrine cut loose from its moorings and ceased to be dependant on any question of agency.

2. Representation Inducing Other Forms of Conduct
(i) Breaking out of the Collen v. Wright situation
In *Starkey* v. *Bank of England*[3], the House of Lords decided that an

---

[1] Just as Grose J. had found nobody to agree with him in *Pasley* v. *Freeman*, above, that the plaintiffs should not have relied on the defendants' statements but made their own inquiries.

[2] See *Wells* v. *Buckland Sand Ltd.* [1965] 2 QB 170.

[3] [1903] AC 114, approving *Firbank's Executors* v. *Humphreys* (1886) 18 QBD 54.

agent could be liable for breach of warranty of authority to a plaintiff who did not enter into any contract with the agent but suffered loss through reliance on the agent's representation in some other way. In this case the Bank of England sued a firm of brokers who had in all good faith presented a forged power of attorney purporting to authorize them to transfer certain Consols. The bank registered the transferee of the Consols as the owner and he later transferred them to a bona fide purchaser for value. This purchaser was entitled, on well-settled principles, to hold the bank liable, and the bank sought an indemnity from the brokers who had presented the forged power of attorney. The case was presented as one of a warranty by the brokers that they had the authority which they appeared to have under the power of attorney. The brokers, however, argued that the case differed from *Collen* v. *Wright* in that the bank's loss derived from the fact that they had registered the transferee of the Consols and not from any contract which they had made with the brokers. This distinction was rejected as 'absolutely immaterial', and the brokers were held liable for breach of warranty.

(ii) The 'request' principle

Two years later *Sheffield Corporation* v. *Barclay*[2] came before the House of Lords. This case was very similar to that of *Starkey* v. *Bank of England*, but it did not involve any question of agency at all. The defendants had accepted in good faith a certificate of Sheffield Corporation stock and a forged transfer as security for a loan. They later sent the certificate and transfer to the corporation for registration; the transfer was registered and the defendants later sold and transferred the stock to a buyer who thus had a valid claim against the corporation. The corporation, also being liable to the true owner, sought an indemnity from the defendants. Thus in all essentials the facts were identical with those in *Starkey's* case except that the defendants had acted as principals throughout. What was alleged against them was that they had represented the transfer to be genuine and not that they represented themselves to have authority. It was thus not possible to treat the case as a case of breach of warranty of authority; but equally the plaintiffs could not succeed in a simple action for damages for misrepresentation having regard to *Derry* v. *Peek*,[3] still fresh in the memory of the profession. It was, therefore, necessary to find a new

---

[1] [1903] AC 117, *per* Lord Halsbury.
[2] [1905] AC 392.
[3] (1889) 14 App. Cas. 337.

principle to support the plaintiffs' action. This principle was found by the House of Lords in an old line of cases dating back to *Adamson* v. *Jarvis* in 1827.[1] According to this principle, whenever one person 'requests' another to do an act which is not manifestly illegal or tortious the former comes under an obligation to indemnify the latter against any loss which he may suffer in consequence. This principle is one of considerable interest and importance and deserves something of a digression.

One of the most interesting features of this principle is that it is so little noticed in the books;[2] the reason for this is doubtless that it is not at all clear to what branch of the law these cases really belong. They hardly look like cases of tort, and are certainly not treated as such in the tort books. But they do not look very like ordinary contracts, either, and they are ignored by the contract books as much as the tort books. There is certainly no express promise to indemnify the plaintiff, nor is there any very obvious consideration. Moreover, they cannot (it seems) be treated as cases of genuine implied-in-fact promises, because in *Dugdale* v. *Lovering*[3] (which was approved in *Sheffield Corporation* v. *Barclay*) no such implication could possibly have been made. In that case the plaintiffs had railway trucks in their possession which had been sent to them by a party who had become bankrupt. The defendant was the trustee in bankruptcy, and he demanded return of the trucks. Third parties, however, claimed that the trucks had been sold to them by the bankrupt. The plaintiffs asked the defendant for an indemnity in the event of their delivering the trucks to him and later being held liable to the third parties; the defendant refused to give any such indemnity but insisted on the trucks being handed over, whereupon the plaintiffs complied. Being later held liable to the third parties, they now sued the defendant for an indemnity. The defendant was held liable although there was no express promise of indemnity and manifestly no promise could have been implied in fact.

If, on the other hand, these cases are to be treated as based on a promise 'implied in law', further questions spring to mind. First, a

---

[1] (1827) 4 Bing. 66; *Betts* v. *Gibbins* (1834) 2 Ad. and El. 57; *Toplis* v. *Crane* (1839) 5 Bing. NC 636; *Dugdale* v. *Lovering* (1875) LR 10 CP 196.

[2] And this may in turn explain why it has been so rarely relied upon in modern cases. See, however, Lord Denning in *Z Ltd.* v. *A–Z* [1982] QB 558, 575, and the Privy Council decision in *Yeung* v. *Hong Kong and Shanghai Banking Corp.* [1981] AC 787.

[3] Above.

promise 'implied in law' looks very like a species of restitutionary liability and indeed the request principle seems to have been treated as such by Lord Wright in *Secretary of State for India* v. *Bank of India*.[1] But this approach too has difficulties: the defendant's liability in these cases is to indemnify the plaintiff against his losses and not to make restitution of any benefits or gains. The principle is not discussed at all in Goff and Jones on *Restitution*.

Moreover, if the request principle depends on a promise 'implied in law' it should be possible to state the circumstances in which such a promise will be implied. Yet the request principle is itself stated in terms which are manifestly too wide. It cannot possibly be asserted that the mere request to another to do an act which turns out to be injurious to him is in all cases sufficient to impose a liability on the former to indemnify the latter. Literally interpreted, such a principle could be made to hold a seller liable to a buyer for leading him into a bad bargain merely because the former has made an offer to sell which the latter has accepted. In *Birmingham and District Land Co.* v. *LNW Railway Co.*,[2] an argument which involved similar reasoning was rejected as obviously untenable. Lord Bowen explained the inapplicability of the 'request' principle merely by asserting that, 'It is idle to say that in a contract for purchase and sale of land there is any request made by one person to the other'.[3] But this is not very helpful. In point of fact there clearly may be a request: if the 'request' principle does not apply then it must be because that principle is too widely stated. Some additional fact is needed before the principle becomes applicable.

Another objection to a literal application of the request principle is that it would convert many credit references into contracts of suretyship. A person to whom application is made for a reference may in a sense request the third party to deal with the applicant, but such a request is not the same as a promise to be answerable in the event of default. It imposes no doubt a duty of honesty[4] and even of care,[5] but it is plainly not a warranty.[6]

It is clear, then, that there is something missing in the traditional formulations of the request principle. In the original version of this essay I suggested that the missing element was a reference to mis-

---

[1] [1938] 1 All ER 797.
[2] (1889) 34 Ch. D. 261.
[3] Ibid., at 275.
[4] *Pasley* v. *Freeman*, above.
[5] *W. B. Anderson & Son Ltd.* v. *Rhodes* [1967] 2 All ER 850.
[6] *Haycraft* v. *Creasy* (1801) 2 East 92.

representation. It was, I then thought, the combination of mis-representation coupled with a request that the promisee should act on the representation which justified the courts in treating the representation as a warranty. It now seems to me that this was mistaken. The basic idea behind the 'request' principle is wider than any notion of misrepresentation. For instance, a principal who requests an agent to do something on his behalf is plainly liable to indemnify the agent against any costs of doing so, and that liability does not depend upon any misrepresentation.

Although doubtless misrepresentation is an element in many of these cases, it now seems to me clear (and was, I believe implicit in the original essay, though I failed then to see the implications of my own reanalysis of the relevant legal concepts) that the basis of the liability can be seen to rest on the twin pillars of benefit and reliance. A person who requests another to do something will prima facie be entitled to be indemnified against the consequences, either if he derives some benefit from the act to be done or if the other justifiably acts in reliance on the request, rather than on his own judgment. Although the way in which the two concepts of benefit and reliance operate here requires further amplification, which is offered below (and was indeed in the original essay) it can now be seen that liability under the 'request' principle is very similar to liability on a promise. The elements of benefit and reliance which, in the case of promises, provide the consideration, here also, it seems, provide the grounds of liability. This, it may be thought, bears out the suggestion made in Essay 8 that a consideration is really a reason for the recognition of an obligation, rather than a reason for the enforcement of a promise. The place of misrepresentation in the operation of the 'request' principle now seems to me to be as one of the factors which make the reliance of the 'requestee' (to coin a word) justifiable, in the sense that it makes it not only reasonable for him to act on the request, but reasonable to shift the risk of his doing so onto the other party.

This also makes it easier to explain the decision in *Sheffield Corporation* v. *Barclay*, where the House of Lords appeared to think that the 'request' principle was quite independent of any misrepresentation by the defendants, but the liability they imposed was nevertheless conceived to be a contractual liability. The interesting thing for present purposes is that *Collen* v. *Wright* was cited by Lord Davey to show that the plaintiffs' action in reliance on the representation could be treated as consideration. This is generally taken as showing that the liability was based on an 'implied promise', because otherwise the reference to consideration seems mysterious; and yet the implication of a promise in such circumstances seems totally fictitious. However, if we see consideration as the reason for the creation of an obligation (as suggested in Essay 8) the result makes perfectly good sense.

I will return later to the 'request' principle because I believe that it sheds light on a number of important policy questions about liability for misrepresentations generally. But for the moment I turn to the question of consideration as a requirement where the misrepresentation has not induced a contract between representor and representee.

C. CONSIDERATION AND MISREPRESENTATION

We have seen how in *Collen* v. *Wright* no difficulty was found in treating the plaintiff's conduct in entering into the transaction as a sufficient consideration to support an action on the agent's representation of authority as a warranty. In *Starkey* v. *Bank of England* no mention was made of the question of consideration from beginning to end of the case, and in the *Sheffield Corporation* case, only Lord Davey felt it to be necessary to affirm that the act of the corporation in registering the transfer was a sufficient consideration. It will be seen that the willingness of the courts to treat such conduct as a sufficient consideration meant that henceforth the consideration problem was largely disposed of. So long as the plaintiff has acted to his detriment in reliance on a representation it is possible to find a consideration, at least where the action was expected or foreseeable by the representor. The fact that action in reliance plays the same role when treated as a ground for relief for misrepresentation and as consideration is well illustrated by *Australasian Brokerage Ltd.* v. *A.N.Z. Banking Corporation.*[1] It was here held that a fraudulent representation by one contracting party to another which induces the latter to perform his contract is not actionable in deceit. This is, of course, merely an application to the tort of deceit of the familiar rule that performance of an existing duty may not be a good consideration.

In the great majority of cases it is precisely the element of reliance that gives rise to the representee's loss and leads to claims for relief for misrepresentation. But as we have already mentioned, it is possible though less common for representations to give rise to expectations

[1] (1934) 52 CLR 430.

just as promises do. At present an 'unacted-upon' representation stand-ing alone resembles a gratuitous promise. Both may give rise to ex-pectations which are not legally enforceable. But the question may still be raised why a representation of this character should be unenforceable if not acted upon. The nature of the question may be illustrated by considering certain types of representation which at present are usually enforced by way of estoppel. For example, A steals a share certificate and forges a transfer in the owner's name. B buys the shares in good faith and is registered by the company who issue him with a new share certificate. This certificate is a representation that B is the owner of the shares. It may well give rise to 'expectations' in B's mind, for example that he will receive dividends. But unless and until he acts to his det-riment upon the representation he will have no relief against the company.[1]

It does not seem that there is anything unreasonable in refusing relief for unacted-upon misrepresentations. If the representor has re-ceived no benefit from his representation, has not intended to undertake any commitment, and is just as innocent as the representee, and the representee's only complaint is that he has been disappointed in the expectations which the representor has raised in him, why should the loss be shifted? No doubt, to the orthodox lawyer, this can be explained by pointing out that a representation differs in the essential respect from a promise, but an alternative view, of course, is that if a rep-resentation has to be acted upon before it becomes actionable, perhaps the same ought to be true of a promise (unless it is a paid-for promise).

D. THE POLICY ISSUES

Apart from doctrinal difficulties, it is important to enquire whether there are significant policy issues wrapped up in the distinction between the representation which induces a contract between the parties and the representation which does not. Given that the consideration di-fficulty can be overcome, is there any reason why the courts should be more willing to find an 'intent to warrant' in the case of a representation which leads to a contract between the parties than a representation which is relied on by the representee so as to cause him loss in some other way?

There seems no doubt that representations will much more readily be treated as warranties in the former case than in the latter case.

[1] *Simm* v. *Anglo-American Telegraph Co.* (1879) 5 QBD 188.

Certainly in contracts of sale of goods we are not today in practice very far removed from the American position whereby an affirmation by the seller is always treated as a warranty. That there may be situations in which justice is better served by denying strict liability for representations, even between contracting parties, is shown by the well-known case of *Oscar-Chess* v. *Williams*,[1] but there is no question that this was an unusual case involving special features, not the least of which was that the buyer was the dealer with presumptively greater knowledge and the seller was the private consumer. Perhaps we have now also arrived at the stage where a representation by a dealer as to the quality of goods will normally be treated as a warranty even if the representee buys the goods from a third party rather than the representor; these are the familiar 'collateral contract' cases.

But when we consider other types of representation leading to conduct in reliance, the general approach of English lawyers is still to categorize the case as a tortious one, and then the 'general principle' that no damages can be awarded for innocent misrepresentation at common law is sure to be advanced (even though liability may exist under the Misrepresentation Act 1967). Why is this so? What, in terms of policy, distinguishes (1) the ordinary representation leading to contract which is called a warranty, (2) a representation not leading to contract between the parties which is also treated as a warranty, and (3) other representations which are not treated as warranties?

I suggest that the answer is largely to be found in the same two factors which operate with the 'request' principle, and of course with the doctrine of consideration, though there is also a third factor here not relevant in the other cases. First, a representation is more likely to be treated as a warranty where the representor derives some benefit from the action which is taken by the representee in reliance on the representation. Secondly, the representation is more likely to be treated as a warranty if the court thinks that as between the parties the primary responsibility for ascertaining the facts rests on the representor rather than the representee, so that the representee's reliance is not only reasonable, but also justifiable. A third more complex factor (I suggest below) concerns the relationship between misrepresentations and the rules relating to the transfer of property in string transactions.

1. Benefit
It is perhaps not surprising that the element of benefit to the representor

[1] [1957] 1 WLR 370.

should be a material factor in these cases. Where there is some element of benefit the whole transaction begins to approximate more closely to the ordinary bargain; detriment to promisee and benefit to promisor are, of course, the hallmarks of the typical bilateral contract. I do not mean to suggest that 'benefit' has a technical meaning here, or that its presence can be tested by study of the cases dealing with what is a sufficient benefit to make a promise actionable. But what I do suggest is that this is one of the factors which lead lawyers to classify such cases as 'warranty' or contractual situations and therefore to impose stricter duties on the representor.[1]

Where the representation induces a contract between the parties to the representation the element of benefit is obviously present. In the ordinary contract of sale of goods the buyer is likely to pay more for goods represented to have certain qualities, at any rate, if he does actually rely on the representations; if the goods do not have these qualities, therefore, the buyer has not only acted to his loss but the seller may have been unjustly enriched. He may have received more than the goods are worth. And this result remains the same even if the representation was wholly innocent. This is, therefore, the strongest case for giving the representee a remedy by way of warranty.[2] In this situation, even on my view, liability for expectation damages will often be justifiable, not necessarily because the representor 'intends' to accept such a liability by his warranty, but because it may be the only way, or the best way, of preventing the unjust enrichment of the seller. But there may be other cases (such as *Sealand of the Pacific* v. *MacHaffie*,[3] discussed in Essay 7) where, despite the misrepresentation, the goods have not been sold for more than they are worth, and in that event (as suggested in Essay 7) I am less clear why there should be any liability for breach of warranty, though there should, of course, still be a liability for reliance losses which will be achieved by treating the mis-representation as tortious.

Where the representee's conduct in reliance takes a different form,

---

[1] For this reason I cannot agree with the views of Fullagar J. in (1951) 25 *Aus. LJ* 278, 283, that the implied warranty of authority cases are 'altogether anomalous', even though I now feel that it is not always appropriate to treat these as contractual cases.

[2] Perhaps this is only so where the seller is selling in the course of business, or where the goods are new. I doubt if the same arguments hold good for the sale of houses, except by a builder or developer. In such transactions the discovery of defects, etc., which have been innocently misrepresented not to exist, seems more analogous to the occurrence of a new loss, the risk of which falls on the buyer.

[3] (1973) 51 DLR (3rd) 702. See p. 176 above.

there may or may not be any element of benefit to the representor. The implied warranty of authority cases are perhaps borderline in this respect, but certainly, in many such cases the agent would derive a direct or indirect benefit from the contract. In many other cases classified as collateral contracts there will also be some indirect benefit to the representor, as in the typical hire-purchase situation where the dealer misrepresents the condition of the goods and induces the representee to acquire them on hire-purchase. Although the representee does not contract with the representor the latter will benefit from the representee's actions. The goods must be sold by the dealer to the finance company in order to be supplied to the hirer. On the other hand there are cases in which the representor gives a wholly disinterested reference about the credit or standing of another. In essence this was the situation in *Pasley* v. *Freeman* and in the *Hedley Byrne* case; in both cases A made a representation to B as a result of which B entered into a contract with C. The basic facts in these cases seem identical with those in many of the collateral contract cases, and yet the legal result is entirely different: the difference seems to lie largely in this element of benefit.[1]

At this point I return to the request principle. In the light of the suggestion made above about the importance of the element of benefit to the representor, it becomes clearer why a 'request' is regarded as so significant. A 'request' to another to act in a certain way is, on the face of it, good evidence that the requestor expects to derive some benefit from the act to be performed. This very argument was relied upon in *Bank of England* v. *Cutler*,[2] where the facts were somewhat similar to those in *Starkey* v. *Bank of England*. But in the *Cutler* case the defendant broker did not put forward any forged power of attorney; he personally attended at the bank's premises and identified one J. P. as M. P., the owner of some stock. The broker acted in complete good faith but was nevertheless held liable by a majority of the Court of Appeal on the principle of *Sheffield Corporation* v. *Barclay*. Counsel for the broker protested that the whole case was in effect an action for damages for misrepresentation, and he went on: 'If every statement upon which it is intended that another shall act is to be treated as involving a request to

---

[1] This probably also explains why in *Low* v. *Bouverie*, above, the court found no 'intention' to contract and no consideration although here again the representee had acted on the representation in a foreseeable way.

[2] [1908] 2 KB 208. Cf. *Gowers* v. *Lloyds & N.P.F. Bank* [1938] 1 All ER 766 where bankers were held not liable for wrongly certifying a customer to be alive as a result of which plaintiffs continued to pay his pension.

him to act, then there is really an end of the principle affirmed in *Derry* v. *Peek*.'[1]

This argument was accepted by Vaughan Williams LJ who dissented, and who thought that the broker had acted more as a witness than as a moving party.

> There must [he said] be a request, and the request or invitation must be under such circumstances that one can as a matter of law imply the intention to warrant; and generally speaking, such intention will not be inferred except in cases where the request or invitation is made by some one who will derive a benefit from compliance with the request.[2]

The majority of the court, however, found a sufficient 'request', though the difference of opinion seems to have been on the interpretation of the facts rather than the law. Vaughan Williams LJ seems to have thought that the broker had attended at the Bank as a disinterested witness; the majority thought, more realistically, that the broker had attended in the ordinary course of his business as a broker. On this view, he plainly expected to derive some benefit, however indirect, from his 'request'.

But although benefit is thus often an important factor, I do not think it can be said that a representation can never be treated as a warranty where there is no benefit to the representor. Where the representor knows that the representee is going to commit himself in some serious step in reliance on the representation, justice may require the representation to be treated as a warranty apart from any element of benefit.[3]

2. Reliance and Responsibility

The second principal factor arises from cases of detrimental reliance, and concerns the relative position of the parties with regard to the facts represented. One important element in this is the means of knowledge. We have seen how in *Collen* v. *Wright* the court thought that an agent ought to know the extent of his own authority. Where the parties have equal means of ascertaining the facts the traditional individualism of the common law led to a disinclination to give relief to the representee;

[1] Ibid., at 215.

[2] Ibid., at 219.

[3] See e.g. *Maunsell* v. *Hedges* (1854) 4 HL Cas 1039, where Lord Cranworth says that a declaration by A to B that he has executed a deed undertaking to leave property to B will become a binding contract if B acts upon it by getting married, assuming A to have known of B's intention.

he should have looked to the facts himself and not trusted to the representor. This line of thought is often to be found in the cases distinguishing between 'statements of fact' and 'statements of opinion', but it also has a bearing on the possibility of treating a representation as a warranty. There are even some cases in which an agent (of sorts) may not know much about his principal. In *Dickson* v. *Reuter's Telegraph Co.*,[1] for instance, the Court of Appeal held that the defendants did not warrant that a telegram delivered by them was in fact dispatched by the person represented. It was pointed out that the defendants were mere messengers who did not necessarily know anything about the identity of a person sending a telegram.

But means of knowledge is not the only factor involved here. There are many cases in which it is evident that the courts have had decided views as to who had the primary responsibility for ascertaining the facts. This appears, for instance, in cases like *Sheffield Corporation* v. *Barclay*, where there was much argument over the corporation's responsibility to maintain a register of its stock. Where the dispute has been between a corporation and a purchaser of shares or stock who has relied on a (false) certificate issued by the company, the courts have laid stress on the fact that it is the company's responsibility to maintain a correct share register.[2] Where, however, as in *Sheffield Corporation* v. *Barclay*, the dispute has been between a party who has in good faith submitted a false or forged transfer and the corporation itself, the courts at first found more difficulty. On the one hand, they evidently felt that it still remained in a sense the responsibility of the corporation to keep a proper register;[3] and arguments have been based on the fact that corporations can and do make inquiries of the registered holder before registering a transfer.[4] On the other hand, it was felt that in practice corporations must often rely on the accuracy or validity of transfers submitted for registration when accompanied by proper certificates. In *Sheffield Corporation* v. *Barclay*, the House of Lords went so far as to say that the act of the corporation in registering transfers was 'ministerial', and this notion was incorporated in the request prin-

---

[1] (1877) 3 CPD 1.

[2] *In Re Bahia and San Fransisco Rail Co.* (1868) LR 3 QB 584.

[3] See *Simm* v. *Anglo-American Telegraph Co.* (1879) 5 QBD 188, 195, where Lindley J. said it was the company's duty 'to look to their own register'. This was overruled in the *Sheffield Corporation* case.

[4] In *Bank of England* v. *Cutler*, above, it was in evidence that the Bank only did this for transfers exceeding £2,000 in view of the very large numbers of transfers of smaller amounts.

ciple as there formulated. It seems plain that use of this word was merely intended to indicate that, as between the corporation and the party submitting the transfer, the corporation's role was a passive one, and did not place upon them the responsibility of ascertaining the validity of the transfer.[1] In other words, in these circumstances, it is the corporation which relies, justifiably, on the party submitting the transfer, and not the other way about.

But it is also clear that, as between a representor and a representee, the primary responsibility may be on the former even though the latter is not acting 'ministerially' and later cases have shown that this is not a necessary requirement of warranty.[2] These cases show that it does not always matter that the representee has not acted 'ministerially', for example, where the representor was legally entitled to call on the representee to act in a certain way on the basis of certain facts being shown. Where this is the case there is a strong ground for saying that prima facie the responsibility for ascertaining the truth of the facts is on the representor—the representee is, after all, *entitled* to rely on what he is told in this situation. So, for instance, where a common carrier was required to carry goods, the court was even willing to imply a representation that the goods were safe and then hold this to be a warranty.[3] Similarly, where the master of a ship was required by a charterparty to sign bills of lading presented to him by the charterers, the primary responsibility for seeing that the bills were in accordance with the terms of the charterparty was held to be on the charterer and he was treated as both representing and warranting that this was so.[4]

3. Representations and the Transfer of Property in String Sales
In determining who, as between representor and representee, should be

---

[1] It is interesting to compare the position in regard to registered land. Originally the principle of *Sheffield Corporation* v. *Barclay* was applied as between a party submitting an invalid application for registration and the Land Registry (*Attorney-General* v. *Odell* [1906] 2 Ch. 47). But the policy behind land registration clearly differed from that behind stock registration: the Land Registry was intended to have the responsibility of thoroughly checking titles, etc. before registering them, and registration was intended to give a guarantee of validity. Accordingly the *Odell* case was reversed by s.83(4) of the Land Registration Act 1925. It has, however, been suggested that the practical effect of the case has been unwittingly restored by the Land Registration Act 1966, see Cretney and Dworkin, 'Rectification and Indemnity: Illusion and Reality', (1968) 84 *Law Q. Rev.* 528.

[2] See, e.g. *Bamfield* v. *Goole Transport Ltd.* [1910] 2 KB 94.

[3] *Bamfield* v. *Goole Transport Ltd.*, above.

[4] *Kruger & Co. Ltd.* v. *Moel Tryvan Ship Co. Ltd.* [1907] AC 272. It was expressly denied that the master's role was purely 'ministerial'—he could have refused to sign; see at 282; *Dawson Line Ltd* v. *Aktiengesellschaft Adler* [1932] 1 KB 433.

regarded as primarily responsible for ascertaining the truth, it is possible that the courts have been influenced by another policy consideration. In many of the actual cases the representation has been wholly innocent and the loss has been caused by some fraudulent party. It is noticeable that, whether by accident or design, the decisions nearly always place the responsibility on the party nearest in the chain to the fraudulent person. In this respect the law relating to the implied conditions as to title in the Sale of Goods Act, the cases of estoppel by representation in share and stock certificates, and many other cases seem to produce a similar result. Thus if a thief steals goods and sells to A who sells to B who resells to C, the loss at common law is nearly always pushed back up the line to A. He, of course, may have a legal remedy against the thief though one which is unlikely to be of much use.

The same seems to be true of other dealings in goods which involve successive conversions. For example, in the Australian case of *Grace Bros. Ltd.* v. *Lawson*,[1] furniture storers were induced by the fraud of a third party to send the goods to auctioneers for sale. The owner recovered damages against the storers who attempted to recover in turn from the auctioneers. The action failed as the plaintiffs had represented to the auctioneers that they had the owner's authority to send the goods for sale; in fact if the owner had sued the auctioneers they could probably have secured an indemnity from the plaintiffs. Here again, it can readily be seen that the question is, who is entitled to rely on who? Is the auctioneer entitled to assume that the storer has the owner's authority, or is the storer entitled to assume that the auctioneer will satisfy himself that he has the legal power to sell before he does so? Similarly in the share certificate cases there is usually an initial fraudulent party who steals a share certificate and forges a transfer. Again the effect of the cases is generally to pass the liability along the chain until it reaches the person who actually dealt with the fraudulent party. But fraud is not always involved. For instance if A 'requests' B to do something which causes loss as a result of the negligence of X, there is a tendency to give B a right of indemnity from A, where A can in turn claim against X but B cannot.[2]

This general policy seems to have been influenced by two obvious considerations. First, if there is any chance of recovery from the original

---

[1] (1922) 31 CLR 130.
[2] See *Groves & Sons* v. *Webb & Kenward* (1916) 85 LJKB 1533.

fraudulent party, the loss must be passed along the chain, for there would be—or at any rate, in earlier law, there would usually have been—no prospect of a successful action being brought against the original defrauder by a person lower down the chain.[1] And secondly, if there is no prospect of recovery from the fraudulent party, the person who dealt directly with him should be left to bear the loss since it was he who in a sense 'started it all' by trusting the defrauder.

The first argument is inapplicable where the last person in the chain has a remedy himself against the fraudulent party, for example, where he has had direct dealings with him. In such circumstances there is no need to pass the liability up the line. And the second argument is also less forceful where the last person has had direct dealings with the fraudulent party, because he is then not in such a good position to accuse the first party of 'starting it all' by trusting the fraudulent party. Accordingly (it seems), in such a case there is less chance of a representation being held to be a warranty. The point is best illustrated by *Guaranty Trust Co.* v. *Hannay*,[2] where it was held that the purchaser of a bill of exchange with shipping documents attached, who presents it for acceptance and receives payment, is not liable to indemnify the acceptor when it later transpires that the shipping documents included a forged bill of lading. At first sight these facts resemble those in *Sheffield Corporation* v. *Barclay*, and it was argued that the defendants had represented the bill of lading to be genuine and requested the plaintiff to act upon that representation by accepting the bill of exchange. In a factual sense this argument is hard to refute; moreover there was plainly a benefit to the representor in the act which he requested the representee to perform. Nevertheless it was held that the defendants were not liable on the ground that there was no 'request' in the relevant sense. The decision is perhaps more easily understandable if it is appreciated that the plaintiffs as the acceptors of the bill of exchange could have sued the fraudulent parties who originally drew the bill and attached to it the forged bill of lading. Stripped to their simplest, the facts in the *Guaranty Trust* case really came down to this: that X had obtained money from A by fraud and that, by arrangement with X, this money was later paid off from other moneys supplied by B. Although A had passed on to B the misrepresentations of X, A was himself acting in good faith and he received the money from B in discharge of a liability due to him. Moreover X was clearly liable to B.

[1] The point was specifically taken in *Groves & Sons* v. *Webb & Kenward*, above.

[2] [1918] 2 KB 623. A very similar case in its essentials is *Porter* v. *Latec Finance (Qld.) Pty. Ltd.* (1964) 111 CLR 177.

II. ESTOPPEL BY REPRESENTATION

1. Introductory

It is well known among lawyers that a representation which cannot be directly sued on in contract or tort may nevertheless be actionable with the assistance of the doctrine of estoppel by representation. But there are a number of very puzzling features about this form of estoppel. The constant assertions that estoppel is not 'a cause of action in itself' and that it is a rule of evidence rather than a rule of law make it very difficult to understand the role of estoppel and its relationship to the rest of the law relating to misrepresentation. How does estoppel fit in with liability for breach of warranty and liability in deceit and in negligence? Is this a form of 'strict liability' analogous to liability on a warranty, or is it more analogous to liability for fraud or negligence? What is the significance of the assertion that estoppel is not 'a cause of action'? Is it really a rule of evidence? And more fundamentally, do we need a doctrine of estoppel by representation at all? Would we have one in a Contract Code? Before I look into these questions, it may be useful to list a number of typical situations in which the courts have in fact used estoppel by representation to enable damages to be awarded.

(i) Share certficates[1]

It is now well-established law that a company which issues a share certificate stating that X is the owner of certain shares is estopped from denying this fact to a purchaser of the shares who has bought in reliance on the certificate. If X was not in fact the owner, the company cannot register the buyer as the owner of those shares for this would infringe the rights of the true owner; but the company is bound to register the buyer as owner of other shares of the same issue, or, if it cannot, it will have to pay him damages.

(ii) Bills of lading[2]

If a shipping company issues a bill of lading which falsely states that the goods were shipped 'in apparent good order and condition', the company will be estopped from denying that they were so shipped when sued by an endorsee of the bill of lading.

[1] *Re Bahia & San Fransisco Railway Co.*, above; *Balkis Consolidation Co.* v. *Tomkinson* [1893] AC 396.
[2] *Compania Naviera* v. *Churchill & Sim* [1906] 1 KB 237; *Brandt* v. *Liverpool etc. Steam Navigation Co.* [1924] 1 KB 416.

(*iii*) *Warehouse keepers, etc.*[1]

A warehouse keeper who issues a warrant or certificate stating that he has certain goods in his possession is estopped from denying this fact if sued by someone who has bought the goods in reliance on such a warrant or certificate.

(*iv*) *Trustees, etc.*[2]

A trustee who, in answer to inquiry by one considering lending money on the security of an assignment of a beneficial interest in a trust, declares that there are no prior charges on the interest, will be estopped from denying this against the party acting upon that representation.

2. Estoppel not a Cause of Action in Itself?

I wish to start by examining the frequent assertion that 'estoppel is not a cause of action in itself'. This is a rather strange phrase particularly when combined with the assertion that estoppel is a rule of evidence. If estoppel is indeed a rule of evidence then it would obviously follow that it could not itself be a cause of action. Whatever the precise meaning of 'cause of action' it is scarcely possible for a rule of evidence ever to be such a thing. It seems that the denial that estoppel can be a cause of action in itself is really intended as a denial that the representation which founds an estoppel can itself be a cause of action. This assertion is commonly explained by insisting that the plaintiff must have an 'independent cause of action' and cannot rely on the representation alone. Thus in the share certificate cases the plaintiff's cause of action is said to be, not the misrepresentation in the share certificate on which the plaintiff relied, but the refusal of the company to register him. Similarly in the bill of lading cases the endorsee's complaint is not that the shipping company have misrepresented the state of the goods but that they have delivered to him damaged goods when (according to their own word) they received them in good order and condition. And so on.

It is my contention that these arguments are transparently fallacious and that a few moments devoted to their consideration will show them to be without any substance. The precise meaning of the phrase 'cause of action' may be a matter of doubt, and it may in any event vary according to context. But it may safely be said that in an action for substantial damages the plaintiff must in every case prove, first that he

---

[1] *Seton, Laing & Co.* v. *Lafone* (1887) 19 QBD 68.
[2] *Burrowes* v. *Lock* (1805) 10 Ves. 470; *Low* v. *Bouverie* [1891] 3 Ch. 82.

has suffered damage, and secondly, that the damage was the result of some facts giving rise to a ground of complaint in law.

Since the first requirement is common to all actions for substantial damages there is a tendency for lawyers to ignore it, and to fasten on the second requirement in discussing 'causes of action'. Thus we say that the plaintiff's 'cause of action' is based on the defendant's negligence or fraud or breach of contract. We do not say that the plaintiff's cause of action is for (say) 'pain and suffering' or 'loss of £X'.

Now the process by which lawyers have (it seems) convinced themselves that estoppel is not 'a cause of action in itself' can be seen to be a very simple one. The representation which is the ground of complaint is ignored and the cause of action is said to be the damage which the plaintiff has suffered. Thus in the share certificate cases the cause of action is the 'failure of the company to register the plaintiff as a shareholder'; in the bill of lading cases it is the 'delivery of damaged goods'; and so on. But it is surely clear that these cannot themselves be treated as causes of action; they are statements of the damage the plaintiff has suffered, not the ground of his complaint in law. The damage in such cases no more amounts to the cause of action than 'pain and suffering' could be a cause of action in a personal injury claim. And the reason is surely plain. The damage when considered alone gives no indication that it has been inflicted in circumstances giving rise to a legal remedy. If a company refuses to register the plaintiff as a shareholder this cannot by itself be a cause of action because there is nothing so far to indicate that the refusal was *wrongful*, or that the plaintiff was *entitled* to be registered. And it is impossible to explain why this should be wrongful without explaining that the company has by its misrepresentation led the plaintiff to believe that he would be entitled to be registered, and that he acted on that belief by buying the shares. Similarly with the bill of lading cases. The delivery of damaged goods is not in itself wrongful; it is only wrongful because the shipping company has misled the endorsee of the bill of lading into taking up the bill in the belief that the goods are not damaged.

I submit, therefore, that it is perfectly plain that the cause of action in a case of estoppel by representation is in fact the representation, and that what is conventionally stated to be the cause of action is merely the damage. The belief that estoppel is not a cause of action in itself is a myth.

It does not, however, follow that every case of estoppel by representation resembles an action for damages for misrepresentation.

There are undoubtedly some peculiar features about estoppel by mis-representation which have (I believe) prevented its true nature from being more clearly observed. In particular it has often been insisted that a person who relies on estoppel by representation is not complaining of misrepresentation.[1] He is not, as he would be in an action of deceit, suing on the basis that the representation is false, but on the basis that it is true. How then can it be asserted that the plaintiff's cause of action is the misrepresentation? I believe that the answer to this objection is as follows. Representations, like promises, may give rise to different remedies. When a promise is broken the promisee may be able to choose between (1) affirming the contract and treating it as still in force even to the extent of suing for specific performance, or (2) accepting the breach, treating the promise as no longer binding, and suing for dam-ages. Equally, it seems to me that the law may offer different remedies to a representee for misrepresentation (although they may not always both be available, any more than in the case of promises). It may offer him the remedy of (1) 'affirming' the representation, that is, treating it as true, and claiming whatever relief would be appropriate if it were true; or (2) accepting that the representation is untrue, and suing for damages accordingly.

Basically my submission is that estoppel by misrepresentation is the first of these two alternatives; it is thus a remedy for misrepresentation which corresponds in some respects with the remedy of specific per-formance for breach of promise. It corresponds with that remedy in that the innocent party is in both cases entitled to hold the other party to his word. A party who is estopped from denying the truth of the facts he has represented is in a similar position to a promisor who has broken his promise, but who is sued for specific performance; he too 'cannot deny' the continued subsistence of his duty to perform the promise. And just as the promisee cannot both accept the repudiation of the contract and hold the contract to be still in existence, so too a representee cannot both insist on the truth and rely on the mis-representation at the same time.[2]

It now also becomes clear what is meant by the assertion that there must be 'an independent cause of action' if an estoppel is to be set up. Plainly if the representee chooses to 'affirm' the truth of the rep-

---

[1] See *Low* v. *Bouverie* [1891] 3 Ch. 82, *per* Kay LJ at 112.

[2] See *Scarf* v. *Jardine* (1882) 7 App. Cas. 345, where it was said that a party cannot rely on the truth and an estoppel at the same time. However, the decision itself seems to have been an unnecessary application of the principle.

resentation and claim such relief as would be appropriate if the representation were true, he must in fact be able to show that there is some such relief available. In all the four types of cases listed at the beginning of this section there would be such relief. In the share certificate cases, the representee would be entitled to be registered as a shareholder if the representation were true; in the bill of lading cases, the representee would be entitled to have undamaged goods delivered to him; in the warehouse keeper cases the representee would be entitled to have the goods delivered to him; and in the trustee cases, the representee would be entitled to the charge on the trust fund of which he has given notice. All this does not mean that the misrepresentation is still not an essential part of the cause of action. The representee is entitled to treat the representation as true; and if it were true he would have an 'independent cause of action'. But if there had never been any representation at all the 'independent cause of action' would never have arisen. The word 'independent' is thus quite inappropriate. The position is almost precisely analogous to a suit for specific performance. Specific performance is not 'itself a cause of action'; a suit for specific performance must be supported by an 'independent cause of action', namely a right of action on a contract. But this does not mean that specific performance is quite independent of the promise which has been broken and which it is sought to enforce. If there had been no promise there would have been no contract; and without a contract there would be nothing to enforce specifically.

But it must be stressed that all this is only the case where the representee claims to rely on the truth of the representation. If he takes the alternative course of 'repudiating' the representation, then no question of estoppel arises at all, and the only question is whether the misrepresentation itself is actionable as a warranty or for fraud or negligence.

Why has this myth that 'estoppel is not a cause of action' grown up? The reason is not far to seek. It grew up as a direct result of the decision in *Derry* v. *Peek*.[1] When the House of Lords affirmed that there was a general principle that no damages could be awarded for innocent misrepresentation a great deal of current law was immediately thrown into doubt. This is not the place to attempt a full survey of the nineteenth century cases at law and in equity in which by some means or another liability had been imposed for innocent misrepresentation; but it is an undoubted fact that there were a large number of such cases,

[1] (1889) 14 App. Cas. 337.

though this has gradually been forgotten as generations of lawyers have grown up to whom *Derry* v. *Peek* was the starting-point in the law of misrepresentation, rather than an unexpected check to a general current of authority. I do not suggest that prior to *Derry* v. *Peek* all misrepresentations were actionable at law or in equity, any more than all promises were actionable. But certainly where the justice of the case required it, relief had been regularly given for misrepresentation either by way of damages or by giving the representee the right to treat the representation as true. In *Low* v. *Bouverie*,[1] only two years after *Derry* v. *Peek*, the Court of Appeal was at pains to insist that that case in no way affected the law of estoppel by representation. It is quite true that even before *Derry* v. *Peek* the courts had sometimes denied that estoppel could constitute a cause of action in itself,[2] but this did not mean that the remedy of estoppel was not founded to some degree on the representation; it merely meant that if the representee affirmed the truth of the representation he had to have some right to relief as a result of that affirmation. After *Derry* v. *Peek* the courts seized on the idea that estoppel was not a cause of action as one way of distinguishing that decision.

3. A Rule of Evidence or a Rule of Law?

It is now possible to understand why the idea of estoppel as a rule of evidence has proved so tenacious. The party estopped 'cannot deny' or 'cannot be allowed to dispute' the truth of the facts he originally asserted; this way of formulating the rule gives way easily enough to a formulation in terms of evidence—'the party estopped cannot produce evidence to deny' the truth of the facts asserted.[3] But, in my submission, it is quite plain that estoppel is no more a rule of evidence than a so-called 'irrebuttable presumption'. Most lawyers are well aware that such a 'presumption' is, so far as its legal effects are concerned, a rule of law masquerading as a rule of evidence, and the same seems to be the case with a 'conclusive admission'. The modern tendency— propounded in Cross on *Evidence*[4] and now adopted in Spencer-Bower

---

[1] [1891] 3 Ch. 82.

[2] See *Seton, Laing & Co.* v. *Lafone* (1887) 19 QBD 68 at 70.

[3] It is, however, much more difficult to apply formulations like this to estoppel based on promises, see Henderson, 'Promissory Estoppel and Traditional Contract Doctrine', (1969) 78 *Yale LJ* 343, 376-7. In Essay 8 I suggested that there was no need for promissory estoppel to be recognized as a form of estoppel at all, but of course current doctrine does recognise it.

[4] 5th edn., at 352.

on *Estoppel*[1]—is still to insist that estoppel is a rule of evidence, but to admit that like other rules of evidence it may have the practical effect of creating substantive rights. No doubt this argument is somewhat academic but I do not believe any real progress can be made in understanding the law until the true nature of estoppel is fully appreciated. And I find it necessary to refuse to embrace even this compromise. The true position, I submit, is as follows. When a party is estopped from denying the truth of his representation he *is not entitled* to deny those representations, and the representee *is entitled* to certain relief as if the facts represented were true. If evidence were admitted which showed that the facts represented were untrue it would be irrelevant; the rights and liabilities of the parties would still be determined by the facts as they were represented to be and not by the facts as they actually are. To ask whether in such circumstances the relevant rule is a rule of law or a rule of evidence is to some extent like asking whether the chicken or the egg came first. Clearly it is possible to argue that, (1) the parties' rights are regulated by the facts as represented rather than the actual facts because no evidence of the actual facts can be given; or (2) that no evidence of the actual facts can be given because such evidence would not affect the rights of the parties which are anyhow regulated by the represented facts. In this situation there is surely only one way of deciding which is correct;[2] namely to ask whether the exclusion of the evidence is based on grounds which are in any way related to the general purposes of the law of evidence, namely proof of relevant facts by satisfactory means. The answer is surely No. The evidence is not excluded because of possible unreliability or any other evidentiary principle. It is excluded because it would be unjust to admit it and allow the rights of the representee to be affected by it.[3] Therefore it seems more correct to say that the evidence is excluded because of the rules of substantive law which make the evidence irrelevant.

But although the true nature of estoppel by representation is now seen to be a remedy in the nature of specific performance, there are still

---

[1] Now Spencer-Bower and Turner, 3rd edn. (1977) at 7-10.

[2] An alternative approach might be to ask which rule came first historically. It is possible that exclusionary rules of evidence may at one time have been introduced and that these rules may have gradually led to rules of substantive law which would then have kept out the evidence as irrelevant. But I do not believe this was the course of development in estoppel by representation. For one thing (as Ewart pointed out long ago, *Estoppel by Misrepresentation* (1900) at 189 *et seq.*) the evidence is nearly always admitted in practice in cases of estoppel by misrepresentation.

[3] See e.g. the formulation by Lord Blackburn in *Burkinshaw* v. *Nicolls* (1878) 3 App. Cas. at 1026.

a number of peculiar features about the doctrine which require further consideration. First, what is the practical effect of estoppel? Secondly, what is the relationship between this remedy and other remedies for misrepresentation? Thirdly, why is it that this remedy seems to be more readily available than the remedy of damages, in contrast to the position regarding promises which is, of course, quite the reverse?

4. Practical Effects of Estoppel

The first question which arises here is how does it come about that the effect of estoppel is so often to give damages to the representee if, as I have suggested, estoppel is a remedy corresponding in some sense to specific performance? The answer to this is simply that in many cases of misrepresentation the plaintiff's ultimate claim will be for damages whether he claims for relief on the basis that the representation was true or not. For example in the share certificate cases the plaintiff might claim relief on the basis that the representation was false, in which case he would acknowledge that he had no right to be registered as the owner of the shares but would (if the law allowed him to) claim damages for the loss he suffered as a result of the misrepresentation. Alternatively he can claim relief on the basis that the representation is true; on this footing he is entitled to be registered as a shareholder, and if the company does not register him, he again recovers damages. Thus in this sort of case the plaintiff's ultimate remedy is for damages, whether he chooses to 'affirm' the representation or to 'accept' the fact that it was false.

There are also many cases in which the representee can set up the representation as a defence to an action against him if he chooses to affirm the truth of the representation; whereas if he claimed relief on the ground of the falsity of the representation his remedy would be a counter-claim of some sort. A good example is to be found in *Greenwood* v. *Martin's Bank Ltd.*,[1] where the plaintiff was held estopped from disputing the authenticity of his signature on some cheques; in fact his signature had been forged by his wife but the plaintiff had not disclosed this fact to his bank until after his wife's death. The House of Lords held that the plaintiff owed a duty to inform the bank of the forgery when he discovered it, and therefore his silence was equivalent to a representation that the signatures were authentic. Accordingly the plaintiff was not entitled to deny the authenticity of the signatures. It

[1] [1933] AC 51.

will be seen that in this situation the representees would clearly have had an alternative remedy, though the net result would have been the same. Instead of claiming relief on the basis of the truth of the implied representation they could presumably have acknowledged the forgery, recredited the plaintiff's account with the amount of the cheques, and then sued the plaintiff for damages. Since the plaintiff was held to be under a duty to inform the bank of the forgery, this duty presumably arose out of the contractual relationship between the parties; breach of this duty would therefore presumably have been actionable had any damage resulted.

In all cases of this sort, the remedy by way of estoppel may have two advantages for the plaintiff. The first is that of avoiding circuity of actions.[1] A defence to a claim is simpler than imposing a liability on one party which is exactly counterbalanced by a corresponding right. But the second advantage is more substantive. To claim damages on the basis of the truth of the representation is, in effect, to claim expectation damages, while to claim on the basis of the falsity of the representation is to claim reliance damages. The point is that if the plaintiff is entitled to treat the representation as true, and obtain the relief appropriate if it were true, his expectations consequent on the truth of the statement are being given full legal protection. On the other hand, if the plaintiff is only entitled to damages on the basis of the falsity of the representation, he is only protected against the consequence of having relied on the statement. Here again, therefore, one observes the parallel between estoppel and specific performance which also protects the plaintiff's expectation interests. But in the ordinary contract case, the damages which are the alternative remedy to specific performance will usually be expectation damages. In the estoppel situation, however, this will not usually be so. I will return to this distinction below when I come to a comparison of warranty and estoppel liability.

I now pass to cases in which the remedy of estoppel is decidedly superior to any form of remedy by way of damages. First, there are cases in which the representee is in a very real sense able to obtain 'specific performance' of the representation which may be more important to him than damages. For instance in *Hopgood* v. *Brown*,[2] contractors built a bungalow and garage for the plaintiff on a site adjoining their own land. In fact the garage was partly built on land

---

[1] See *Swan* v. *North British Australasian Co.* (1863) 2 H. and C. 175, 190 *per* Cockburn CJ; *London Joint Stock Bank* v. *Macmillan* [1918] AC 777 at 818 *per* Lord Haldane.
[2] [1955] 1 All ER 550.

owned by the contractors, the boundary never having been clearly
identified. It was held that the contractors were estopped from claiming
the land: they had represented the land to be the defendant's and he
was entitled to treat that representation as true. The result of this was
that the defendant remained in undisturbed possession of this land,
though it is perhaps not clear if he could have transferred a title to the
disputed area. Clearly from his point of view, this was a more satisfactory result than an action for damages for misrepresentation could
have been.

The second type of case in which the superiority of estoppel as a
remedy manifests itself concerns a variety of situations in which title to
goods is in question. For example, A represents to B that C has A's
authority to sell A's goods. Relying on this, B buys some of A's goods
from C who has in fact acted without authority, for example, because
he has sold below the price stipulated by A. Here again B may have
alternative remedies: (1) to acknowledge that the representation was
false, that therefore he has acquired no title to the goods, and to sue A
for his damages; or (2) to insist that he is entitled to treat this representation as true, and that therefore he has acquired title to the
goods. Clearly (2) is so advantageous to the representee that it is hardly
surprising if the first remedy is rarely invoked and it may even be
doubtful whether it is available. In recent years it has been confirmed
that the representee acquires a 'real' title in this situation and not merely
a 'metaphorical title by estoppel'.[1] This seems to confirm that the
rightful place of estoppel by representation is with the rules of substantive law rather than with the rules of evidence.

5. Incidental Advantages of Estoppel

I have so far been considering those advantages of estoppel by representation which are inherent in the nature of the remedy. There may,
however, be other advantages which are, in a sense, accidental; they
are advantages which do not derive from the real nature of estoppel but
from the fact that the courts have denied its real nature. In particular, by
using the doctrine of estoppel by representation the courts have been
able in many cases to give adequate remedies where the Statute of
Frauds would have raised difficulties if a different basis of liability had
been urged.

The Statute of Frauds lies in the background to a very large number

[1] *Eastern Distributors* v. *Goldring* [1957] 2 QB 600.

of nineteenth-century cases of representation and estoppel. In *Pickard* v. *Sears*,[1] which is generally regarded as the foundation case of the whole doctrine of estoppel by representation, Lord Denman specifically refers to the requirement of written evidence for contracts of sale of goods (above £10) as a ground for the introduction of the rule on which the court acted. In this famous case the plaintiff was the mortgagee of some machinery which had been owned by one M. Execution was levied by creditors of M and the sheriff took possession of the goods. The plaintiff knew what was going on, and explained that he was a creditor of M but never disclosed his ownership of the goods nor produced his bill of sale. The sheriff sold the property to the defendants who were then sued in trover by the plaintiff. After pointing out that the plaintiff clearly had a title to the goods, Lord Denman went on to say that the title could only be divested by gift or sale, of which no specific act was even surmised. He then enunciated the principle, which still forms the basis of the law today, that the plaintiff was 'concluded from averring' his title against the defendant, and added significantly,[2] 'the plaintiff, in this case might have parted with his interest in the property by verbal gift or sale without any of those formalities that throw technical obstacles in the way of legal evidence'.

A simple modern example of a case where estoppel by representation succeeded where difficulties might have arisen under the Statute of Frauds is *Hopgood* v. *Brown*, referred to above.

I have tried to show in Essay 8 how the idea of action in reliance on a representation as a ground for estoppel was at this stage closely linked with the notion of 'part-performance' as a ground for not insisting on compliance with the Statute of Frauds; and how *Jorden* v. *Money*[3] attempted to prevent the further evasions of the statute by refusing to treat promises in the same way as representations. I have not space here to trace the full story of these nineteenth-century cases; it is enough to note that evasion of the Statute of Frauds has played a large role in the development of the law of misrepresentations. The invention of the action of deceit in *Pasley* v. *Freeman* was also attributed to a desire to evade the statute,[4] and the story has not stopped even now. For one result of *Pasley* v. *Freeman* was the extension of the Statute of Frauds to cover the action in deceit by the Statute of Frauds Amendment Act

---

[1] (1837) 6 Ad. and E. 469.
[2] At 474.
[3] (1854) 5 HL Cas. 185.
[4] See *Ashlin* v. *White* (1816) Holt, 387 at 388.

1828; and in 1967 it was held that this extension did not cover the new action for negligent misrepresentation.[1]

6. The Relationship between Estoppel and Other Remedies for Misrepresentation

Before proceeding any further it may be helpful here to list the various remedies which the law provides in different cases of misrepresentation. (I leave out of account the 1967 Act which provides no assistance on the present question.)

1. The action of deceit.
2. The action for damages for negligent misrepresentation.
3. Defence to an action for breach of contract.
4. Rescission of a contract.
5. Damages for breach of warranty.
6. Estoppel.

Now it is clear enough that the first two remedies require respectively proof of fraud and negligence; it is equally clear that remedies 3, 4, and 5 require no such proof. They are instances of 'strict liability'. The question which I now wish to consider is the relationship of estoppel to these other remedies. Does it require proof of fraud or negligence or is it a species of strict liability? And if it is the latter, how can it be reconciled with the principle that damages cannot be awarded for innocent misrepresentation?

These questions have been surprisingly little discussed. But it is reasonably clear on the authorities that estoppel by representation can be a form of strict liability. When the doctrine was first propounded in *Pickard* v. *Sears* in 1837, liability for negligence was scarcely thought of, and there was basically only the single choice between liability for intentional wrongs and strict liability. In *Pickard* v. *Sears* itself the court seemed at first to confine estoppel to the former category, because the formulation of the principle in that case referred to the representor 'wilfully' causing another to believe in the existence of the facts represented. But, as is well known, this word was explained away in *Freeman* v. *Cooke*.[2] What was now said to be required was an 'intention' that the representation should be acted upon; and even this was qualified by explaining that the appearance of intention sufficed. So long

[1] *W. B. Anderson & Sons Ltd.* v. *Rhodes* [1967] 2 All ER 850; *UBAF Ltd.* v. *European American Banking Corp.* [1984] QB 713.

[2] (1848) 2 Ex. 654. See also *Jorden* v. *Money* (1854) 5 HL Cas 185 at 212.

as the representee understood, as a reasonable man, that the representation was 'meant' to be acted upon, that was sufficient.

Later still this requirement became even more attenuated. In 1887 Lord Esher said that it was sufficient if 'it was reasonable as a matter of business for the plaintiff to do what he did as a result of his belief in the defendant's statement'.[1] And during the present century, at least in the bill of lading cases, the Court of Appeal has indicated that no evidence is necessary to show that an endorsee of a bill of lading has acted on the statements contained in it;[2] this may be presumed.[3]

It will be seen that what originally appeared to be a requirement closely analogous to fraud has been totally discarded. Indeed, the requirement has passed completely out of the area of 'fault' on the part of the representor, and has simply become part of the 'inducement' which must be shown by the representee. No help is obtainable, therefore, from these cases as to any requirement of 'fault' in the modern law.

But there are a number of other cases towards the end of the nineteenth century in which the courts began to analyse this question in more modern terms. In *Carr* v. *LNW Railway*,[4] Brett J. introduced the possibility of 'culpable negligence' as a possible ground for supporting an estoppel. But, as is pointed out very clearly in Spencer-Bower's classic work,[5] negligence in this context does not have its modern meaning of a breach of a duty of reasonable care. It is used in the sense of 'neglect' or 'omission'; the point which Brett J. was making was that a party might be estopped by silence (culpable neglect to speak) as much as by actual misrepresentation. Thus this dictum in no way supports the view that negligence is relevant to estoppel by representation; it does not deal with cases of positive misrepresentation at all. But the same cannot be said of Lord Esher's next discussion of this question in the *Seton, Laing* case.[6] In this case he does quite plainly introduce the modern notion of negligence into the doctrine.

An estoppel does not in itself give a cause of action; it prevents a person from denying a certain state of facts. One ground of estoppel is where a man makes a fraudulent misrepresentation and another man acts upon it to his detriment. Another may be where a man makes a false statement negligently, though

---

[1] *Seton, Laing & Co.* v. *Lafone* (1887) 19 QBD 68, at 72-3.
[2] *Silver* v. *Ocean S.S. Co. Ltd.* [1930] 1 KB 416.
[3] But the presumption is not irrebuttable: *The Skarp* [1935] P. 134.
[4] (1875) LR 10 CP 307.
[5] 3rd edn., at p. 72 *et seq.*
[6] Above.

without fraud, and another person acts upon it. And there may be circumstances under which, where a misrepresentation is made without fraud and
without negligence, there may be an estoppel.

The next important case is *Low* v. *Bouverie*,[1] which contains what is
probably still the fullest judicial examination of estoppel by representation in the law reports. In this case Kay LJ ignored the possibility
of negligence and declared that estoppel could be founded on a fraudulent or an innocent statement, though he gave no indication whether
fraud was ever required to found estoppel. In the first of the bill of
lading cases in 1906, it was held by Channell J. that as the estoppel
arose on 'a direct statement of fact which [was] incorrect', the question
of negligence did not really arise. But estoppel always arises 'on a direct
statement of fact' except where it is alleged to arise from silence; this,
therefore, seems to imply that estoppel can always be founded on an
innocent misrepresentation, except in cases of silence.

In the more modern decision of *Mercantile Credit Ltd.* v. *Hamblin*,[2]
it again seems to be suggested that negligence may be essential to some
types of estoppel. In this case the owner of a car signed various forms
in blank and left them with a dealer to see if he could raise a loan on
the car; the dealer, without further authority, completed the forms and
sent them in to the finance company who thought they were thereby
buying the car from the dealer and letting it on hire-purchase to the
defendant. It was held that the defendant was not estopped because in
the circumstances the plaintiffs had to show 'an ostensible authority
based on negligence' and there was in fact no negligence. The discussion
of the legal concepts in this case is not at all easy to follow. Perhaps the
defendant was thought not to have made any representation herself
but merely to have, by her silence, enabled the dealer to make the
representation. But it is surely unsafe to take the decision as holding
that negligence is always a requirement of estoppel. This certainly
accords with Ewart's view,[3] which (though never explicitly adopted by
the courts[4]) seems sound. According to Ewart, negligence is immaterial
to a case of actual misrepresentation by the representor; moreover,
there can be no such thing as estoppel by negligence without mis-

[1] [1891] 3 Ch. 82.

[2] [1965] 2 QB 242; see also *Moorgate Mercantile Ltd.* v. *Twitchings* [1977] AC 890,
where it was assumed throughout that negligence had to be shown to raise an estoppel if
no direct representation had been made.

[3] Above, p. 311, n. 2 at Ch. ix, especially the Summary at 121–2.

[4] Though it seems to be supported by Dixon J. in *Thompson* v. *Palmer* (1933) 49 CLR
at 547. It is also similar to the rule adopted in the Restatement of Torts: § 894.

representation—the foundation of all estoppels of this species is a misrepresentation. Negligence, therefore, is only relevant where the representation was made by a third party and the party alleged to be estopped *by his negligence* facilitated or permitted the deception to be made. Most probably the courts have moved unconsciously from the notion of 'neglect' to the notion of 'negligence'. There is certainly support for the view that estoppel by silence does require proof of negligence or something akin to it. For instance, if A directly represents that B has authority to sell certain property to C, A will be estopped from setting up any interest of his own in the property as against C, even though he may not have known that he had any such interest.[1] But if A has not made any such direct representation, but has simply stood by while B dealt with the property, A will not be estopped unless he knew of his interest.[2] Similarly, in other cases of estoppel by silence something is required to make the silence culpable, and that something must at least amount to negligence, although there were earlier doubts whether even that was enough.[3]

Whatever the true position where there is silence rather than active misrepresentation, there cannot, I think, be any doubt that there are many situations in which estoppel arises even where there is no fraud or negligence. This leads to the next major question.

7. Estoppel and Warranty
If estoppel by misrepresentation can arise without fraud or negligence, it begins to look as though estoppel by misrepresentation is closely analogous to warranty liability. Certainly the relationship between estoppel and warranty requires further consideration. A number of basic similarities and two obvious distinctions between these two legal concepts need to be noted.

(i) *Warranty and estoppel: basic similarities*
Estoppel and warranty-liability have a large number of features in common.

1. Both depend on a representation of fact.[4]

---

[1] *Sarat Chunder Dey* v. *Gopal Chunder Laha* (1892) LR 19 Ind. App. 203 (PC).

[2] *Svenson* v. *Payne* (1945) 71 CLR 531.

[3] See *Swan* v. *North British Australasian Co.* (1863) 2 H. and C. 175.

[4] There is one type of case—'conventional' estoppel or estoppel by agreement—where no representation is required, but the parties simply agree to regulate their rights on the basis of certain assumed facts, see *Amalgamated Investment & Pty. Co.* v. *Texas Commercial Int'l Bank* [1982] QB 84, affirmed, ibid, on different grounds, and see also *The Leila, Financial Times*, 8 March 1985. Such cases are governed by their own rules and have no real connection with the estoppel by representation cases.

2. In both cases the representation must be acted upon.
3. In both cases the representor must have intended or at least foreseen as reasonably probable that the representee would act upon the representation.
4. In both cases the legal result is independent of fraud or negligence.
5. In both cases the representee may be entitled to the contractual measure of damages, and not just the tort measure, though (as we have seen) this result remains dubious in some estoppel cases.

The first four points are clear enough and need no elaboration. The fifth has been touched upon above, but now needs further elaboration. It is clear law that a representee who sues for breach of warranty is entitled to damages which will place him, so far as possible, in the position in which he would be if the representation had been true.[1] In the case of a breach of warranty of quality in a contract of sale this is specifically provided for by s. 53(3) of the Sale of Goods Act 1979. Where the warranty induces a contract between representor and representee this is the result of usual contractual principles, because the whole approach of the law is to treat the warranty as part of the bargain; and the normal measure of damages in contract is intended to compensate the plaintiff for loss of the bargain. The plaintiff has not got what he bargained for, and is entitled to damages which will give him what he bargained for. I have already indicated my doubts in Essay 7, and again above, as to whether this result is justifiable, particularly where the representee has obtained the goods sold at their normal market value, but there can be no doubt that for the present this is the law.

But it is, of course, well known that the measure of damages for misrepresentation in tort is not the same. Here the representee's complaint is not loss of bargain; he complains because he has suffered loss as a result of being induced to act on the representation. Accordingly the damages here are merely intended to place him in the position in which he would have been if he had not acted on the misrepresentation, and not to place him in the position in which he would have been if it were true. The distinction appears clearly from the following situation:[2]

---

[1] Yet this is not apparently the correct measure where a principal sues his agent for loss accruing from a misrepresentation made by the agent: *Salvesen & Co.* v. *Rederi Aktiebolaget* [1905] AC 302. The reason for this is not clear, but may have something to do with the fact that an agent's remuneration is much more limited than that of a principal.

[2] See *Hart* v. *Frontino* (1870) LR 5 Ex. 111.

A sells shares to B and gives B a (stolen) share certificate and a signed transfer which is not registered by B. The company makes a call on the shares which has to be paid by A who is purporting to be the owner. A demands payment of the calls from B. Before payment B insists that he be registered, and the company accordingly registers him and issues him with a certificate. In reliance on the certificate he pays A the amount of the call. It is later discovered that A had no title to the shares, and the company removes B's name from the register.

Now it is clear that the company has represented to B that he is the owner of the shares, that it intends or expects him to act on that representation, and that he has done so. The question then is whether B can recover damages from the company (1) for his loss, that is the amount of the calls paid to A, or (2) for the full value of the shares. The former is the tort measure, the latter is the warranty measure. In fact the courts have had no hesitation in giving the warranty measure of damages in such cases.[1] They have treated this as naturally following from the basic principle that the representee is entitled to sue on his 'independent cause of action' as though the representation were true. But the net result is that estoppel seems even more akin to warranty than it does to fraud or negligent misrepresentation.

In the case last discussed there would be no action in reliance at all before the representee has done something with the shares, so the whole question is whether the representee's pure expectations deserve protection. But (just as in the parallel cases concerning promises) it may happen that the representee does act to some degree on the representation, but his reliance loss may still fall far short of the expectations he had from believing in the truth of the representation. In *Avon C.C.* v. *Howlett*,[2] for instance, the defendant, an employee of the plaintiffs, was overpaid by mistake when he was away from work during sickness. He queried the amounts but was assured that they were correct. Later the mistake was discovered and the plaintiffs claimed the money back. It was proved (or assumed) that the defendant had spent some of the money overpaid on abnormal expenses in reliance on the assurances, so all the ingredients of estoppel were present. But it was

---

[1] See Spencer-Bower and Turner, above, at pp. 112–14.

[2] [1983] 1 All ER 1073; see also *Greenwood* v. *Martin's Bank*, above, where the plaintiff's representation (by silence) led to inaction by the bank as a result of which they took no steps to sue the plaintiff's wife before she died, even though they might in fact have recovered very little from such an action. (But in this case there might have been grounds for treating the representation as a warranty.)

unclear—and the point was left unresolved by the Court of Appeal—
whether this meant that the defendant was entitled to treat the representations as true (which meant that he would not have had to repay
any of the money) or whether he was only protected to the extent of
his reliance (in which case he would have had to refund the unspent
money). On the one hand, the principle that 'estoppel is a rule of
evidence', which I have criticized above, was thought to lead to the
conclusion that the plaintiff was entitled to treat the representation as
true, so that his expectations would have been fully protected. This was
thought to follow from the fact that evidence of the untruth of the
misrepresentation could not be given at all, so that the plaintiffs' action
would have failed *in limine*. On the other hand, some members of the
court were clearly troubled by the possible implications of this conclusion which would seem to mean that if the defendant had spent five
pounds out of an overpayment of £1000, he could have kept the lot.

It should be evident that the apparently 'logical' conclusion to which
the courts have felt driven in some of these cases is not an inexorable
result at all. As I have already suggested, the idea that estoppel is a
rule of evidence is itself unsupportable. The question is one of legal
rights, not evidence. A representee is prima facie entitled to treat a
representation acted upon by him as true; but if the rule is formulated
in this way, it is clear that the conclusion that the plaintiff should be
protected in full is not a logical necessity at all. Although a representee
may have a prima facie right to treat a representation as true, it does
not follow that he is entitled to treat it as true to a greater extent than
is necessary to protect his legitimate interests. Whether that is the result
is, of course, the very question at issue in such cases, and whether the
law should permit such a result should surely depend upon better
reasons than supposed logic.

The strange result of allowing the representee to claim protection to
a greater degree than his reliance requires is that it seems at least
theoretically possible for a representee to obtain expectation damages
for misrepresentation via estoppel without having to prove the additional requirements of warranty. No 'intent' to warrant need be proved, and none of the policy factors to which we have referred need be
present. In short there seem to be no 'control devices' by which the
courts can limit liability of this kind if they find it unjust, as they can
with a claim openly based on warranty. In the original essay, I consoled
myself with the thought that no claim for damages seems to have
succeeded except in circumstances in which it would be quite reasonable

to find a warranty to be present. But *Avon C.C.* v. *Howlett* shows that this is a very real possibility, although it is not difficult for a court to refuse damages via estoppel by holding that, for example, the representation was ambiguous or that the representee acted unreasonably in relying on it.[1]

(*ii*) *Warranty and estoppel: two obvious differences*

Estoppel is (as we have seen) a remedy which allows the representee such relief as would be appropriate if the representation were true. Warranty primarily allows the representee to claim damages on the basis that the representation is false. But in this respect warranty is clearly the superior or higher remedy; there can, I think, be no doubt that whenever damages are recoverable for breach of warranty the representee could rely on estoppel in the alternative if he chose to do so. All the ingredients of estoppel are necessarily present in a case of warranty, namely a statement of fact, acted upon by the representee, the intention, or at least reasonable probability that he would so act, and detriment to him from so acting. But as we have seen, warranty requires in addition other factors, conventionally treated as the 'intent to warrant'. Therefore every case of warranty could be treated as a case of estoppel whereas the converse is clearly not true.

Thus the two distinctions between warranty and estoppel are, first that warranty has additional requirements over and above those needed for estoppel, and secondly, that warranty provides the representee with a choice of two remedies, while estoppel is limited to one. The question which now arises is whether there is a rational connection between these two distinctions. Are these distinctions due to a series of accidental chances in the historical development of the law, are they mere quirks, or is there some sensible foundation to them? If we were to start with a clean slate would we retain these distinctions or sweep them away? Is there any policy reason why every set of facts sufficient to support an estoppel should not be treated as a warranty giving the representee the choice (where this is in fact possible) of either suing for damages on the basis of the falsity of the representation, or claiming whatever relief would be appropriate if it were true?

(*iii*) *Warranty and estoppel: are the distinctions worth retaining?*

In favour of retaining the present distinctions it could be argued that

---

[1] See *Low* v. *Bouverie*, above, where the courts' obvious views as to the merits of the case were given effect to by an extraordinary finding of fact.

the remedy of estoppel is naturally a secondary or inferior remedy to the remedy of damages; therefore less justification needs to be shown for this remedy than for treating a representation as a warranty. The mere making of a false statement with knowledge that it is likely to be acted upon is a good ground for regulating the rights of the parties by reference to the supposed facts. But where expectation damages are sought from an innocent representor it should surely be necessary to go further, for example to show some benefit to him from the representee's conduct and some element of responsibility for ascertaining the truth of his statement. Even according to the accepted theory of the law (let alone according to my more extreme views) it seems anomalous to allow the protection of expectations by estoppel, given that it is in a sense an 'inferior' remedy.

It may, however, be objected that it is incorrect to treat estoppel as an 'inferior' or 'secondary' remedy. Certainly this cannot be said of the remedy of specific performance for breach of promise with which I suggested estoppel has affinities. The answer seems to be that it is correct to treat estoppel as an inferior remedy where it operates purely as a defensive device. It can be argued that it is rational policy to require less justification for giving a party a defence to an action, than for giving him an affirmative cause of action. Prima facie, it can be urged that some justification needs to be shown for disturbing the status quo: the onus of proof is on a party who starts legal proceedings. But a defence to an action is an attempt to maintain, not to upset, the status quo. The chief objection to this argument is (as we have seen) that in many of the principal situations in which estoppel by representation is applied, it does in fact assist the representee to take the initiative and obtain damages for the misrepresentation. In the share certificate cases, the bill of lading cases, and the warehouse keeper cases the plaintiff can in fact recover damages via estoppel for the misrepresentation. Similarly, where a person claims to have acquired a title to goods by estoppel he is using estoppel to disturb the status quo and not to maintain it, at least where he has not obtained possession of the goods.[1]

But there may, in turn, be an answer to this objection. It is, I think, strongly arguable that many of the typical cases of estoppel in which the representee is enabled to recover damages at present have really got into the wrong legal category. These cases could, and perhaps should, be treated as warranty cases pure and simple. Little doctrinal difficulty would be met by following this course, and in some cases,

[1] As in *Mercantile Credit Ltd.* v. *Hamblin*, above, where the claim failed.

indeed, it seems purely accidental that this is not how the law has actually developed.[1] For instance, the statement in a bill of lading that the goods are 'shipped in apparent good order and condition' could (it seems) quite easily be treated as a warranty to the endorsee of the bill of lading. In fact an argument to this effect was put to the court in the first of these cases,[2] but was rejected by Channell J. for a reason which now seems unsound; he thought that if these words were contractual they must be part of the original contract of carriage which was transferred to the endorsee of the bill of lading under the Bills of Lading Act 1855. In that event the words would have had no effect because the original shipper must have known that the goods were not in apparent good order and condition and could not have sued for breach of warranty; therefore (reasoned Channell J.) the endorsee of the bill of lading would not have been able to sue for breach of warranty either. But this is fallacious. If it is sound policy to give the endorsee of the bill of lading a remedy, the words 'shipped in apparent good order and condition' could be treated as a warranty addressed directly to an endorsee of the bill of lading; the endorsee could then rely on it in his own right, and not as transferee of the original contract.[3] If, on the other hand, sound policy should deny the endorsee the right to sue where the original shipper cannot, the estoppel decision is just an evasion of the earlier part of the judgment.

In later cases Channell J.'s reasons for not treating the case as one of warranty seem to have been forgotten and the courts have fastened on another part of his judgment in which he said:[4] 'The words 'shipped in good order and condition' are not words of contract in the sense of a promise or understanding. The words are an affirmation of fact . . . '

This seems plain enough; the words are a representation of fact, not a promise, but that does not mean they may not amount to a warranty.

---

[1] In *Freeman* v. *Cooke*, above, it was in fact suggested that most cases of estoppel would be cases of contract or licence, and in *Cornish* v. *Abington* (1859) 4 H. and N. 549 it was even said that the rule of estoppel only applied where this was so: 'No doubt, unless the representation amounts to an agreement or licence, or is understood by the party to whom it is made as amounting to that, the rule would not apply', *per* Pollock CB at 555. Moreover, as I have argued in Essay 8, this is precisely what did happen with promises.

[2] *Compania Naviera* v. *Churchill & Sim* [1906] 1 KB 237, though (it seems) without the assistance of the *Sheffield Corporation* case which had been decided a few months earlier.

[3] That such a warranty is possible doctrinally seems confirmed by *V/O Rasnoimport* v. *Guthrie* [1966] 1 Lloyd's Rep. 1.

[4] *Compania Naviera* v. *Churchill & Sim*, above, at 247.

But in *Silver* v. *Ocean S.S. Co. Ltd.*[1] it was said that Channell J. had decided that the words 'shipped in good order and condition' are *not words of contract* in the sense that they do not constitute a warranty. The result is that these words have ever since been treated as sufficient to raise an estoppel but not a warranty. There seems no justification for this. Every feature of warranty is present: statement of fact, intended to be acted upon, benefit to the shipowner,[2] and responsibility for ascertaining the facts on the part of the representor.

Furthermore, this is, I think, clearly the sort of case in which expectation damages are more likely to be appropriate on any view. Businessmen who buy goods at sea are usually buying for resale, and the expectation of profit is not only an essential part of such transactions, but is likely to be treated as real wealth before it is received. Moreover, in so far as expectation damages may contain a penal element, this sort of case—falsely certifying the condition of goods shipped on board—may be just the kind of case in which penalties are justifiable.

The same is, I believe, true of many other cases which are commonly treated as cases of estoppel. For example, consider the 'classic' case of *Western* v. *Fairbridge*:[3] the plaintiff's husband wanted to borrow money on the security of some furniture and fittings which belonged to her. She made a statutory declaration that the goods belonged to her husband, and in reliance on this the defendant made a loan to the husband on the security of a bill of sale. The plaintiff was held estopped from asserting her title. But why could this not be treated as a case of warranty? Every element of warranty seems present, but it was plainly simpler and preferable for the representee to claim the relief appropriate on the footing that the statement was true (namely a charge on the goods) than damages. In *Brownlie* v. *Campbell*[4] Lord Blackburn virtually confessed his failure to see any distinction between cases in which damages are obtained via estoppel and cases of warranty. 'Most of the cases', he says, '(the leading one is *Burrowes* v. *Lock*[5] and it is sufficient to mention that, though there were others) when looked at, if they do not absolutely amount to contract come uncommonly near it'. He then stated the facts of *Burrowes* v. *Lock* and added that if that was not

[1] [1930] 1 KB 416.

[2] Indirect benefit, of course, but very real; a shipowner who refused to issue bills of lading would soon find himself out of business.

[3] [1923] 1 KB 667.

[4] (1880) 5 App. Cas. 925, 952-3.

[5] (1805) 10 Ves. 470.

warranty or contract 'it was so uncommonly like it that I cannot make the distinction myself'. Yet in *Low* v. *Bouverie*[1] the Court of Appeal held that *Burrowes* v. *Lock* could only be supported as a case of estoppel and not as a case of contract.

In many of these cases the application of estoppel serves the representee perfectly well and nobody is ever likely to argue that such statements should be treated as warranties, but in any restatement or reform of the law the correct classification of such cases would assume greater importance. My suggestion, then is that cases of representation where the warranty elements are present should all be treated as cases of warranty. But it should then be recognized that what we now term 'estoppel by representation' is an alternative remedy open to the representee where the facts permit, that is where he would have some relief other than damages if the representation had been true. Estoppel would then cease to be a weapon of offence, and it would never be possible to claim damages for misrepresentation by way of estoppel. Such a claim would have to be based on warranty or fraud or negligence.

If this were done, it would remain only to consider whether there may not be other cases where estoppel could operate as a defence even though the statement is not actionable as a warranty, or for fraud or negligence. Thus, where the representor has no real interest in the action taken by the representee as the result of the representation, and where the representor has no special responsibility for ascertaining the truth of the statement—that is, where there is neither benefit nor justifiable reliance—estoppel could still be used purely as a defence to an action. In this way it would operate as an extension of the principle that misrepresentation is a defence to an action for breach of contract, though not *per se* giving rise to a claim for damages. If this were done, estoppel without warranty could be left to perform a much more minor function than it does today: namely to offer a purely defensive role to a representee who is sued by the representor. In this limited sphere it would seem justifiable to impose strict liability on the representor and recognize a defence based on estoppel even though the additional factors which justify the creation of warranty liability are not present. Thus even if the representor was wholly disinterested in the statement which he made and even if the representee may have had equal (or

---

[1] Above. Much of the present confusion in the law is traceable to this case where the court took the notion of 'intent' to warrant too seriously, even though the plaintiff's claim was for a reliance loss and not for protection of an expectation. The whole approach of the court here is quite inconsistent with the *Sheffield Corporation* case.

greater) responsibility for ascertaining the truth of the facts, the representation could give rise to a defence: the representee could claim to be entitled to treat the representation as true, even though he could not take the initiative and sue the representor for damages. I believe the role left for estoppel in this situation would be a small one for there are unlikely to be many situations in which a representor who has made representations with no real interest in, or responsibility for, what he says will bring suit against the representee in connection with the same matter. But this need not cause any undue alarm. So long as estoppel is recognized as an alternative remedy available in all cases of actionable misrepresentation (whether for fraud, negligence, or warranty) the courts will have a sufficient armoury to enable justice to be done in most circumstances. There will then be few cases in which reliance will need to be placed on estoppel as a defence where there is no actionable misrepresentation.

Contract and Fair Exchange

It has for many years, even centuries, been part of the traditional dogma of contract law that the adequacy of the consideration is immaterial to the validity of a contract. It is for the parties to make their own bargain, not for the courts. Each party to a contract must himself decide how much the other's performance is worth to him, and then decide whether to enter into the contract, yea or nay. If the contract is concluded then it must be assumed that each party is content with his bargain, or he would not have made it. There is simply no room for any inquiry into the fairness of the exchange. If the parties knew what they were at, then the exchange must, by definition, be fair—or at least, it must be as fair as the law cares. Of course if one of the parties did not know what he was at, then the result might be different, but that had nothing to do with the doctrine of consideration. To be sure the doctrine did require that there must be some consideration for a promise; a wholly gratuitous promise, not under seal, was of course not a contract at all. But once the law's attention was shifted from performance to promises, so that an exchange of promises was regarded as a binding contract in its inception, even this requirement was diluted.[1] While the completely one-sided promise remained outside the scope of contract law, an exchange of promises has for many years been thought wellnigh impregnable on grounds of inadequacy of consideration.[2] Even the purely nominal consideration has retained its validity in English law,[3] though the position is more doubtful in modern American law.[4]

This apparent abdication by the courts from any interest in the fairness of an exchange has, however, long been tempered by two bodies of legal doctrine. In the first place, there were, and there remain today, the defences of fraud, misrepresentation, and duress and undue influence; and perhaps some cases of mistake and even frustration. Traditionally, these were cases in which the defence was grounded not on

---

[1] See *Freedom of Contract*, especially at pp. 419-54.
[2] See Fuller, 'Consideration and Form', (1941) 41 *Col. L. Rev.* 799, 816.
[3] *Mountford* v. *Scott* [1975] Ch. 258.
[4] Restatement, Second, Contracts, §71, illustration 5; Farnsworth, *Contracts* (1982), pp. 66-9.

the unfairness of the ensuing transaction but on the deficiencies of the will of one of the contracting parties. Thus a consent extracted by fraud or misrepresentation, or granted under some fundamental mistake, might be treated as negativing or vitiating the consent apparently given. Even a consent extracted by duress was traditionally dealt with in the same way; indeed, until very recently, English courts have continued to assert that the defences of duress and undue influence rest upon the theory that one party has overborne the will of the other, whose apparent consent is thus no real consent at all.[1]

In modern times these defences have sometimes been subsumed under the generic heading of 'cognitive weaknesses'. They can thus be seen, it is urged, as concerned with fair procedures and not with the fairness of the substantive result. On this view, the law is not concerned with the fairness of any particular transaction but merely with the fairness of the bargaining process. Procedural fairness requires that nobody shall retain the fruits of a bargain extracted by fraud or force; but if both parties understand fully what they are doing and participate freely in the process, then the result is no concern of the law. This may be explained on the ground that the result of a fair bargain must by definition be fair; or, as it was put by counsel in the eighteenth-century case of *Keen* v. *Stuckeley*,[2] a man 'was obliged to perform a bargain, though it was a hard one; and where he was obliged in conscience, it was no hardship upon him to be compelled thereto'. Or alternatively it may be explained by saying that law has simply no concern with the fairness of the bargain—the adequacy of the consideration is immaterial.

The second set of rules or principles concerning adequacy of consideration was exclusively equitable in origin, and many of them have a long history. The usury laws limiting rates of interest have existed in some shape or form since the Reformation, though there was half a century between 1854 and 1900 when all statutory restraints disappeared;[3] the law of mortgages has for centuries limited the power of the mortgagee to demand more than a fair return on his loan;[4] the law of penalties has at least since the seventeenth century protected

---

[1] At least they have generally used this theory in contract cases despite its rejection by the House of Lords in the criminal law, but see 'Economic Duress and the "Overborne Will"', 98 *Law Q. Rev.* 197, and see now dicta in *Universe Tankships of Monrovia* v. *ITWF* [1983] 1 AC 366, at 384 and 400.

[2] (1721) Gilb. Rep. 155, 156.

[3] Simpson, *A History of the Common Law of Contract* (1975), pp. 510-18.

[4] See Turner, *The Equity of Redemption* (1931).

contracting parties from liability freely entered into quite irrespective of the promisor's understanding of the nature of the terms;[1] and the law relating to the sale of reversions or the purchase of annuities has also provided relief in certain circumstances to the victims of harsh and unconscionable bargains.[2] These equitable doctrines, unlike the broader defences of fraud, misrepresentation, and duress, were mostly limited to particular types of transaction or particular types of promise; but on the other hand they could not be treated as merely concerned with the reality of consent or procedural fairness. It is clear that these were doctrines concerned with the substantive fairness of transactions or exchanges. Probably for that very reason they came to seem anomalous during the nineteenth century, and many of them were gradually whittled down. Only in very recent times have they shown renewed signs of life,[3] but even today they are not usually regarded as qualifications to the doctrine that adequacy of consideration is immaterial. Somehow, the purity of that doctrine has remained substantially unqualified in modern English law, despite these doctrines,[4] and despite, also, the huge growth of statutory interventions in contract law, much of which is quite avowedly designed to ensure substantive fairness in exchange.

But, like much else in the heritage of classical contract doctrine, the principle that the adequacy of consideration is immaterial seems to me to be seriously misleading. It is my view that in fact the law of contract is today greatly concerned with substantive fairness of exchange; and in the remainder of this essay I want to illustrate some of the ways in which courts strive to secure fairness in exchange, sometimes with, but often without, the assistance of statute. I begin, however, with three preliminary comments. The first is that no observant person can today be unaware of the strength of public feeling on matters of this kind. The idea of a 'fair deal', fair wages', 'fair prices', or 'fair rents', and so on is today deeply embedded in most Western societies, though I write

---

[1] Simpson, op. cit, pp. 118-22.

[2] *Freedom of Contract*, pp. 172-3; for a sample of the large case-law, see *Davis* v. *Duke of Marlborough* (1819) 2 Swans. 108; *Aylesford* v. *Morris* (1873) LR 8 Ch. App. 483; *O'Rorke* v. *Bolingbroke* (1877) 2 App. Cas. 814.

[3] For instance, *Lloyd's Bank* v. *Bundy* [1975] QB 326; though cf. *National Westminster Bank* v. *Morgan* [1985] 2 WLR 588. There does, however, seem to be a hardening against the extension of equitable relief in the penalty/forfeiture area, see *Hyundai Heavy Industries Ltd.* v. *Papadopoulos* [1980] 1 WLR 1129 and *Scandinavian Trading Tanker Co* v. *Flota Petrolera Ecuatoriana* [1983] 2 All ER 763; but cf. *BICC* v. *Burndy Corp.* [1985] 1 All ER 417.

[4] See e.g. Treitel, *Law of Contract* (6th edn., 1983) pp. 57-8. Treitel concedes that there are a limited number of exceptions and that the courts 'are by no means insensitive to the problem of unequal bargains', but he insists that even in these exceptional cases relief can never be obtained merely for inadequacy of consideration (p. 58).

particularly of the English experience. No one who reads newspapers or listens to political debate can for a moment suppose that procedural fairness is all that people have in mind when they demand fairness in exchange in such contexts as these. Some demands of this kind can no doubt be discounted as simply being the complaints of those who have lost a game according to the rules and then cry 'Foul'. And others may be part of the general, universal, and ageless protests of the 'have-nots' that transactions between them and the 'haves' are unfair just because the 'haves' already have so much more. But it is hard to believe that this is all that lies behind the insistent demands for fair wages, fair prices, or fair rents. Whether or not this demand is sensible or economically desirable is not a question I address for the moment: I merely assert that it exists, that it is powerful and deep-rooted and pervasive, that it shows little sign of being submerged by the ideological fervour of the new right, and that it has played a major role in much modern statute law. I approach the subject, therefore, with the belief that it would be surprising if ideas of this kind had failed to permeate the legal profession and the judges or to have any influence on common law decisions in the ordinary law of contract.

My second preliminary comment concerns the way in which the principle about adequacy of consideration is traditionally formulated. It is, of course, well known that the principle is always stated in terms of the validity of a contract.[1] Because consideration itself is regarded as a requirement of contractual validity, it is natural that the principle has always been said to be that inadequacy of consideration does not invalidate a contract. What I wish to point out here is that, as traditionally formulated, this principle is really of quite limited application. It does not say that inadequacy of consideration is no ground for relief or remedy any kind: it merely states that inadequacy of consideration is no ground for invalidity. But to invalidate a prima-facie contract at the suit of one party is merely one way to give redress or relief. It is clearly not the only way. Where adequacy of consideration is in issue, it might well be thought that a more appropriate way of giving relief—if this is desired—is to adjust the contractual obligations of the parties so that, in the result, the consideration is brought into line with the promise. This can, of course, be done in one of two ways: adjusting the consideration or adjusting the promise. There is no a priori reason for supposing that either of these ways is superior or more obviously appropriate than the other. I hope it is clear that I am not

[1] See ibid., pp. 57-8.

making a purely verbal argument about the way in which the adequacy principle is usually formulated; still less am I making a logical argument that the adequacy principle does not impede alternative ways of ensuring fairness in exchange. All that I am saying is that—as I hope to demonstrate—there are many ways in which the law can and does strive to give effect to ideas of substantive fairness in exchange despite the dogma that adequacy of consideration is not *per se* a ground of invalidity. If I succeed in making this contention good, if I can show that the adequacy principle does not today reflect any deep-rooted commitment to the idea that the law should have nothing to do with the substantive fairness of an exchange, then it will be time enough to consider whether the adequacy principle itself ought to be retained.

My third preliminary comment has to do with the distinction between procedural and substantive fairness in exchange, or—looking at it from the other side—between procedural and substantive unconscionability.[1] While this distinction may have utility for some purposes, I want to utter a word of caution against the belief that we can wholly separate our ideas of fair procedures from our ideas of fair results. Procedures, after all, do affect results, and that is one reason we are interested in fair procedures. When we set contracts aside because fraud or threats have been used by one party, it is surely idle to suppose that we are indifferent to the fact that the usual consequence of fraud or threats is to produce an unfair or one-sided contract. No doubt once in a while a perfectly fair contract may be the outcome of fraud or threats, but all our instincts make us sceptical about this possibility. If this is, indeed, what seems to have been proved, we are apt to look for ways of upholding the contract. Perhaps the fraud or threats concerned immaterial facts? Perhaps no reasonable man would have been influenced by them? Perhaps the other party would have entered into the contract on the same terms anyhow? And even if, which I am prepared to concede sometimes does happen, a court actually sets aside a completely fair exchange because of fraud or threats, this is not enough to demonstrate that our interest in fair procedures *per se* determines this result.

---

[1] This distinction originated in the well-known article by Leff, 'Unconscionability and the Code—The Emperor's New Clause', 115 *U. Pa. L. Rev.* 485, 487 (1967), and has been almost universally adopted in America since then. See Farnsworth, *Contracts*, pp. 314-15. But other writers have not always found the distinction so helpful, see, e.g., Waddams, 'Unconscionability in Contracts', 39 *Mod. L. Rev.* 369 (1976) which doesn't mention Leff's article; and Reiter, 'The Control of Contract Power', 1 *Ox. J. Leg. St.* 347 (1981), which treats both forms of unconscionability without suggesting that the distinction is of general importance.

Perhaps the reality is that fraud and threats so often lead to unfair exchanges that we wish to deter their use, irrespective of the result in a particular case.

But there is another point: ideas of procedural and substantive fairness feed upon each other. Imagine a society in which fraud is regarded as a permissible bargaining procedure and negotiating parties are simply expected to be more careful of trusting anything the other party says. Perhaps this leads to inefficiency since both parties have to devote more resources to ascertaining the facts from more trustworthy sources. Still, it is an imaginable state of affairs; as I recollect my schoolboy days, the market in comics and marbles was conducted somewhat along these lines. Naturally, if skill in lying and dissembling is an accepted attribute of the bargaining procedure, the outcome of bargains will be different. But it will not only be different in fact, it will probably seem acceptably different. It is unlikely that such a bargaining procedure would be found acceptable except in a society which had some admiration for the plausible rogue, the skill of the lying cheat. What is a fair outcome may thus depend on our views about fair procedures.

The process also works in the reverse direction. Suppose a contract in which the outcome favours one party vastly more than the other; our natural reaction today is to believe that something must have gone wrong with the bargaining process. How could a rational person have entered into this contract if he had known what he was about, had not been subject to undue pressures, or the like? We may be so sceptical that such a contract could have been the result of the ordinary and proper bargaining processes that we examine the case with a strong, almost conclusive presumption that a sufficiently unfair contract must have been the result of improper procedures. This is partly, but only partly, because there is a reasonable presumption of fact that a very unfair or imbalanced contract was the result of some procedural improprieties; but it is also partly due to a normative idea. We want people to behave like reasonable people; our laws and institutions are based on the assumption that man is a rational being—and a rational being with particular characteristics. One of these characteristics is that a person is presumed not to want or intend to give away his property without some good reason. When the most plausible explanation of a contract is that one of the parties must have behaved in an irrational manner, something clearly has gone wrong and there is a lack of fit between what ought to have happened and what has happened. So in this way also there are serious problems about drawing a sharp line between procedural and substantive fairness or procedural and substantive unconscionability.

I turn now to examine some of the ways in which the law of contract has—in spite of the adequacy of the consideration principle—demonstrated its concern with fundamental ideas of fairness in exchange.

Let me begin with some old and absolutely fundamental rules of contract law, rules so well established that we are probably mostly unaware that they actually represent a choice, and that there are imaginable alternative rules. Consider first the traditional and elementary distinction between a unilateral and a bilateral contract. Observe how difficult it is to fit in a third category between these two, in which one party to a contract is, for any length of time, bound, while the other is not. The distinction between these two classes is always taken to be exhaustive and is based on the premise that either both parties must be bound, or neither can be bound. Of course we know today that there are special circumstances in which it would be convenient and perfectly reasonable to have a transaction in which one party is bound while the other is not. The option is a standard modern device, so common and well established indeed, that proposals have from time to time been mooted to convert every offer which is declared to be open for a specified time into a binding option. I am very far from being convinced that such a change would accord with the morality of the man in the street or even perhaps of the commercial community.[1] The traditional common law rule may well reflect a common understanding to the effect that gratuitous undertakings are concessions, freely withdrawable on notice given, at least so long as they have not been relied upon.

But whatever may be the case where a clear promise is made to keep an offer open for a specified time, I am more interested in the normal understanding of the ordinary offer, and the rules governing acceptance. The common law rules of offer and acceptance have never permitted an offeree to accept an offer in such a way as to impose an immediate binding obligation on the offeror, except by tendering his own counter-promise in exchange. If someone offers to sell me Blackacre for £100,000 I cannot reply by saying, 'Thank you very much. I accept your offer, though of course I remain free myself to buy or not as I choose; but you are as from this moment committed to convey if and when I tender the £100,000.' Indeed, not only can I not do this, but if I simply reply to the offer by saying, 'I accept', or even just 'Done' or 'That's a deal', I am in law now just as committed as the other party

[1] See Lewis, 'Contracts between Businessmen', 9 *Br. J of Law and Soc.* 153 (1982).

(subject to requirements of writing). Why am I so committed? The traditional answer is to say that my acceptance 'amounts' to a promise, and that my promise also converts the offer into a binding promise. Yet neither offer nor acceptance may be couched in the language of promises at all, and I see no a priori reason to suppose that this is the only or even the most plausible interpretation of what an offer and an acceptance are actually intended to mean. No doubt in some contexts this is the case, but in many others it seems unlikely. Yet lawyers rarely pause over the context before deciding that an accepted offer creates mutual binding obligations on both sides; and even where they do, the only alternative is to treat the transaction as a unilateral contract in which prima facie both sides remain free, at any rate prior to some significant acts of performance or reliance. My own view is that these rules reflect a deep-seated belief that it is somehow unfair that one party to a transaction should be bound while the other remains free. An inchoate exchange of this character is so unbalanced that it simply offends the sense of justice.

If it is said that there would be nothing unfair about it so long as the party bound fully understands what he is at and accepts the consequences, I am prepared to agree that this may be the case in certain contexts; but it seems to me clearly wrong to suppose that the only norms we recognize in this bargaining process derive from the deliberate promises of the parties. Suppose that while the bargaining is taking place one of the parties asks the other to commit himself, while the former wishes to remain free until some later stage in the transaction; in other words, he asks for an option. It seems to me likely that the prima-facie reaction of the second party would be to say that it is unfair to ask him to bind himself while the other remains uncommitted. This would thus be an appeal to norms which do not derive and cannot derive from the bargain itself, because by hypothesis the bargain has not yet been concluded. Once again, I freely concede that differing contexts may lead to different results. A person may have some good reason for granting an option; or indeed he may be paid an actual price for the option itself. But like much else in the law of contract, the treatment of options seems to me to be based on the underlying supposition that people do not normally give things away or do something for nothing. A transaction in which one person is bound and the other is not is suspect; given the way in which behaviour and customary ideas react upon each other, it would not be inaccurate to suggest that such arrangements are unusual because they are felt to be unfair, and are felt to be unfair because they are unusual.

I suspect that similar ideas underlie the many difficulties which English[1] and—more commonly—American[2] courts have had with requirement and output contracts. As with options, the basic problem with these arrangements is that they seem one-sided and for that reason unfair; however, the fact is that most such arrangements are to be found in commercial contexts where they do in fact make perfectly good sense and where there is no serious element of unfairness, so that in the result such contracts are today normally upheld without too much difficulty.[3]

I turn now to another of the principal ways in which contract law strives after the ideal of the fair exchange, namely the ordinary processes of construction and interpretation and implication. This is such an everyday part of the work of the contract lawyer that we are perhaps apt to underrate both its importance and the extent to which our preconceptions of what is fair enter into the process. Traditionally, of course, we attribute results here to the presumed intent of the parties, but this is much criticized as a fictional exercise. Most lawyers—at least most academic lawyers—nowadays prefer to acknowledge that courts are, at least in part, giving effect to their sense of justice in construing contracts or implying terms. I have myself said this on many occasions and have no desire to backtrack today; nevertheless it is perhaps worth noting once again how ideas of fairness and customary behaviour interact on each other. We imply a term to give effect to our sense of justice rather than to give effect to what these particular parties intended; but our sense of justice does derive in part from patterns of customary behaviour. Because most people enter into exchange transactions of a certain type and at certain prices on certain terms, we come to regard these as fair and reasonable; and when they are not specifically included in a contract we are apt to read them in very easily.

Unfortunately, the extreme reluctance of courts to acknowledge openly that they are trying to ensure that a contract operates as a fair exchange means that the conceptual apparatus of the law is highly complex and often obscures what is actually going on. Consider the simple possibility of a purchaser of a second-hand car who—without any fraud or other procedural impropriety—is induced to buy the car

---

[1] See Adams, 'Consideration for Requirements Contracts', 94 *Law Q. Rev.* 73 (1978).
[2] See Farnsworth, *Contracts*, pp. 79-82.
[3] UCC 2-306 (1).

for a price which is far in excess of its reasonable market value. No lawyer would suggest that, on these facts alone, the buyer could upset the contract or obtain relief of any kind. It seems too clear for argument: adequacy of consideration is not material, the contract price is for the parties to fix, and so on. Yet this all contains an air of unreality about it, because although the court may have no power directly to reduce the price paid by the buyer, it does have the power to interpret the contract and decide what the seller's responsibilities are as regards the quality and fitness of the goods. Suppose the car breaks down, some new part is needed, or repairs to this or that are required at substantial cost; it at once becomes possible to think of claiming that the car was unmerchantable. What is merchantable quality? According to the English statutory definition,[1] merchantable means more or less what a reasonable buyer is entitled to expect having regard to all the circumstances, including the price. Thus, the higher the price, the higher the quality and condition you are entitled to expect. What is all this except a roundabout and complicated way of saying that—within certain broad parameters—the buyer is entitled to some reasonable approximation of value for money?

Of course it goes without saying that we are only concerned with a rough and ready fairness of exchange. There is no question of attempting to ensure any precise correspondence between the two sides of a contract. As in many other spheres, the common law has never worked well as an administrative procedure designed to mass-regulate all human activity in detail. It works on the assumption that most human activity can be left to the parties immediately concerned, and that the intervention of the courts is reserved for serious cases where there is some gross deviation from the norm. What that means in the area under discussion is that courts will not interfere to iron out every trivial imbalance in an exchange; but what I am suggesting is that when there is some gross imbalance, something serious enough to offend our sense of justice, it will usually be found that some remedy is available.

Let me give one other example of a standard kind of implied term, akin to the implied warranties in contracts of sale of goods, which seems to me to involve much the same sort of concern with fair exchange, but which is also wrapped up in obscuring circumlocutions. In contracts of employment the question sometimes arises whether the employer is obliged to provide work for his employee or whether he fully complies

[1] Sale of Goods Act 1979, s. 14 (6); see Atiyah, *The Sale of Goods*, (7th edn., 1985), pp. 132-5.

with his contractual obligations by simply paying the employee his agreed wage or salary. The courts have answered this question by saying that in general mere payment of wage or salary is sufficient compliance, but that there are a number of exceptional cases in which the employer will be in breach if he does not actually provide the work or the opportunities for the work contemplated by the contract. The stock example of this exception is provided by the case of the actor or other public performer who is entitled to claim the opportunity to perform as contemplated by the contract, in addition to receiving his contractual remuneration.[1] This is justified by the courts by saying that in this situation the contractual remuneration is only part of the consideration, because the actor expects that the opportunity to perform on the public stage will give him the chance to enhance his reputation and thus gain additional benefits in the future. But it is to be noted that it is the courts themselves who declare that the specified remuneration is not the sole consideration in such contracts; it is not necessarily expressly stipulated thus by the parties. In effect the court says that the fair exchange in these circumstances requires the employee to have the opportunity to perform publicly as agreed, as well as to receive his contractual pay. Of course the court gets its ideas of fairness here, as elsewhere, by looking at the normal, usual situation; if it were customary for theatrical producers to demand and receive a share of the enhanced earning capacity of an actor whose performance was a smash hit, our ideas and the courts' ideas of what is a fair exchange in this type of situation might well be different.

But it is not only in the implication of standard terms in standard contracts that one can see the interest of the courts in ideas of fair exchange; one finds it also in virtually any case in which the court is called upon to construe ambiguous or vague contractual provision or to supply some kind of implied term. As a third example of this process of construing contracts so as to give effect to some idea, however crude, of fairness in exchange, let me cite the decision of the House of Lords in *Liverpool City Council* v. *Irwin.*[2] This case concerned a council tenancy—a lease of a flat or apartment by the local city council to a tenant. However, the documentary and formal sides of such council tenancies were, at this time, somewhat neglected. (Statute has intervened since then.) A document entitled 'Conditions of Tenancy' was signed by the

---

[1] See e.g. *Clayton* v. *Waller & Oliver* [1930] AC 209; *Withers* v. *General Theatre Corp.* [1933] 2 KB 536.
[2] [1977] AC 239.

tenant and contained a list of obligations on the tenant—a simple list of 'dos and don'ts'. But, and I quote from Lord Wilberforce's judgment, 'On the landlords' side there is nothing, no signature, no demise, no covenant.'[1] Thus the entire nature of the landlords' obligations under the lease had to be constructed by the court out of the flimsiest material. There was nothing which could seriously be called evidence of the intention of the parties. The obligations of the landlord simply had to be constructed out of the nature of the relationship. In the event the House of Lords held that the landlords were under an obligation to take reasonable care to maintain the common facilities available to the tenants—lifts, stairways, and rubbish disposal chutes. Strict orthodoxy was maintained in rejection of Lord Denning's heretical suggestion that the court could imply any 'reasonable term'. Not so, said their lordships, the courts could only imply terms when 'necessary', not when 'reasonable'. But observe, once again, what the actual outcome was. A term of 'reasonable care' to maintain the common services was implied. But given the scanty nature of the material available from which to fill in the actual content of the duty of reasonable care in such a case, the House necessarily had to rely heavily on the particular nature of the tenancy—a council tenancy at a low rent. The fact that the entire rental paid by all the tenants in the block had been swallowed up in maintenance and repair, leaving nothing whatever with which to service the capital costs of the building, not unnaturally weighed in the result. Fairly minimal standards of maintenance and repair were all that reasonableness demanded in the circumstances. Clearly, the obligation imposed on the landlords was very largely determined by the type of the relationship and the size of the rent. Had the flat been in a luxury block at a high rent in a fashionable quarter it is inconceivable that a much higher duty would not have been imposed on the landlords.

So here we have a situation in which the price paid by one of the parties very largely determines the extent of the obligations which will be imposed on the other. Is there anything surprising about this result? Surely only if we misconceive the whole nature of the process of implication in contract. Over-emphasis on the importance of the 'presumed intent' of the parties may divert attention away from the fact that underlying presumed intent is the idea of fairness in exchange. As I have already said, ideas of fairness and customary patterns of behaviour obviously interact, so it doesn't much matter whether we say that reasonable parties would have intended a fair exchange, or that a fair

[1] Ibid., at p. 253.

exchange is the sort of exchange that reasonable parties would have made in this kind of situation. At least it doesn't much matter if we adopt the sort of broad approach to matters of interpretation that the House of Lords did adopt in this case. But it would be a serious matter if the search for presumed intent was conducted by literal-minded analysis of the written word, because we would then be liable to find the search for presumed intent going in one direction and arguments based on fair exchange in quite a different direction.

There is no doubt that this kind of thing has often happened in the past, nor that it probably still does happen today. But there are also signs that fair exchange ideas are beginning to dominate over literal interpretation in certain circumstances. A striking example of such a case is the Court of Appeal decision in *Staffs. Area Health Authority* v. *S. Staffs Waterworks*,[1] which concerned a contract made in 1929 for the supply of water to a hospital at seven old pence per thousand gallons and expressed to continue for 'all times hereafter'. By 1975, the price of water was fifteen times what it had been in 1929, so the contract was clearly operating in a very imbalanced fashion. Yet the nominalist principle still generally prevents courts from rewriting long-term contracts to adjust the price payable in the absence of express provision in the contract. Few long-term contracts made in these highly inflationary times would fail to include some such provision, but in 1929 nobody could have foreseen the economic conditions of today, and this contract contained no price adjustment clause. Nevertheless, the court held the contract to be terminable on reasonable notice, which was, in the circumstances, simply a way of enabling the suppliers to increase the price.

I want now to draw attention to a number of other principles of law, well known enough in their own contexts, which I believe to be further important illustrations of the ways and means by which ideas of fair exchange can be used by the courts. The principles I have in mind are often dignified by being cast in the language of maxims: a person cannot blow hot and cold,[2] a person cannot affirm and disaffirm an instrument,[3] a person must elect between inconsistent remedies,[4] and

[1] [1978] 1 WLR 1387.

[2] See *Lissenden* v. *CAV Bosch Ltd.* [1940] AC 412 for a discussion of the maxim that a person cannot 'approbate and reprobate'.

[3] *Ker* v. *Wauchope* (1819) 1 Bli. 1, 21; *Codrington* v. *Codrington* (1875) LR 7 HL 854; *G.* v. *M.* (1885) 10 App. Cas. 171.

[4] The application of this principle has been cut down in *United Australia* v. *Barclays Bank* [1941] AC 1 and *Johnson* v. *Agnew* [1980] AC 367, but nobody doubts that it is still applicable in appropriate circumstances.

so forth. But many of these principles seem to be little more than illustrations of the rather more homely maxim that you cannot both have your cake and eat it, the attempt to do which could, I suppose, be characterized as an attempt to subvert the whole idea of fair exchange. Consider some of the simplest applications of these principles. A person induced to enter a contract through fraud or misrepresentation must elect to affirm or avoid it; he cannot keep the benefit of the contract while repudiating liabilities under it. Like so many other contract doctrines, this one has been seen for many years through nineteenth-century spectacles; that is, the principle has often been cast in terms of the innocent party's choice. He has to choose between affirming and repudiating the contract. But in fact few cases turn on express affirmation or repudiation: more commonly the court is asked to 'infer' an affirmation or repudiation from what has been done; and on analysis it will often be found that the court is in effect insisting that the innocent party remains liable because he has accepted the benefits of the contract;[1] it is, in other words, maintaining the integrity of the exchange transaction.

Or consider a similar principle, the idea that a person cannot take the benefit of a contract without accepting the burdens. Recently, Sir Robert Megarry adopted a principle in these very terms as a way of avoiding the somewhat limited and technical English rules governing assignment and novation. In the *Ocean Island* case[2] the defendants had taken over a business and mined lands owned by the plaintiffs and leased to the defendants' predecessors in title. The question was whether they were liable under covenants entered into by their predecessors, the original contracting parties, with respect to the restoration of the condition of the lands on expiry of the leases. The defendants' argument that they were not parties to the contracts was, of course, technical in the extreme; the proper way, according to classical law, to render the defendants liable on the contracts was to show that they had consented to them, that there had been novations properly agreed to by all. No such novations could be proved or even implied, however. Nevertheless

---

[1] Or that he has so behaved as to induce the breaching party to act to his prejudice (to act in reliance, in other words): *Peyman* v. *Lanjani* [1984] 3 All ER 704. Nothing was said about benefit in this case (where it was not relevant) but it is to be expected that the courts will subsume benefit cases under the reliance principle enunciated in this case. (If the innocent party elects to retain benefits obtained under the contract he will surely be held to have induced the other to believe that he does not intend to repudiate the contract.)

[2] *Sub. nom. Tito v Waddell* [1977] Ch 106.

by invoking the benefit-and-burden principle, to which I have referred, Megarry VC was able to hold the defendants liable on the contracts.

A closely related idea, which I have no space to explore here, but which was of great significance in eighteenth century law, was the principle that a person who stood to gain from the profits of an enterprise or venture should also be liable for the losses.[1] The arrival of limited liability and modern corporate ways of doing business went a long way to destroying this principle, but I do not think it is quite dead; and indeed, abuse of the one-man corporate form may well lead to a revival of this principle in the future.

While these and similar ideas of substantive fair exchange appear to be increasing in importance today, it is not surprising to find that traditional contractual doctrines concerned with procedural fairness have also shown signs of increased vigour in recent times; nor is it suprising that the lines between the two are, as I have already suggested, increasingly difficult to draw. Thus there are many trends, both in case-law and in statute law, to give protection to consumers or non-business parties who enter into contracts not wholly appreciating or understanding the full implications. Thus we have, for instance, the well-known decision in *Lloyd's Bank* v. *Bundy*[2] in which the court invalidated a mortgage granted by way of guarantee of the mortgagor's son's business debts. The bank to whom the mortgage was given, as creditor of the son, was, said the court, in the special circumstances of the case, under a duty to advise their client to obtain independent advice. This looks therefore like a case of procedural impropriety, an extension of traditional doctrines of undue influence; and, indeed, it is in chapters of that heading that the textbooks deal with the case. Yet is it so clear that substantive unfairness played no part in the decision? Certainly Lord Denning paid attention to it, in amalgamating procedural and substantive unfairness in his new doctrine of inequality of bargaining power; and even though the House of Lords later repudiated some of these dicta,[3] they have made it clear that transactions are not to be set aside in such circumstances unless there is substantial unfairness in the result.

The majority of the court in *Bundy's* case followed a more orthodox analysis, like the House of Lords in the more recent *Morgan*[4] case,

---

[1] *Freedom of Contract*, pp. 177-8, 497-9.
[2] [1975] QB 326.
[3] *National Westminster Bank* v. *Morgan* [1985] 2 WLR 588.
[4] Ibid.

and they concentrated on the procedural improprieties, stressing that independent advice should have been obtained. But the passage in the judgment of Sir Erich Sachs in which this point is made suggests that there was only one piece of advice which an independent adviser could possibly have given Mr Bundy, namely on no account to grant the mortgage without some further consideration from the bank in the form of an agreement to hold its hand for some minimum period. This is, indeed, not an uncommon feature of cases in which contracts have been invalidated for lack of any such independent advice. In the great majority of cases, it is clear that any such adviser would have been bound to urge the party concerned not to enter into the transaction at all. Moreover it is pretty clear that the whole need for independent advice in a case like *Bundy's* arises precisely because the contract was so one-sided in terms of the consideration, a point now confirmed by the *Morgan* case. There is therefore an element of circularity in insisting that cases like this concern purely procedural fairness or impropriety. The fact is that, as in most cases of this kind, breach of the procedural proprieties in the bargaining process was largely inferred from the gross inadequacy of the consideration.

Much the same seems to be true of the decisions in *Cresswell* v. *Cresswell*[1] and *Backhouse* v. *Backhouse*,[2] both of which concerned agreement by separating spouses whereby the wives surrendered their interest in the matrimonial home in return for an indemnity against liability on the mortgages. The consideration in each case was, of course, of the barest and most technical character, and the transactions were plainly grossly unfair or unequal exchanges. There has been some suggestion that these contracts were entered into by the wives under some sort of emotional disturbance, and that therefore the cases can be characterized as involving cognitive flaws and therefore procedural unfairness.[3] But in both cases the judgments say very little about any element of emotional disturbance or stress; the decisions are based primarily on the suggestion that a sale at an undervalue by a person who has no independent advice can be set aside if that person can somehow be treated as belonging to the modern equivalent of the 'poor and ignorant' class of persons who sometimes appear in similar nineteenth-century cases. And the interpretation placed on these words in these two cases is so generous that they seem to have virtually

[1] [1978] 1 WLR 225 n.
[2] [1978] 1 WLR 243.
[3] See *Sutton v Sutton* [1984] 1 All ER 168, 174.

disappeared as independent requirements of the principle. Once again, it is to be noted that it is really the gross substantive inequality of the exchange which is used to justify the argument or inference that independent advice ought to have been obtained; there is little in the circumstances themselves, apart from the unfairness of the exchange, to justify the need for independent advice.

A similar blurring of the lines between procedural and substantive fairness seems to me to be illustrated by some recent English decisions on economic duress. In particular, the case of *The Atlantic Baron*[1] nicely demonstrates how concern with substantive fairness can lead the courts to develop principles ostensibly intended to regulate the bargaining process rather than its results. It is well known that the doctrine of consideration was at one time used to strike down contractual modifications which benefited only one party to the contract. Later it came to be felt that this apparent concern with fairness was unjustified and that the purpose of the law was chiefly to prevent contractual modifications being extracted by unfair pressure or other improper means. Furthermore, as the doctrine of consideration was assumed to pay no regard to adequacy, it naturally followed that a contractual modification which involved a slight concession on one side and a much more substantial concession on the other would be valid even though it might appear to be very unfair. Thus, it came to be thought that cases of this nature could be more satisfactorily dealt with by developing a law of duress or improper pressure, rather than by using the doctrine of consideration. But until very recently, English courts had been unwilling to treat a threat to breach a contract as amounting to duress which could invalidate a concession or modification thereby obtained. In *The Atlantic Baron*, however, this step was finally taken. A seller's threat to refuse delivery of a ship under construction unless the buyer agreed to a substantial increase in the price was now held to be improper duress which in principle could have been relied upon by the buyer despite a minor variation in the terms of payment which might have been a sufficient legal consideration for the price increase.

Once again, it will be seen how difficult it is to keep separate the procedural and substantive issues. The shift from using consideration to using economic duress suggests that the courts have moved from ideas of substantive fairness to procedural ones. Yet this seems too simplistic a view. For the fact is that it is precisely the impropriety of

[1] *North Ocean Shipping Co. Ltd* v. *Hyundai Construction Co. Ltd.* [1979] QB 705.

using the threat to breach the contract in such circumstances which leads to the resultant contractual modifications being so one-sided and hence substantively unfair. If the modifications had been fairly equally balanced, there would presumably have been no need for the seller to use the improper threat in the first place. The modifications could have been negotiated in an ordinary commercial manner. Thus, use of the doctrine of duress in this situation was functionally equivalent to using the doctrine of consideration without the limiting exclusion of the relevance of adequacy. One difference only remains, as with the analogous cases of fraud and misrepresentation mentioned earlier, namely that in theory, even if the modification secured by the duress had been completely fair, the duress, once established, would still have been an invalidating factor. But one can only say that this seems of very little practical importance; for it is surely almost certain that if the resultant modification were substantively fair the court would deny that the alleged threat had amounted to improper pressure. Only where the threat is of an obviously gross and improper kind—for example, a threat of personal violence—is it in the least likely that a court would use it to invalidate a perfectly fair transaction or modification; and in that unlikely event, there would be independent policy goals to justify the result, irrespective of fairness in exchange. This suggestion, first made in the original version of this essay, now gains strong support from the decision of the House of Lords in *National Westminster Bank plc* v. *Morgan*,[1] in which it was firmly laid down that the court will not set aside a contract for undue influence where the resulting transaction is not itself unfair—or where (as it was put) no actual advantage has been taken of the victim of the undue influence. This case concerned alleged undue influence between a bank manager and a client, and was obviously of a highly technical character, if it could be shown to have existed at all. No doubt the result may still be different where the actions of the defendant are of a kind which are seriously wrongful in themselves, and need to be deterred by the courts, apart altogether from the result in the particular case.

By now I have, I hope, adduced enough evidence to suggest that it is no longer possible to accept without serious qualification the idea that the law is today solely concerned with the bargaining process and not with the result. For one thing, I have cast doubt on the reality of this distinction, and for another I have cited evidence suggesting a real concern with substantive fairness. There is, I believe, a great deal more evidence which could be adduced, especially if regard is had, as it must

---

[1] [1985] 2 WLR 588.

be if the subject is to be fully explored, to statutory interventions. As we all know, the area within which the pure doctrines of the common law actually operate are continuously being confined by the ever-encroaching tide of statute law; and when it comes to statutes nobody feels the least inhibition about trying to ensure that contracts should actually be, in some sense, fair. However, this is obviously not the place to attempt an exhaustive enumeration of examples, so I turn from what has hitherto been largely a descriptive exercise to the more troublesome normative questions.

Is this concern of contract law with substantive fairness desirable or legitimate? Is it all part of the general movement away from the free market, a search for what Hayek calls 'the mirage of social justice'?[1] Is the greater legislative willingness to pursue openly the ideal of fair contracts the result of the democratic process falling into the hands of egalitarians, and if so, what does this mean for the legitimacy of judicial attempts in the same direction—or for the counter-revolutionary attempts of some judges and some academics to restore faith in the pure common law of contract?

Let me begin with a pretty fundamental question: is the idea of fairness in exchange itself a theoretically defensible idea? Many supporters of the liberal theory of justice (discussed in Essay 6) and of the modern versions of economic theories of contract (discussed in Essay 7) would say that it is not. Adherents of the subjective theory of value sometimes seem to suggest that the very idea of a fair exchange is a chimera. Each party assesses the value to himself of the other's performance, and there are no objective criteria against which to measure these values. The fact that both parties freely and voluntarily enter into the contract is evidence that they both benefit by it, that there are gains from trade; and the precise division of those gains is not a matter of fairness but the result of market forces and bargaining position. On this view, all that the law can do is to police the bargaining process, to try to ensure that contracts are indeed the result of free and voluntary and, perhaps we should add, informed, processes; but once we have done that, the result must be accepted. There simply is no basis for saying that a free and voluntary exchange is unfair.[2]

This extreme view bears a certain resemblance to the argument that there is no such thing as justice in the abstract, and that therefore all

---

[1] This is the sub-title of vol. ii of F. A. Hayek's trilogy, *Law, Legislation and Liberty* (1976).

[2] This seems to be the position of Trebilcock, 'The Doctrine of Inequality of Bargaining Power: Post-Benthamite Economics in the House of Lords', 26 *U. Tor. LJ* 359

laws and all administrative decision-making should be structured round ideas of due process rather than pursue the fantasy of actual justice.[1] Thus (it may be urged), constitutional laws and institutions should merely provide a framework in which conflicting ideals can be pitted against each other in some fair procedures and should have no bias or tendency to produce laws of any particular kind. Similarly, it sometimes seems to be suggested, there is no way in which courts can actually arrive at just decisions, because, once again, there is no such thing as justice in the abstract.[2] Hence, fair procedures are more important than actual results, even if there is such a thing as a fair result at all.

I hope it will be clear why I reject this extreme position in all three spheres, the constitutional, the judicial, and the contractual. Procedures influence and indeed often determine results in all three spheres. In the constitutional or political sphere, electoral laws would normally be thought of as largely procedural, and yet in particular contexts the selection of one or other type of electoral law may determine the general composition of an elected assembly for generations. And so too, it is hardly a novel insight to suggest that procedural rules will often determine the result of judicial decisions. Similarly, as I have already demonstrated, contractual results are profoundly influenced by the bargaining procedures. So unless there is some reason to suppose that

at pp. 376-7 (1976). Duncan Kennedy, from a radical left perspective, also attacks the doctrine of inequality of bargaining power as conceptually incoherent: 'Distributive and Paternalist Motives in Contract and Tort with Special Reference to Compulsory Terms and Unequal Bargaining Power', 41 *Maryland L. Rev.* 563 (1982). But this, of course, is because Kennedy wishes to replace this doctrine with open use of contract law for redistributive purposes. English judges sometimes seem to agree with Trebilock's view, see e.g. *Multiservice Bookbinding* v. *Malden* [1979] Ch. 84, but cf. *Cityland & Property (Holdings) Ltd.* v. *Dabrah* [1978] Ch. 166, where in a traditional mortgage case the contractual terms were set aside even though there was no allegation of procedural impropriety.

[1] I find it hard to pin this 'theory' on any particular individual, but it seems to me to underlie a great deal of modern American legal theory, beginning perhaps with Roscoe Pound, see e.g. his *Introduction to the Philosophy of Law* (reprinted 1961) 46. It also seems to underlie the American 'theory of legislation', see e.g. Posner, *The Federal Courts: Crisis and Reform* (1985), 262ff.

[2] For a striking example, see *B.P. Exploration Ltd.* v. *Hunt* [1981] 1 WLR 232, 238 (affirmed on a different point [1983] 2 AC 352) where the CA refused to interfere with the trial judge's mode of assessing the 'just sum' to be awarded under s. 1(3) of the Law Reform (Frustrated Contracts) Act 1943, on the ground that there were several ways of arriving at a 'just sum', none of which had a claim to be regarded as exclusively correct, or 'more just' than the others: 'The concept of what is just is not an absolute one. Opinions among right thinking people may, and probably will, differ as to what is just in a particular case.'

fair and neutral procedures are more readily identifiable than fair results, the position of the extreme sceptic must result in throwing away the baby with the bathwater. If there is no such thing as justice in the abstract, then there is equally no such thing as a just procedure in the abstract. There are, of course, liberal theorists like John Rawls, who believe that it is possible to identify neutral principles of fair procedure—whether in the constitutional, judicial, or contractual sphere— and who have made great efforts to explain why these principles would be assented to by all rational people; but whatever the plausibility of all this in the constitutional sphere, it is really quite impossible to accept it in the contractual sphere. For it must be remembered that even the proceduralist, he who argues for neutral rules of fair bargaining, takes as his starting point the assumption that a bargain once made is legally binding. As I tried to demonstrate in Essays 6 and 7, that is not a rule of procedure but a very solid substantive rule, which is quite incapable of being justified by neutral principles. Indeed, it is surely only too manifest that the substantive principle which declares executory bargains to be binding is a principle with clear distributive implications.[1]

One must also remember that courts are in the business of fixing just prices and fair prices, however conceptually difficult it may be to explain what they are supposed to be doing. Many, if not most, tort actions involve the courts in fixing, *ex post*, the fair or reasonable price which the defendant has to pay for what he has 'taken' from the plaintiff; in contract and restitution actions, also, the courts are often required to fix prices, as in the simplest sort of case where a contract is made on the basis of an unspecified 'reasonable' price; and there are, too, statutory procedures of compulsory acquisition and the like in which courts or other tribunals have the task of fixing just compensation for deprivation of property. Similarly, as I have already pointed out, the implication of terms in a contract, even at common law, necessarily involves a court decision as to what is the fair and reasonable consideration which one party is entitled to receive for his price.

Now it may be said that all this activity is parasitic on the free market. Court attempts to fix fair and reasonable prices or their equivalent are, it may be thought, attempts to discover the market price which the parties would have negotiated for themselves if they, and not the court, had actually done this. I do not doubt that the market price of a

---

[1] See Essay 6; Kronman, 'Contract Law and Distributive Justice,' 89 *Yale LJ* 472 (1980).

commodity often plays a significant part in any judicial decision determining a fair and reasonable price, but there are difficulties in treating this entire judicial exercise as parasitic on the market. First, there are some commodities for which there is no market at all, such as pain and suffering and personal injury, and yet courts have to fix prices for these in tort actions.

Furthermore, the prices fixed by the courts in tort actions then feed into or affect the market price for other goods for which there is a market, for example, liability insurance; perhaps also the market value of legal services may be affected by this legal fixing of prices for personal injury, since one only has to look at American practice in this area to see how the price of legal services may be closely correlated with the price of personal injuries. Thirdly, even where the court makes some attempt to look at the hypothetical contract which the parties might have made in order to fix the fair and reasonable price to be paid by one for some good obtained or taken from the other, it is for the court itself to determine under what rules this hypothetical bargain would have been conducted. For example, in *Bracewell* v. *Appleby*[1] the defendant had built a house whose only access was over a private road owned by six adjoining landowners, including himself. Damages were awarded for infringement of the plaintiffs' rights, but the judge held that the damages were to be assessed on the footing that the plaintiffs were willing to sell, and not 'as if they were in the extremely powerful bargaining position which an interlocutory injunction would have given them'.[2]

Finally, there is the more general point I have already made, namely that even the market itself is not a construct of neutral rules. The extent to which the market is based on the enforcement of binding contracts and the nature of the permissible bargaining process—permitting, for instance, the use of skill and foresight but not force or fraud—are such that ideas of justice in any event have a role to play in the fixing of prices. So it is hardly surprising that the courts, when they are required to construct prices in lieu of leaving this exercise to the market, should themselves inject an important normative element into the exercise.

All this may be highly controversial. But what should surely not be controversial is that in any event the market is riddled with imperfections, and the notion that there is no such thing as a just or fair price other than a market price fails to provide answers to many difficult

[1] [1975] Ch. 408.
[2] Ibid., at p. 419.

questions. First, what is the law to do with contracts where the price agreed is clearly out of line with the market price? It is totally unrealistic to suppose that even in highly competitive markets this kind of thing does not happen. One only has to think of the unsophisticated consumer who buys a second-hand car from a plausible dealer at well above the market price to realize that cases of this kind must present a problem to the legal system. Nor is it enough to wave aside a case of this kind by claiming that the consumer must have made a conscious decision that any attempt to get more information about market prices was not worth the costs involved. Of course this may have been the case, but that is an empirical question, not a logical deduction from the facts. An alternative explanation for what has happened may be that the consumer assumes—takes it for granted—that the dealer's prices are more or less in line with other dealers' prices, that they are, in other words, market prices. As Archdeacon Paley suggested nearly two hundred years ago, it is not an unreasonable implication that a person who sells in the market-place is selling at market prices—indeed impliedly undertakes to sell at market prices.[1] If that is what is in the consumer's mind when he makes a contract at much above market prices, then I see no economic or other justification for refusing some form of relief. So if the most recent case law on the implied terms of merchantability is—as I have suggested—getting close to offering relief for grossly unfair contract prices, I see nothing in economic or market theory to suggest that this is an illegitimate result.

Secondly, there are all the other common market imperfections much discussed in the literature, such as the existence of monopolies, externalities, informational difficulties, and so on. It is interesting to note that some common law courts seem to have had an intuitive understanding of some of these problems; or perhaps it would be more accurate to say that market imperfections often give rise to ideas of unfairness which closely parallel the economic arguments. I have, in Essay 6, already referred to the problem of 'micro-monopolies', and the traditional common law anxiety about contractual modification seems to reflect awareness that the parties negotiating a modification are in a bilateral monopoly situation. Judges do not of course use this kind of language, but they do refer to the fact that a party may have had 'no choice' but to accept a proposed variation to a contract, and whether they use consideration arguments[2] or the new doctrine of

---

[1] *Principles of Moral and Political Philosophy* (first published 1785, reprinted in *Works of William Paley* (1888)), pp. 526-7.

[2] As in *D. & C. Builders Ltd.* v. *Rees* [1966] 2 QB 617.

economic duress,[1] it seems clear that the underlying idea is the same as that discussed by the economist under the heading of monopoly. Precisely the same is true of maritime salvage contracts, which have for many years been subject to control where an exorbitant price has been demanded by the salvor—almost invariably, of course, in a monopoly situation.[2]

There are also other, surprisingly old cases in which courts have set aside contracts for the sale of information at grossly unfair prices, and these too are classic illustrations of market difficulties.[3] How can one assess the value of a piece of information until it has been disclosed? Then there is the problem of externalities—far too large a question to be seriously addressed here. But it is perhaps worth suggesting that this question is of much greater importance than is generally recognized in the legal or even the law-and-economics literature. As Ian Macneil pointed out in his 1979 Rosenthal lectures, a great deal of modern contracting seems to be undertaken by agents in a world without principals.[4] The legal nature of corporate or group personality must not obscure the fact that contracts entered into by such parties necessarily externalize most of their costs and benefits, so far at least as concerns the actual agents who make them. Business executives may, of course, participate to some extent in the profits or losses of their employers, but only to some extent, and public employees only do so to a minimal extent. So when governments or other public bodies complain about contracts at excessive or unfair prices,[5] it is not a priori obvious that these complaints have no economic justification.

I cannot, of course, attempt here any comprehensive assessment of how far modern derogations from freedom of contract in the name of justice and fairness have any adequate justification in economic theory. But I have said enough, I hope, to suggest that this is a far more complex issue than it is sometimes assumed to be. But if the search for fairness in exchange cannot therefore be condemned wholesale as a violation of market principles, are there any other grounds on which it can be rejected as illegitimate in principle? The only such ground which occurs to me is that to give effect to some notion of fairness in exchange may often involve overriding the consent of the parties to the ar-

---

[1] See *The Atlantic Baron*, above, p. 345; *Pao On v Lau Yiu* [1980] AC 614.

[2] *Akerblom* v. *Price* (1881) 7 QBD 129, and *The Port Caledonia and The Anna* [1903] P. 184 are two of many cases.

[3] *Rees* v. *De Barnardy* [1896] 2 Ch 437.

[4] Macneil, *The New Social Contract* (1980), pp. 78-84.

[5] See Turpin, *Government Contracts*, (1972), p. 171.

rangement. Of course, this will not always be the case because the traditional processes of construction, implication, and interpretation do not necessarily involve the rejection of express contractually agreed provisions. But undoubtedly any serious attempt to pursue the ideal of fairness in exchange—even to the limited extent, as I have suggested, of dealing only with gross departures from the norm—will sometimes require that express consents be rejected as not conclusive. To some theorists this seems to be the ultimate in illegitimacy. But I suggest this is to overdramatize the issue. Many of the reasons for rejecting the conclusiveness of market arrangements apply with equal force when the argument is dressed up in terms of overriding consent. The victim of monopoly who consents to an arrangement because he has no effective choice is surely entitled to attack the result notwithstanding his consent. His position scarcely differs from the victim of fraud or duress who knowingly consents and then seeks to repudiate afterwards. So too the lack of information which often means that a party has mistakenly overvalued the other party's performance surely weakens the persuasive force of holding him bound by his consent, just as it weakens the argument that the exchange was a Pareto-optimal transaction. More generally, it seems to me that the trend of modern law is to look into the *reasons* for the agreed arrangements or transaction. Consent alone, without an inquiry into the reasons for which the consent was given, seems a barren thing. It is, indeed, an example of formal reasoning, which can easily become formalistic if not fetishistic, to insist that consent must bind, no matter what the reason for which consent was given.[1] As I said earlier, one explanation of why we have traditionally refused to look into the adequacy of the reasons for the consent—the adequacy of the consideration, that is—is that the law is based on assumptions about rational behaviour. We do not generally ask why a person consents to arrangements, because most people do not consent without good and adequate reasons. Unfortunately, human experience demonstrates that this general assumption is not universally valid. People do occasionally consent to arrangements on inadequate or irrational grounds. It is particularly easy to do this when the procedure for indicating assent is simple and formalized, such as merely writing one's name at the bottom of a page, but much more striking instances occur

---

[1] I do not mean that there are not powerful arguments for a prima-facie adherence to formal requirements, as I believe there are: see Essay 5. But the question posed in the text relates to cases where there may be reasons outweighing the prima facie desirability of adhering to formal requirements.

of persons consenting to arrangements without good grounds, as where a manifestly innocent person pleads guilty to a crime. This kind of thing has happened too often in recent times for lawyers to be unaware of it; and an adequate institutional response is now needed.

I have doubtless skated over many difficult questions. There are, for instance, troublesome problems about reconciling ideas of fairness in exchange with market flexibility in times of shortage; the difficulties of fashioning suitable legal remedies to deal with contracts made in imperfect markets are complex; the relationship between the problem of externalities on the one hand and legal classifications such as illegality and public policy on the other need further analysis from the legal side. And so on. But I have, I hope, done enough to suggest that the relationship between bargaining procedures and the bargain which is the outcome of those procedures is not as simple as has sometimes been suggested; and that once the law takes an interest, as it always has, and must, in the procedures themselves, it is of necessity compelled to take an interest in the substantive justice of contracts.

Freedom of Contract and the New Right

1. The Swinging Pendulum

The concept of Freedom of Contract, it is widely agreed, reached some sort of intellectual pinnacle in the nineteenth century. One can argue about the precise dating, and this probably varied anyhow from one country to another, but in my book, *The Rise and Fall of Freedom of Contract*, I put the very high point of Freedom of Contract in England in the year 1870—and it is mainly with the modern English experience that this Essay deals.

Now Freedom of Contract was, at that time, by no means exclusively a legal concept, or a concept of interest only to lawyers. In fact I argued in my book, and tried to demonstrate with a good deal of supporting evidence, that Freedom of Contract began as an economic and even a political ideal, which probably had its roots in the personal, religious, and intellectual freedoms which had their origins in the Reformation and the beginnings of Protestantism. Although no doubt there were from the earliest times some subjects—for instance, usury—in which lawyers were closely involved, the movement towards Freedom of Contract was not primarily a legal movement. Nevertheless, at least from the middle of the eighteenth century, and perhaps earlier, there were clear signs that English lawyers began to be increasingly influenced by political and economic arguments in favour of Freedom of Contract. After the publication of Adam Smith's famous book *The Wealth of Nations* in 1776—a book which is generally thought to be the beginning of modern economic thought—the lawyers became more receptive and more involved in the movement to Freedom of Contract. By the beginning of the nineteenth century the law was itself beginning to reflect the new ideology. First there was a strong movement to repeal much obsolete legislation of a highly paternalistic character, interfering with Freedom of Contract, and later the common law itself began to show signs of modification, reaching a peak, as I have said, around 1870. Then the tide turned, and perhaps for a hundred years or so—I suggested from around 1870 to 1970, or perhaps 1980—the movement was the other way.

Freedom of choice was whittled down in many directions, government regulation replaced free contract, bureaucracies replaced private parties operating in the open market, markets themselves began to be increasingly dominated by monopolies, and paternalism once again was the order of the day. When I was writing my book on Freedom of Contract in the late 1970s I sensed that the pendulum had swung to its furthest point away from the ideology of Freedom of Contract. My book was published in 1979, a few months after the election of Mrs Thatcher's first administration. So this is an attempt to bring the story up to date.

To anyone with some knowledge of the historical background, the past decade or so must convey a strong sense of *déjà vu*. English lawyers may be forgiven for placing the beginnings of this new movement of the pendulum with the election of Mrs Thatcher's Government in May 1979, but the same signs of the swinging pendulum are to be observed almost all over the Western world. Once again, we find a strong ideological current, basing itself on the need for political and economic freedom. We find the same faith in Adam Smith and the operation of market forces, the same distrust of government bureaucracies, the same belief in the rights of individual choice. If the term 'Freedom of Contract' is not today very prominent on the lips of members of the New Right, as I shall call it, the ideas themselves look very similar indeed to those which were being so vigorously propagated in England some 150 years ago.

The question I want to address in this Essay is what this new swing of the pendulum is doing and is likely to do to the law of contract. Are we going to see the same kinds of change in contract doctrine in the next few decades as those which took place between 1770 and 1870? Are we going to see a reversal of the tide in the same way as happened during that century? Will Freedom of Contract once again become the paramount value in the private law of obligations, and, if so, what are the consequences likely to be?

Now these attempts to look at broad movements of ideology and their influence on the law over a short period of time are very difficult indeed. It is one thing to discern such movements over a century or two, but it is quite another to study their effects from day to day in the very hurly burly of politics and daily controversy. Of course one reason for this difficulty is that these great ideological swings are never monolithic. There are always violent controversies, there are those who fight the changes, threatening to reverse them at the earliest opportunity, there are also countervailing trends and swings in particular fields, and so on. Only in the long perspective of history does it become clearer which 'side' of the particular spectrum has been the ideologically dominant one.

Today, as we all know, the New Right appear to be politically supreme. They are in power, they win elections, and they are changing the law. The Left are almost everywhere in disarray, and in many ways the whole political discourse seems to have shifted ground, so that even the Left are now defending and fighting for policies which seem well to the right of the positions they were arguing for a decade ago. On the other hand, it is far too early to say that the ideology of the New Right has won out. By no means everyone agrees with them. Many passionately disagree with much of what they stand for. And some of those who disagree are always to be found in positions of authority and influence. Although they do not today control Parliament, they may still have an influence on ideas—for instance as academics whose views may powerfully influence the next generation, or as lawyers in bureaucracies such as Law Reform bodies, or the EEC, which may put up proposals for change and reform which are not always thrown out by the New Right, or even as judges who (being mostly over the age of 50) will have received most of their training and ideas in their youth when the ideology of Freedom of Contract was at a very low ebb.

All this means that it is very difficult to pore over the current scene and try to detect the influence of massive shifts of ideology, in the same way I tried to do in my book for 200 years of history. But I want to try.

However, I must first point out a number of respects in which the situation today, despite superficial appearances, does differ profoundly from the situation in the last century. First, the nineteenth-century movement to Freedom of Contract was, politically speaking, a left-wing movement, closely associated with the movement towards democracy in England. Radical politicians argued that the people could be trusted to look after themselves, to see to their own interests, and this led them to reject paternalism both in law and in politics. The people should be left free to vote, and to make their own contracts.

Today, of course, Freedom of Contract is a right-wing ideology, and it has largely lost its close association with democracy. The result may seem paradoxical: no one argues that the people cannot be trusted with the vote, but many still argue that they cannot be trusted in the market-place.

In the second place, we in the Western countries live today in an age of almost universal education and literacy. Nineteenth-century politicians who argued that the people could be trusted were relying heavily on their optimistic views of the probable effects of mass education. Although they knew that in their own time there were many socially inadequate people who would not fare well in the market-place, the ill-educated, the mentally weak and simple, the alcoholics, the elderly, and no doubt other groups, they had such unbounded confidence in the future that they assumed that most of these problems would disappear with the spread of education. Today, I doubt whether this extreme optimism would find many supporters. Surely we now know that if people *are* left to look after their own interests and make their own choices in the market-place, many of them will not choose wisely. Consequently, the New Right must be willing to face one of the unpleasant consequences of Freedom of Contract—namely, that there will always be losers, as well as winners, and, unfortunately, that the losers will often be the same people in many different fields of activity.

In the past decade or so, some of these losers have become more numerous and more visible than they once were in England. We see and hear today more, for example, about people who are turned out of their houses because they have failed to pay their mortgage instalments, or who have gas or electricity or even water supplies disconnected because they have not paid their bills. These are distressing events, and much can be done to reduce the risk of their occurrence, as well as to alleviate the distress they cause. But if the New Right is to prevail, it must be recognized that this kind of thing is an inescapable result of the return to Freedom of Contract. At the same time the New Right are entitled to remind us that these losers are balanced by gainers—nor should it be thought that the gainers are always rich capitalists. For example, one reason why there are more mortgage defaulters today is that there are more mortgages, and lenders as well as borrowers are prepared to take more risks in the market. Most of the borrowers will not default, so an increasing number of defaulters may be more than balanced by an increased number of successful and contented home-owners.

2. Nullification of Contract Terms

It is time for me to turn now from these generalities and speculations to consider what evidence there is of legal change in the face of these ideological and political changes. I wish to discuss in particular two main sets of questions. The first relates to those cases in which the law explicitly overrides the freely arrived at agreement of the parties— the deliberate nullification of express contractual terms—and therefore challenges the fundamental principle of Freedom of Contract. And the second concerns the more general relationship of contract law and contractual obligation to other principles of the law of obligations, even where there is no express nullification of express contractual terms.

I will begin then with the case of deliberate nullification of express terms. Of course such nullification can occur for many purposes. One of the differences between the present position on these matters, and the position as it was 100 or 200 years ago, is that we understand today a great deal more about the problem of externalities. In the first part of the nineteenth century, English economists as well as English lawyers were much more confident that a private agreement which was in the interests of both parties must also be in the interest of the public at large. There was a widespread belief in the harmony of interests, an idea which underlays much classical economic thought and also much English utilitarian thought. Today we know that, even if we accept the fundamentals of private enterprise economics, it can only be assumed that private agreements are in the public interest if we ignore the effects of a contract on third parties. And where there are grounds to think that a contract may have harmful effects on third parties or the public at large, there is nothing contrary to economic theory in recognizing these harmful effects and nullifying or even prohibiting such contracts.

This is, of course, one reason why today we have, in most countries, large and very complex bodies of law concerning monopolies and anti-trust matters. But this recognition of the effect of externalities may also justify other modern legislation designed to interfere with Freedom of Contract. In *Johnson* v. *Moreton*[1] in 1980 the House of Lords had to consider the effect of a 1948 statute which was designed to give security of tenure to agricultural tenancies. After reviewing the history of British agriculture over the previous century the judges concluded that the purpose of the Act was to promote the efficiency

[1] [1980] AC 37.

of British agriculture as a matter of national policy, and they therefore held that contracting out of the statute was not permissible. They went out of their way, thus, to insist that the statute was not mere paternalism, it was not designed simply for the protection of the weak against the strong, but for the protection of the nation itself.

I must now point out that there are various situations in which statutory interferences with Freedom of Contract can be justified both on paternalistic grounds and also on public policy grounds. For instance, much modern anti-discrimination legislation raises issues of fairness and equity, but also raises matters of profound national policy. We now reach a very important point, and one on which the New Right is making a major impact in its thinking. In one sense the effect of private contracts on the public interest is very much wider than was recognized even when the problem of externalities first came to be appreciated. This is precisely because modern Western societies are so socially committed to the relief of the poor and the disabled and those unable to care adequately for themselves, that any contract which affects a person's ability to care for himself and his family almost necessarily comes to have some potential impact on the public interest. If an employee is not paid a wage which is adequate for him and his family to live on, the state may be forced to help him out; so the state becomes interested in employment contracts. If a tenant is in danger of being thrown out on to the street by his landlord, or if he cannot afford to pay a rent on the open market, the state may be called upon to house him, so the state becomes interested in residential tenancies. This is obviously a very slippery slope, and it was down this slope that many Western societies found themselves increasingly slithering as the pendulum swung to its furthest point against Freedom of Contract in the 1970s. But what has been increasingly under challenge since then is the assumption that because Freedom of Contract has potential externalities in so many situations, the appropriate response is therefore to interfere with that Freedom of Contract. During the past decade or so the view has been gaining ground, certainly in England, that these contracts should still be left to the market, while we should try to control or handle the externalities by other governmental action. If a tenant is too poor to pay an open market rent, then the tenant should receive some state financial benefit, but the market should be left to operate freely. If employees are not paid a sufficient wage to maintain a family, then the state should contribute some family income support, rather than try to interfere in the employment contract by imposing requirements for minimum wages. Only in this way, it is now being urged, can we avoid the distorting effects on supply and demand of violent interferences with Freedom of Contract, such as result from controlled rents, or minimum wages. Of course, changes of this nature take many years to implement because another feature of modern Western democracies is an extreme tenderness to all vested rights and often even expectations derived from many years of governmental action. So, although the ideology of the New Right on these issues is becoming plain enough, we shall still have controlled tenancies and minimum wages for many years, even under the New Right themselves.

I turn now to consider those interferences with Freedom of Contract which have traditionally been justified on simple grounds of fairness or equity, without any reference to the public interest or externalities. Such interference is, of course, a highly paternalistic process, and at first sight, it seems to fly in the face of the basic principle of Freedom of Contract. The whole point of Freedom of Contract is to reject paternalism and leave the parties to their own bargain. Yet, as all lawyers know, there are many types of circumstances in which for fifty years and more the law has been busy interfering with express contractual terms on grounds of unfairness.

Furthermore, most lawyers brought up in the atmosphere prevailing after the Second World War have shown considerable sympathy with these legislative interferences with Freedom of Contract. I myself have often argued that it is impossible to ignore the idea of a fair exchange in contract law. In Essay 11 I pointed out that there are all sorts of legal doctrines which enable the courts to pursue normative criteria of fairness in handling contractual disputes, and I rejected the idea that the express terms of the contract can always be treated as a conclusive and definitive decision on what is fair. On the other hand, I must admit to a good deal of sympathy with the ideology of the New Right, so a major problem for those who think as I do is to reconcile much traditional and apparently paternalistic interference with free contract with this new ideology.

I will start by looking at a number of areas of the law in which interference with free contract has been sanctioned by many years of legislative activity. Take, for instance, the field of consumer credit. There has been a movement extending back for at least 50 years in England, but with roots going back much further than this, to protect contracting parties who enter into small credit transactions. In

England, the statutory protection of small borrowers and small credit-users against harsh and unreasonable contract terms goes back to the late nineteenth century when the first Moneylenders Act was passed, and the law was modernized and ovehauled as recently as 1974 in the Consumer Credit Act. This Act involves massive interventions with the express terms of contracts for consumer credit. The making of such contracts is regulated in minute detail, with 'cooling-off periods' enabling the debtor to withdraw from a transaction within specified periods, and requirements imposed with respect to documents and copies to be served on the debtor, some contract terms are declared void altogether, many of the creditor's remedies are restricted by the Act, for example, with respect to retaking possession of goods sold under a credit transaction. And so on. The details do not matter for present purposes: the broad outline will be familiar to lawyers in most countries where similar provisions have been introduced.

To what extent can this sort of interference with contractual freedom be reconciled with the ideology of the New Right? So far, it must be admitted, there is no sign that the New Right has any intention of turning its back on this sort of consumer protection, but that may only be because they have had weightier and more urgent matters on their agenda. In the long run, it may be questioned how far this kind of massive intervention with Freedom of Contract can be justified. But if the New Right does turn its attention to this sort of protective legislation in the future, some important distinctions will need to be drawn.

First, there is surely nothing seriously objectionable about the provisions requiring information to be given to the consumer, nor even about the cooling-off provisions. It is true that even these may seem unnecessarily fussy and over-protective in the more robust market favoured by the New Right, but the main purpose here is to ensure that the contracts do indeed have the full consent and understanding of the consumer. There is nothing contrary to Freedom of Contract ideology in that. In fact, the giving of information about true rates of interest available from suppliers of credit can be justified as an aid to the competitive market.

But I would go much further, and suggest that there is nothing in Freedom of Contract ideology which requires us to accept without question the binding validity of pages of small print, simply because they are signed by contracting parties, whether they are consumers or even commercial organizations. The truth perhaps is that the practical convenience of treating signed printed forms as binding on the parties is so great that we have far too readily accepted these forms as conclusive evidence of what the parties really intended. This may well have been a wrong turning from the beginning, and if modern protective legislation is ever to be challenged by the New Right, some fundamental rethinking on this question will surely be in order. This could be a major gain, because much of our protective legislation, like the Consumer Credit Act itself, draws no distinction between the consumer who truly understands the nature and essential terms of the contract he is entering into, and the consumer who does not. Nor will it suffice today to insist blandly that no consumers can understand the essential elements of a credit transaction. Some consumers are well informed, and others may have independent advice.

In this connection it is interesting to note that there are at least some recent judicial decisions which do seem more willing to treat consumers as rational adults, at least where they have been advised by their own lawyers. Of course this is not likely to happen with the purchase of consumer goods, but in two recent cases dealing with mortgage-loan transactions, in which consumers were advised by their own lawyers, and fully understood the nature and essential elements of the transactions, the contracts were upheld by the courts even though the terms were arguably harsh or unfair.[1] So here perhaps is a small pointer suggesting that the message of the New Right is being heard in the law courts as well as in the City of London.

The provisions of the Consumer Credit Act dealing with the creditor's security, and restricting his rights (for instance as to the retaking of possession of consumer goods) may perhaps be justified on rather different grounds. These are, of course, largely provisions dealing with security, and as the history of the English law of mortgages shows, there has long been an acceptance that interference with contractual freedom in this area is more easily justified. Not that it is sufficient to invoke history to reconcile this kind of legislation with the ideology of the New Right; but I will postpone further discussion of this for the moment because it links up with a number of other modern developments I want to address in a moment.

[1] *Multiservice Bookbinding Ltd.* v. *Malden* [1979] Ch. 84 (which did not fall within the Consumer Credit Act at all, but was challenged under traditional equity jurisdiction over unfair mortgages); *Davies* v. *Directloans* [1986] 1 WLR 823 (where the judge rejected a claim that the contract was an 'extortionate credit bargain' and so void under s. 137 of the Consumer Credit Act).

3. The Unfair Contract Terms Act 1977

The Consumer Credit Act, of course, deals with one relatively small corner of the field. But shortly after this Act was passed the consumer protection movement (which was running very strongly before the emergence of the New Right) secured the enactment of the Unfair Contract Terms Act 1977. This Act is also a highly paternalistic measure, which extends to all kinds of contracts and in that sense is much wider in scope than the Consumer Credit Act. On the other hand, it only deals, broadly speaking, with exclusion and limitation clauses, and the remedies it offers for abuse are limited to the striking down of unacceptable contract terms, so in that sense this Act is actually narrower in operation that the Consumer Credit Act.

I will not attempt any detailed summary of the Act here because it is a very intricate and complex measure. Enough to say that the Act in broad terms prohibits altogether the use of some exclusion clauses in certain types of consumer contract, particularly in contracts of sale, and subjects many other exclusion clauses (including 'standard business terms') to a test of reasonableness. This seems to mean much the same thing as a test of 'fairness', but English lawyers always prefer the word 'reasonable', with its hint of pragmatic common sense, to the word 'fairness' with its moral suggestions.

This Act was the culmination of many years of patient work by the Law Commissions, and this was itself preceded by many years of protest by academic lawyers, in particular, at the apparent harshness of many contractual exclusion clauses. So it seems almost paradoxical that so soon after the passing of this legislation the New Right should have arrived on the scene, with their renewed commitment to Freedom of Contract. What are we to make of all this? What has been the effect on this Act and the question of unfair exclusion clauses, of the appearance of the New Right? Does the 1977 Act already represent an outdated ideology? Is it doomed to be shunted into a side-line leading to a dead end? Should we already reconsider its purposes in the light of renewed faith in Freedom of Contract? How are we to answer the proponents of the New Right when they claim that even a consumer is perfectly capable of looking after his own interests, and should be bound by a contractual exclusion provided that he clearly understood and agreed to it? And some kind of answer we must give because this consumer may well protest that he is paying more for his goods or services as a result of this sort of protective legislation. That the 'beneficiaries' of protective legislation may not always appreciate the value of these benefits in the modern age of the New Right has already been demonstrated in a different field. In 1986 the Sex Discrimination Act of that year repealed many statutory restrictions on the working hours of women, because the Government and also many feminist bodies took the view that such restrictions actually penalized women in the labour market. Though it may also be that the requirements of the law of the EEC determined this result, it is easy to see that in the modern world most women do not feel that they are in fact benefited by such protective legislation. If they do not want to work for longer house than the law permits, they need not accept that particular employment; while if they think that the extra hours are adequately compensated by the remuneration, the law prohibits them from acting as they think best. How are we to say whether the ordinary consumer who is now protected against unfair or un-reasonable exclusion clauses is not in the same way being given a protection he does not want, for a price he does not wish to pay?

One thing at least has happened since the New Right appeared on the scene, and that is that the judges appear to have decided that paternalistic interference with Freedom of Contract should now be left to Parliament. In the *Photo Productions* case[1] in 1980 the House of Lords, after the passing of the Unfair Contract Terms Act, reaffirmed their general faith in the freedom anyhow of commercial parties to make their own contracts, subject only to the terms of the Act. The idea that the common law actually restricts the freedom of business parties to protect themselves against the consequences even of the most fundamental breaches of contract was finally and summarily rejected. More recently, in *National Westminster Bank* v. *Morgan*[2] the House of Lords has 'questioned' whether any general principle of 'unconscionability' is needed to protect even consumers against unfair contracts after the passing of the Act. Thus Freedom of Contract seems to have been re-established as the ideology of the common law, in accordance with the views of the New Right. So we are left with the 1977 Act, and with the questions I posed a moment ago about its compatibility with the ideology of the New Right.

I do not think that these are easy questions. So far the English answer to them has either been non-existent or highly pragmatic. When we look at some of the exclusion clauses in the cases they seem so absurd or outrageous that little theoretical justification seems to

[1] [1980] AC 827.
[2] [1985] AC 686.

be needed to strike them down. But the outcome leaves me uneasy. We must always remember that what seems absurd or outrageous to lawyers is often merely the result of professional traditions and culture. The House of Lords itself has, for instance, recently pointed out[1] that a clause in a building contract which freed the builder from responsibility for damage done by fire could not be considered absurd or outrageous (as the lower court had thought) merely because the builder might have to redo the work damaged by the fire and thereby earn extra profit from his own negligence. The point of the clause was simply to allocate responsibility for insurance, insisted the House of Lords, and this was a perfectly normal commercial arrangement, even though it might produce anomalous results in some respects.

So it is hardly good enough to rely on a common sense intuition about absurdity or outrageousness if we want to strike down exclusion clauses, even where they have clearly been understood and agreed to. Some more principled answers, some satisfactory theoretical justification for doing so must be found if we are to head off the New Right before they turn their attention to these statutory provisions. I will not pretend to offer any definitive answers here, but I will suggest a number of lines which seem to me to provide us with possible answers to these questions.

The first I have already hinted at. I do not think that we can continue to assume that written or printed contracts, signed or not, are conclusive evidence of what contracting parties have agreed to. No matter how much sanctity one is prepared to allow to genuine bargains and agreements it surely flies in the face of all reality to treat written or printed contracts as though they themselves had been gone through clause by clause, word by word, and thoroughly accepted and understood by both parties. Of course I do not say this is never the case, but only that it is very often *not* the case, even in commercial contexts, and still more in consumer contexts, and that we cannot just assume, because the parties have adopted the written documents as their contract, whether by signature or otherwise, that this somehow proves that they have done so.

In this connection I must stress that it is not merely the written terms of the contract which are important. It is also their legal effect, indeed their effect is actually more important than the words themselves. Now the legal effect of contractual terms includes many matters which constitute huge chapters of the law of contract itself,

[1] *Scottish Special Housing Association* v. *Wimpey Construction UK Ltd.* [1986] 1

such as, for example, the implication of terms concerning the duties of the parties, and the law relating to remoteness of damages, and what kinds of damages a party is liable for in the event of breach. These great bodies of contract law are voluminous; many of us have devoted years to their study, and even at the most elementary level, a whole year's course on the Law of Contract is to be found in almost every law school in the world. When most contracting parties adopt the terms of a written contract they know very little about such matters. If they think about these matters at all, they rely on the law to provide fair and reasonable answers to the questions which may arise. Of course I do not deny that customary and reasonable standards of behaviour will often assist the courts to arrive at what the fair and reasonable answer to these legal questions may be. But what I do deny is that these results can sensibly be attributed in most cases to what the parties actually agreed to or intended. As Lord Reid once said, only a lawyer would think of saying that because the natural result of the bad stroke which a golfer has played is that his ball has gone into the bunker, it must be assumed that he intended to hit the ball into the bunker.

Now some adherents of the New Right have a sort of answer to these arguments. They urge that even though the contracting parties may not actually have foreseen or contemplated all the problems which may arise, and assented to all the legal effects which the terms of their contract will be held to import, still we must treat them as though they had done so. The reason for this, they say, is that contracting parties must realize that the law provides some solution to the various possible problems, and if they choose not to inquire into the precise nature of that solution, this is because they are willing to assume the risk of the solution being adverse to their rights, in the interests of saving costs. So although they may not *actually* know or understand or agree to the full meaning and implication of the contract terms, we must treat them as though they have done so, since they have consciously decided that it is not worth the extra cost of themselves doing these things. Now this 'fast shuffle' as Professor Fried has called it,[1] by which ignorance is somehow deemed to be knowledge, must, it seems to me, be rejected. As I have pointed out on a previous occasion,[2] this is an empirical question, and not a

WLR 995.

[1] See Fried, *Right and Wrong* (1978), p. 101.
[2] See Essay 11, p. 351 above.

necessary deduction from the facts. There are many cases in which the parties have not even appreciated the risk of the problem arising, let alone the risk that the law may deal with it in a particular way, and therefore the parties have made no further examination of these questions, not because they decide the benefits are not worth the risk, but because they do not perceive the risks at all. This therefore takes me back to my starting-point: we cannot just assume that all written and printed contract terms represent the full understanding and agreement of contracting parties, although in some particular cases they may do so.

However, this is an answer which lawyers are naturally very reluctant to accept because they perceive at once that there are enormous practical conveniences in treating the written terms of a contractual document as conclusive of these matters, and they do not see where we could draw the line if once we permit a general inquiry into whether the parties really did agree to and understand the implications of their contract. I share these feelings, though I am pretty sure that more rigid adherence to Freedom of Contract will simply not be found tolerable unless we can find some practical way to modify the law on this question. While I have no general solution to this difficulty to offer now, I want to suggest that there are at least some circumstances in which we can know or perhaps guess with reasonable accuracy that the terms of a written contract do not actually represent what the parties either did intend or agree to, or even what they would have intended or agreed to if they had thought about it. Furthermore, I want to suggest that the common law has over many centuries already been groping its way to recognition of this fact, although the new legislation has brought to light certain additional points which the law now needs to develop more fully.

4. Written Contracts not Reflecting True Intentions
So I turn now to examine some of these cases. A clue to the nature of the circumstances I have in mind may be provided if we start by asking why the contracting parties should ever prepare their contracts in such a way that they do not represent what they really intended. Although at first sight this may seem an odd thing to do, legal experience at once provides some answers. Consider first, the penalty clause which is inserted in a contract, not because either party intends that it should be invoked, but as a deterrent and a threat. The party

threatened plainly does not intend to face the consequences because he does not intend to breach the contract; but even the other party has no wish that the clause should be invoked, nor does he expect to receive the benefits of the penalty clause as part of the price of his bargain. Indeed, the very definition of a penalty clause is designed to distinguish between such a clause and a liquidated damages clause which *does* represent part of the price of the bargain. When a contract is so breached that the innocent party's primary purposes are no longer capable of fulfilment, he is no doubt entitled to be compensated for that, because the intent of the parties in making the contract is that these primary purposes should be fulfilled, or compensation paid for their non-fulfilment. But the enforcement of a penalty clause is never one of the primary purposes of the contract, and nobody wishes, *ex ante*, that the clause should ever be enforced. The purpose of a penalty clause is to bring pressure, to threaten, and if the contract is broken anyhow, the clause has failed of its purpose. Just as the threat of criminal punishment fails when a crime is committed, so this is true also of a penalty clause; equally, infliction of the penalty could then be justified for the purposes of deterring future breaches, like future crimes, but it cannot be justified by treating it as part of a bargained-for contractual price.

So it seems to me clear that the common law's traditional refusal to enforce penalty clauses shows an intuitive understanding that such clauses are not genuine contractual promises or obligations. They are fakes, masquerading as contractual promises. Any attempt by the New Right to argue that the non-enforcement of penalty clauses is inconsistent with the ideology of Freedom of Contract would therefore be, in my view, erroneous, and simplistic. Unhappily, it must be recorded that for the last decade the House of Lords, apparently strongly influenced by the New Right, has been turning its back on the traditional common law approach to this field, and has insisted repeatedly on the literal enforcement of provisions which in substance and often in intent also, appear penal.

There are, in particular, two sets of cases which seem to me to show a formalistic approach to the question of enforcement of penalties, a failure to understand when the enforcement of such clauses is, and when it is not, inconsistent with the fundamental principle of Freedom of Contract. The first case relates to a problem which surprisingly surfaced relatively recently in English law, namely, does the law of penalties apply to any payment clause in a contract, or only to a clause requiring payments to be made in the event of a breach of contract? The problem first came to prominence in hire-purchase contracts which commonly used to provide (before modern legislation made the practice ineffective) that if the hiring was prematurely terminated *either* by breach, *or* by the hirer returning the goods (which he was entitled to do), he would then be liable to make additional payments to the owner, which were often penal in amount. In such a case it was clear law that if the hirer broke the contract, the court could strike down the additional payments clause as a penalty. But suppose the hirer honestly and lawfully returned the goods, what then? In *Bridge* v. *Campbell Discount Co.*[1] the Court of Appeal held that the law relating to penalties had no application in that case, and the hirer had to pay in full. On appeal to the House of Lords,[2] it was held that the hirer had actually broken his contract so that the clause could be struck down as a penalty, but the judges were evenly divided on whether this would still have been possible if the hirer had not breached the contract. Little comment was made in the appeal on the absurd fact that the hirer won his appeal by persuading the House of Lords that he had been guilty of a breach of contract—surely (as I once wrote) the first contracting party in history to do that! Now, in the *ECGD*[3] case in 1983 the House of Lords has finally confirmed the absurdity of this situation as part of the common law. The law relating to penalties, it was held, does not apply to any payment to be made on an event other than a breach of contract. The actual result in this case may well have been quite sound, but the reasoning, as I have suggested, looks formalistic. Surely the question should be what the clause is designed to achieve, what is the purpose of the clause, and that is not something which should be settled definitively by the terms of the written contract. I fear that the case illustrates a modern and simplistic belief that Freedom of Contract requires such clauses to be enforced.

The second field in which the House of Lords has shown its determination to enforce what are in substance penal clauses concerns forfeiture provisions, an area in which the law had not until recently been fully developed. There has of course been a very long tradition that the forfeiture of mortgaged lands is not permissible in Equity, whatever the mortgage contract may say, merely because of a failure

[1] [1961] 1 QB 445.
[2] [1962] AC 600.
[3] [1983] 1 WLR 399.

by the borrower to pay interest or repay the capital on the due date. But in other fields it has not been clear whether such equitable relief is available to help a defaulting party. As late as 1973 there were important dicta in the House of Lords indicating that a residual equitable jurisdiction remained and could be invoked to strike down forfeiture clauses of various kinds,[1] but since then the House of Lords has repeatedly declined to do this. A whole stream of new cases can unfortunately be cited to show this modern trend in the House of Lords. First, there has been a series of charter-party cases, in which a ship-owner has been held entitled to withdraw the vessel on the failure of the hirer to pay the charter money, promptly and precisely on the due date.[2] In this connection it must be remembered that in the common law, it is not necessary for an innocent party to give notice of default, or to call on the other party to perform, before he invokes his rights under the contract, so that these decisions enable a ship-owner to cancel a charter, even when the ship is already *en route*, loaded with a cargo, for the most technical and trivial of breaches.

Another drastic decision was to come in 1984.[3] In this case the plaintiffs were the makers of sports shoes overseas, and they had licensed the defendants to distribute their goods in England and to use their trade name. The parties had already litigated, and compromised their dispute in an agreement under which the defendants were to pay £105,000 to the plaintiffs for continuation of a licence to use the plaintiffs' name. The money was to be paid in three instalments, the first at once, which was paid, the second and third over a period of time. The defendants also agreed to provide a bank guarantee for payment of the second and third instalments. The guarantee was duly provided for the second instalment, and when that instalment was paid, the defendants intended and expected the guarantee to be rolled over to secure the payment of the third. Unfortunately there was a technical hitch, partly at least because the bank would not allow the guarantee to cover the third instalment until they were assured that the second had been paid, and the plaintiffs failed to provide immediate assurance to this effect. It was held that this trivial delay was a sufficient breach to entitle the plaintiffs to cancel the agreement and withdraw the defendants' licence to use their name. Of course this

[1] *Shiloh Spinners* case [1973] AC 691, at 722; see also *The Georgias C* [1971] 1 All ER 193, which as overruled in *The Laconia* [1977] AC 850.

[2] *The Laconia*, above; *The Chikuma* [1981] 1 All ER 652; *The Scaptrade* [1983] 2 AC 694.

[3] *Sport International Bussum BV* v. *InterFootwear Ltd.* [1984] 2 All ER 321.

was a highly penal result. It is interesting to note that the leading speech of Lord Templeman insists here that the court did not know the purpose of the forfeiture clause, or how much importance the parties attached to it; in other words, the House of Lords was taking refuge in the Freedom of Contract idea that the parties were the best and only judges of what they were trying to achieve. Here again, one gets an echo of nineteenth-century cases,[1] where equally the courts refused to speculate on the purpose of contract clauses although some modern cases had already departed from this doctrine,[2] and it seems obvious enough that penalty clauses cannot be identified without an examination of the purpose behind the clause.

Eventually, the Court of Appeal drew back from some of these extreme positions in 1985 in *BICC* v. *Burndy Ltd.*[3] where the court refused to allow a party to insist on forfeiting the other's share in some valuable patent rights in accordance with the terms of the contract, as a result of a relatively trivial breach in paying a sum demanded by the plaintiffs. The court insisted that there still was a jurisdiction to relieve against forfeiture of property rights although not of purely contractual rights, and patent rights were property rights for this purpose. So we are left with an absurd distinction between patent rights and commercial licensing agreements, though perhaps that is only because the *BICC* case did not go to the House of Lords.

Other cases could also be cited in which the House of Lords has recently declined to contemplate relief against forfeiture, in effect enforcing contracts with literalness and apparent harshness.[4] Given the dating of these cases, and the apparent change of front since the 1970s, they certainly provide some ground for thinking that the ideology of the New Right has been influential here. As I have already said, these cases seem to me mistaken in thinking that this is what a sophisticated analysis of the demands of the New Right should really require.

---

[1] See e.g. *Bowes* v. *Shand* (1877) 2 App. Cas. 455 (buyer entitled to reject goods shipped too soon because court could not speculate why buyer wanted the goods shipped then).

[2] See e.g. *Reardon Smith Lines* v. *Hansen Tangen* [1976] 1 WLR 989 (House of Lords inquired into purpose of a clause that a ship be built at a particular named shipyard, and held this to be of no practical importance).

[3] [1985] Ch. 232.

[4] See e.g. *Hyundai Heavy Industries* v. *Papadopoulos* [1980] 1 WLR 1129 (defaulting buyer of ship obliged to pay instalment due before seller cancelled contract, regardless of amount of seller's loss).

A second type of case where contracting parties put things into their contracts which they do not necessarily intend to adhere to is illustrated by the first case to reach the House of Lords under the Unfair Contract Terms Act. In the *George Mitchell* case,[1] the sellers sold early cabbage seed to the buyers, but supplied a different and inferior variety which totally failed. The contract contained a very tight limitation clause under which the seller's liability would have been confined to refunding the value of the seeds, even though in fact the buyers had actually lost many thousands of pounds, through wasted expenditure on planting the seed, and later clearing the failed crop. The House of Lords held that the clause was unreasonable under the new Act, and the most important point, which seemed almost conclusive, was that suppliers of seeds were shown not to rely on such clauses in practice. Compensation was usually paid despite the presence of such a clause. Why then did the suppliers use the clause, and why did they not pay in the instant case? The answer is surely clear enough: suppliers put such clauses into their contracts because they want to reserve the right to judge for themselves whether they think a claim is well founded, and not be dragged before courts and judges who (they believe) may not understand the realities or may be deceived by the buyers. And presumably they refused to pay in the instant case because they doubted the legitimacy of the claim, though once before the courts they made no attempt to suggest that the claim was not bona fide.

Now if that is indeed the purpose of such clauses, (and there are other cases illustrating that purpose also[2]) then there is, I think, very good ground for striking them down, even though that appears contrary to the principle of Freedom of Contract. Because it will be seen that in this case the contracting parties do not intend to deny the right to compensation for legitimate complaints, they only intend to deny the jurisdiction of the courts to decide on what is a legitimate complaint. And that in turn is totally inadmissible because it seeks to make the guilty party a judge in his own cause—a procedural monstrosity which is contrary to the most fundamental principles of

[1] [1983] 2 AC 803.

[2] For other examples of contracting parties using terms designed to enable them to judge of the validity of such claims, see *The Zinnia* [1984] 2 Lloyd's Rep. 211 (shiprepairers' contract required ship to be returned to their yard to ascertain if work faulty); perhaps also *R. W. Green* v. *Cade Bros. Farms* [1978] 1 Lloyd's Rep. 602 (sale of defective potatoes, clause requiring defects to be notified in three days, but defects not discoverable till crop began to grow).

justice, and to ancient principles of the common law. So here too it seems to me that there are very good grounds for striking down exclusion or limitation clauses which appear to have this end in view, and that doing so should not be thought to violate the fundamental principle of Freedom of Contract. The intention of the parties on a side issue is negatived but only in order to give effect to their intention on the fundamentals.

5. Paternalism and the New Right

So far I have argued that there are real grounds for interfering with Freedom of Contract which do not conflict with the ideology of the New Right, at least on a sophisticated understanding of what the New Right stands for. But I now come to a more difficult area. It is not a novel insight that many forms of consumer protection operate in effect like insurance policies. When a consumer is given statutory rights in respect of defective goods, or misleading holiday brochures, the other contracting party is liable to some degree as though he were insuring the consumer against the risk of buying a defective car or a miserable holiday. And when these rights cannot be bargained away by exclusion clauses, the consumer is in effect being given a form of compulsory insurance. But nothing is free in this world, and this compulsory insurance has to be paid for. Indeed, in the long run, it must be paid for by the consumers themselves in the form of increased charges. The problem then is that if we force the consumer to pay for insurance which he does not want, we are making him spend his money contrary to his own inclination, and thus distorting the operation of the market, as well as interfering with the private rights of the consumer to choose how he wishes to spend his money. So there undoubtedly is a real form of paternalism in this sort of legislative interference with Freedom of Contract, and the New Right has certainly made many of us more aware that there are risks involved.

Still, compulsory insurance can sometimes be justified, and perhaps even reconciled with the ideology of the New Right. For instance, legislation which compels working people to make provision for their retirement pensions is no doubt partly paternalistic but it can be justified because if elderly people have no income when they are unable to work, the rest of the population will, in Western societies, be obliged to care for them. This is, therefore, an example of paternalism which is closely linked with the externalities problem.[1]

But this justification does not hold good for many of the modern forms of statutory protection. The provisions of the Unfair Contract Terms Act, for instance, which prevent a seller of goods from contracting out of his liability for selling defective goods, cannot be justified in this way. There are great difficulties in reconciling these provisions with the general stand of the New Right. After all, their primary effect is not to give rights to those who would choose to buy them anyhow—because those who would choose to buy those rights should be able to do so in the market in the ordinary way. The primary effect of the Act is to prevent those who would not choose to buy these rights in the market from buying the goods or services without the rights attached. Why should we prevent these buyers from exercising their freedom of choice? This is on the face of it pure paternalism: the law tells the buyer that he does not know what is in his own best interest, and that if he wants to buy certain goods or services he must buy certain rights as a sort of compulsory extra. I can only think of three possible ways in which this interference with free choice can be justified according to the ideology of the New Right. First, it might be justified by arguing that too many buyers do not in fact understand what is involved in buying such goods or services without protective rights. But in that case the right course seems to be to insist that contractual terms must reflect real understandings more closely than the present law requires. It would not be difficult, for instance, to throw an onus on to a seller requiring him to show that exclusion clauses have been clearly brought home to the mind of the buyer so that the buyer really understood what he was giving up. A mere signature on a printed document should not suffice.

Second, it might be said that markets are in practice very imperfect and that too often buyers do not really have the choice to buy goods or services with or without protective rights. Certainly this was largely true of the situation in England (and perhaps other countries) at the

---

[1] It is interesting to see how even in the Conservative Government's new Social Security Act 1986 which entitles employed people to make their own pension arrangements if they choose, rather than be compelled to join an occupational pension scheme, the enhancement of freedom of choice in the first respect requires that the employee's freedom of contract should be restricted: see s. 15 of the Act which makes void any contractual clause in an employment contract compelling employees to join the employers' own pension scheme in future.

time when exclusion clauses first became a major legal problem. But
I do not think it is true today. Consumers today do often have a wide
choice, not only as to the kinds of goods or services they want to
buy, but also as to the terms on which they are supplied. Paradoxically,
the Unfair Contract Terms Act actually restricts the freedom of choice
of the market in this respect. Without the Act, goods and services
might be very generally available today, with and without protective
terms, depending on the prices charged. And if the market fails to
provide this degree of choice, the right solution should be to free the
market so that the choices are available.

Thirdly, it might be argued that the overwhelming majority of
consumers would, if given the choice, buy the protective terms, and
pay the extra costs involved, and that in practice the best way of
ensuring that they are not misled or confused is to prohibit the
contracting out process altogether. So although a few people may
suffer a diminution of their freedom of choice in the market, this
would prove a small price to pay for the benefit of the great majority.
It does, however, depend on an empirical base, whose foundations
may be uncertain. It must, of course, be clear that the argument
depends on the assumption that the overwhelming majority of
consumers would choose to buy the statutory rights if given the choice,
and it will not do to suggest merely that a bare majority of them
might do so. On the whole I think this argument is probably well
founded, and is the best justification of the Act which is consistent
with the New Right.

This discussion does show that the justification for statutory
provisions of this kind is going to be a much more difficult matter in
the future, if they are going to be tested by the criteria favoured by
the New Right. And indeed, the application of the 'reasonableness'
test under the statutory provisions already gives rise to difficulties of
this kind. I will give here just one very difficult illustration of this
problem, which is, indeed, raised in some cases recently decided by
the House of Lords.[1] This problem arises from the use of disclaimer
clauses by surveyors who value houses and flats on behalf of
mortgagees. Unfortunately, it sometimes happens today that houses
turn out to have serious hidden defects which are not discovered by
surveyors or buyers until long after the buyer has completed his
purchase and gone into occupation.

Until recently the buyer had no remedy in this situation unless he

[1] *Smith* v. *Eric S. Bush* [1989] 2 All ER 514.

had instructed his own surveyor under a separate contract. But most buyers do not do this. They have to pay for the mortgagee's valuation, and although they are often not permitted to see the valuer's report, they may well assume that if a mortgage is offered to them, this is proof that the valuer has found nothing seriously wrong with the house. In 1982 it was held for the first time in England that a buyer could sue a surveyor in tort for a negligent valuation in these circumstances.[1] Surveyors were divided in their reaction to this decision. Some accepted it, and doubtless modified their charges accordingly. But others inserted disclaimers into their reports and insisted that mortgagees inform the buyer that the surveyor accepted no liability to him. These clauses raised the question of the applicability of the Unfair Contract Terms Act, and they also raised an issue of reasonableness under that Act.

In the result the House of Lords held that these disclaimers were governed by the Unfair Contract Terms Act, and they then went on to hold that the disclaimers in the cases before them were void as unreasonable. Are these results defensible in light of the ideology of the New Right? Should buyers, in effect, be compelled to buy this form of insurance protection? Would the overwhelming majority choose to do so if they had the choice? It may be said that they do have the choice, because they could instruct their own surveyors, but they do not generally do this. So it may seem that they have already demonstrated that they do not want this form of insurance. But I do not think this is a full answer, simply because of the practicalities of the situation. Buyers who instruct their own surveyors are normally expected to pay for a full structural survey which is much more costly than a simple valuation—all that the mortgage survey covers. And it seems absurd for a buyer to commission his own valuation when he already has to pay (through the mortgagee) for the mortgagee's valuation. Another argument pressed on the House of Lords was that some building societies (not involved in the cases before them) did actually offer to accept liability but only in return for a very much higher fee—a fee which the House of Lords clearly thought bore no relationship to the extra risks entailed. Thus the market does not at present effectively give the buyer a free choice. Only if a market

[1] *Yianni* v. *Edwin Evans* [1982] QB 438.

developed in which this form of insurance[1] was clearly and easily available to buyers would this be an adequate answer.[2]

I have two other illustrations of this sort of problem, both of which relate to consumer remedies rather than the substantive rights themselves. But the issue with regard to the extensiveness of the legal remedies is identical with the issues with regard to the actual rights. The more generous the remedies, the more expensive the rights are, and the greater the cost the consumer ultimately has to pay. So we must be sure, not only that the consumer would nearly always believe it is worth buying the rights we are forcing him to buy, but that he also would agree to buy the remedies which go with those rights.

My first illustration of this kind relates to a common consumer complaint in England. It is widely suggested that manufacturers and retailers are hardly ever willing to accept the rejection of a new car or other vehicle, however defective it may prove to be, and whatever the consumer's theoretical legal rights may be. Some redress may be obtained out of court, in the form of free repairs, or even monetary compensation, but a consumer who actually wishes to reject a new vehicle will nearly always be compelled to litigate; and furthermore, the right to reject is generally held to have been lost within a very short time.[3] Now, speaking for myself, I should really like to know how much it would add to the cost of new car if consumers were entitled to reject them for defects much more easily than they are today. It seems to me quite possible that the extra cost could be a significant item which I, and many other consumers, would perhaps prefer not to pay. If this is the situation, then any attempt to force the consumer to 'buy' this right by interfering with his Freedom of Contract may well turn out to be unacceptable. Nor is it an adequate answer to this to say that if consumers could reject more easily, manufacturers would be compelled to take more care to ensure cars were not defective, because that too would cost more money which the consumer would have to pay for in the end.

A second illustration of a similar problem arises from the present practice of the courts of awarding substantial damages for distress

[1] Of course even then it would only be limited insurance, since it only operates if the valuer has been negligent.

[2] For the same reason it is not an adequate answer to say that the buyer, in the individualist world favoured by the New Right, should not rely on the mortgagee's surveyor, but on himself (or advice he has paid for): the market arrangements are too imperfect to make this a satisfactory answer.

[3] See *Bernstein* v. *Pamson Motors* (*Golders Green*) *Ltd.* [1987] 2 All ER 220.

and vexation to disappointed holidaymakers who are able to establish a breach of contract by holiday operators.[1] As we all know, some people take minor disappointments of this kind lightly, or shrug them off altogether; others become very indignant and magnify their grievances. The present position seems to require the former group to pay insurance premiums to compensate the latter. The lessons which the New Right teaches may make us challenge the acceptability of this kind of result of interfering with Freedom of Contract.

6. Non-consensual Liability and the New Right

I come now to some more general questions about the interrelationship between the law of contract and the rest of the law of private obligations, and, in particular, the law of tort. In the past few decades it has become obvious, certainly in England, and I suspect elsewhere also, that the great expansions which have been taking place in the law of tort are to some extent related to the law of contract. Tort law, and to some degree also the law of unjust enrichment, expand into areas where there is, or was in classical contract theory, no liability at all. It is obvious that these developments have a profound effect on the law of contract, because that law (to borrow a phrase which has been used of tort law) was not only a law of liability but also a law of no-liability. If, and in so far as, modern tort law or the law of unjust enrichment expand into areas where there was no liability in contract law, is this, then, somehow illegitimate? Is it in derogation of proper principles of contract law? Or, to put the question in a form specially relevant to the theme of this Essay, is it contrary to the ideology of the New Right?

In the past I and a number of other writers have crossed swords with Professor Fried on this issue. He has argued[2] that there is nothing inconsistent with classical contract theory in developing and expanding non-consensual forms of liability, through the medium of tort and unjust enrichment; and classical contract theory updated and refined by Professor Fried is pretty close, if not identical, to what I have called the ideology of the New Right. The fact that there is no liability in contract law is, he says, simply no reason at all why community

---

[1] The practice was first sanctioned by the decision in *Jarvis* v. *Swan Tours* [1973] QB 233, and though little High Court litigation has been reported since then, it is apparent (for example, from cases noted in *Current Law*) that many County Court cases are brought every year in which such damages are obtained, sometimes on a surprisingly generous scale.

[2] See Charles Fried, *Contract as Promise: A Study in Contractual Obligation* (1981).

values, expressed through tort and unjust enrichment principles, should not create a liability. On the other hand I have previously argued[1] that this is unreal, that classical contract theory historically rested on a background of very restricted non-consensual forms of liability, and that if these forms of liability are to be expanded in all directions to fill in real or apparent gaps in the law of contract, this is to make nonsense of classical theory.

I now want to offer some further reflections on this theme, a theme which gains greatly in importance as, on the one hand, the ideology of the New Right spreads, and, on the other hand, the law of tort is increasingly relied upon in new areas and cases where traditionally contract law alone held sway. I suggest that the expansion of non-consensual forms of liability into areas left vacant by the law of contract is sometimes inconsistent with the ideology of the New Right, and sometimes not. It is, I suggest, inconsistent with that ideology where the reason for the absence of contractual liability is that the party who it is sought to make liable clearly did not wish to accept that liability. On the other hand, it is not inconsistent with the ideology of the New Right to impose liability in tort or through unjust enrichment principles where the reason why there is no contractual liability is that the law of contract contains arbitrary and perhaps technical restrictions on liability not themselves dependent on the intentions of the parties concerned.

This distinction will not answer all the problems, but is does provide some sort of matrix, I suggest, by which to test or measure some of the current problems concerning the existence of tort liability in new areas. Let me now look at some recent cases with which I can illustrate this distinction. It will be seen that although a few of these recent cases lend support to my suggestion, others do not. However, I am not disheartened by this. My purpose is to offer a framework which can be relied upon in the future, rather than to provide a theory which explains what is happening today. Indeed, I doubt whether any theory can explain what is happening in English tort law today because the judges seem to me to be floundering around with a total absence of theoretical help, on an entirely *ad hoc*, case by case, basis.

Let me start with a case of no great authority, which has even escaped being reported in the major series of Law Reports, but which is a very good illustration of the distinction I have drawn. In *Crossan*

---

[1] See my review of Fried's book, in 95 *Harv. Law Rev.* 509 (1981).

v. *Ward Bracewell*[1] the plaintiff, who had been involved in a road accident causing much damage, was charged with reckless driving, and he consulted the defendant, a solicitor. The defendant started by telling the plaintiff that he could either plead guilty to the charge, in which case he would not need a solicitor, or he could plead not guilty, in which case the defendant would act for him but would require a deposit of £50 against his costs. The plaintiff decided to plead guilty, and left without instructing the defendant. Later the plaintiff was sued for the damage involved, and it transpired that he had failed to inform his insurers of the reckless driving charge, so they repudiated liability under the policy as they were entitled to do. The plaintiff now sued the defendant in tort for negligence, claiming that a reasonable solicitor should have realized that the plaintiff's insurance probably provided cover against the costs of a criminal charge, and if he had investigated the policy, he would have seen that this was indeed so. Further, if the defendant had done that, the plaintiff would then have instructed him to act for him, and the defendant would then have informed the insurers who would not then have been able to repudiate liability. So the defendant was held liable. Now this case seems to me very questionable if it is tested by the criteria I have suggested. The defendant clearly did not enter into a contract with the plaintiff, and showed an unwillingness to do so unless the plaintiff made the £50 deposit. That may have been foolish and careless for the reasons already given, but Freedom of Contract demands that we all be free to make or refuse to make contracts for reasons which appear good to us, not for reasons which appear good to judges. Indeed, even conventional tort doctrine says that in circumstances like these, a defendant should not be liable unless he has voluntarily assumed a liability, almost the equivalent of contract.[2] Why then was he held liable here? Apparently because the judge thought that by telling the plaintiff the two courses open to him, the defendant had voluntarily assumed a responsibility for giving him careful advice as to how he was to meet the criminal charge. But this seems wrong to me: if the case is thought of along contractual lines, the matter had clearly not proceeded beyond the stage of negotiation. The parties were discussing a contract, that is they were discussing the possible voluntary assumption of responsibility by the defendant solicitor, but he had not yet reached the stage of accepting that responsibility. To make a

---

[1] (1986) 136 New LJ 849.

[2] This is the principle of the *Hedley Byrne* case [1964] AC 465.

defendant liable in tort in such circumstances seems to me to flout the fundamental principle of contract law that a person should not have a liability imposed on him without his consent, in circumstances where *that consent is the very basis of the tort liability suggested.*

My second illustration involves a number of recent English cases concerning the liability in tort of subcontractors or suppliers of materials to contractors for use in building contracts. This line of cases starts, in one sense, with *Donoghue* v. *Stevenson*[1] as far back as 1932, where liability was imposed on the manufacturer of defective products for bodily injuries suffered by a consumer of those products. But in modern times the problem became far more serious with the *Junior Books*[2] case in 1982. In this case a building owner was permitted to sue a subcontractor in tort for the bad construction of a floor which had to be replaced. The House of Lords here relied heavily on *Donoghue* v. *Stevenson* for the proposition that an absence of liability in contract was no ground for denying liability in tort. What the House of Lords do not seem to have appreciated, however, is that the mere absence of liability in contract is a different matter from a deliberate *refusal* to accept responsibility in contract. In the case of large and complex building and engineering works, the modern practice has for a long time been to separate the role of subcontractors and suppliers from the role of the contractor. There simply is no point in this elaborate set of commercial arrangements if the various parties are all liable for negligence in tort anyhow; for if they are liable in tort, it will only be a short time before they are held entitled to sue in unjust enrichment for the benefits they confer and the whole commercial edifice will be stripped away. If we follow the ideology of the New Right we must assume that businessmen who adopt these sorts of contractual arrangements deliberately intend *not* to assume tort liabilities to the other contracting parties involved. Fortunately, in this instance, it now seems reasonably clear that the *Junior Books* case is one of those cases which is destined to be cast aside, for a whole new line of cases has restricted its authority as a precedent in a number of different directions. In particular, there are now several decisions[3] which do take very much the line I have been suggesting, and conclude that suppliers of components or goods to manufacturers

---

[1] [1932] AC 562.

[2] [1983] 1 AC 520.

[3] *Muirhead* v. *Industrial Tank Specialities* [1986] QB 507; *Simaan General Contracting Co.* v. *Pilkington Glass Ltd.* [1988] 1 All ER 791; *D. & F. Estates Ltd.* v. *Church Commissioners* [1988] 2 All ER 992.

or builders are not to have imposed on them a liability in tort which makes a mockery of the contractual arrangements. In one of these cases, decided in 1988, indeed, Bingham LJ specifically denied tort liability on the very ground that the supplier of the goods in question had not assumed a direct liability to the contractor, because such a liability 'would be inconsistent with the structure of the contract the parties ha[d] chosen to make.'[1]

My third illustration here is the case of *Ross* v. *Caunters*[2] decided in 1979. Here it was held that a solicitor whose negligence in the preparation of a will causes a legacy to fail can be sued by the disappointed legatee in tort, even though there is no contractual liability. Approached along the lines I have suggested, this decision seems perfectly acceptable. The absence of liability in contract in such circumstances is not because the solicitor did not want or intend to assume a responsibility to the third party, but because this person was debarred from suing by the privity of contract doctrine. Since this doctrine often obstructs the implementation of contracting parties' intentions, there is nothing against the ideology of the New Right in outflanking the doctrine where that is the case. Of course there will often be difficulty in saying whether the effects of the privity doctrine are in line with the parties' intentions—as in the building contract cases mentioned above—or conflict with the parties' intentions. Very often, as in *Ross* v. *Caunters*, the parties probably have no intention on the matter at all, and in this situation I see no objection to liability being imposed in tort. Perhaps the decision in *The Aliakmon*[3] is another example of a case in which the elaborate commercial arrangements of the parties would have been evaded if liability had been imposed in tort, although that is a difficult and border-line case from this point of view.

There is, however, one broader and very difficult issue which cannot be explored in any detail here, but which I shall just mention, and that concerns the expanding area of liability for economic loss in tort. Because contract law has traditionally imposed liability for economic loss, while such claims have hitherto been generally denied in tort in the common law at least, it seems plausible to suggest that many modern claims for economic loss in tort are attempts to evade restrictions on contractual liability. The question then arises whether

---

[1] [1988] 1 All ER at p. 803.
[2] [1979] 3 All ER 590.
[3] [1986] AC 875.

this evasion is at odds with the New Right. Are there good reasons why economic loss claims should not be more readily permitted in tort law in those cases where contract law denies liability?

Sometimes it does seem to me clear that these claims for economic loss in tort are attempts to evade limits on contractual liability, and that these limits are perfectly sound in principle, and should not be evaded. The *Muirhead* case[1] illustrates this well enough. Here the plaintiff used the defendant manufacturer's electric pumps to maintain the water circulation in his lobster tanks, and when the pumps proved defective for English conditions, he lost many of the lobsters. The Court of Appeal allowed his claim for the actual death of the lobsters but refused his claim for lost profits. When the figures are looked at, it will be seen that by far the greater part of this claim was for loss of anticipated profits from a new and untried business. These losses were claimed on a generous scale, and the attempt to secure recovery in tort for such losses seems to me quite illegitimate. It only derives apparent plausibility because of the long-standing tradition and practice of our lawyers of separating out issues of liability from issues of quantum. Yet contract liability is meaningless except in the context of liability for a particular kind of damages. Now economic loss is nearly always a species of expectation damages—an economic loss must be a loss of an expectation, unless the loss is the quantification of a physical loss or injury—and expectation damages are the hallmark of contractual liability. But this is because in the traditional bargain or exchange relationship the parties specifically contract with a view to certain expectations. Where expectations are genuinely and legitimately protected in contract law it is because (I suggest) the defendant has *contracted* to guarantee those expectations. A person who sells goods with an explicit warranty of fitness is, in some circumstances at least, offering such a guarantee; but the manufacturer in the *Muirhead* case, who knew nothing of the plaintiff's lobster business, plainly did not intend to offer any such guarantee.

This suggestion of mine—that non-consensual forms of liability can be legitimately developed so long as we do not tread on genuinely contractual ground—derives support also from the great expansion in modern times of reliance-based liability,[2] usually through the various forms of estoppel. Here also liability is usually imposed in cir-

[1] Above.

[2] To such a degree that Lord Diplock was able to speak in 1983 of 'a general principle of English law that injurious reliance on what another person did may be a source of legal rights against him': *The Hannah Blumenthal* [1983] 1 AC 834, 916.

cumstances which could be said to involve a voluntary assumption of responsibility, but the typical case plainly does not involve protection of the relying party's expectations.[1] Only his actual reliance losses are usually protected.[2]

This entire problem, concerning the relationship of consensual and non-consensual liabilities, is obviously a matter of great importance, not only because it is such a pressing problem in practical terms today as the courts are flooded with tort claims in circumstances where there is no liability in contract law, but also because it does very vividly illustrate the profound importance of some overall theoretical structure to the law of obligations. In the context of the great revival in belief in Freedom of Contract which I have called the ideology of the New Right, I have tried here to offer some suggestions which have implications for this overall theoretical structure; but to go beyond this would be a formidable task, and well beyond the confines of this Essay.

[1] An important decision here is *A.-G. for Hong Kong* v. *Humphrey's Estate (Queen's Gardens)* [1987] 2 WLR 343 which suggests that if the relying party seeks protection of his expectations, detrimental reliance is not enough to create liability unless an expectation has been encouraged that the transaction is irrevocable.

[2] No doubt there are exceptional cases, one of which seems to be *Pascoe* v. *Turner* [1979] 1 WLR 431; another more doubtful case is illustrated by *Avon CC* v. *Howlett* [1983] 1 All ER 1073.

Table of Cases

Index